Social PERSONS, PRODUCTS & IMAGES OF WELL-BEING
Communication
in Advertising

Second Edition, Revised and Enlarged

• WILLIAM LEISS • STEPHEN KLINE • SUT JHALLY •

ROUTLEDGE

17986

© Nelson Canada,
A Division of Thomson Canada Limited, 1990
1120 Birchmount Road
Scarborough, Ontario
M1K 5G4

Published in Australia by
Thomas Nelson Australia
480 La Trobe Street, Melbourne 3001
Victoria, Australia

Published in the United States of America by
Routledge, A Division of Routledge, Chapman and Hall, Inc.
29 West 35th Street, New York NY 10001

Published in the United Kingdom by
Routledge,
11 New Fetter Lane, London EC4P 4EE

Canadian Cataloguing in Publication Data

Leiss, William, 1939-
Social communication in advertising

2nd ed.
Includes bibliographical references.
ISBN 0-17-603491-9

1. Advertising – Social aspects.   2. Advertising –
Psychological aspects.   I. Kline, Stephen.
II. Jhally, Sut.   III. Title.

HF5827.L45   1990   659.1'042   C90-093732-7

Library of Congress Cataloguing in Publication Data

Library of Congress Data available.
ISBN 0-415-90354-8

British Library Cataloguing in Publication Data

British Cataloguing Data available.

The University of California Press has generously given permission to use
material from *Advertising the American Dream*, by Roland Marchand.
Copyright © 1985 by The Regents of the University of California Press.

Printed and bound in Canada
  2 3 4

OTABIND

Bound to stay open

Publisher's Note

Otabind (Ota-bind). This book has been bound
using the patented Otabind process. You can
open this book at any page, gently run your
finger down the spine, and the pages will lie flat.

Contents

Preface to the Second Edition

For the second edition, we have prepared three new chapters, made additions to other chapters, included some new illustrations, and updated the bibliography. Chapter 13, on political marketing, is entirely new. Both Chapter 7, on the advertising industry, and Chapter 12, on social policy issues, are substantially new, although they retain the basic thrust—and some of the content—of the first edition; in addition, Chapter 7 contains new interview materials. A new section, entitled "The Ad Industry Discovers Art," appears in Chapter 4.

We incurred many debts in the course of this project, which was begun in 1976 as a modest contract assignment with a federal government department in Ottawa (the officials were intently disinterested in our report, and injured pride spurred us to further study). Arlin Hackman and Judy Wright assisted us on that assignment, which resulted in the first version of our protocol for analyzing advertisements. When the final protocol was ready, in 1980, Edwine Hugenholtz supervised the team of coders for the ad sample at York University; we are especially grateful to her and to the other coders for their diligence and patience during this arduous task. Special thanks also is owing to Liss Jeffrey, who conducted most of the interviews with industry professionals that are quoted at many points throughout the book. Later JoAnne Stone, David McRobert and Glenn Ponthier at York University, and Leslie Wallace at Simon Fraser, helped us as research assistants. Professor Brent Rutherford of York University gave us astute guidance in configuring and interpreting our data from the ad sample.

Along the way we had the good fortune to encounter Professor Richard Pollay, Faculty of Commerce, University of British Columbia, who was engaged on a separate historical study of magazine advertising content. Those who work in this area know his extensive series of publications and research reports; he has been exceptionally generous to us with advice, encouragement, good humour, and gentle criticisms. We also happened upon Stan Shapiro, professor of marketing in the Faculty of Business Administration at Simon Fraser University. Professor Shapiro welcomed our novitiate amid the marketing literature, and pardoned our many interpretive errors; he has also championed our work among the members of his profession, cheerfully disdaining the possible adverse consequences for his own reputation, for which he has earned our admiration. Our copy editor for the first edition, Elizabeth Reid, vexed us with her line-by-line sifting of our manuscript, but finally won our admiration and thanks for her insistence on clarity and precision of expression. We thank many publishers for permission to quote passages of text. Companies that allowed us to reproduce advertisements featuring their products are listed below; their cooperation in providing illustrations enhanced the effectiveness of our text. For permission to make use of earlier versions of some parts of this book, we would like to thank the following: University of Toronto Press, publisher of *The Limits to Satisfaction* (1976) by William Leiss; the editors of the *Canadian Journal of Political and Social Theory,* publisher of three essays by us (1978, 1985); and the editors of *Theory, Culture and Society,* publisher of "The Icons of the Marketplace" (1983).

Sut Jhally extends special gratitude to Eileen McNutt; to his colleagues and graduate students in the Department of Communication at the University of Massachusetts, Amherst; and to Bill Livant.

Stephen Kline records his gratitude to Jill, Daniel, and Meghan Kline, for their support and tolerance; and thanks friends and colleagues Grahame Beakhust, Dian Marino, Peter Penz, and Neil Evernden.

William Leiss is deeply indebted to three dear friends and colleagues—Gaetan Tremblay, Liora Salter, and Arthur Kroker—for many kindnesses; to his departmental colleagues and Roman Onufrijchuk at Simon Fraser; to Folke Olander and Preben Sepstrup, Aarhus University, Denmark; to members of communications programs in Quebec: Bernard Schiele and others at Université du Québec à Montréal, Annie Méar and others at Université de Montréal, Gail Valaskakis and others at Concordia University, Gertrude Robinson and others at McGill University, and Michel de Repentigny and others at Université Laval. And, beyond measure, to Marilyn Lawrence.

During and after our book's gestation period, graduate and undergraduate students at York University, Simon Fraser University, and the University of Massachusetts nourished our project with their keen interest in the course materials through which we were developing our ideas. We are very grateful for their encouragement.

We are grateful to Mr. David Ward and his colleagues at Nelson Canada for their continued support of our book. We would also like to thank the New York ad industry executives for the interviews they granted to Sut Jhally in Summer 1989, and Mr. Jim Dosman of Vancouver, B.C., who did some valuable photography work on the illustrations for this edition.

We have made every effort to trace the ownership of all copyrighted material and to secure permission from copyright holders. In the event of any question arising as to the use of any material, we will be pleased to make the necessary corrections in future printings.

Vancouver, B.C.
Amherst, Mass.

January 1990

PART 1
DEBATES ON ADVERTISING AND SOCIETY

1

Introduction

A single thread of argument is drawn through this book: in industrial societies in this century, national consumer product advertising has become one of the great vehicles of social communication. Regarded individually and superficially, advertisements promote goods and services. Looked at in depth and as a whole, the ways in which messages are presented in advertising reach deeply into our most serious concerns: interpersonal and family relations, the sense of happiness and contentment, sex roles and stereotyping, the uses of affluence, the fading away of older cultural traditions, influences on younger generations, the role of business in society, persuasion and personal autonomy, and many others.

Advertising represents a "privileged form of discourse" about such concerns in modern society—meaning simply that we accord what it says a place of special prominence in our lives. A century ago in North America and western Europe, the forms of privileged discourse that touched the lives of ordinary persons were church sermons, political oratory, and the words and precepts of family elders. Such influences remain with us, but their prominence within the affairs of everyday life and the rhetorical force and moral authority that they carry are generally sharply diminished now; among industrial societies, only in the United States does a significant part of the population retain a passion for religious rhetoric.

The space left as these influences have diminished has been filled largely by *the discourse through and about objects.* We intend this phrase to convey the idea that communications among persons, in which individuals send "signals" to others about their attitudes, expectations, and sense of identity, are strongly associated with—and expressed through—patterns of preferences for consumer goods. People in contemporary society come together in "taste cultures," "lifestyle groupings," or "market segments," which represent distinctive consumption patterns. Such subsidiary formations are quite informal in nature but can be identified quite precisely; businesses try to aim their product design and advertising messages carefully at them. We also intend this phrase to convey something more specific: a significant portion of our daily public "talk" and action is about objects (consumer goods), and about what they can do or should mean for us.

This discourse is privileged in two senses. In "market-industrial societies" (North America, Western Europe, Japan, and a few others), economic affairs and marketplace transactions occupy a preponderant place in public life. For example, much of our political debate deals with "managing" the national and international economy. The talk about our economy's fortunes overawes everything else and indeed forces most other concerns to be expressed in its terms; the "bottom line" for all this talk is "delivering the goods" to consumers.

At the individual level, too, the discourse through and about objects sidles up to us everywhere, beckoning, teasing, haranguing, instructing, cajoling. Advertisements, the most accomplished vehicles of this discourse, are expertly and sometimes brilliantly constructed; it has been said with some justice that commercials are the best thing on television. Advertisements also make up the most consistent body of material in the mass media, something we have come to expect when we turn on the radio or television or open a magazine or newspaper. They are present in the most personal settings in our lives, at home and in leisure activities, just those times and places in which we relax and have the opportunity for self-expression.

How do we react to this omnipresent discourse? Typically, with matters that are major "fixtures" in everyday life, that are regarded as permanently troublesome but also indispensable—such as public education—we are ambivalent. So it is with advertising. Extensive public opinion surveys show that a high proportion of people enjoy ads as an art form, think that neither our economy nor the mass media could exist without advertising, and regard it as playing a generally positive role in society. In a major Canadian survey, respondents were asked whether the public school system or advertising had the greater influence on society: 54 percent identified schools, 42 percent ads. In the same study, an equally high proportion responded that good products do not have to be advertised at all; that ads cannot be believed, make products more expensive, do not influence consumer choice, and cause people to spend money on things they do not need. In another major Canadian survey, 60 percent of respondents agreed with the statement: "Most advertising is an insult to one's intelligence" (Canadian Radio-television and Telecommunications Commission 1978).

Many individuals hold contradictory and sometimes diametrically opposed views on advertising, mirroring the divergence of opinion in society as a whole. Advertising has given rise to harsh criticism ever since it became prominent in the national media, on the grounds that it has a negative impact in general—for example, it encourages people to overvalue "material" things in life. Suggestions that subliminal messages hidden in ads affect us without our being aware of their influence are alarming, although this sort of claim usually turns out to be groundless. Advertising is defended with equal ardour as a valuable contributor to the efficiency and freedom of a market economy. Recently, it has been acknowledged as a form of artistic expression; each year, prizes are awarded at an international competition held in Cannes (site of the famous film festival), and a collection of the year's best commercials makes the rounds of movie theatres.

Should we consider advertising and its effects on us (whatever they might be) as important issues? Does advertising, in fact, have a significant and measurable impact on our basic attitudes and behaviour patterns? Criticisms of advertising often are based on the presumption that it does have such an impact; rejoinders are made with equal conviction that no decent proof has been offered. The main difficulty here is to pin down what exactly it is that the two sides are arguing about. By now researchers are quite convinced that, as John Driver and Gordon Foxall (1984) conclude in a recent review of the literature, "advertising is helpless when it comes to establishing long-term purchasing patterns."

Notice that Driver and Foxall phrase the point in very specific terms. The debate about advertising is often vaguely cast, as demonstrated in the opinion surveys mentioned above. Driver and Foxall remark that many economists, advertisers, marketing managers, and policy makers still "cling to the conventional notion" that advertising exerts a strong influence on consumer behaviour. Research, they say, does not bear this out: "By and large, advertising does not act forcefully via intra-personal, mental processes to create attitudes which determine behavior." However, they are discussing a very narrowly defined issue — purchasing decisions for highly competitive consumer brands.

On the other hand, they are prepared to entertain a different perspective on the more general issue, conceding that "the aggregate effect of advertising on a materialistic society may be very great" (Driver and Foxall 1984, 98–104). Indeed, advertising's overwhelming presence today leaves little doubt that it is a factor to be reckoned with. In part, society tries to keep tabs on what the industry is doing by regulating it. Laws and industry codes of ethics are supposed to discourage unfair or misleading practices. All regulation is an attempt to work out a compromise among parties with conflicting viewpoints, but regulating advertising has not, by and large, ended the disagreements about its influence or appropriateness.

Fortunately, a welcome spate of studies has appeared in recent years, so that, even if we cannot yet decide what (if anything) we should do about advertising, we are in a much better position to understand it. Most of these studies are referred to and made use of in the following pages. Notable among the more recent of them are Daniel Pope's *The Making of Modern Advertising* (1983), the first extensive historical study to connect the industry's development with broader currents of change; Michael Schudson's *Advertising, the Uneasy Persuasion* (1984), a judicious, wide-ranging commentary on major cultural and social issues, with a wealth of references to relevant literature; Stephen Fox's *The Mirror Makers* (1984), a sophisticated historical study of the industry, focusing on dominant firms and personalities and including materials drawn from manuscript collections; and Roland Marchand's *Advertising the American Dream* (1985), a superbly illustrated study of the period 1920–1940 and undoubtedly the finest historical account of a segment in advertising history ever written.

A series of insightful works published a few years earlier stimulated these efforts, especially Stuart Ewen's *Captains of Consciousness* (1976), Judith Williamson's *Decoding Advertisements* (1978), Erving Goffman's *Gender Advertisements* (1979), and Gillian Dyer's *Advertising as Communication* (1982). In a sense, the maturing of advertising studies as a domain for serious research was heralded by the invaluable annotated bibliography compiled by Richard Pollay, *Information Sources in Advertising History* (1979), and by the growing literature in essays and articles, especially the series of research reports issued by Pollay and his collaborators.

The recent literature seeks to set the serious study of advertising firmly on the twin pillars of history and culture—an objective we share.

The pillar of history is reflected in the consensus that we can grasp the implications of present-day practices best by seeing how they were composed and put into place step by step during this century. The works by Ewen, Pope, Pollay, Fox, Schudson, and many others reflect this conviction, as does our own book. Older advertisements are a treasure house of fascinating and often amusing illustrations of how people and products used to look; exhuming and examining them turns out to be a pleasant chore. They are also a "condensed" and graphic representation of certain aspects of life in times past. Robert Atwan and his associates put together a selection of ads spanning this century in *Edsels, Luckies and Frigidaires* (1979), remarking quite accurately in their preface that "advertisements tell us in miniature a great deal about an entire civilization, its actual material life and interlocking collective fantasies."

Even a cursory glance at the past helps to persuade us that what exists now is by no means the inevitable outcome of prior events, that things could be other than they are. For example, if some of the businesspeople who controlled media industries in the 1920s had had their way, there would be no commercials on radio and television. Had this happened, we would have grown up knowing only noncommercial broadcasting, which would appear "normal" to us, and under such circumstances most of us would be offended at the very idea of having commercial messages on the electronic media. Our present-day situation, considered all by itself, always appears at first glance to be a "whole": everything seems to be linked naturally to everything else.

Thus, to understand the present we must first, so to speak, disassemble it. In this book, we will devote a good deal of space to inquiries into the historical evolution of various institutions: consumer goods marketing, the mass media of communication, popular culture, and the advertising agencies. Then we will put the pieces together again. The advertising industry is a complex mechanism, made up of many parts, and its products reflect that complexity; by taking it apart and reassembling it we hope to show how it works.

The second pillar for the study of advertising is culture. Many controversies about the real or imagined effects of ads on specific aspects of attitudes and behaviour are bound up with our cultural traditions; see, for example, the comprehensive review of sex-role stereotyping in Courtenoy and Whipple (1983). We have in mind, however, the more general issue of the decline of older European cultures and the creation of a twentieth-century "consumer culture." Here it is not a matter of advertising "causing" this or that, but rather of it being one actor among others in a powerful social drama. Stuart Ewen's *Captains of Consciousness* (1976) pioneered in this area; the collection of essays edited by Richard W. Fox and Jackson Lears, *The Culture of Consumption* (1983), made important further contributions. Stephen Fox contends in *The Mirror Makers* (1984) that advertising was a "primary, independent force in the molding of American culture and mores" in the 1920s, but thereafter served more as a mirror for "deeper cultural tendencies."

Our main point is a simple one: **Advertising is not just a business expenditure undertaken in the hope of moving some merchandise off the store shelves, but is rather an integral part of modern culture. Its creations appropriate and transform a vast range of symbols and ideas; its unsurpassed communicative powers recycle cultural models and references back through the networks of social interactions. This venture is unified by the discourse through and about objects, which bonds together images of persons, products, and well-being.**

In seeking to analyze and understand this discourse and its historical evolution, it is necessary to weave together and synthesize elements from a number of different perspectives within the general domains of history and culture. Table 1.1, "The Development of Media, Marketing, and Advertising," summarizes our main argument and findings about the development and place of advertising as social communication in modern culture. It reflects our belief that only through an integration of insights from a number of different approaches is it possible to fully understand the role of advertising in the discourse through and about objects. Table 1.1 draws upon five main perspectives to aid us in this.

First, we focus on broad *economic* changes that characterize the transition in societies from largely agricultural and artisanal modes of production to a predominantly industrial mode of production. This tran-

TABLE 1.1
The Development of Media, Marketing, and Advertising

	NEWSPAPERS/ MAGAZINES	RADIO	TELEVISION	
MEDIA FOR ADVERTISING*	NEWSPAPERS/ MAGAZINES	RADIO	TELEVISION	
MARKETING STRATEGY	RATIONAL	NON-RATIONAL	BEHAVIOURIST	SEGMENTATION
ADVERTISING STRATEGY	UTILITY[a]	PRODUCT SYMBOLS[b]	PERSONIFICATION[c]	LIFESTYLE[d]
PERIOD	1890 1900 1910	1920 1930 1940	1950 1960	1970 1980
ELEMENTS IN ADS	product **qualities, price, use**	product **qualities**	product	product
		symbolic attributes	**person prototype**	**activity (person-setting)**
METAPHORIC-EMOTIVE THEMES IN ADS	quality, useful, descriptive	status, family, health, white magic, social authority	glamour, romance, sensuality, black magic, self-transformation	leisure, health, groups, friendship

* Pre-1890: Posters and billboards.
[a] See Figure 1.1.   [c] See Figure 1.3.
[b] See Figure 1.2.   [d] See Figure 1.4.

sition necessitated not simply the adaptation to new ways to produce goods, but also required the development of new mechanisms for the distribution and circulation of goods.

Second, we draw upon *sociocultural* perspectives in seeking to understand how these economic changes influenced the way in which people related to goods. We pay special attention to the way in which the cultural forms that give meaning to the world of things undergo a drastic repositioning, such that in the consumer society marketplace institutions come to replace the family, community, and religious institutions that were important in agricultural societies and earlier forms of industrial society.

Third, we pay special attention to the specific manner in which these economic and sociocultural changes were *institutionally* mediated by the emergence and development of two key symbiotically related industries: the commercial mass media and the advertising agencies. In terms of the mass media, we focus on the way in which the successive integration of newspapers, magazines, radio, and television into the sphere of marketplace communications that deal with the discourse through and about objects profoundly influences the nature of that discourse. Different media offer different potentialities for advertising formats and strategies. This dimension is reflected in the "Media for Advertising" categories in Table 1.1. The commercial media are the delivery system for advertisements, which are actually planned and created by advertising agencies who act on behalf of their manufacturing clients. It is important to find out how the agencies and advertisers are thinking about consumers and ways to appeal to them. We identify four main phases in the development of "marketing strategy" throughout the twentieth century (see line two in Table 1.1).

Fourth, we closely *analyze advertisements* from all periods of this century to see how the economic, sociocultural, and institutional contexts influence their form and content. Specifically, we identify four main stages in the development of "advertising strategy." (See lines three to six in Table 1.1, as well as Figures 1.1–1.4).

Fifth, drawing upon our previous analysis of advertising content, we ask how this framework impacts upon our general understanding of goods and the ways in which they are integrated into the process of satisfaction and communication in the consumer society throughout the twentieth century. Particularly, we focus on the predominant set of images, values, and forms of communication in any period that provide a *"cultural frame for goods."* We identify four major cultural frames that have historically given some definition to the relationship between people and things (see below and Chapter 11, especially Table 11.1, line 7).

We have just described our general approach to the understanding of advertising as a form of social communication. More specifically, chapter by chapter, in taking apart and reassembling the mechanism of modern

FIGURE 1.1
Utility: A Discourse about Product Quality

The story of a muslin sack

THE real wonder-story of the tobacco that is smoked by *more millions of men* than all other good tobaccos *combined*—

GENUINE
"BULL" DURHAM
SMOKING TOBACCO

In quaint old Durham, North Carolina—that's where the story starts.

That's where those golden leaves first grew in the sunny fields of Greene's farm. That's where they first filled those simple muslin sacks with good, sweet, native tobacco—fifty-two years ago.

No thought then of fancy packages—or of "processes" for improving on Nature.

Just surprisingly good tobacco! *That* was what they had *discovered* —that was what interested those critical Southern smokers who gave a rousing welcome to "Bull" Durham as the greatest tobacco they had ever tasted.

And then the soldiers came. They came—and smoked—and were captured!

Scattering to their homes all over the nation, they carried the fame of this wonderful smoke.

Wasn't that Durham postmaster busy with letters from up and down the land asking how to get *more* of that "Bull" Durham!

And—for over half a century, just because it's so down-right *good*—it's been *earning* and *winning* and hold-ing new friends faster than any other tobacco ever grown.

Faster! Twenty-two million pounds — 362 million packages — were sold and smoked last year! Yet this was merely the normal growth over the year before.

That sack might have been displaced by a fancy box. But the increasing millions of smokers who have an affection for this plain, convenient muslin cover have shown that *they* want the value where it belongs—in the tobacco. You can't smoke the cover!

"Bull" Durham has stood the long test. Its purity—its natural, undoctored goodness as a smoke—have held and splendidly multiplied its friends—have won for it the leadership over all the tobaccos of the world.

Wherever they sell tobacco you can buy "Bull" Durham

Blackwell's Durham Tobacco Co.

Source: Courtesy of The American Tobacco Company.

FIGURE 1.2
Product Symbols: A Discourse about Social Values and Tastes

LUXURIOUS TRANSPORTATION

PACKARD luxury, once enjoyed, is seldom relinquished. Records indicate that 96% of all Packard owners remain in the family—replace their old Packards with new ones.

Packard has always been a luxury car. It has sought and found its patronage among those who know and appreciate fine things.

When such owners, after long, proud years of satisfaction, have come to part with their cars, they have naturally turned again to Packard. And Packard has always been ready with new and finer vehicles—improved mechanically and more luxurious than ever, but retaining the characteristic beauty of style and design so distinctly Packard's own.

New customers, too, have turned to Packard when seeking supreme motor car luxury. Two-thirds of today's Packard Standard Eights are bought by those who give up other makes of cars to do so.

What greater tribute to quality and reputation and engineering leadership can there be than that which old customers and new thus bestow on Packard? Act upon the Packard slogan and—

All the treasures of ancient Egypt contributed to the splendor and luxury of Cleopatra's lavish barge

ASK THE MAN WHO OWNS ONE

PACKARD

FIGURE 1.3
Personalization: A Discourse about Individual Feelings

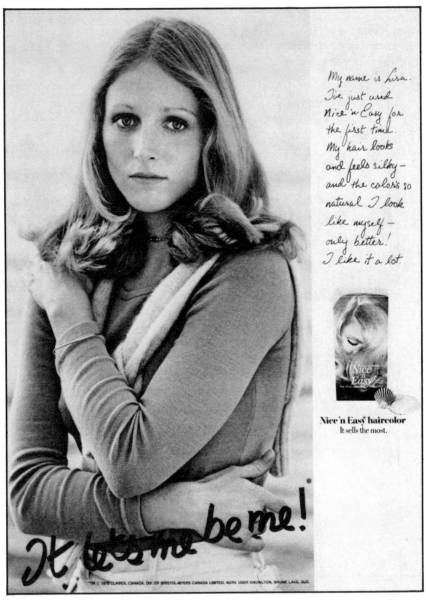

FIGURE 1.4
Lifestyles: A Discourse about Social Groups and their Activities

Dubonnet s'il vous plaît

Source: Courtesy of Schenley Industries.

advertising and its linkups with other social institutions, we shall run through the following steps. In the next two chapters, we put our workbench in order by arranging and inspecting the principal arguments concerning the relationship between advertising and society. On the critical side, we review concerns about the creation of wants, the manipulation of psychological processes, and the promotion of unworthy ideals. On advertising's behalf we take up the rational information model of consumer choice, the nature of persuasion, and the importance of symbolism in forming the individual's sense of satisfaction. On neither side do we get very far. The critics turn out to be interested chiefly in attacking the "materialist ethos" in general and, except for brief rhetorical flourishes, pay little or no attention to the actual workings of advertising. Most of the defenders downplay advertising's importance in the evolution of the consumer society, and from them, too, we learn relatively little about its wider social significance.

In Part 2, Advertising and Media, each of the major institutional components that set in motion the interplay between society and culture, media, and advertising is examined in turn. Chapter 4 sketches the main differences between the earlier form of industrial society and the consumer culture that has replaced it over the course of the twentieth century. We now have a society unique in human history—one wherein most individuals depend on a continuously growing array of marketed goods for the satisfaction of all their needs. This has been made possible by the succession of technological triumphs in industry, by the rationalization of the market economy by manufacturers and financiers, and by the long and bitter struggles of workers to win a decent standard of living and a semblance of social democracy.

Chapter 5 traces the emergence of the mass communications media in modern society, from print (newspapers and magazines) to broadcasting (radio and television), and attempts to foster a proper appreciation of these media as autonomous institutional actors. By the end of the nineteenth century, the print media had established new forms of communication; created the "public" that they addressed; and, above all, set up the fertile interaction between media strategy and audience segment—all this before the sale of commercial advertising space began to generate significant revenues. So well established was the framework for the transactions between media and their audiences by this time that, when the new electronic broadcasting media appeared on the scene, they slipped relatively easily into the mould established by the print media.

Chapters 6 and 7 present the advertising industry and its key actors, the national agencies, as the institutional force at the crossroads where all other forces meet. The agencies worked out the strategies for the common enterprise of the consumer culture. Over time the agencies learned to operate on a triple front: they stood between industry and media, helping to create new forms for messages about products; between industry and consumers, helping to develop comprehensive marketing campaigns; and between media and consumers, helping to do the research on audiences that led to what we know as "market segmentation." The fruits of these activities are realized and displayed in the agencies' creations: advertisements.

These activities are not necessarily apparent. Can we devise a way to look at ads so that—out of their own form and content—they yield up this story? Chapter 8 reviews the methodological problems encountered when we try to do this and some in-depth studies of advertising content. In Chapter 9, we present our own research design for analyzing advertisements and the results obtained in two extensive applications of it. One looks at modern television commercials; the other involves a large sample of magazine ads drawn from the period 1910–1980 and provides detailed information about what has been happening in ads over the entire course of the twentieth century.

In the total system of advertising, the agencies turned out scene after scene and act after act of a never-ending "drama of consumer satisfaction," using images of persons, products, and forms of well-being as their players. Our research design enables us to follow each of the players and its lines separately, as well as to keep track of their interactions, revealing significant patterns in each period and changes in them over time.

What do these changing patterns mean? These two chapters open the discussion of Part 3, The Theatre of Consumption. Chapter 10 contends that the success of both the advertising message formats, and the major shifts in their content (from description of the product to the linking of persons, products, and settings in symbolic representations), was not due primarily to their intrinsic merits as artistic creations; rather, it was due to the fact that they evolved alongside other, more general changes in society that "loosened up" and diversified the range of approved cultural models that guide the search for personal satisfaction. These models are later baptized "lifestyles."

Chapter 11, "Goods as Communicators," seeks to put the pieces back together again. Anthropological studies tell us that, in human societies, material objects have always served to convey meanings and messages about rank, status, privilege, roles, caste, sex, class; about how such social subgroups were formed; and about what rules groups devised to dictate their conduct to each other. We look at the modern consumer society as an "anthropological type" and find that the age-old function of goods as communicators is now combined with the special capabilities of the new technologies of mass communication, the immense productive resources of modern industry, and the diverse array of lifestyle models for personal satisfaction, to generate the discourse through and about objects. Advertising makes all this possible, for it is the place at which industry, media, and lifestyles converge. Chapter 11 concludes with a fuller explanation of the stages of development outlined in Table 1.1.

In Part 4 (In the Heat of Controversy—Advertising, Culture, and Politics), Chapter 12, "Issues in Social Policy," looks at a number of areas in which advertising has been especially controversial (for example, advertising to children, and tobacco/alcohol advertising), in the light of both industry and governmental attempts to regulate the contents of ads. These attempts have never been very satisfactory. Modern advertising draws upon so many diverse cultural resources, and is so dependent upon a collaboration with its audience for constructing the meaning of its messages, that the rather clumsy tools of social regulation almost inevitably fail to achieve their objectives. It seems pretty clear by now that the only effective way of constraining advertising's impact—where social concerns about that impact are sufficiently grave—is to deny or restrict access by advertisers to specific audiences or media.

Finally, Chapter 13, "Fantasia for the Citizen," presents some scenes from what is perhaps the most telling evidence that advertising is, above all, a *general* method of persuasive communication, exerting a pervasive influence throughout our society. This chapter is about politics. Over the last thirty years, the ad industry has revolutionized political activity in North America. No major election campaigns (and fewer and fewer minor ones) can be conducted without the expert services provided by ad agencies. This fact, more than anything else, underlines the continuing need to understand advertising's place at the very heart of the process of dynamic change in our culture and institutions.

2

Criticisms of Advertising

When considering advertising's role in society, most commentators have concentrated on its *economic* function in the modern marketplace. Opinions are widely divergent as to whether advertising is a beneficial or a negative factor. Many critics charge that advertising is a wasteful and inefficient business tool, and that, although the present standard of living in western societies is high, it would be higher still if the marketplace could be freed from the negative influence of advertising.

From this perspective, advertising raises the prices of goods because it is an unnecessary business cost whose main effect is to circulate a great deal of superfluous puffery in unsuitable places (for example, between the episodes in television programs); whatever real information there is behind the puffery could be better provided on product information labels and by salespersons in stores. Thus, considerable amounts of money are expended without resulting in a net consumer benefit.

In response, many other economists have claimed that advertising is, in fact, a beneficial component of modern economies, and that significant increases in the standard of living and consumer satisfaction can be attributed to it. Because advertising increases the overall sales of a particular brand, it permits economies of scale that are reflected in lower prices for consumers. In general, its defenders argue, advertising is an efficient means of distributing information—more so than salespersons, for example—about the huge, ever-changing array of available products. This results in continuous product innovation and improvement, because there is an effective and relatively cheap means available to inform consumers of new and improved products.

Is, then, advertising productive, or is it a wasteful business practice that creates distortions and inefficiencies in the overall functioning of the marketplace? The present standard of living is high in western societies, but would it be even higher if the market were freed from the negative influence of advertising? Does advertising channel or diffuse competition and creative energies that would otherwise stimulate productivity? Kaldor and Silverman (1948) were among the first economists to attempt to assess advertising's contribution to the industrial economy—a theme that persists in recent writings such as Pope (1983). A number of specially commissioned studies such as Harris and Seldon (1962)in England and

Nicosia (1974) in the United States have been explicitly undertaken to identify the underlying issues. Nicosia (1974), in particular, views advertising as an important institutional factor in the overall functioning of the marketplace.

Without a mechanism for mass distribution of information about products, the significant economies of scale achieved by national producers for the mass market might never have occurred. But it remains unclear whether other information mechanisms might also be compatible with mass production and retailing, and, of course, whether the concentrations of ownership in particular industries results in reductions in the competitiveness of the marketplace. The innovator of mass production lines, Henry Ford himself, resisted advertising well into the early 1920s and was only forced to adopt it as a strategy because other car manufacturers were doing so. Historical analysis has been unable to determine just how much advertising, as distinct from other factors, increased overall sales and stimulated mass production and distribution. The growth of advertising is correlated to the growth of the industrial economy, but whether as cause or effect is difficult to determine.

In fact, the Ford case highlights the other criticism of advertising's role, especially in the mature marketplace where, it is argued, advertising raises the price of goods because it is an unnecessary business cost. Advertisers are forced to advertise in order to forestall the incursions of brand enemies without significant alterations in product or price. Per capita expenditure on advertising has remained at about 2.5 percent of share of consumer spending; in 1980, it was $241 per person in the United States, a cost added to the price of goods. If the main effect of advertising is merely to draw consumers away from competitive brands, it is an expenditure without benefit to the consumer or to the competitiveness of the market in terms of price or quality of goods.

In addition, advertising allows inefficient large manufacturers to dominate the scene because newer (and presumably more efficient) producers cannot allocate the large advertising budgets required to break into the market. Thus advertising becomes an entrance barrier discouraging competition and promoting conditions in which a few manufacturers have an unhealthy oligopolistic control of prices and supplies of goods—a significant deviation from the hypothetical perfect market. Research has not shown conclusively, however, that advertising has led to inefficient oligopolies and barriers to competitiveness, even for particular types of goods (Pope 1983; Nicosia 1974). What is clear is that not all industries advertise equally intensively and some specific markets function competitively without advertising much at all.

Advertisers themselves view this strictly economic perspective as a major limitation on the growth of their industry (Frank 1963, 440). Many economists argue that advertising distorts the adequate and uniform distribution of information the market needs to ensure that consumers are properly informed about new products as they become available, so that they can make choices and express their preferences and promote innovation and competitiveness, and that this is likely to have disturbing economic effects. Moreover, they continue, until advertising has been definitely shown to achieve economic benefits, it should be regarded as a wasteful and inefficient business practice. What definite proof one way or the other would look like, however, is hard to imagine. Without hard data, economic critiques of advertising's larger role are likely to remain rhetorical.

Thus, although the literature on the economic effects of advertising is substantial by now, no consensus has been reached about whether it is wasteful or beneficial from a strictly economic standpoint. However, some commentators have sought to broaden the terms of debate by interpreting advertising's role in social as well as economic terms (Aaker and Myers 1975, 535–53). In this chapter, we review the general arguments advanced in defining and criticizing advertising's social impact in modern society.

It is difficult to think of another contemporary institution that has come under such sustained attack from so many different angles. For instance, advertising is assailed by conservative groups affiliated with the so-called Moral Majority for contributing to the moral breakdown of society because it presents images of hedonistic pleasure and draws upon overtly sexual themes to promote products. The Moral Majority views advertising as one of the most visible arenas in which the "blasphemous" ideology of secular humanism is celebrated. Advertising is just as severely attacked by left-wing groups, who see in its deceitful promises of material pleasure the means by which potentially revolutionary groups of working people are "bought off by the system."

Advertising has been taken to task for how it affects the relationship between people and objects (making people buy more goods than is really necessary by creating false needs), for the bad role models that advertising presents (especially to women and children), and for having too much influence on programming content in the mass media. This diversity makes it difficult to present a coherent and succinct summary that reflects adequately the full range of concerns, and in this chapter we cannot hope to address them all. Rather, we will focus on what is the main theme of this book: the place of advertising in the interactions between people and goods in modern society.

We have referred to the views of economists who think that advertising hampers the free development of market forces by setting up barriers of entry to other potential producers and by raising the prices of goods.

These writers can be labelled loosely as "liberal" critics, who see advertising as upsetting the delicate balance of the marketplace upon which the health of modern society depends.

This group has been less influential of late than "neoliberal" writers, who are more likely to concede that market forces must be constrained by public policy and government action. The neoliberals maintain that there are serious problems in how modern society is organized, but that these can be solved by modifications in the existing social system, such as a more equitable distribution of wealth. The left wing of the Democratic Party in the United States, the New Democratic Party in Canada, and the Social Democratic/Liberal alliance in Britain are examples of neoliberal groups. For them, capitalism's drawbacks can be remedied by overhauling, rather than dismantling, its institutional structures.

On the other hand, there are the social critics, reflecting variants of "Marxist" thought, who think that the problems of modern society (capitalism) are far from superficial, based as they are on its fundamental mode of organization. Solving these problems, therefore, entails a total transformation of the system rather than its modification.

Curiously enough, while neoliberals and Marxists look at society very differently, their criticisms of the institution of advertising are sufficiently similar for us to be able to treat them as a single argument that runs as follows. National consumer product advertising arose as an economic necessity as modern society progressed from a competitive to an oligopoly situation in the early years of this century. Its function was, and still is, to create demand among consumers to ensure that the goods produced in such large numbers by mass production are bought in equally large numbers, so that the owners of the factories producing them can secure adequate returns on their investments. To this end, advertising is a manipulative tool, controlling the market by creating false needs in consumers, and by extolling a general ethos of consumption whereby all needs come to be fulfilled through the purchase of goods in the marketplace. This overemphasis on consumption of goods as a means of satisfaction for needs leads ultimately to general feelings of dissatisfaction rather than to happiness and content, because goods simply cannot deliver the promised happiness shown in advertisements.

The remainder of this chapter will be devoted to further elucidation of these arguments. The discussion is divided into three topics: (1) why advertising exists; (2) how advertising works; and (3) what effects advertising has on society.

WHY DOES ADVERTISING EXIST?

The prime contention of the critics is that advertising *creates demand* among consumers. The neoliberal position is that a managed economy is desirable, but within such an economy advertising is seen as unnecessary and disadvantageous to the public welfare. The Marxist position sees advertising as essential to the maintenance of the exploitative relations of advanced capitalism.

The Neoliberal Position

The most celebrated attack on the role that advertising plays in creating demand for goods comes from the writings of John Kenneth Galbraith, especially *The Affluent Society* (1958) and *The New Industrial State* (1967). Galbraith thinks that modern society's emphasis on the production of goods and economic growth has harmfully affected such areas as resource use, the environment, and labour–management relations. He therefore asks, "How are these effects justified by the proponents of the theory of economic growth?" and finds two basic claims of legitimacy proposed for the present organization of society and its emphasis on production: first, that industrial production provides high levels of employment, and second, that the goods that are produced satisfy the needs of consumers.

Although the issue of employment is important, Galbraith thinks it is the satisfaction of consumer need that is the key to justifying the harmful effects of modern industrial production. Traditional economic theory assumes that consumers are the most important decision makers in the economy, controlling what and how much is produced as manufacturers of goods respond to consumers' needs. This is known as the theory of consumer sovereignty. Galbraith thinks that to be accepted, this theory must convince us that consumer wants and needs are *independently determined*—in other words, that wants and needs originate with the consumer:

> Consumer wants can have bizarre, frivolous, or even immoral origins, and an admirable case can be made for a society that seeks to satisfy them. But the case cannot stand if it is the process of satisfying wants that creates the wants. (Galbraith 1958, 140)

The existence of a massive advertising industry proves that the theory of consumer sovereignty is not applicable here. The institutions of salesmanship and advertising cannot be "reconciled with the notion of independently determined desires, for their central function is to create desires—to bring into being wants that previously did not exist" (Galbraith 1958, 141). Galbraith thereupon reverses the theory of consumer sovereignty ("the accepted sequence") into what he labels "the revised sequence," in which producers clearly control demand.

In this new sequence, the business firm is the key decision maker and the system operates in the firm's interests, not those of the consumer.

The present emphasis on production is based upon firms' pursuing private profit by creating demand rather than by seeking to satisfy existing consumer needs. In short, wants are created by producers through advertising.

Galbraith's work is a good example of the neoliberal critique of corporate capitalism and the role of advertising in it. It calls for a halt to the blind support of increased production as a moral imperative. Instead, we should divert social resources to other, more needy areas in society. The rallying cry is "social-welfare capitalism." What is required is not overturning the whole economic system, but modifying it so that the rewards that capitalism can produce are more equitably distributed.

The Marxist Critique

The Marxist account of the creation of demand through advertising is similar, except for one major element. In Marxist theory, advertising is such a vital and integral part of the *system* of capitalism that the one could not survive without the other. Capitalism's productive capacity is so great that it would threaten its own existence were it not for the aid it gets to stave off the threat of overproduction from institutions such as advertising. The problem is this: although the process of production places value in goods (the value of labour and raw materials), profit is only extracted when those goods are sold in the marketplace and the value in goods is converted into a usable form (money). Once the basic needs of food, shelter, and clothing are satisfied for most people, capitalism faces the problem of "realization," of making sure that the huge numbers of goods produced beyond this minimal level are consumed. If capitalism cannot overcome this, it will collapse, because if goods cannot be sold there will be no further investment in production, resulting in a stagnant economy. In the absence of counteracting forces, advanced capitalism would sink into a permanent depression. The problem is one of overproduction—of "too much." According to Paul Baran and Paul Sweezy in *Monopoly Capital* (1966), only in capitalism does "too much" appear as an economic problem. In a rational (that is, socialist) society, they argue, the appearance of "too much" would simply be a signal that attention should be switched to areas of "too little" or that prices should be lowered, thus increasing consumers' purchasing power. Neither option is open to capitalists. Instead, the dilemma of "too much" supply is turned into that of "too little" demand. In order to survive, the system has to stimulate demand "on pain of death," and what accomplishes this is advertising.

British cultural theorist Raymond Williams says that modern capitalism "could not function" without advertising. And Marxist economist

Ernest Mandel (1978, 399) holds that the enormous expansion of the service sector, of which advertising is a part, within the economy as a whole is "an unmistakable expression of the growing difficulties of realization in late capitalism." While these writers consider advertising to be only part of the larger system for stimulating or creating demand that also includes package design, planned obsolescence, model changes, consumer credit, and so on, they see advertising as the "principal weapon" in this strategy.

In his critical study of the beginnings of national advertising, *Captains of Consciousness* (1976), Stuart Ewen comments on the way a fledgling advertising industry reacted to the role thrust upon it in the first decades of this century. The crisis of overproduction created the imperative to expand markets to the poorer social classes and on a national scale, and the advertising industry offered business a means of "creating" consumers and controlling the consumption of products.

> Such social production of consumers represented a shift in social and political priorities which has since characterized much of the "life" of American industrial capitalism. The functional goal of national advertising was the creation of desires and habits. (Ewen 1976, 37)

The tremendous growth in the scale of national advertising in the period from 1890 to 1920 is seen by Ewen as an indication of the way that capitalist domination and control would seek to affect the mass of the working population beyond the boundary of the factory gate.

There are similarities and contrasts in the neoliberal and the Marxist positions. (Neither acknowledges one of the more straightforward economic arguments in favour of advertising: that it arose in part to displace intermediaries or "middlemen" in the distribution sector and thereby contributes to consumer welfare.) The neoliberal critique is that the market cannot be trusted to make good decisions about allocating resources, because advertising distorts the composition of needs and wants that producers are engaged in satisfying. The market economy (and advertising) should be replaced by a more rational planning institution. The Marxist critique sees advertising as a response to the needs of advanced capitalism for a solution to the problem of realization. Advertising is a willing accomplice in creating and perpetuating the unhealthy features of the social system in which it evolved, and moreover has become indispensable to its continued existence; therefore, one cannot contemplate its abolition except in the context of rejecting capitalism as such. Although they differ with respect to solutions, neoliberals and Marxists agree that advertising creates demand for products, and that it makes people buy more than they really need.

HOW DOES ADVERTISING CREATE DEMAND?

Underlying the argument that advertising creates demand is, of course, the tacit assumption that advertising actually succeeds in its attempt to induce and increase consumption. In fact, a belief in the enormous manipulative powers of mass-media advertising was one of the most widely accepted tenets of the radical movement in the 1960s and 1970s. Consequently, criticisms of advertising have been directed not only at advertising's creation of demand, but also at the way in which it does so. One contention is that advertising influences us without our being aware of it, that it affects us behind our back.

Technological Manipulation

Two writers in particular are associated with this view. The first is Vance Packard, who started his enormously popular *The Hidden Persuaders* by explaining that is was about

> the way many of us are being influenced and manipulated — far more than we realize — in the patterns of our everyday lives. Large scale efforts are being made, often with impressive success, to channel our unthinking habits, our purchasing decisions and our thought processes by the use of insights gleaned from psychiatry and the social sciences. Typically, these efforts take place beneath our level of awareness. (Packard 1957, 11)

Citing the use of motivational research (using focus groups of audiences to discover the basis of behaviour, particularly consumer behaviour) by growing numbers of advertisers, Packard attempted to show that consumers were becoming creatures of conditioned reflex rather than of rational thought. Most importantly, he alleged, this manipulation took place at a subconscious level. Packard's criticism is not levelled at all advertising but only that which is underhanded and covert; indeed, for most advertising Packard has nothing but praise, referring to many advertisements as "tasteful, honest works of artistry." His main theme, however, concerns the obnoxious character of what he regards as devious forms of advertising.

Packard's dark vision of the manipulative and hidden impacts of advertising was reinforced by Wilson Bryan Key's discussions (1972 and 1976) of the alleged technique of subliminal perception in advertising. Key is concerned not so much with the use of motivational research and nonrational techniques of persuasion, but with ascertaining whether techniques impossible to perceive at the conscious level of awareness are concealed within the construction of the advertising message itself and whether they can influence behaviour. For example, Key claims to find the word "sex" baked into the surface of Ritz crackers and deeply symbolic sexual imagery used in the depiction of ice cubes in alcohol advertising.

This "secret technology," he asserts, "modifies behaviour invisibly, channels basic value systems and manages human motives in the interest of special power structures. . . . Subliminal stimuli assault the psyches of everyone in North America throughout each day of their lives" (Key 1976, 2). Neither Packard nor Key, it should be noted, was ever able to point to actual instances in which such alleged manipulative techniques induced consumers to do anything that they would not otherwise have freely chosen to do. But at least Packard could point to actual programs for motivational research; no other commentator, either within the advertising industry or outside it, has ever corroborated Key's assertions about advertising practices, nor is there any evidence that motivational effects result from subliminal stimuli. The popularity of these attacks appears to rest on the general impression they create that advertising is a powerful and omnipresent apparatus with better knowledge of consumers than they have of themselves, and that this knowledge is used to manipulate them into buying goods they do not need.

More cautious writers have concentrated on examining the general powers of the mass media that carry advertising. For Galbraith, the need to manage demand was matched by the development of a technology to accomplish this goal. Radio and television, appealing to a mass audience and requiring of it no special literacy skills, admirably filled the needs of producers to be in "comprehensive, repetitive, and compelling communication" with consumers. Indeed, the persuasive communication of commercial television (as opposed to the rationality of print) is so crucial, Galbraith conjectures, that the industrial system could not survive in its present form without it. Other writers, such as Jerry Mander (1977), reinforce this idea, contending that there is something deeply disturbing about the very technology of television that invites persuasion and manipulation and stops the critical thought process.

False Symbolism

Consumer demand is manipulated not only by subtle technologies but also by the obvious content of commercial messages, which show people how to use commodities. In this connection, advertising has been criticized for the arbitrary manner in which goods are linked to various attributes presented as being socially desirable. Stuart Ewen calls attention to a transition period in the 1920s when advertising messages shifted from focusing on products to defining consumers as an integral part of the social meaning of goods. If advertising's task was to create demand in consumers rather than simply to reflect their innate desires, it would have to stop talking merely about the product and incorporate direct references to the audience as well.

Advertisers, therefore, effected a "self-conscious change in the psychic economy" (Ewen 1976) by flooding the marketplace with suggestions that individuals should buy products in order to encounter something in the realm of social or psychological experience that previously had been unavailable to them. Material objects thus came to play an increasingly important role in social interaction and everyday life as symbols of prestige and status. Stuart Hall and Paddy Wannell (1965) also have argued that the main trend in modern advertising shows a move away from the presentation of information and toward persuasion, and that, as such, advertising today has both an economic and a cultural function.

In an important and influential essay first published in 1962, Raymond Williams wrote that the social and symbolic significance conferred upon goods by advertising shows us that it is wrong to regard modern society as being too materialistic, as putting too much emphasis on the possession of goods. Rather, we are *not materialistic enough*:

> If we were sensibly materialist, in that part of our living in which we use things, we should find most advertising to be of insane irrelevance. Beer would be enough for us, without the additional promise that in drinking it we show ourselves to be manly, young at heart, or neighborly. A washing machine would be a useful machine to wash clothes, rather than an indication that we are forward-looking or an object of envy to our neighbors. But if these associations sell beer and washing machines, as some of the evidence suggests, it is clear that we have a cultural pattern in which the objects are not enough but must be validated, if only in fantasy, by association with social and personal meanings which in a different cultural pattern might be more directly available. (Williams [1962] 1980, 185)

Williams then distinguishes between a rational use of goods, based on their utility alone (what they can do for us), and an irrational use of goods, based on what they symbolize (what they mean to us) — a distinction between use and symbol.

Thus, capitalist consumption is characterized by irrationality because of the symbolic system of meaning within which goods are located. But note that for Williams *any* symbolic system is irrational, for rationality is based only on utility, only on the objective performance features of the product. For goods to take on any other meaning is unhealthy. Fred Inglis also sees the consumption of objects based on such arbitrary characteristics as socially harmful:

> Attainment of the values is signalled by acquiring the appropriate objects, using them, throwing them away and acquiring replacements. Continuous and conspicuous consumption is the driving energy of this fiction. . . . The objects advertised are drenched in a certain light and smell. They give off the powerful fragrance of the very rich and instead of leaving the object in an intelligible domestic world, remove it to a fantastic one. (Inglis 1972, 17)

Once again, the constrast is between an "intelligible domestic world" and a "fantastic one," between use and symbol. One of the cornerstones of the critical approach appears to be, then, that goods should have no meaning over and above their functions as conceived in strictly utilitarian terms, because any additional meaning is false.

As well as attacking the content of advertising, critics also have zeroed in on the mode of presentation, which favours persuasion rather than sober decision. In their study of the rhetoric of advertising, Andren and his collaborators distinguish between nonrational influences, or persuasion, and rational influences, or argument. The latter operates in the public or consumer interest whereas the former does not. The rhetoric of advertising (the form of presentation) would have to conform to a particular set of criteria if the communication were to qualify as sensible guidance to the consumer. Andren et al. (1978, 112) conclude, not surprisingly, that advertising does not contain sufficient information to be the basis of reflective choice among products, and that "advertising does not serve the consumer or the public interest."

Magic in the Marketplace

Consumers are also manipulated by an advertisement's promise that the product will do something special for them—something magical that will transform their lives. Commercials promise all kinds of things: goods can make us stunningly attractive in an instant, give us power over other people's affections, cure us of all illness, capture and package nature for our use, lift our emotions, act as a passport into a fantastic community of desirable persons.

In an essay appropriately entitled "The Magic System," Raymond Williams (1980 [1962]) refers to advertising as a "highly organized and professional system of magical inducements and satisfactions" that co-exist strangely with the rest of a highly developed technological society. Varda Leymore (1975) suggests that advertising works much as mythology does in primitive societies, providing simple, anxiety reducing answers to the complex problems of modern life by playing on the deep symbolic structures of the human imagination. Fred Inglis (1972, 78) thinks that, while the advertiser does not command the prestige of a shaman, "his anonymous vantage in society permits him to circulate a novel magic which offers to mute the familiar pains of a particular society and history, to soften or sharpen ambition, bitterness, solitude, lust, failure and repacity."

Howard Luck Gossage, ad-man turned social critic, argues that magical stewardship in any society is associated with its most important domain; in western capitalism, this is the consumption of goods. Further, because advertisements must have wide appeal, they have to play on very basic human emotions: "They go beyond reason into something even more basic, the most common denominator of all, magic" (Gossage 1967,

364). Advertisements draw upon the entire magical repertoire, including contagious magic, charms to avoid dire consequences, taboos, command over the supernatural, incantations (jingles), and even the devil's blandishments.

> Mephistopheles grants a boon: eternal life, youth, prowess, togetherness, unfulfilled dreams. His price is always something. When it is such a small thing as a pack of cigarettes, or a soft drink, or a lipstick, why should we not take a chance? (Gossage 1967, 367)

People are magically changed—but so are goods, from inanimate objects into living things. Products dance and sing, engage in relations with humans as if they themselves were alive, and sometimes direct human actions because of the consumer's confusion in the marketplace. At the same time, because human personalities are correlated with specific qualities ascribed to products, people become more like goods. In this dual exchange, things appear as animate and people appear as inanimate. In a 1984 television commercial for Renault, for example, a man announces, "You are what you drive," and as he continues speaking he is transformed into the automobile whose virtues he has been praising. Television advertising especially presents us with an enchanted kingdom where goods and people are equal citizens in the democracy created by the magic of the marketplace.

Some critics maintain that the blurring of the distinction between humans and goods is not just innocuous fun, for it has serious implications for the ways in which "real" people are treated in the "real" world. Judith Williamson (1978, 169) offers the following warning about the possible effects of enveloping people within arbitrary symbolic structures in advertising:

> There is nothing "wrong" about symbols as such—obviously systems of signification are necessary and inevitable. . . . [But] there is a danger in having *people* involved as part of the currency in these systems. When people become symbols they need not be treated as human beings. . . . Women are especially liable to this phenomenon. But in all areas of life it is clearly very dangerous to see only what people "mean" (e.g. a threat, a status symbol) rather than what they are.

Advertising's imagery and symbolism replaces "real" people with artificial "types" and situations, and thus turns people into *things*, purchasable and exchangeable in the marketplace.

WHAT EFFECTS DOES ADVERTISING HAVE ON SOCIETY?

At the heart of both the liberal and radical critiques lies the claim that from the economic necessity to create demand, and from the existence of the technological means to achieve this, arises advertising's power to induce false needs in people.

The Creation of False Needs

There are two variations on this theme, the best known of which is found in the work of Herbert Marcuse. Here, false needs are defined as those that are superimposed upon the individual to aid repression and that

> perpetuate toil, aggressiveness, misery and injustice. . . . Most of the prevailing needs to relax, to have fun, to behave and consume in accordance with the advertisements, to love and hate what others love and hate, belong to this category of false needs. Such needs have a societal content and function which are determined by external powers over which the individual has no control. . . . No matter how much such needs may have become the individual's own, . . . they continue to be what they were from the beginning — products of a society whose dominant interests demand repression. (Marcuse 1964, 19)

The only "true" needs, it would appear, are for nourishment, clothing, and housing. When pressed for a definition of who decides what needs are true and what are not, Marcuse retreats into the distant (socialist) future and answers that individuals themselves must define these, but only when they are truly free to give their own answer. This is impossible as long as they are "kept incapable of being autonomous, as long as they are indoctrinated and manipulated."

In a similar vein, the French situationist writer Guy Debord suggests that the whole enterprise of the consumer society is simply fraudulent:

> When economic necessity is replaced by the necessity for boundless economic development, the satisfaction of primary needs is replaced by an uninterrupted fabrication of pseudo-needs which are reduced to the single pseudo-need of maintaining the reign of the autonomous economy. (Debord 1970, 51)

The phrase "pseudo-need" puts one in mind of Daniel Boorstin's *The Image* (1962). Boorstin is convinced that the contemporary scene is riddled with "pseudo-events" — happenings that appear to be natural or spontaneous but are, in fact, stage-managed, planned, and executed by interested parties in order to make an impression on public opinion. "News conferences" and "photo opportunities" by politicians, "information" supplied on a not-for-attribution basis by "usually reliable sources," and the comings-and-goings of celebrities are examples of pseudo-events.

Pseudo-events are constructed occurrences in the world of fact; images of pseudo-ideals, on the other hand, represent a kind of "short-circuiting" of values, in that models of behaviour are displayed in a compressed, impressionistic form often constructed from bits and pieces of older values thrown together helter-skelter. Boorstin connects "the rise of image-thinking" with the new technologies of mass communication, and regards it as virtually synonymous with the increasing prominence of advertising, whose special power is derived from its capacity to unite pseudo-events and pseudo-ideals into a single statement. Advertisements combine a constructed or imaginary event (how junior got his clothes so filthy) with a simplified but vivid ideal (mother's passionate concern for whiteness) so as to generate a desired outcome in reality (brand loyalty in a laundry detergent). Boorstin worries not that advertising lies, but that it "befuddles" or blurs our experiences with values, making everything ambiguous, so that it becomes harder and harder to distinguish true ideals from pseudo-ideals.

A minor variation on the false-needs theme comes from Ernest Mandel (1978), who criticizes capitalism not because it stretches the boundaries of needing, but because its actual configurations of human needs "restrict man's development, making it narrow and one-sided," discouraging individuals from developing and expressing all those needs and activities (such as self-created popular entertainment and fuller participation in managing organizations) that have nothing to do with buying products. "Socially manipulative compulsions" such as advertising thus work against the full development of individuals and serve instead the needs of the owners of capital. Stuart Ewen (1976, 36), too, sees the underlying dynamic of the system of needs as being based not on the interests of consumers but rather on "the real, historic needs of capitalist productive machinery."

Thus, the unifying theme in the Marxist approach is that advertising brings into existence false needs that would not be felt in its absence. This view differs significantly from the critique of mass society offered by writers such as Packard (1957) and C. Wright Mills (*The Power Elite*, 1956), who complained not that false needs were being instilled in people, but that genuine, deeply rooted human needs were being appealed to in unscrupulous ways. Needs for emotional security, self-esteem, ego-gratification, creativity, a sense of power, and so forth already exist. Advertising merely draws these needs out in order to create demand for particular products. It subverts rational decision making by aiming persuasive communications at the psychological domains where consumers are apt to be most vulnerable.

John Berger in *Ways of Seeing* (1972) states that advertising works through the passions of envy and pleasure on a deep and powerful level of human emotions, and that it directs its appeals toward the psychological domains in which people have only weak capacity to resist types of behaviour that cannot bring them real happiness and contentment in the long run.

Galbraith (1958) takes a slightly different position: the creation of demand is not a matter of appeals to strong, basic needs but rather to relatively weak psychological drives such as vanity, envy, and insecurity. Simply because these drives are weak, they are subject to manipulation and influence.

The Propaganda of Commodities

It is claimed that without advertising people would not develop "false needs," nor would they try to satisfy such needs in misdirected ways through purchasing commodities. According to Raymond Williams (1980 [1962]), much of human satisfaction takes place in nonmaterial domains, where objects are largely inconsequential, but the magic system of advertising distracts us by channelling all needs through the object-laden rituals in the consumer marketplace.

In the Marxist tradition, this process is referred to as "reification," which encourages people to satisfy their needs with things that can be bought and sold. Thus, the capitalist marketplace controls the basic pattern and content of social interactions. Leisure, play, and other personal activities increasingly are absorbed by a kind of generalized "fashion consciousness" that connects our activities with the inescapable presence of commercial objects.

Indeed, a growing number of social commentators (many of whom are not Marxists) view this process of reification as the most sinister feature of advertising in western societies. Charles Lindblom (1977) and Morris Janowitz (1978), for example, think that advertising's main cultural function is not to sell us particular goods but rather to persuade us that *only* in consumption can we find satisfaction and happiness. Similarly, Christopher Lasch in *The Culture of Narcissism* (1979) refers to "the propaganda of commodities" by which "advertising serves not so much to advertise products as to promote consumption as a way of life." This propaganda has two functions: to offer consumption as an alternative to rebellion or protest, and to turn alienation or reification itself into a commodity. While Lasch looks upon advertising as a force that in general maintains the social relations of capitalism, he also regards it as a revolutionary institution that has fundamentally altered the traditional authority structures within capitalist society:

> The "education" of the masses has altered the balance of forces within the family, weakening the authority of the husband in relation to the wife and parents in relation to their children. It emancipates women and children from patriarchal authority, however, only to subject them to the new paternalism of the advertising industry, the industrial corporation and the state. (Lasch 1979, 140)

For Jerry Mander (1977), the most dangerous consequence of this process of reification is that the "natural" satisfaction of needs is replaced by the "artificial" mediation of commodities. A good example is the marketing of milk products in the Third World. In the 1970s, the multinational food company Nestlé advertised powdered milk for babies as an alternative to breast feeding in countries such as Kenya. The attractiveness of the product was undoubtedly enhanced by the positive image of "modernity" that western technologies and social practices carry in developing nations. In this case, however, the results were tragic, because the powdered formula required sanitary conditions that were not available; many babies who were fed in this way became ill and died.

Mander compares the experience of "commodity people" to that of experimental laboratory animals used in medical and psychological research. To accept the notion that the capitalist marketplace offers consumers "free choice," he maintains, is to perpetuate a cruel and dangerous myth:

> We have been removed from the environment within which we evolved and with which we are uniquely designed to interact. Now we interact and coevolve with only the grosser, more monolithic, human-made commercial forms which remain available within our new laboratory-space station. Because we live inside the new environment, we are not aware that any tradeoff has been made. (Mander 1977, 122)

Far from offering a diversity of choices for the satisfaction of needs, advertisements offer only one—purchasing a commodity. In this way, advertisers intervene between people and their needs, separating them from the possibility of direct and true fulfilment. Debord (1970) seconds this complaint, holding that in the "society of the spectacle" everything that used to be experienced directly has been moved away into "representations" (what Boorstin would call "images"). Advertising "represents" our experiences, but in a distorted and artifical manner. Its images come to replace reality; since they are composed of pseudo-events and pseudo-ideals, however, we cannot experience full and true satisfaction (Boorstin 1962).

In such a context, commodities become separated from people, loosed from their control, hostile to their autonomy and search for self-realization. Since advertising must perpetually create new demand, it must also continually produce unsatisfied consumers. Mander (1977) writes that "the goal of all advertising is discontent, ... an internal scarcity of contentment." Advertising plays on our fears, insecurities, and anxieties by constantly reminding us that our lives could be better if only we were to buy this or that. This is the reason for advertising's existence. As *Printer's Ink* remarked as early as 1930: "Advertising helps to keep the masses dissatisfied with their mode of life, discontented with *ugly things* around them. Satisfied customers are not as profitable as discontented ones" (Ewen 1976, 39).

Advertising as Social Control and Ideology

False needs and reification bring about a redefinition of what is important in social life. In the Marxist critique of capitalism, the productive sphere is held to be the key both to the way the system operates and to the way that it will eventually be overthrown; problems in the way goods are produced will lead to the disintegration of capitalism. This theory has serious weaknesses, however. During the course of this century, capitalism has survived numerous crises in its productive sphere — in part, by modifying its structure and operation. In trying to explain why capitalism has been able to survive so long, the radical critique has had to look to other institutions that contain and "deflect" the crisis at the heart of capitalism's productive relations. Thus, explaining capitalism's longevity or why the working class (caught in oppressive class relations) has not yet developed a critical view of capitalism has become increasingly important. As Alan Swingewood writes: "For many contemporary Marxists the term 'late capitalism' implies that the historically necessary collapse of capitalism has been averted by the conscious ideological and cultural manipulation of the bourgeoisie over the proletariat" (1977, *x*).

Such manipulation is illustrated, for example, in the way that advertising encouraged people to think of themselves as *consumers* rather than as *producers.* Advertising addressed both production and consumption domains: while creating demand to solve the problem of over-production, advertising would simultaneously persuade workers that the satisfactions not available in the workplace were available in consumption; though they could not control the conditions under which they laboured, they could buy consumer goods and thus control, in some measure, their personal lives. Judith Williamson writes,

> In our society, while the real distinctions between people are created by their role in the *process* of production as workers, it is the *products* of their work that are used in the false categories invoked by advertising, to obscure the real structure of society by replacing class with the distinction made by the consumption of particular goods. (Williamson 1978, 13)

The deflection from production to consumption is a deflection from the real world to the imaginary world. The world of production is where the important decisions of our society are made, yet advertising encourages us to leave this world to others and stresses instead consumption as the realm for decision making. Raymond Williams thinks that modern society offers us a fundamental choice in whether we see people primarily as producers or as consumers, and that "the system of organized magic [advertising] is primarily important as a functional obscuring of this choice" (1980 [1962], 186).

Many writers also claim that advertising plays a more straightforward role in transmitting an ideology that perpetuates the status quo and its exploitative social relations, through the presentation of a world view that encourages the audience to interpret reality in ways that work to the benefit of those who already possess economic power. For David Potter (*People of Plenty*, 1954), advertising is a major factor in socialization. The danger is that, while advertising wields great social power, there is little social accountability for its operations. In this respect, it differs from institutions such as churches and schools.

Advertising "communicates directly and indirectly, evaluations, norms and propositions about matters other than the products that are to be sold" (Andren et al. 1978, 113). Advertising ideology is a set of false and misleading concepts about reality, and in two major dimensions this ideology actually works: the stress on satisfaction through consumption rather than work, and the "Hollywood set," in which the world is portrayed as free from racial and class conflict, "idyllic and false." As Williamson puts it:

> Advertisements are selling us something else beside consumer goods: in providing us with a structure in which we and those goods are interchangeable, they are selling us ourselves. . . . Ideology is the meaning made necessary by the condition of society while helping to *perpetuate* those conditions. We feel a need to belong, to have a social place; it can be hard to find. Instead we may be given an imaginary one. (Williamson 1978, 13)

CONCLUSION

Many critics maintain that advertising exists primarily to create demand among consumers. People have certain types of wants and needs, and they are perfectly capable of discovering for themselves what they are. All that is required for the efficient functioning of a market economy is that when consumers visit retail establishments or examine product labels or descriptive brochures, they are made aware that certain items will satisfy those wants. Everything else—and especially, all of national consumer product advertising—is superfluous puffery.

Advertising creates demand, which would not exist in its absence, by manipulating people's normal motivational impulses. Advertisers, it is held, manipulate people by subtly mixing reality and fantasy, by creating a "magic show" that makes it hard to tell what one's "real needs" are or where to draw the line between sensible behaviour and careless overindulgence.

Finally, some say that advertising is a powerful mechanism that distorts our whole society's values and priorities, resulting in an overemphasis on the private pursuit of material satisfaction and a serious neglect of public spaces and common concerns such as creating safe and pleasing urban environments.

Serious criticisms of advertising have been around almost as long as their target has and doubtless will remain with us, ranging from mild, general unease to sharper, more specific forms of attack. The continued debate lends support to the common perception that advertising has some influence on serious issues in modern social life.

One overall observation about advertising's critics will be ventured here. Objections directed at advertisements, the industry, and its alleged social impacts are often indirect attacks on the so-called materialistic ethos of industrial society, or on capitalism in general as a social system; these are critiques of society masquerading as critiques of advertising. We have not presumed to evaluate their merits, but we do think that when advertising is used as a surrogate for these larger concerns, its critics are aiming at the wrong target.

3

Defences of Advertising

As we have seen, critics of advertising usually regard advertising as so persuasive, powerful, and manipulative that consumers are unable to decide rationally what exactly their real needs are or how best to satisfy them. The consumer is seen, from this perspective, as the confused and hapless victim of the advertising industry's clever machinations.

Not surprisingly, defenders of the advertising industry seek to portray the typical consumer in a distinctly different light. Their starting point is not the "bewildered" but the "rational" consumer who uses the goods of the capitalist marketplace and the information provided by advertising to satisfy his or her needs. This concept of how things *should* work, rooted in classical liberal economic theory, is something many defenders and critics of advertising share, but while the defenders claim that, with the help of advertising, the market actually operates in this way to match people's needs with suitable products, many of the critics think that advertising actually destroys the competitive and rational nature of the free market.

Another major point of divergence concerns the question of needs. The critics hold that advertising creates needs in people; the defenders say that this attributes too much power to advertising. They see advertising as one component among many of the "marketing concept," helping people to match their needs with products that will satisfy them. Marketers are the democrats of the marketplace, discovering (not creating) consumer needs, designing products to meet them, and using advertisements to communicate the availability and desirability of products.

Proponents of the marketing concept believe that marketing and advertising are essential in our complex, market-oriented economy. Marketing seeks to overcome some of the disadvantages of the specialization of labour, through which most persons become unfamiliar with the characteristics of mass-produced goods. The marketing system should be seen as a "provisioning technology" that confronts the enormous task of matching tens of millions of consuming units with tens of thousands of producing units. Its strategies are based on the premise that the consumer, as ultimate decision maker, is a rational problem solver who takes full advantage of this technology. The marketing concept involves the coordination of the "four Ps": product (shaping and designing products to meet consumer needs); price (pricing appropriately to generate sales); promotion (promoting sales through advertising, store displays, and selling strategy); and place (placing products in appropriate retail outlets).

Ironically, marketing proponents can agree with much of Stuart Ewen's explanation of how, in the past, advertising was used to solve problems in distribution and consumption caused by mass production. In *Marketing: Concepts and Strategy,* Martin Bell concedes that national advertising of the 1920s and 1930s did, indeed, seek to manipulate consumer demand:

> The high-powered, skillful manipulator of consumer opinion, using personal salesmanship and aggressive advertising, took charge in many American businesses. His was the specialized task of selling the goods that had been mass produced and mass distributed. He found that almost anything could be sold with enough expense and effort. (Bell 1966, 7)

But during the 1930s, social criticism of this aggressive approach increased, and the marketing industry, recognizing the limits of coercive persuasion, framed a new orientation based on intensive market research and the effective design of new products instead of merely producing goods and then looking for ways to sell them. "The marketing concept starts with the firm's target customers and their needs and wants; it plans a co-ordinated set of products and programs to serve their needs and wants; and it derives profits through creating customer satisfaction" (Kotler and Turner 1981, 31).

Implicit in the marketing concept is the assumption that the most efficient way for the market to function is to allow consumers to direct producers, rather than the reverse. Under classic liberal theory, market behaviour of consumers is based upon deliberate and calculated action. Rational consumers faced with many products will only purchase those they truly require to satisfy their wants; rational producers of goods (in the face of competition from other marketers) will only produce what consumers want. Thus, the self-interested actions of buyers and sellers together within the free, competitive market will ensure the most efficient functioning of the system.

Martin Bell has outlined how the consumer behaves according to the rational approach. The satisfaction of a want involves four stages: (1) the recognition of a want; (2) the search for means to satisfy the want; (3) the evaluation of competing alternatives; and (4) a decision. Advertising plays its part in the search and evaluation stages (Bell 1966).

Marketing literature's basic contention is that the rational consumer and the responsible producer are the cornerstones of the marketing system. The consumer is not manipulated and controlled, but rather is a free agent who searches the market for suitable means to satisfy his or her own needs and desires. The producer of goods tries not to create wants but to discover what wants exist and to design and manufacture products to respond to those wants. Advertising informs consumers about the result.

THE "MYTH" OF MANIPULATION

The persistent criticism that advertising creates a demand for products that otherwise would not exist puts the advertising industry in a peculiar position. Advertisers contend there is little evidence to show that advertising has any affect on aggregate sales—that is, it does nothing to increase the overall level of consumption. Seldom does one find an industry so strenuously arguing the *ineffectiveness* of its product.

What exactly is the influence of advertising on the level of consumption in our society? The classic work in this field, Neil Borden's *Advertising in Our Economy* (1947), concluded that, while advertising may accelerate trends in consumption patterns, it cannot by itself create these patterns. Twenty-four years later, Julian Simon stated that advertisements for products such as alcohol, soap, and drugs—the products at the heart of the controversy about advertising—do not seem to have much effect on the economy and "hence from an economic point of view, it is immaterial whether they are present or absent. . . . All this implies that the economic study of advertising is not deserving of great attention" (1970, 285).

The issues have continued to attract attention, however. Mark Albion and Paul Ferris write:

> We believe strongly that advertising, as an efficient form of mass communication, can *accelerate* the growth of new markets and new entries into markets. We doubt that advertising significantly determines the ultimate size of a market. . . . Other factors appear to be much more important in increasing demand. The effectiveness of advertising is severely limited, relegated mostly to new products and new services. (1981, 179)

Michael Schudson (1984) concludes that, while advertising cannot create new needs, it can help to satisfy an old need in a new way and accelerate trends in consumption. To illustrate his argument, he looks at the cigarette industry, which on the face of it seems to provide solid support for the critics' case about need creation. Advertising has been accused of breaking down traditional taboos against smoking by women and young persons and thereby contributing to the creation of new needs. Schudson points out that, while cigarette sales have grown enormously this century, overall tobacco consumption has increased much less; for example, in the period from 1918 to 1940, cigarette consumption increased steadily, but the overall level of tobacco consumption was unchanged, suggesting that, if advertising indeed was having an effect, it was to switch cigar and pipe smokers to cigarettes, thus satisfying an old need in a new way.

What advertising did was to latch onto a change in consumption patterns. Compared to traditional smoking practices, cigarette smoking is a short, simple activity involving little skill or fuss, and well suited to modern urban living, which does not normally allow long breaks during a day. Schudson thinks that the success of the cigarette industry has less to do with advertising and more to do with its suitability for modern living (1984, ch. 6).

This kind of thinking is reflected within the advertising industry itself. Retired advertising executive Bud Turner says,

> Advertising follows, it doesn't lead. You have to discover there's a market for what you're producing—you have to have a dream. . . . Advertising follows this through to its logical conclusion and uses whatever is the fashionable way to describe that product and the strongest medium. Even the fashion has to precede the expression of it in the ad. The product and the ad reflect society. If it's well placed on the consumer spectrum it will be successful. (Interview)

Similarly, Bruce Morrison, testifying before the U.S. Federal Trade Commission in 1971, agreed that advertising may cultivate "dormant or previously unperceived desires" but maintained that it cannot create them or force people to buy things they do not need. He cited estimates that about 46 percent of new products fail in testing and that another 50 percent do not last a year on the market. (Other estimates of market failure rates range up to 80 percent depending on how the concept is defined.) These figures point to the successful functioning of a competitive market, where poor products, regardless of the amount of advertising lavished upon them, are weeded out by the consumer. Morrison ended with a simple challenge: "To anyone who truly believes he can manipulate consumers, I would offer this humble advice: try it" (in Moskin 1973, 38).

Downplaying advertising's social role is a familiar refrain of the industry. Advertisers claim they simply do not have the knowledge or tools required for manipulating people (no matter how much they might want to do so). Indeed, after reviewing the literature one is tempted to conclude that in no other domain has so much effort yielded so little insight. Market research has provided remarkably little reliable information on the kind of advertising that works with various market segments, or why consumers react to commercials as they do.

People who work in the advertising industry certainly do not feel that they are all-powerful manipulators, as these comments indicate.

> The recipients think that advertising is a powerful tool, capable of great things. We in the business see it as a fragile tool—if we could sell everything there would not be so many failures.

> The thing that intrigues me is that everyone thinks the advertising business is so sophisticated and that we have all sorts of research. We always laugh at

that. We're working on something and come up with a dumb idea and laugh. Things happen so simply. In a lot of cases you don't need years of experience. If you are a good lateral thinker and approach it from a different way then you can present it to the consumer.

> Manipulating wizards? It's one of the misconceptions and I wish it were true—we'd be running the country and sitting in the sun somewhere if I knew absolutely how to manipulate people. The fact of the matter is that human beings can't be thus manipulated—if they could we could banish war and apply the same techniques to larger theaters of life and control whole populations. We can't because fundamentally human beings refuse to be categorized and are finally unpredictable. (Interviews)

Testifying before the Federal Trade Commission in 1971, Alfred Seeman said,

> I can see why people outside the advertising business think we have an unlimited supply of scientific tools and techniques—so magical that we can manipulate almost anything. The fact of the matter is that we are successful in selling good products and unsuccessful in selling poor ones. In the end consumer satisfaction—or lack of it—is more powerful than all our tools and ingenuity put together. The economics of the marketplace insist that an advertiser must satisfy the consumer—that is, get repeat purchases—or fail. Often we think, after using all our techniques, we have a sure bet in a new product, for instance, only to find that it fails in the marketplace. You know the story: we had the perfect dog food except for one thing—the dogs wouldn't eat it. . . . The use of language is not a science, it is an art. (in Moskin 1973, 44)

The overall impression one derives from this self-deprecating view is that advertisers do not know how to manipulate. Advertising is an art form. It is incapable of steering audience responses reliably in one direction or another.

Studies on the economic effect of advertising have focused on advertising's role in developed western economies, particularly the American economy. Some researchers have sought to measure the claims of manipulation and demand creation in cross-national terms. In a 1980 paper, Rachael Querles and her colleagues sought to test Galbraith's thesis that advertising creates demand by asking a wider question: What factors determine how much we buy? Two broad answers are usually given. Galbraith thinks that advertising (and specifically television advertising) is an important element in governing how much a society consumes. Classical liberal economic theorists believe that the level of consumption is based more on how much people have to spend that it is on advertising; the level of affluence, in other words, is the dominant factor in explaining how much a society consumes.

Querles and her coworkers quantified the subsidiary elements of these two explanations. They measured the level of consumption in each society in terms of consumption per household; the level of advertising as the amount spent on advertising; and affluence in terms of a society's per capita gross national product (GNP). By comparing different societies along these dimensions, they hoped to be able to see the relative influences of advertising and affluence on the level of consumption in general; that is, whether high levels of consumption are more dependent on advertising or on wealth. Using data from forty-two nations representing the industrialized nations of western Europe and North America and the developing nations of Latin America, Africa, and Asia, they performed a regression analysis to determine which of the factors was more significant.

The results were far from clear-cut. When total advertising expenditures (both broadcast and print) were included in the calculations, it seemed that Galbraith's contention that advertising creates demand was upheld, because consumption seemed to correlate more closely to it than to the relative level of affluence. However, when advertising expenditures were broken down into broadcast and print expenditures and treated separately, a curious result appeared. Broadcast advertising, which according to Galbraith is the most important tool in the creation of demand, was much less of an influence upon the level of consumption than was print advertising. Galbraith states that print advertising is primarily informational rather than persuasive and is therefore less of a manipulative tool. The findings of the Querles study indicate that the rational information of print is more influential than television's persuasive formats.

If the Querles study is assumed to be valid, what conclusions follow? The authors suggest that "it is possible that consumers are not really manipulated by advertising but are instead beneficiaries of a more efficient distribution system made possible by advertising" (Querles, Jeffres, and Schnuerer 1980, 11). Advertising may actually increase the level of consumption, not because it is persuading us to do things we would not otherwise do, but by making the system work more efficiently for the benefit of both consumers and producers. In the light of such empirical evidence and the plausible protestations of innocence from the advertising industry, the notion of the malleable consumer appears more and more implausible. As we will see later, consumers may well be bewildered and confused, but, if they are, it is not because advertising is manipulating them.

ADVERTISING AS INFORMATION

Few would go far as to suggest that advertising has no relation whatsoever to consumption patterns. After all, if this were the case, advertisers would not hand over the many billions of dollars they do each year. Why, then, do they spend so much?

There are two answers. First, producers advertise not because they know it will work, but because they do not know for sure that it will not. As Schudson (1984, 42) puts it: "Advertisers use advertising as one way of coping with the ever uncertain world of changeable consumers and wily competitors, but they hedge the bets they place on it." Advertisers cannot risk not advertising, even though they can never be entirely sure it is worth the money. Second, while advertising may not influence aggregate demand for a particular product group, it influences substantially the market share commanded by any company at a given time. As advertising executive Frank Convery says: "The task of most advertising is to keep the product on the market or increase its share from someone else. This is share-oriented advertising, pushing brands. Most, even for tobacco, is brand oriented—it doesn't make people smoke" (Interview).

From this perspective, advertising cannot increase the total quantity of a particular product type (for example, cigarettes) bought on any day, but it can persuade people who are going to smoke anyway to buy a particular brand. Advertising as a whole, therefore, is geared for the seemingly inconsistent goals of celebrating brand loyalty and of drawing consumers away from competitors, and can be viewed as a device that consumers use to evaluate alternatives in the marketplace prior to purchase. In other words, it is a form of information. This is, of course, the standard industry defence, and indeed a powerful theoretical position can be constructed around it, based on the social benefits of information flow.

In an industrialized economy, consumers will have imperfect information about the goods circulating around them. In contrast, a small-scale, self-sufficient community has no need for media advertising, because the sources of supply are nearby and personal observation and word-of-mouth communication are adequate as sources of product information. According to the standard textbook accounts, which are admittedly somewhat simplistic in this regard, as the production of goods is centralized and begins to undermine local and regional economies, unfamiliar goods appear and advertising steps in to provide the required information.

The belief that advertising primarily affects market share gains further credence when we examine the historical roots of national brand advertising from a slightly different perspective. Vince Norris (in Rotzoll, Haefner, and Sandage 1976) claims that the impetus behind the development of national advertising was only partly centralized production and problems of distribution. The dynamic element, he opines, is the relation between wholesalers and producers.

In the last thirty years of the nineteenth century, there were four key players in the production and consumption of goods: consumers, retailers, wholesalers, and producers. The wholesaler occupied the pivotal position, serving as a link between a limited number of producers and a much larger number of retailers. In the absence of branded goods, the wholesaler fulfilled retailer demand by buying a product from the manufacturer with the lowest price. Obviously, such practices were not very advantageous to manufacturers and kept profit margins rather small.

To escape the stranglehold of the wholesalers, manufacturers started to create brand names for their products, differentiating them from other producers' output (usually only in image) and appealing through advertising directly to the consumer. Norris concludes:

> To the extent that consumers could be induced to request a particular manufacturer's brand from the retailer, the retailer would order it from the wholesaler who in turn would be forced to buy it from that manufacturer and no other. Now the manufacturer, not the wholesaler, was dominant, and he could name his price. (Rotzoll, Haefner, and Sandage 1976, 23)

The ascendancy of the manufacturer changed the pattern of economic activity, and while it resulted in higher prices and lack of price competition, it gave consumers a "choice" regarding the brand of product they purchased. The "information" that advertising provided gave the producer and consumer more autonomy at the wholesaler's expense.

The seminal article on the relation between advertising and information is George Stigler's "The Economics of Information" (1961), in which advertising is presented as an important source of consumer information. Provisioning oneself with goods takes time, because one needs to "search" for products. Advertising provides a service for which consumers are willing to pay, since it reduces their search costs. Stigler admits his remarks are more appropriate to classified and retail advertising, which does little more than to show that a product is available at a particular place at a specific price, but he also argues that they can be extended to the more spectacular national product advertising on television." "The assimilation of information is not an easy or pleasant task for most people and they may well be willing to pay more for information when supplied in an enjoyable form" (1961, 222).

Philip Nelson (1974b) sought to give a complete account of the consumer's sources of information. Because consumers do not have perfect information about goods, he writes, they have to rely on past consumption experiences, the advice of friends and relatives, consumer reports, and, of course, advertising. Nelson is aware that the information argument appears to be weakest in the case of national television advertising, but he attempts to construct a model that will accept this as a form of information as well. Conceding the point that much national advertising offers no help in ranking competing brands on any "informational" criteria (because all claim to be the best and only experience can differentiate them), he still believes that it conveys some vital information—

namely, that a brand advertises. The more a brand advertises the more the consumer is likely to believe it is a better buy. The mere existence of the commercial is its total informational role:

> The consumer is right in his belief that advertised brands are better. The better brands have more incentive to advertise than the poorer brands. . . . Simply put, it pays to advertise winners rather than losers. In consequence, the amount of advertising gives consumers a clue as to which brands are winners and which brands are losers. (Nelson 1974b, 50)

Nelson meets the controversy over the "irrational" nature of national advertising by ignoring it.

Further support for the necessity of advertising in making market economies function efficiently can be found in an analysis of advertising's role in some "socialist" societies. In *Advertising and Socialism* (1974), Philip Hanson reported that advertising expenditures—although very small by comparison with western economies—vary greatly among these countries. The deciding factor seems to be the amount of centralized planning in the production and distribution of goods. The more centrally run a society is, the less need it has for advertising. For example, in the most highly centralized of them all, the Soviet Union, whatever advertising does take place is initiated by the distributive rather than the productive sector, and its main function seems to be to encourage the disposal of "surplus goods." On the other hand, in societies (such as Hungary and Yugoslavia) that practise some form of market socialism— independent production units dealing with buyers through the market— advertising expenditures are markedly higher. The more active the marketplace, the greater advertising's role. This hypothesis supports the view that advertising is one indispensable means for providing the information that all market-oriented industrialized societies need for their economies to function efficiently.

ADVERTISING AS PERSUASION AND AS SYMBOLISM

Driver and Foxall believe that detailed studies on consumer choices show that "the depiction of consumers as rational, problem-solving beings is actually a highly limited description of buyer behaviour" (Driver and Foxall 1984, 87). In fact, most purchasing decisions appear to be "situationally determined" and to be the most strongly influenced by interpersonal communications, especially word-of-mouth information. Even more significant is the typical consumer's "low involvement"; the consumer is "essentially passive," selecting among products without developing much interest, on average, in the whole enterprise of shopping (except perhaps for consumer durables, fashion clothing, and personal care items).

The upshot is simple: most people are indifferent to most of the "information" about goods already circulating around them, and are uninterested in obtaining more. "For many purchases a decision process never occurs, not even on the first purchase" (Driver and Foxall 1984, 92). Advertising, then, doesn't matter very much. This opinion reinforces other judgments noted earlier, that advertising's impact lies primarily in stimulating trials of new goods and in "defensive" propaganda by brand-name producers against each other. Driver and Foxall (1984, 93) conclude that advertising seems to have "no power beyond engendering passing interest and, perhaps, cursory comparative evaluation; it is certainly, of itself, incapable of building preference or conviction." Since their book is copublished by the Advertising Association of Great Britain, one can assume that this finding is at least a quasi-official stance by the industry there.

Notwithstanding the denigration of the informative role of advertising in much of the recent literature, information has always been the major reason for classified and retail advertising. In our opinion, the information model has never had much relevance for national consumer product advertising. The explicit function of spectacular image-based, nonrational advertising is not so much to inform as it is to persuade. There must be a convincing case on behalf of such advertising. And, indeed, one has been made. Charles Sandage argues that the persuasive function of advertising has been thrust upon it by the culture and economy of which it is a part: "Modern society emphasizes the right of every person to be employed. To achieve this, high-level consumption is essential. . . . This will require persuasion. This is the function of advertising" (in Sandage and Fryburger 1960, 149). To the extent that advertising can persuade people to buy goods they would not otherwise buy, it provides employment within the economy as a whole by ensuring that investment in production is profitable.

Moreover, Sandage sees nothing wrong with persuasion in settings where other sources of persuasion are also present. Thus, advertising enhances freedom of choice by raising the consumer's level of education. Rotzoll et al. (1976, 20–21) tell us that, "under the assumption that man is rational, it is quite appropriate to attempt to persuade. For it is assumed that rational man will be able to detect truth in the clashing views of self-interested individuals in the economic marketplace in the same manner that his discerning nature would enable truth to arise in the political arena." Advertising is only one among many capable players in the free marketplace of ideas, and there is no good reason for singling it out for special attention.

In Canada, a royal commission report on "consumer problems" stated bluntly, "the view that persuasion is bad . . . must be rejected out of hand. Persuasion is an inherent part of the democratic process." Supporting this standpoint, a group of theologians from Toronto upheld the position that persuasion is "legitimate and valid and entirely defensible" because the consumer is always more than a mere spectator in events (Oliver 1981).

A Swedish economist, Staffan Linder (1970), has taken the case for persuasion one step further. He claims that persuasion is not only good for society as a whole but that, in fact, consumers *want to be persuaded.* Affluent societies are characterized by a scarcity of time, because as we produce more and more goods, we require correspondingly more and more time to enjoy them fully. The time available for each activity (and for enjoying the goods that accompany it) decreases because we must spread our available leisure time across an ever-enlarging array of activities and goods. As such, the "leisure class" in modern societies is "harried"—surely one of the most peculiar paradoxes of modern affluence.

The search for consumer goods takes time, but, because time is limited, consumers cannot make fully rational decisions in the strict sense of weighing all available competing product information. The only properly rational course of action, then, is to be *irrational.* A fully rational decision, based on complete product information and the study of consumer research reports, would require far too much time to complete— time that could better be allocated to other activities:

> But as soon as one lacks complete information, one is also exposed to the possibility of being influenced by advertising. One actually *wants* to be influenced by advertising to get an instant feeling that one has a perfectly good reason to buy this or that commodity, the true properties of which one knows dismally little about. Only unintelligent buyers acquire complete information. . . . People can be made the victims of persuasion, not because they are irrational, but because they are rational. (Linder 1970, 73–74)

According to Linder, then, we want to be persuaded in the shortest time possible so that we have at least some basis, however irrational, for our decisions and enough time left over after shopping to actually use and enjoy the many things we come to possess. To behave rationally is to accept cheerfully and at face value advertising's persuasive appeals.

Can we, then, view acceptance of persuasion as a rational process for those being persuaded? At first glance, much of the national advertising we encounter today contains neither much information nor much explicit persuasion. What strikes us is the linking of abstract qualities (such as social status) with products. In order to legitimate this type of persuasion, the advertising industry has had to redefine what constitutes persuasion. In particular, there has been an attempt to distinguish manipulation from persuasion.

While manipulation involves outright deception (lying or falsehood), persuasion is supposed to harbour only allowable exaggeration and embellishment—what is known in the trade as "puffery" (Aaker and Myers 1975, 567-77). This distinction has been important to the advertising industry in controlling the boundaries of debate about its product. In essence, it says that while advertisers are not to lie, they are not necessarily bound to tell the whole truth and nothing but the truth—a vital distinction. Alvin Achenbaum, Senior Vice-President at J. Walter Thompson, put it this way: "To the degree that an advertiser intends to deceive his prospects and succeeds, he is manipulating. . . . But what constitutes deception is not always clear-cut. And to say that emotion, subjectivity, incompleteness are deceptive is not necessarily so" [*sic*] (Moskin 1973, 48).

Theodore Levitt extends this line of argument by equating advertising with art. The latter, by definition, presents a "distortion" or interpretation of reality with the aim of influencing an audience to think in a certain way—beyond functionality and practicality to abstraction. Advertising has the same goals and uses similar means, and so it should be evaluated by the same criteria.

> Civilization is man's attempt to transcend his ancient animality: and this includes both art and advertising. . . . Both represent a pervasive and I believe *universal* characteristic of human nature—the human audience *demands* symbolic interpretation in everything it sees and knows. If it doesn't get it, it will return a verdict of "no interest" (Levitt 1970, 87–89)

Thus, human beings are not confined to rationality in their market behaviour but may also be nonrational (as distinct from irrational). Human subjectivity and the need for symbolism is now part and parcel of the case for the defence: *we want and desire the symbolism of advertising.* What is at stake here is a deeply felt human need. We never relate to goods only for their plain utility; there is always a symbolic aspect to our interactions with them. In fact, the need and desire for symbolism is one of the defining features of human nature.

Most people, we think, would agree that appeals to people's emotions and feelings are perfectly legitimate. Michael Schudson (1984) reminds us that in all cultures goods have always carried symbolic baggage with them. If advertising is to be criticized at all, he continues, objections should be directed not at its love of symbolic representation in general, but rather at specific acts of omission or distortion. Levitt (1970) agrees: since the relationship between use and symbolism is a fundamental part of all human interactions with objects, there cannot be anything wrong in principle with advertising's participation in this universal process, so long as its audiences are not subject to acts of outright deceit.

CONCLUSION

The defences for advertising are, in essence, remarkably simple: advertising is part and parcel of a highly industrialized, market-oriented society.

Information and persuasion from uncounted sources swirl around all the individuals who live, work, and shop in this setting. Both informative and persuasive communications are vital and indeed necessary ingredients of decision-making processes in politics, in social relations, and in the marketplace. Advertisements include both communication formats but constitute only one ingredient in the mix, and not a particularly outstanding one at that. In short, there is nothing special about advertising.

Thus, both the usual criticisms and the usual defences end up at the same point, although they arrive there by quite different routes. In the defences, as in the criticisms, we are hard pressed to identify either advertising's uniqueness as a form of modern mass communication or its unique place and function among the many overlapping social forces in modern life.

PART 2

ADVERTISING AND MEDIA

4

Origins of the Consumer Culture

WITH ROMAN ONUFRIJCHUK

The arguments recounted in the preceding two chapters leave us with a curious result. Throughout the twentieth century, the nature of the disagreements between the staunch defenders and equally resolute critics of advertising does not seem to have changed very much. Advertising's defenders maintain that a modern economy relies upon the provision of both straightforward factual information and persuasive messages about products to consumers; they exclude only blatantly misleading or deceptive statements from the set of legitimate means of influencing consumer choices. Advertising's critics, on the other hand, believe that consumers get very little useful information from advertisements and could make more sensible choices if they were not bombarded constantly with messages about products, most of which are somewhat misleading or deceptive anyway.

The debate has reached an impasse, which is unfortunate because issues of advertising and its role in contemporary society are important for us all. We can see a way around the impasse, however, as soon as we realize that the debate has been framed too narrowly. To put the point in provocative terms, perhaps the least important aspect of advertising's significance for modern society is its role in influencing specific consumer choices—whether wise or unwise—about purchasing products.

Then what *is* advertising about, if it is not about influencing consumer choices? To avoid misunderstanding, we wish to emphasize a key point here: all forms of advertising from classified ads and grocery store flyers to nationwide TV campaigns transmit some information about goods or services from those who own them to those who may wish to acquire them. Furthermore, it is reasonable to assume that such information has *some* influence on *some* of the decisions about acquiring goods and services that most people make every day.

Exactly *what* kind of influence is exerted on *which* people and whether or not this influence is beneficial for society are matters of longstanding controversy that will not be settled in the near future or, perhaps, ever. Meanwhile, however, both modern society and advertising have been undergoing major changes that have affected every aspect of their interaction: the type of persons addressed by advertisements, the type of information presented in them, the media through which they are transmitted, and so forth.

The course of the twentieth century has seen a dramatic and sustained rise in the real income and purchasing power of the average person in western consumer societies, where most people have access to a huge and constantly changing array of goods. At the same time, technological innovations in mass communications have transformed the message formats for advertisements themselves; compare a typical magazine ad at the beginning of the century with a national television ad today! The entire social context and social significance of advertising has altered radically. If we continue to think about advertising as being mostly about the transmittal of specifics about item X from person (or company) A to person B, we will remain unaware of the most interesting and important developments affecting it.

Research undertaken in the past ten years on changes in advertising content during the twentieth century encourages us to take a broader perspective. R.W. Pollay divides the communication function of advertising into two aspects: "informational" and "transformational." Through the informational function, consumers are told something about product characteristics; through the transformational function, advertisers try to alter the *attitudes* of consumers toward brands, expenditure patterns, lifestyles, techniques for achieving personal and social success, and so forth. After studying a sample of magazine ads covering the period from 1900 to 1979, Pollay concluded: "There are clearly some large-scale historical trends in advertising copy, in particular the trend toward selling consumer benefits rather than product attributes and the trend toward creating favorable attitudes rather than communicating cognitive content" (1984,73).

Why did advertisers decide to devote less and less copy to talking about products, shifting their emphasis instead to claims about how those products could change the lives of people? Because the consumer society evolved and matured, and marketing and advertising evolved with it. For despite the fact that the modern consumer society makes available so many more goods, it shares with earlier economies a fundamental characteristic: material objects produced for consumption not only satisfy immediate needs (such as for food and shelter), but also serve as "markers" and communicators for interpersonal distinctions—honour, prestige, power, rank—in social groups.

As twentieth-century consumer societies matured, they demonstrated this key "communications" aspect of the consumption process more and more clearly, particularly through dramatic changes in marketing and advertising strategies. Therein lies the real importance of advertising in modern society: **it is the privileged discourse for the circulation of messages and social cues about the interplay between persons and objects**. As explained earlier, the "discourse through and about objects" is privileged—that is, it occupies a special place in our lives—for two reasons: first, because the state of the economy is the predominant concern in public affairs; and second, because messages about goods surround us through our interactions with communications media. In comparison with the importance of this service, advertising's transmittal of details about product characteristics is a trivial sidelight.

Goods produced by sophisticated industrial technologies in consumer societies fulfil the twin functions served by goods in all human economies: they satisfy immediate needs and they mark and communicate social distinctions. They are in all cultures the material embodiments and the transmission lines for the dense network of exchanges and interactions among persons that is never still. Those who interpret the term "marketing" as coterminous with social exchanges see marketing activity as "essential to satisfying all the functional prerequisites of society"—generating meaning in the environment, role differentiation, communication, and social cohesion (Levy and Zaltman 1975, 2–4). In all human cultures, material objects are social communicators. Modern market-industrial societies are noted for a progressive specialization of functions—hence the emergence of a specific industry (advertising), which is charged with the task of displaying the communicative function of goods.

FROM INDUSTRIAL TO CONSUMER SOCIETY

The world we see appears "natural" to us, and it is easy to take it for granted. We can understand today's world, however, only if we step back from it and realize just how novel it is. In all earlier epochs, the common pattern was to seek to satisfy one's needs with what was, for the most part, produced locally by familiar handicraft skills and tools. With few exceptions, people knew how the items they consumed were produced, even if, as individuals, they specialized in producing only one thing; the world of objects was familiar.

The coming of a market-industrial society introduced a radical change. For the first time, the majority of the population was surrounded by goods produced in settings that were no longer familiar, although initially most goods and the materials they were made from resembled those that had been used at home and in local shops. But gradually the consumer marketplace became flooded with items whose purposes and benefits could not be ascertained by the shopper's unaided senses and intellect alone.

An example may help. The advertisement in Figure 4.1 explains for a female audience the addition of "ethyl" (tetraethyl lead compound) to gasoline by suggesting that adding lead to gasoline is like adding grated cheese to the family's macaroni supper dish! The ad strategy is simply to draw an analogy between a thoroughly familiar activity and social role (mother making dinner) and an unfamiliar activity (choosing the correct

FIGURE 4.1
Advertising's strategy for the new consumer—associating something unfamiliar with something well known.

product for the car); it should be noted that the effect is achieved largely with visual imagery.

The developed phase of the market-industrial society is the consumer society, where a truly enormous assortment of goods confronts the individual—and where the characteristics of those goods change constantly. The dramatic rise in real incomes, discretionary spending, and leisure time also meant that a far higher proportion of the marketing effort could be devoted to human wants not directly tied to basic necessities. More precisely, messages about necessities such as food could be incorporated within broader "transformational" message formats, which culminated in the present "lifestyle" image. Just as most individuals in the consumer society had been freed from concentrating on the bare necessities of existence, so marketers and advertisers could now, for the most part, safely ignore life's humdrum aspects and play freely, and apparently endlessly, with structures of imagery for the consumption process.

What marketers had realized was that, with the population as a whole having far greater discretionary income, leisure time, and employment security than ever before, work was no longer the focus of everyday life. The sphere of consumption could take its place. By linking consumption through electronic media to popular entertainment and sports, marketers and advertisers eventually fashioned a richly decorated setting for an elaborate play of messages (increasingly in imagistic or iconic form) about the ways to happiness and social success.

Marketing practices had realized that the market-industrial society was becoming a consumer society long before most social commentators did. Until quite recently, our thinking about consumption was almost primitive. Reinforced by economists, a powerful cultural tradition lauded the moral benefits of hard work and obedience to authority and concentrated its attention on increasing production; the process of consuming the things so assiduously produced was regarded as a less worthy enterprise, which in any case would take care of itself. Indeed, as the economic historian A. O. Hirschman has noted, attacks on "consumerism" are as old as the literature on economic development itself: the new productive possibilities, which began to be glimpsed in the eighteenth century, have always led to fears that the availability of new types of goods would corrupt society and individuals alike (Hirschman 1982, ch. 3).

Around the turn of this century, the realization dawned that a satisfactory application for the industrial system's vast productive capacities could be found in unfettered mass consumption. (Later it was discovered that protracted warfare on a global scale, and even more protracted preparation for a war that must never be allowed to happen, would also occasion reinvestment and help to absorb the output.) This discovery caused concern because commentators believed that ordinary folk could not handle more than a modest array of goods without becoming dissolute—a diagnosis that reflected the dominant social interests in the earlier phases of industrialism.

Factory owners and shopkeepers seeking to teach the new discipline of market relations—regular hours and days of work, punctuality, subordination to the machine, wage income as the sole means of subsistence—to a workforce steeped in peasant rhythms had encountered a recalcitrant and often hostile audience who had little reason to be grateful to its teachers. Employers lamented their employees' love of cheap but debilitating spirits and the "Blue Mondays" that shortened the working week; their frequent absences for long celebrations of traditional festive occasions or just for going hunting or attending to domestic business; and their stubborn resistance in general to the new work discipline that offended customary practices and the profound sense of personal dignity rooted in them.

These themes are nicely illustrated in a splendid essay by the historian Herbert Gutman, who also shows how European immigrants to North America constructed defences against oppression out of their popular cultures: "Peasant parades and rituals, religious oaths and food riots, and much else in the culture and behavior of early twentieth-century immigrant American factory workers were . . . natural and effective forms of self-assertion and self-protection" (1977, 66). Both secular and religious elements in transplanted ethnic communities were called upon to sustain labour solidarity, especially in the bitter and all-too-frequent strikes. Group traditions supplied not only the means to struggle against degradation and injustice, but also to retain a foothold in a remembered world via an elemental coherence fashioned out of custom, venerated objects, ancient loyalties, and intergenerational memory.

Gradually, however, the older patterns of life and culture fell apart. The unity and continuity of daily life in village settlements could not be sustained amid increasing urbanization, especially when workplace, domicile, and commerce were separated. Linked intimately with craft labour, the old ways of life could not stamp their accumulated meanings on the anonymous products that were beginning to pour off the assembly lines. And the highly restrictive codes of personal behaviour shaped by the closed worlds of religious values and distinct ethnic communities could not survive the more subtle blows of industrialism: the cultural relativism resulting from the quick amalgamation of so many different groups; the erosion of the economic function of the extended family; and the dawning of a new type of leisure time highly individualized in nature and no longer bound to the traditional collective forms of popular entertainment or domestic routine.

These diverse but interconnected changes affected the principal channels of public intercourse and also the smallest details of everyday life. For example, they are represented both in the character formation and values of individuals. David Riesman summarizes these changes in *The Lonely Crowd* (1950) by contrasting "inner-directed" and "other-directed" characters. The former's goals are set early in life and remain largely unaffected by later events; the latter are influenced continuously by what is happening around them, and their goals shift with circumstances. Inner-directed characters emphasize production, and other-directed characters, consumption. Riesman contends that there has been a shift from the former to the latter as the predominant character type in modern society.

The recognition that the progress of industrialism itself would require society to change its emphasis from a "production ethic" to a "consumption ethic" began to dawn at the close of the nineteenth century. Rosalind Williams has spotted in French thought of the period the evocation of what she calls "dream worlds of the consumer." At this time, the large urban department stores were established, and the great expositions that had started with the Crystal Palace in 1851, where the wonders of science, technology, and machinery were at the forefront, completed the transition from production to consumption with the Paris Exposition of 1900: "At the 1900 exposition the sensual pleasures of consumption clearly triumphed over the abstract intellectual enjoyment of contemplating the progress of knowledge" (Williams 1982, 59–60). As soon as cheap consumer goods began to appear in large quantities, commentators started to fret about the levelling of tastes, that is, the collapse of the distinction, formerly so clear, between items of refined design possessed by the rich and the rough possessions of the poor. Industry' s cleverness was beginning to devise passable mass-produced imitations of objects that the poor had only dreamed of owning in the past (see Figure 4.2).

Once again, we have to make an effort to think back in time to visualize an epoch vastly different from our own. At the turn of the twentieth century, many of those in more fortunate circumstances felt two sensations when they surveyed the common run of humanity: first, terror that the police and army might one day be unable to stifle the upwellings of violence against property and order; and second, dread that this teeming mass might some day discard the shackles of moral restraint so carefully fashioned by religion and traditional culture. Curiously enough, few among the scions of the propertied classes, wrapped so thoroughly in the finely spun cocoon of conservatism, imagined that even a paltry share of nature's bounty and humanity's skill, along with a modicum of dignity and self-respect, would cause the same conservatism to take root among the general population as well.

But that world view was slipping away irretrievably in the industrializing nations. The restraint on worldly desires preached for so long to

FIGURE 4.2
Advertising helped industrialism to bring products associated with "refined"
life to the ordinary person.

the poor made less and less sense as the factory system's astonishing productive capacities became apparent. For the only arena capable of absorbing the system's output was the one occupied by those who had been poor for so long. The American writer Simon N. Patten (1852–1922) was one of the first to see this clearly. In *The New Basis of Civilization* (1907), he argued that society should preach not renunciation of desire but expansion of consumption and should accept as its goal the attainment of a general state of abundance (in Horowitz 1980, 303–304).

Patten's call for plenitude marks the origin of what has been called "the culture of consumption." The foundation stone for everything that was to emerge from this culture was a new type of personality and "social self" based on individuality, which has the qualities ascribed by David Riesman to the other-directed character. Gradually set loose from restrictive behavioural codes by the crumbling of older cultures that measured persons against fixed standards of achievement and moral worth, persons became oriented instead to the ever fuller consumer marketplace—a marketplace *that had begun to address them as individuals.* The new social self was set against an open-ended scale of success set to whatever criteria happened to be applicable at the time. It is no accident that income eventually emerged as the single most important status indicator in the United States, where the culture of consumption is most fully developed: "Income is of overwhelming importance in how Americans think about social standing" (Coleman and Rainwater 1978, 220). Income provides access to whatever visible and tangible tokens of success happen to be most prized at any given moment.

For Riesman, the other-directed character is open to ever-shifting environmental influences, especially peer-group pressures. Given the predominant features of the new social environment of the early twentieth century, it is hardly surprising that a tendency toward other-directedness should arise. Older extended family and ethnic community bonds were unravelling, urbanization and the personal anonymity it confers were proceeding apace; and individuals were being confronted more and more with the fact of incessant change in everyday life, as industrial technologies and design were applied to proliferating consumer products.

Judging from the great popularity of the "anxiety format" in advertising during the period between the two world wars, the new social self was tormented by anxiety as it looked for a safe niche in largely uncharted domains of social approval. Jackson Lears quotes a classic example from a Brunswick toilet seat ad of 1930. Beneath a scene of well-dressed women drinking coffee the text runs as follows:

> "And . . . did you notice the bathroom?" At that moment the hostess reentered the room. She had just barely overheard. But it was more than enough. She began talking about Junior, about bridge, anything—but like chain

lightning her mind reviewed the bathroom. She saw it suddenly as a guest must see it, saw the one offending detail that positively clamored for criticism. (Fox and Lears 1983, 25)

The detail in question was a wooden toilet seat! The charming aspect of this tale is that two generations later the descendants of these anxiety-stricken women, responding to the beat of a different peer-group drummer, scoured junkyards and used furniture stores for the surviving population of old wooden toilet seats, carefully refinished them, and reinstalled them proudly in their bathrooms. This recent practice, it should be noted, ran counter to prevailing contemporary industry advertising.

Jackson Lears suggests that in the social environment we have just sketched, the new social self experienced a feeling of "unreality," in response to which a "therapeutic ethos" flourished. With the erosion of social group supports for personal identity sustained by older cultures, the generation and maintenance of selfhood became a lifetime task for individuals—an endless series of exercises in self-improvement, personal development, self-expression, mental and physical tone, "selling oneself," cultivating approval, "winning friends and influencing people," continuing down to the present outpouring of manuals on such subjects as "power lunching" for teaching aggressive (and by now somewhat hysterical) self-assertion.

Lears sees the therapeutic ethos as a cultural response to the uncertainties introduced into the social environment by urbanization, industrial technology, and market relations. He also suggests that it prepared fertile ground for the rising prominence of national consumer product advertising, in that the "longings for reintegrated selfhood and intense experience" could be employed by advertisers "to arouse consumer demand by associating products with imaginary states of well-being." The erosion of older cultures created a void in personal life. For all practical purposes, there was an empty slate on which to write, and advertisers seized the pen: "The decline of symbolic structures outside the self has been a central process in the development of a consumer culture, joining advertising strategies and the therapeutic ethos" (Fox and Lears 1983, 17–21).

There is, of course, another side to the story. Business and industry had awakened at the same time to the need for a greatly intensified selling effort in order to "move the goods" cascading off their assembly lines. Daniel Pope, discussing "industry's need for advertising" around the turn of this century, mentions exactly the same key factors, looked at from the business angle, as Lears does in examining the culture of consumption: industrialization, urbanization, and new forms of communication. Marketing emerged as a recognized professional activity, and corporations established marketing departments in their organizational structures.

During this period, advertising came to constitute the largest share of print media revenues, and by 1920 it accounted for about two-thirds of all newspaper and magazine income. More important than the volume of advertising was the fact that "the lead in advertising had passed to manufacturers of nationally distributed, brand-named goods" (Pope 1983, 30), for it was in the formation of a national consumer market that the advertising industry as we know it today was born and nurtured.

We have now encountered the three constituents of modern advertising's social significance identified in Chapter 1: mass media of communications, a national consumer culture, and the advertising industry, with the third as the linchpin.

The importance of advertising is highlighted in Daniel Boorstin's concept of "consumption communities" that, formed by popular styles and expenditure patterns among consumers, became a principal force for social cohesion in the twentieth century, replacing the ethnic bonds that people had brought with them to the industrial city. Advertising was the unifying force that brought these new communities into being: "Advertising could not be understood as simply another form of salesmanship. It arrived at something new—the creation of consumption communities"(Boorstin 1973, 145).

The transition from older to newer forms of community was traced in a famous sociological study, *Middletown* (1929), by Helen and Robert Lynd, which reported research done in Muncie, Indiana, in 1924. In seeking to depict the cultural changes that had occurred in the preceding thirty years, the Lynds chronicled what they saw as the systematic replacing of personal interactions with "services" for which cash payment was made. They also thought they detected a fundamental shift in attitudes toward work; what had once been a considerable source of intrinsic personal satisfaction was becoming chiefly a means of earning income — a change that more recent studies have confirmed as being deeply entrenched in popular attitudes (Coleman and Rainwater 1978). The Lynds saw what Richard Wightman Fox has also pointed out: that already in the 1920s, consumption had begun to serve as "compensatory fulfilment" for the older, largely interpersonal, forms of life-satisfaction that were disappearing (Fox and Lears 1983, 125). The transition from industrial culture to consumer culture had taken place.

Figures 4.3 and 4.4 offer a diagrammatic sketch of the main elements of the changes in social structure we have been discussing.

Figure 4.3 suggests that, in industrial societies (western Europe and North America) until the turn of this century, social classes were by and large formed directly through the operation of economic and political institutions (the marketplace and government). In other words, persons were formed into social classes as a direct result of how economic and political power was distributed; the "lower class" was defined by poverty and oppression, the "upper class" by wealth and political influence, and so forth. In everyday life—in types of housing, dress, recreation, for example—the social classes existed in quite distinct spheres, although, of course, the dividing lines between them were not always rigid, especially in North America, and some social mobility existed.

FIGURE 4.3
Industrial Society about 1900

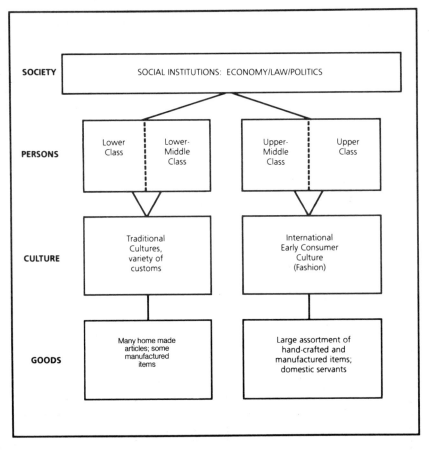

A very important point is that older cultural traditions were still flourishing; in North America, immigrants had brought a variety of traditions with them from Europe and elsewhere. Consumer articles still included many things made partially or completely at home, and activities in popular culture (festivals, ceremonies, entertainments) still showed the strong influence of regional, ethnic, and linguistic differences. This is why we represent "culture" as standing between "persons" and "goods": For the most part, cultural traditions defined acceptable consumption patterns for each group, and in so doing these traditions shaped the sense of satisfaction individuals felt in their uses of things.

Change, however, was imminent. The wealthier classes (being ever more closely attuned to international currents in fashions and tastes) had already become accustomed to drawing upon an ever-widening array of consumer articles, both handicraft and manufactured, shipped from every corner of the globe.

In contrast, Figure 4.4 represents the assimilation or "homogenization" of cultural traditons into the common framework of the "consumer culture" that began to gather strength during the 1920s and was firmly rooted by the 1960s. A unified realm of popular culture that cut across income and wealth strata in the population had emerged. The consumer culture is differentiated by voluntary and temporary affinities between persons who share a set of tastes and complementary values—a "lifestyle." These affinity groups can also be categorized as "market segments," which are the object of audience research (by media firms) and

FIGURE 4.4
Modern Consumer Culture

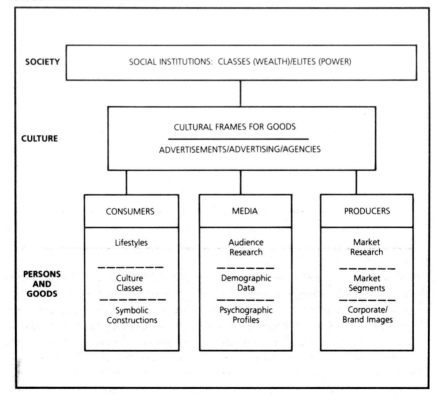

market research (by goods producers) as coordinated by advertising agencies. In addition, the separate domains of "persons" and "goods" have collapsed and been absorbed into a more general, fluid setting where symbolic constructions play with an infinite variety of possible pathways to personal satisfaction. The functions of older cultural traditions in shaping consumption partterns and the sense of satisfaction for individuals have been taken over by media-based messages through which are circulated a great assortment of cues and images about the relationship between persons and goods.

In other words, the realm of consumption practices, or the marketplace itself through messages about products and their possible meanings for an individual, gradually absorbed the functions of cultural traditions in providing guideposts for personal and social identity—telling one "who one is" or "where one belongs" or "what one might become" in life. Neil Harris points out that a number of important changes occurred during the first quarter of this century—more attractive product design and store merchandising, the power of the movies in conveying images of extravagant consumption, more striking photographic reproduction in magazines—and he suggests that some prominent contemporary novelists, notably Sinclair Lewis, had noticed this and begun to examine "the relationship between the objects of consumer desire and the creation of personality" (Harris 1981, 211–12). From then on, the "world of goods" was increasingly a key feature of personal and social experience for most people.

Figure 4.4 suggests that social class and elite distinctions are in part "hidden" in the consumer culture by the "flow of symbols" across social groupings, as in the use of symbols signifying upper-class status in consumer goods ads directed at the "ordinary person". The flow of symbols stands between social institutions, which embody the uneven distribution of wealth and power, and the "democracy of consumption," in which equal access to the symbols of status and influence is guaranteed to everyone on the same terms.

Figure 4.4 also illustrates the central place of media institutions in the consumer culture and the place of advertising as the unifying force through which the flow of symbols and meanings is managed. Finally, the phrase "Cultural Frames for Goods" is our designation for what holds together the "message system" about the relations between persons and objects in the consumer culture. A cultural frame is the predominant set of images, values, and forms of communication in a particular period that arises out of the interplay between marketing and advertising strategies, the mass media, and popular culture. We have identified four cultural frames over the course of the twentieth century; each is explained and illustrated in the final section of Chapter 11 as we attempt to summarize how national consumer product advertising has become one of the great vehicles of social communication in contemporary society.

THE SENSE OF SATISFACTION

Politicians and other opinion leaders today devote much attention to the management of the nation's economy. They carefully inspect the quarterly and monthly economic performance reports for signs that all is well, reminding us of the ancient soothsayers who sought similar assurances in the entrails of animals. Sometimes it seems that so far as public policy debates are concerned, our leaders have time for little save nursing the gross national product.

How well we manage to produce things now seems to be a matter of public concern, but still we often think of consumption as a private affair. It is up to the individual to allocate his or her time and resources as a consumer in order to experience an adequate sense of satisfaction and well-being.

Even the most casual observer can see, however, that marketing and advertising do not regard the consumer's search for satisfaction in this manner. Their full realization, which took hold in the 1920s, of how much the act of consumption goes beyond the private enjoyment of the individual marks a major turning point in modern society. The transformational function of advertising, as noted above, is to change consumers' attitudes toward products and brands. The new approach of the industry was far broader and more radical: the consumer, not the product, was to be henceforth the key ingredient in the message system.

Two main features of this new approach stand out with increasing clarity in marketing and advertising from the 1920s onward. First, at the heart of the sales effort are images of persons and social groups, that is, visible expressions of human contentment in the associations between persons and products. Second, these images are embedded in background settings made up of both natural and cultural environments. Taken together, they mark the transition from a market-industrial society to a consumer society. Illustrations of both will be presented and discussed at different points in this book.

In the preceding section, we introduced some of the special characteristics of these two types of society. Here we shall identify the impact of the transition on the satisfaction of needs in the consumption process to show why marketing and advertising had to concentrate on these two key features (images of persons and settings for satisfaction).

Beginning in the last quarter of the nineteenth century, the market-industrial system pulled individuals away from traditional sources, such as handicraft objects, of need satisfaction and toward the marketplace, which was being filled with increasing quantities and varieties of mass-produced products. Beginning in the 1920s, the coming of the consumer culture constructed an entirely new social framework for need satisfaction specifically tailored to a market-oriented society and based on the realization that individuals required help in learning *how* to find satisfaction amid those great heaps of new products.

In fact, all human cultures devise socialization processes to teach men and women how to "match" their needs and wants with the satisfactions possible within socially approved ensembles of material objects and cultural practices. We will give a brief account of these processes, adapted from William Leiss's *The Limits to Satisfaction* (University of Toronto Press 1976).

Two general aspects of needs may be labelled the "material" and the "symbolic": humankind is a material entity that is dependent upon the material world for the maintenance of life, yet we rarely appropriate the fruits of this world just as they are found, but rather transform them into specific types of goods—foods, clothing, ornamentation—according to the limitless ideas, images, and symbols fashioned by the human mind.

This point is easy to understand if we think about the traditional cultures that may be part of our family background or that we may have seen recreated at "ethnic festivals" or portrayed in film and television productions—for example, Greek, Basque, Navaho, Japanese, Burmese, Kurdish, Ethiopian, the Indians of Peru. Each has distinctive types of foods, clothing, housing, personal ornamentation, religious practices, and popular entertainments that provide socially approved forms of need satisfaction; these are the formats within which all members of the culture are expected to find an adequate sense of contentment and self-identity. A culture never imposes absolute uniformity; all cultures provide for variation and for greater or lesser degrees of individual expression within those basic formats. But all attempt to control deviance and maintain the viability of established customs, and to channel the individual's needs for physiological maintenance and psychological self-expression so as to ensure that some adequate "match" for them may be found in the existing ensemble of traditional objects and cultural practices.

A primary objective for traditional cultures is to maintain continuity and stability in these formats for need satisfaction. Indeed, their relative success in so doing is why we can still recognize an ethnic group in a particular style of embroidery on costumes, a characteristic food dish, or a special object crafted for festivals that has been part of its activities from time immemorial. Changes, including borrowings from other cultures, certainly occur over long periods of time, but every effort is made to preserve some continuity with the past, even if there remains only a fading memory of how things used to be done. This is the general pattern for every human culture that ever existed down to the point in our own century at which the market-industrial society was poised to undergo its metamorphosis into the consumer society.

Market exchanges have played a significant role in almost all human societies that are rooted in permanent settlements. This in itself does not mean that marketplace transactions determine the forms of need satisfaction or even have a major influence on them. The primary determinants are cultural traditions, which orient needs to specific, relatively stable sets of material things and to the accepted ways of carrying out everyday life with them.

However, as far back as the sixteenth century the system of price-directed market exchanges gathered strength in modern European societies. The field of satisfaction began to be concentrated increasingly in marketplace transactions (Mukerji 1983). More and more individuals received cash incomes and were required to purchase consumption goods, rather than producing most of what they required for themselves and obtaining the rest in local barter arrangements. But only when the market system was combined with industrialization and sustained technological innovation, bringing both mass production and rapid changes in the assortment of goods, did the revolutionary effects of the new system make themselves felt in everyday life.

As we have seen, the market-industrial society led to dissolution of the distinctive and relatively stable forms of need satisfaction created by traditional cultures. Industrialization uprooted great numbers of people from age-old rural settlements and relocated them in cities; only in the early stages could their traditional cultures sustain them amid the poverty of urban industrial life.

As the tradition-bound forms of need satisfaction began to disintegrate, the marketplace itself began to assume the tasks of instructing individuals how to match their needs and wants with the available stock of goods and consumption styles. Quite simply, individuals need guidance on what foods to choose and how to prepare them, on how to dress and wear ornamentation, on how to select and arrange their home furnishings, on how to entertain guests, and on innumerable other points of daily life. When traditional cultures have been weakened and the field of satisfaction filled with an ever-changing variety of unfamiliar, mass-produced goods, such guidance, or "social cues," must be furnished in other ways.

In the consumer society, marketing and advertising assumed the role once played by cultural traditions and became the privileged forum for the transmission of such social cues. This was not inevitable; beginning in the 1920s, marketers simply seized the opportunity to put the transformation of consumer attitudes at the heart of the sales effort. That the need for social cues in the sphere of consumption exists in industrial societies is evident in the Soviet Union and other countries whose economies, until recently, have been based on the principles of state socialism (principles that now appear to have lost all public support). In such countries, where the ruling ideology has traditionally frowned upon marketing but has devised no adequate substitute, consumption styles are an uneasy association between the pre-socialist traditional culture and (especially for the elite) the imported western influences; what stands out glaringly is the absence of any indigenous contemporary style or social identity for their populations.

In a consumer society such as our own, where private business firms are the predominant institutions in the marketplace, the transmission of social cues for consumption styles is generated by these firms' wishes to deliver messages about products and services. It does not follow automatically, however, that such wishes are the most important element in the *social impact* of marketing and advertising. Having oriented the population toward marketplace transactions as the forum for need satisfaction, the market society then broke with the fundamental proposition of traditional cultures—that there is a virtue in fixed and stable forms of satisfaction—and instituted the radically different idea that enhanced satisfaction could be found in discovering new wants and experimenting with new products and consumption styles in order to gratify them.

Advertisers knew full well that they were not dealing merely with messages about product characteristics, but with important ingredients in the lives of individuals, such as social roles. Their message formats show this clearly. A nice illustration is provided by a 1928 ad for "Magic Baking Powder" (Figure 4.5). The text acknowledges that "modern mothers" in cities tend to do less home baking for their families than mothers used to do, but it goes on to assure readers that despite this mothers still care for their children. In the course of selling a fairly simple product, the ad tells a reassuring story about the maintenance of traditional family roles and interpersonal relations in the context of changing social conditions.

Such matters are by no means trivial. Today in many traditional cultures around the world the baking of bread by the mother for the family's evening meal persists as an indispensable daily function, an essential part of an overall social role. Such functions often change, but they cannot be eliminated without providing substitute functions or rationalizations (for example, that the suburban mother requires more time for new activities, such as shepherding the children to social activities in the family station wagon) that are likely to win social approval. In the consumer society, advertisements are an important means for transmitting, in specific forms that are consistent with product messages, cues about new styles of personal behaviour.

Now let us examine more closely the underlying processes in the

FIGURE 4.5
Advertising reassured people that traditional roles would not disappear in the "modern" era.

consumer society that play upon this willingness to experiment with new wants and consumption styles.

Human needs and wants are inherently complex, and the range of cultural forms in various domains (for example, foods and styles of food preparation) is virtually unlimited. And specific needs are not isolated but are part of a network that places individuals in relation to each other in social groups and roles—for example, men may hunt and women tend crops and prepare meals. These universal characteristics of the human personality are what makes it possible for marketers in the consumer society to play endlessly with new ways of expressing wants, to combine them in different ensembles (lifestyles), and to be confident that most people will continue to participate—with varying degrees of intensity and resources—in the game.

And what about the things that are produced in such numbers and variety for the satisfaction of needs? The twin engines of mass production and mass marketing have turned them into unstable collections of characteristics. Most consumer items today are combinations of two types of characteristics—physical and imputed. Let us imagine a new brand of deodorant soap. On one level it is a collection of physical characteristics determined by the chemical ingredients from which it is made that give it a distinctive texture, smell, and lather. On another level, it is a collection of imputed characteristics determined by the way it is marketed—for a male or female market, with a "macho" or a "refined" image, for a special age profile, and so forth. These imputed characteristics are the kinds of personal/group attributes and lifestyle images that are attached to the product through sales promotions and advertisements.

Exactly the same—or only slightly different—chemical ingredients may be used as the material basis for products intended for quite different market niches. The relations between sets of physical and imputed characteristics are purely arbitrary. The more sophisticated industry becomes, with the availability of new chemicals and production techniques, the more varied and artful are its combinations of physical characteristics. The more sophisticated marketing becomes, with its new message formats and media technologies, the more varied and artful are its combinations of imputed characteristics. Together, physical and imputed characteristics provide a richly textured field for individuals to experiment in satisfying the many facets of their wants and needs.

What is likely to happen to the individual's sense of satisfaction and well-being in this setting? When the characteristics of goods change quickly and continuously, the needs through which individuals relate to them must also be in a state of permanent fluidity. When goods are little more than changing collections of characteristics, judgments about the suitability of particular goods for particular needs are, so to speak, destabilized. It becomes more difficult to match a specific personal need with the qualities of the things that may be touted as suitable satisfiers for it.

Characteristics are distributed and redistributed across previously distinct categories of needs, experiences, and objects. For example, the taste of menthol in a cigarette is said to be "like" Spring, and the ownership of a new automobile model "like" gaining a new personality. The expression of needs is progressively fragmented into smaller and smaller discrete "bits," which are then recombined in response to marketplace cues into temporary patterns. For example, a generation ago, a teenager, in order to appear "presentable" at school, had to respect certain very broad behavioural determinants—neatness and cleanliness, gender identity, and provision of basic supplies (book bag, notebooks, pencils). Now the presentation of self in this setting requires minute attention to aspects of dress, ornamentation, hairstyles, and accoutrements that are determined by heavily marketed popular music subcultures. Each facet of self-presentation has been broken down into component parts, and related in astonishingly varied ways to changing assortments of products and consumption styles.

The consumer society tends, as we have noted, to abandon the fixed forms of need-satisfaction typical of traditional cultures and to experiment continuously with newly constructed formats. However, it is often hard to predict how audiences will respond to new formats. So we find that advertisements preserve traces of the more stable formats inherited from the past, linking new goods and styles with traditional images of well-being: the slower pace, quiet and serenity, open space, and closeness to nature of rural life; happiness of loved ones in a close family setting that includes multiple generations; the attainment of goals set in accordance with personal, rather than institutional, demands; the concern for quality and good taste in judging fine foods, wine, and clothing.

An advertisement's composition often connects background imagery with products having not the slightest intrinsic relation to it—the automobile or cigarette package displayed against a stunning picture of unspoiled wilderness, the liquor bottle set in a farmhouse room full of hand-crafted furniture—in a straightforward attempt to effect a transfer of the positive feelings evoked by the imagery to the product. The message structure as a whole plays upon ambiguous feelings for the well-established, traditional formats for satisfying needs on the one hand and for the attractions of new products on the other; the undertone of nostalgia reflects our awareness that our commitment to "newness" means that those older formats must become ever more remote.

As we shall see more fully later, advertising has a unique capacity for sustaining a productive tension and ambiguity in its juxtaposing of images and symbols. Images from quite different contexts can coexist without contradiction because the message is not being communicated as a "rational argument"; they are meant rather to evoke the realm of "meaning"—and, since the symbols are only "suggestive" (of whatever meaning may occur to the viewer), the ordinary rules of logical inference simply do not apply. The essence of modern advertising is not truth but "believability" (Boorstin 1962, 226).

To return to our main theme, if, as we suppose, personal satisfaction results from successfully matching the qualities of needs with the characteristics of goods, consumer experiences today must be very curious. There cannot be direct correlations between the properties of individual wants and the properties of goods. Individuals experiment with their wants, producers shuffle the characteristics and assortment of goods, and marketers try various strategies in market segmentation, message formats, lifestyle imagery, and media technologies. This is indeed a fluid and unstable setting for the satisfaction of needs.

We should therefore expect to find not a clear, overall sense of satisfaction or its opposite, but rather an indistinct grouping of particular satisfations and dissatisfactions existing uneasily together. In personal reports about happiness and unhappiness with respect to such things as jobs and marital relations, researchers found analogous configurations, with no unified feelings but rather two independent dimensions of negative and positive feelings, with the two sets failing to interact or cancel each other out (Bradburn and Caplovitz 1965).

In the consumer society, where marketing has penetrated every domain of needs and the forms of satisfaction, advertising carries a double message in its "deep" structure, not visible in the actual text or images, into every nook and cranny of personal experience: that one should search diligently and ceaselessly among the product-centred formats to satisfy one's needs, and that one should be at least somewhat dissatisfied with what one has or is doing now.

Thus, there is a double ambiguity in the individual person's experience of needs and satisfactions that corresponds to this double message. Needs no longer have an integrated form of expression running in well-defined channels maintained by cultural traditions. Instead they are fragmented into an unordered array of ever smaller bits of desire that may be assembled in many different ways. The ambiguity in personal experience, wherein individuals maintain separate domains of happiness and unhappiness, is rooted in this fragmented state of needs; elements of different types of desire exist side by side to be combined temporarily and then rearranged as the latest opportunity for satisfaction is presented.

This fragmentation of needs stands in reciprocal relation to the disintegration of goods as determinate objects. Many mass-produced goods are now temporary assocations of physical and imputed characteristics, unlike the products of traditional crafts, which changed slowly in shape and composition over long periods. So there is an ambiguity implanted in goods themselves; identical chemical substances used to manufacture various brands of soft drinks may be combined with sharply differing images of social group dynamics in sports or rock music settings.

Advertising stands at the crossroads where the two sets of ambiguities meet and interact.

MEDITATIONS ON A CATALOGUE

In this chapter, we have focused on the significance of the transition from a market-industrial society to a consumer society with respect to the relations between persons and goods, and especially to the interpretation of needs. In later chapters, we will assess the significance of changes in communications media and associated changes in advertising practice that were occurring at the same time.

Many of these themes can be illustrated by an outstanding social document that appeared regularly at the turn of the century: the *Sears* catalogue.

Richard W. Sears began his career in 1887 as a railroad station agent, thus serving the most important transportation system of the time. Some small manufacturers who were plagued with surplus goods hit upon the practice of shipping consignments to local merchants who had not ordered them. If the goods were refused, they offered them to the station agents at cut-rate prices, suggesting that they resell them to other agents on the line or to anyone else they encountered. Sears soon discovered that this was a profitable sideline, in part because station agents were bonded and thus could be relied upon to honour their commitments.

Sears went on to become one of the great media and advertising innovators of his time: by 1907 Sears, Roebuck were printing six million copies a year of their catalogue, and their total readership was undoubtedly some multiple of that (Boorstin 1973, 118–29). Nor was the catalogue a slender volume; the 1908 edition was almost twelve hundred pages long and contained nearly three million words, the equivalent of about thirty average books today. Much of the copy was written by Sears himself.

The arrival of the catalogue became a major social event, especially in rural areas. In the early days, people wrote letters about their lives when mailing orders to the company, and lonely farmers inquired of Sears whether they might acquire wives through its facilities. One of the authors of this book grew up in rural Pennsylvania in the 1950s and can remember the special excitement among children when, twice a year, the *Sears* catalogue arrived in the mail.

In the early years, the catalogue contained not only advertisements for goods but also opened with much puffery about the reliability of the firm, including testimonials from its bankers in Chicago, evidence that people had to be persuaded to put their hard-earned money in the mail and engage in transactions that were not face to face. There were drawings of the firm's headquarters and of the factories where its goods were made: safes and stoves in New Jersey, cameras in Minnesota, shoes in New Hampshire, furniture in New York, guns in Connecticut, wire fence in Indiana, and saws in Michigan. Page after page of densely printed, unadorned text at the front—up to four thousand words per page—explained the firm's criteria for ensuring high quality and low cost. And the company managers knew the social etiquette of small towns. A special section explained that the goods would always be shipped to the railroad terminal in unmarked packages, so that local merchants (who might well include the buyer's employer) would not discover the disloyalty of customers who were, of course, known to them personally.

This catalogue merchandising was enormously successful. Yet, curiously enough, the *Sears* catalogue was not a forward-looking enterprise. In fact, it can serve as a metaphor for the industrial age that was coming to a close, an age dominated by a system of manufacturing with a hitherto undreamed-of productive capacity that had been erected helter-skelter at the price of enormous human suffering. The industrial age had come into being without any notion among the "captains of industry" who were its leading figures that it could offer material abundance to the masses who toiled in its service.

The *Sears* catalogue itself stood at the transition point between the industrial and the consumer age, promising to bring "luxuries to thousands who formerly enjoyed only the necessities." It is not the content of its message, however, but its language and imagery—in other words, its communicative format—that looks backward; the "missionary" approach of the catalogue as a whole, with its implicit promise of general abundance, and the strategy for communicating it, are inconsistent and at war with each other. The task of the advertising industry beginning in the 1920s was to resolve and overcome this inconsistency.

In the first place, the catalogue's message content is saturated with what we might call "artisanal" or "craft" values; it refers to goods in ways that presuppose an intimate knowledge of functions and uses or an interest in acquiring such knowledge about unfamiliar items. It is addressing a population that, for the most part, produces and consumes the goods it needs rather than purchasing them. The catalogue did not present goods as if they were mass-produced in factories, but treated them like the things that people used to make for themselves, except for the fact that they were now available in much greater numbers and variety. The text remains innocent of the marketing outlook that one must forge innovative selling tools in order to dispose of a world of goods that have not been (and indeed could not be) made by the consumer personally.

A nice example is provided by the frequent illustrations of the factories where the goods are made: they look like icons, not actual places of production. There are exterior views only, in peaceful, landscaped settings with no workers or machinery visible; the text calls attention mostly to their size, even giving the exterior dimensions of some buildings. (Such illustrations, emphasizing the size, efficiency, and order of the mass-production factory setting, were common in this period.) In short, this is a symbolic representation of the industrial age, referring only in abstract terms to its immense productivity; the implicit message is that nothing has really changed in the social world of values and behaviour.

Artisanal values pervade the catalogue's circumlocutionary rhetoric and its meticulously detailed descriptions of the many objects on offer. The introductory section to the 1908 edition on the high quality of the company's products mentions the expertise of its buyer for harnesses, an expert harness maker trained in a small country firm who oversees the curing and tanning operations of the suppliers as closely "as if he were the owner." His mission is straightforward: "He is only called upon by us to know everything about a harness." The lead-in for this edition is a seven-page story about the newest cream separator, which is analyzed in loving detail (see Figures 4.6a – 4.6d). The catalogue was directed primarily at a rural audience, so it is not surprising that its opening pages should focus on farm needs; but the amount of space devoted to one item and the exhaustive scrutiny of its characteristics reveal much about the underlying values being appealed to. Lest the reader think that other needs were neglected, we hasten to add that bicycles receive four full pages of densely packed text, followed by five pages devoted to bicycle parts. Coming upon almost twenty pages of text and illustrations for pianos and organs, the reader is admonished at the outset to "read every word in the pages that follow"!

A high proportion of goods made of multiple components are first shown intact and then broken down into their subordinate units, which are, of course, also for sale separately. Craftspeople are concerned with how a thing is put together, with "what makes it work," and with being able to repair rather than to discard it. Industrial goods are meant to be unambiguous in their utility and, in a sense, the fact that they are shown in their component parts is an assurance that they have nothing to hide, that there is nothing frivolous or unnecessary to them.

The commitment to craft values also dictates linguistic style. Heavy matter-of-fact, overlong, and repetitive descriptions of product qualities predominate—interspersed far too infrequently with fanciful observations—and preachy exhortations appeal to the "good sense" of the potential buyer, who, as a careful, sagacious, and, above all, highly suspicious consumer ever alert for the slightest whiff of chicanery, clearly

FIGURE 4.6a
Products were described in loving detail.

FIGURE 4.6b

FIGURE 4.6c

FIGURE 4.6d

can judge the products' highest standards of craftsmanship. One should not be misled by the frequency with which the buyer is addressed directly, as "you." The emphasis is always on the product and its marvellous attributes, constituting the "active" dimension in the message format; the text is devoid of personal references, and in those twelve hundred pages there are few drawings of people except for the clothing section where they look like mannequins. (Magazine advertisements at this time were already including many more illustrations of persons).

The flat, self-assured tone that characterizes so much of advertising text in this era is deceptive, however, for some of its seemingly candid and innocuous statements are just hyperbolic nonsense. In the notorious patent-medicine field, most advertisements were simply fraudulent, but a few were downright sinister. Here is just a part of the pitch from *The Cosmopolitan* magazine of December, 1899 for the "Turkish Bath Cabinet," which appears to be just a large wooden box that fits snugly around a person seated on a chair with a small alcohol stove that supplies enough heat to cause sweating.

> Our Cabinet is recommended by 27,000 best physicians, and it will cure Nervous Troubles and Debility, Sleeplessness, Obesity, Lagrippe, Neuralgia. Cures Rheumatism [we have offered for four years a standing reward of $50.00 for a case not relieved]. Cures Woman's Troubles, Headache, Gout, Piles, Dropsy, Diabetes, all Blood and Skin Diseases, Liver and Kidney Troubles . . . With the Cabinet, if desired, is a Head and Complexion Steaming Attachment, . . . which makes clear skin, beautiful complexion, cures and prevents pimples, blotches, blackheads, skin eruptions and diseases.

The manufacturer claimed one million satisfied customers.

Note especially the way in which the promised cure takes on everything from diabetes to pimples. This is not really a medical claim at all, but a random juxtaposition of words held together only by the ad's commitment to the "matter-of-fact" communicative format. It is a narrative form gone mad, a universe of discourse that resembles nothing so much as an uninspired version of *Alice in Wonderland.*

Many other nostrums were touted for piles, headaches, debility, nervousness, "blood diseases," and so on (the lists are often remarkably similar). The 1902 *Sears* catalogue offered "Peruvian Wine of Coca," just one of a flood of cocaine-based elixirs (including the original formula for Coca-Cola and a failed imitator that carried the brand name "Dope Cola") that reached a wide market in the twenty years after 1885 (*Life Magazine* May 1984).

Whether the text was (at least in retrospect) utterly fraudulent, or absolutely frank and honest as in Sears' ads for bicycles or cream separators, its appearance and rhetorical style were identical. In the honest ads, there is a charming undertone of genuine pride in the technological accomplishments that were making such useful devices so widely available to those who deserved to have them; yet there is a slightly intimidating undertone as well, for, as far as the *Sears* catalogue is concerned, the dominant image is of the immense, startling ingenuity of industrial technology itself. The handwriting is on the wall: although the words paid homage to artisanal values, the life and society sustained by artisanal labour was fast vanishing.

In some respects, the mail-order catalogue was a precursor of the modern mass media. Unlike newspapers or magazines of the period, it was sufficiently comprehensive to project a vision of an entire "consumption universe" of products to satisfy all wants—including wants conceived only in the act of perusing the catalogue itself. Together with the urban department stores, it promised an all-embracing, unified, and ordered *mediation* between persons and their social environment. But it could not serve for long as such a model because its communicative format was too restrictive. Great ingenuity had brought mass-produced consumer goods to the marketplace, but the passage from industrial to consumer society called for bold and fresh initiatives. This call would soon be taken up with relish by the advertising agencies.

THE AD INDUSTRY DISCOVERS ART

As Roland Marchand has written, advertising was to become the "apostle of modernity" for its audience, going beyond its role as the seller of goods to develop broad "strategies for accommodating the public to modern complexities" of twentieth-century life (1985, 9). The larger social role that advertising came to play in modern society had its basis in a simple fact: the vast outpouring of new consumer products from assembly-line production would not sell themselves. In other words, prospective consumers had to be told not just what the new product could do, but why it was important that they should adopt the type of life made possible by that product. For example, the safety razor could not be sold on the basis of its technical attributes alone; the male populace had to be persuaded that good society in the modern age approved of the universal clean-shaven look. This strategy involved promoting the product in close association with an account of what we may call the social benefit that the consumer could be expected to derive from the activity associated with the product.

The philosophy on which this marketing approach was based soon spread, in the 1920s, throughout the advertising industry. Marchand observes:

> The result of this trend toward emphasis on consumer satisfactions was called "dramatic realism"—a style derived from the romantic novel and soon institutionalized in the radio soap opera. It intensified everyday problems and triumphs by tearing them out of humdrum routine, spotlighting them as

crucial to immediate life decisions, or fantasizing them within enhanced, luxurious social settings. (1985, 24)

Marchand shows how advertisers worked at creating successful formats for calming popular concerns about the decay of traditional values and the triumph of "new ways"—formats such as parables, tableaux, and visual clichés. For example, many ads dealt with women's roles, some providing reassurance that there was still an important place for the woman as the superintendent of the home (now filled with marvellous domestic appliances). Thus, a 1928 Canadian ad for "Magic Baking Powder" (Figure 4.2) began: "Some people say that modern mothers are not such good home-makers as were the mothers of olden days. But that's not true. Human nature doesn't change a great deal." Such easily repeatable formulas—used time and again so that consumers became intimately acquainted with them—served as a bridge between the older, familiar, and traditional world that was disappearing and the new mass-consumer age.

But another problem had to be dealt with first. Many of the goods now being promoted to a wide audience were, to put the point simply, quite ugly. If industry could just be persuaded to pay more attention to the appearances of things, advertising could then do its proper work by surrounding its products with attractive images. As one of the great pioneers in this endeavour, Earnest Elmo Calkins, put the point in his 1927 article (as cited by Ewen 1988) entitled "Beauty, the New Business Tool":

> The first step toward making the advertising attractive was to make the goods attractive. It was frequently necessary to introduce the article sold into the advertisement, or at least its package, and most products and packages were so ugly or so commonplace they spoiled the picture; and thus began that steady, unremitting pressure on the manufacturer to make his goods or packages worthy of being placed in an artistic setting. Bales and boxes and cans and wrappers and labels and trademarks were revised and redesigned.

As we shall explain in the following pages, Calkins and his associates, together with the manufacturers they won over to this new way of approaching the marketplace, worked their magic on fashion goods and cosmetics, automobiles (led by General Motors), the General Electric products, radios and phonographs, and so on. And they went on to promote change in the whole area of retail merchandising as well, particularly in department stores. (Ewen 1988, 45ff).

In the 1920s, the advertising business took three important steps that revolutionized both consumption practices and the actual expression of consumer aspiration. These three steps can be expressed as a deceptively simple statement: in the 1920s, the advertising business discovered art; more precisely, advertisers discovered the significance of aesthetics and how to harness the human desire for expression. This discovery was made up of three smaller ones: first, people are eager for expressive things; second, people are prone to organizing their collections of material objects into a thematically coherent system; and third, people are fascinated by novelty. Design and fashion, mobilized in response to the human ability to organize a personal material world, proved to be an enormously versatile force that contributed greatly to the transformation from industrial to consumer society.

It would be unfair to say that the advertising industry had a master plan. However, in the 1920s it was advertising that began to create a bridge between the manufacturing sector and the whole gambit of "creatives"—artists of various kinds. The purpose of this union was to improve American products, to make them more desirable and therefore more salable. As the 1920s unfolded, American consumer-goods manufacturers became apprehensive that consumer spending might hit a saturation point. One by-product of this concern was the following formula: make things attractive, make them in a variety of forms and colours so that they can be combined in specific ways, and change their appearance and some of their features regularly and often. From this bridging process rose the American industrial design profession and the products of its imagination—that is, much of the material world we all inhabit today.

As early as the middle of the previous century, American product design had enjoyed a reputation for innovation and good engineering, and little else. When American products were exhibited in the Crystal Palace in Great Britain in the first world exhibition (1851), they were met with derision by the European press because of their ugliness, and with admiration by the same press for their efficiency and effectiveness. Neither the McCormack Reaper nor the Six Shot Repeater Pistol manufactured by Colt were much to look at, but both were genuine engineering advances. When it came to other products, American industrial product design was so much based on the copying of European models that the French and Swedes were afraid to exhibit their glassware and carpeting in the United States!

Product design was developing very differently in Europe. With few notable exceptions, such as the arts and crafts movement in Britain and the early years of modernist design, products associated with care, quality materials, and the attentions of a professional "designer" were usually conceived of and produced only for the upper classes. It was not until after World War II that even appliances such as the vacuum cleaner were thought to be appropriate consumer goods for a wide market. European designers tended to see themselves as either being in service of the rich or in service of "art." In other words, they either created things that were modelled on the past expressions of class privilege, or they sought to develop a philosophy of design and the built environment that was based on abstract notions of what was good for people. Design in Europe, then, was either a very highly developed decorative art—as was the case with art deco—or it was an aspect of an applied philosophy of the built environment and a form of morality, as was the case with the modernism that was epitomized in the German architectural school known as Bauhaus. More than simply creating a style of building construction and industrial design, the Bauhaus developed a philosophy that combined a social vision with aesthetic and engineering principles. This applied philosophy enriched the entire design field, through its insights into the social and cultural implications of an increasingly technological and industrialized human environment.

The situation in America was quite different. Early American experience had emphasized the necessity of efficient and reliable tools and weapons—be they the double-bit axe or the Kentucky Flintlock. Product design was informed by the spirit of durability, mechanical ingenuity and quality, and the no-nonsense approach of the engineer. Indeed, it was an American grain elevator that served as one of the models favoured by the design avant-garde in Europe. While in America various periods and groups had produced beautiful objects and craft traditions (Quaker furniture is just one example), no tradition of product design as such existed except for those brought by settlers and immigrants. If the Americans did have a tradition, then, it was one of survival, entrepreneurship, ingenuity, and the ideology of equality. This is illustrated by Henry Ford's intentions when he first began producing automobiles. The Ford Model T was to be a very durable product—Ford thought a person would only need to buy one and it would last a lifetime. It would be reliable, it would be easy to service and fix, and it would be black—and it would be so cheap that everyone could have one. As American design historian Arthur Pulos (1986) puts it, the product would be a "type form." In other words, the product, having reached its most developed form, would be reproduced thereafter just as it was; henceforth, there would be no need to tinker with its design. But as it turned out, the future of product design in America did not follow such a pattern.

The literature in the field is consistent on this point—product design in America came out of the advertising industry. First, advertising agencies in the 1920s and 1930s encouraged manufacturers to change their goods and to employ designers to achieve those changes. Second, a number of the innovators of American product design either began their careers in advertising, or else they moved into product design, from such things as theatre design, through the connections that were being made for them by the advertising industry. The professional origins of American product design largely explains both the emergence of a distinct American approach known as "styling" and the derisive attitudes of

Europeans toward the design efforts taking place in America. While the modernist designers of Europe were talking about the social implications of technology and design—designing products from the inside to the outside, debating the nature of function, and applying a formal method to design—their American counterparts were concerned with making products visually interesting and appealing in order to increase sales. It is not entirely true that all American design was surface only; ergonomic research was done, and there were scientific approaches to design. But it is the surface design of American goods that became known universally and associated with the consumer utopia that the United States was perceived to be.

Stuart Ewen (1988) has drawn attention to the discovery of design by the advertising profession. He points out that Earnest Elmo Calkins, partner in the agency Calkins and Holden, was one of the earliest proponents of coordinated image management in America. In the 1920s, this business visionary began pioneering creative services and arguing that businesses had to recognize the relationship between product appearance and consumer preference. Calkins and his partner advocated a systematic integration between aesthetics and industry, and they hired two men who would be among the founders of the American design profession, Walter Dorwin Teague and Egmont Arens. Teague, who began his career as a graphic designer of advertisements, went on to redesign products such as the Kodak Brownie and later the Bantam Special cameras. Egmont Arens, who began as an editor and writer, became a leading specialist in packaging and product design. It was Arens who coined the phrase "consumer engineering" to explain his philosophy, which was that industry had to match its products to the public's interests and demands.

The Calkins and Holden firm also opened a Fashion Coordination Bureau. According to Roland Marchand (1985), the Fashion Coordination Bureau supplied twelve thousand department stores with directives on how to harmonize products in display and merchandising. Calkins was among the first to advocate the use of modern art in advertising, suggesting that modern art techniques such as those developed by the European avant-garde movements of Surrealism, Cubism, Expressionism, and so on, were very well suited to developing powerfully expressive advertisements. What made these techniques so ideal in Calkins's mind was the fact that they possessed immense communicative power. In this, Calkins anticipated and promoted an approach to advertising that is still in place today. As the art historian John Walker has pointed out in his *Art in the Age of Mass Media* (1983), the artistic avant-garde has become and remains the "R & D" (research and development) department for the commercial industry.

Calkins was a major influence on the consciousness of American industry in his day. His argument that good mechanical function was not enough soon began to gain converts. If people were to be compelled to buy, then it would be through an appeal to their sense of the attractive or the expressive, not merely the useful. Attractiveness and expressiveness could be achieved through design, and "consumer engineering" could then help to stimulate the compulsion to buy. If American business were to thrive it would have to appeal to the feeling of pleasure in ownership and consumption that the ordinary citizen was presumed to have.

Perhaps the most well-known of all the designers who became active in the 1920s in America was Raymond Loewy (discussed in Forty 1986; Hillier 1983; Pulos 1986). Many of his designs, or the designs that came out of his large office, have persisted to this day. Loewy's office produced the Singer Sewing Machine logo, as well as those of International Harvester, Shell Oil, and Coca-Cola. Like the Lucky Strike cigarette package, which he redesigned before World War II, many of Loewy's designs are still in use today. The Greyhound Scenicruiser, the red Coke dispenser of the 1940s and 1950s, the Gestetner Machine, the Studebaker, numerous train locomotives, the Avanti, "Air Force One" of the Kennedy era, even the interior of Sky Lab—all flowed either out of this own fertile imagination or from those working under his supervision. Following his death in 1987, a commemorative edition of *ID*, a trade journal of the American product design profession, called him "one of the greatest form givers in America."

Like Teague and Arens, Loewy began his career in advertising and illustration. Immigrating to America from France following World War I, Loewy began his career as a fashion and advertising illustrator. By the 1930s, he was redesigning products for industry. It was also in this era that he, along with Walter Dorwin Teague, Henry Dreyfuss, and Norman Bel Geddes, founded and institutionalized the American product design profession. Indeed, probably no one contributed more to the public image of the designer than did this technological romantic, who was in love all his life with transportation and the image of speed, and whose designs were characterized by a slenderness and grace. The idiom he is most often identified with, and which he helped to popularize in the 1930s, is "streamlining." Streamline design was characterized by its appearance of being aerodynamic. When applied to planes and cars it was functional; however, when applied to furniture, pencil sharpeners, and manure-spreaders, streamlining was an evocation of the fascination with a forward-looking progress. This idiom had a "futuristic" feel to it, as did much of the design that Loewy produced. In the Depression world of shortages, unemployment, and bank foreclosures, there was a great deal of appeal to objects that bespoke a utopian future.

But the essence of Loewy's approach is best captured in his credo— the MAYA dictum. MAYA, an acronym for "most advanced yet acceptable," was the article of faith on which Loewy's fortunes rode. Loewy reasoned that people wanted novelty, but not too much novelty. In short, anything too new frightened people and they would not buy such a product. Thus, if new technology permitted moving an automobile's external gas tank under the vehicle, a fake gas tank was left on top. The consumer who had expected to see the gas tank there still saw what he or she expected, even if it now contained a hideaway extra seat. The MAYA dictum was not invented by Loewy, but he gave it its most elegant articulation.

The MAYA principle was not the only motivating force in Loewy's design imagination. His overall intent was to simplify the lives of the people who, like himself, kept running into poorly made and unimaginatively conceived products. His Gestetner commission of 1929 is a good example of his approach. Prior to its redesign, the Gestetner Copier looked like an industrial printing machine. The "guts" of the machine were exposed, it was messy to operate, and because its moving parts were exposed, it was dangerous to use—not the sort of thing you would want high-school students or teachers operating. On receiving the commission, Loewy sheathed the machine in a metal covering, altered the handle a bit, and produced the device that two generations saw in nearly every school in North America. The machine was now safe and hardly messy at all, except when one had to change the stencils. In this simple redesign, Loewy demonstrated the use of design to eliminate the characteristics of products that inhibited their wider use.

Although he was born in and trained in Europe, Loewy's approach was distinctly non-European. For example, he never believed that design could produce an eternal masterpiece and would have had serious doubts about Pulos's assertion of type form. As far as this "master form-giver" was concerned, every design was just a step in the evolution of the product. While Loewy might have called it an evolution toward technical perfection, it often meant cosmetic or surface design. This approach meshed well with the increasing "fashionableness" of material culture discussed later in the chapter. If every product was but a step, what better justification for annual style changes? Whatever we may think of this, it was an approach consistent with the attitudes of a man whose autobiography was entitled *Never Leave Well Enough Alone*.

Loewy and other early designers all sought an idiom or style. That is to say, they worked within a systematic set of expressions. As the 1920s ran into the 1930s, the predominant idioms in the United States began to move from art deco into streamlining and the skyscraper style. Design historian Bevis Hillier (1983) suggests that art deco was a kind of "domesticated Cubism," which replicated the vibration of machinery and the massing of volumes. The skyscraper style, indigenous to America, emphasized an upwardly-stepped massing that arrived at a peak, like the tall buildings of the late 1920s and early 1930s. Streamlining gave the object the feel of aerodynamics, forward motion, and speed. These idioms or styles, when applied to everything from turnstiles to pencil sharpeners, would become a key building block in the strategy that was emerging in the advertising profession in its capacity as consultant to industry. In the fashion-driven phase of material culture that was then beginning, such idioms and their variations (as well as the idioms that were to displace them) would come to play a key role. For fashion is a process, and style or idiom is its currency. Once the profession understood this, and once they discovered the significance of the human propensity to create ensembles or stylistically or expressively coherent complements of goods, the fashion-orientation of our entire material culture was the next logical step.

The Ensemble

Most people live their lives in a world that contains their own "space" or personal domain. This domain contains goods or artifacts of various kinds that tend to be organized into some sort of system that normally reflects the cultures we inhabit and interact with and within; in other words, our goods are organized into totalities or unities, or, to use Roland Marchand's term, *ensembles.*

We can think of these ensembles in three ways: as stylistic, functional, or a combination of the two. For example, one might buy a bicycle, in the interests of health or transportation. One might then buy a helmet, then a water bottle, then a pair of gloves, then appropriate shoes, then shorts, shirt, and so on, up to the limit on one's credit card. All these parts form a "functional ensemble," and, because they are used in interactions with other people, they might be said to form an "interactive ensemble." Other examples of such ensembles are stereo or home entertainment equipment, kitchen paraphernalia, personal computers, do-it-yourself tools, ski and other sports gear, and so on.

The ensembles that the advertising profession discovered and learned to respond to were primarily stylistic in nature. Clothing and home furnishings were the first two domains to be industrialized, commercialized, and marketed as ensembles. The idea of the production and purchase of items that when put together would match or complement one another, thereby creating an expressive unity, can be clearly noted in fashion and interior décor going back as far as the sixteenth century. However, the early production of items with an eye to their coordination was aimed at an elite market of the bourgeoisie and nobility. The recognition that ensemble-based marketing could be utilized for a mass-consumer market was the second key discovery made by the American advertising profession in the 1920s.

As Marchand points out, the realization of the ensemble as a marketing strategy began with the increased use of colour. By the mid-1920s, through the efforts of advertisers like Calkins, product design took its place alongside of, and then superseded, colour in the creation of products destined to create new ensembles in the consumer's domestic world. The ensemble offered marketing and merchandising a new set of incentives that could be mobilized to increase sales. The ensemble expanded the consumer's conception of necessity; it "schooled the eye in the recognition of obsolescence" (Marchand 1985, 132). In addition, the ensemble became a key device in the transferral of elite tastes to a wider populace, and also offered a vehicle for the personalization of mass-produced goods. Nestled within this idea of the ensemble may be one of the most important clues to how consumer culture interacts with material culture. We can gain some of the insight by considering the four functions of the ensemble listed by Marchand.

Ensemble-based marketing offered industry a way to encourage an expanding definition of necessity. A wonderful example of this is given by Grant McCracken (1988) in his discussion of the "Diderot Effect" (McCracken's term for the ensemble). This effect describes the human experience of producing expressive and functional unities, the fact that we experience some things as going together. It is taken from an essay by Denis Diderot, in which the eighteenth-century French philosopher recalls parting with his old dressing gown. Sitting in his study, and feeling utterly alienated in the neat room filled with a new desk and bookcases, Diderot remembers that it was when he received a new dressing gown as a gift that his study began to change. Having ditched his old threadbare dressing gown and donned the new, he had sat down at his old desk in his cluttered but comfortable study. But he felt how old and shabby his desk and other accoutrements appeared when compared with the new dressing gown, which had schooled his eye for obsolescence. Well, quite literally, one thing led to another, and all the old things were replaced by new ones, with strangely unsatisfying results.

Marchand also argues that the ensemble was a device for the "transferral of elite tastes" (1985, 132). The idea here is that a concern with thematic unity, and the presentation of self as a work of art through such a unity, primarily describes the behaviour of social and economic elites. In the America of the 1920s, the social elites were the rich who took as models for themselves the lifestyles of the "rich and famous" of Europe; and it was these elites who were used as models of consumer aspirations in much of the marketing efforts of the 1920s.

Perhaps the most interesting of Marchand's four points about the ensemble is that it provided a vehicle for the personalization of mass-produced goods. If more and more material needs had to be satisfied through a market filled with prefabricated goods, then it was just the diversity and variety that could provide an opportunity to distinguish one's own ensemble from the ensembles of others. To do so would be to create a material representation for an experience of being somehow distinct or different from everyone else. Marchand reports an increasing awareness in the industry that consumers were willing to forego costliness for variety. The ad industry did not invent the ensemble, but it did learn to combine industrial production with an old and powerful human propensity—the desire for a coherent, expressive, and intelligible world. That so much of this world was now based on surface appearances, and was subject to the effects of stylistic and artificial obsolescence, was a logical outcome of the industrial age.

The Rule of Fashion in a Consumer Culture

To be sure, fashion, like the ensemble and the pleasure of ownership, is hardly something new in human society, nor is the rule of fashion today confined only to consumer-oriented societies. Rather, it is the striking generalization of fashion, spreading both throughout a population and across a wide range of goods, that is novel. As many commentators have pointed out, a concern with fashion is a concern with the apparently contradictory desires of "being unique" and "being the same as." Fashion identifies—quickly, at a glance—a person with respect to others, both those who are playing the same fashion game and those who are not. In this way, fashion situates people in time (being *au courant* or *passé*) and within a social space (who one's models are and are not). Fashion also contains simultaneously an orientation to the future and to the past. One of the ironies of the fashion world is the inevitability of the "novelty" of retro styles and idioms.

In their study of fashion, Ted Polehmus and Lynn Procter (1978) offer an insight that brings us full circle back to the Diderot Effect, the ensemble, and design. Polehmus and Procter identify two cultural approaches to clothing and adornment. In one modality, anti-fashion, we have a traditional culture that uses its material culture as a barrier to the entry of new and potentially subversive ideas. In the fashion modality, on the other hand, we have a society that uses material culture to continuously subvert certain accepted values and to favour an expression of novelty. In a similar vein, McCracken (1988) notes that the Diderot Effect can work in two ways: it can be a stabilizing force that one uses to affirm who and what one is; or, in its radical mode, it can transform not only one's immediate physical world but also one's experience of oneself.

In its conservative mode, the Diderot Effect can protect an individual's sense of self. Thus, we quite often choose things that are consistent with those we already own and with our preconceptions of who and what we are. Such conceptions are communicated to us continually by the things that we have chosen to admit into our lives. On the other hand, we may desire a "make-over" in our lives, as often happens after some significant emotional event has shaken up our previous ideas of ourselves; this make-over is expressed by discarding whole sets of possessions and acquiring different types.

By means of their increased employment of design and ensemble-based marketing, the advertising profession and those who retained its services sought to activate the Diderot Effect in its radical mode, to turn a material culture that had been fundamentally anti-fashion (except for the narrow elites) into the pre-eminent site of fashion. With the arrival of design and ensemble-based production for the mass-consumer market, it was the goods themselves, in their stylistic (and later their functional) relations with each other, that entered consumer culture in a new and importantly transformative way. Having learned how to "fashionalize" the ensemble, and thus how to school the eye for obsolescence, advertisers chipped away at the traditional conservatism in popular culture, urging the ordinary citizen to affirm the styles and values of modernity. When that older traditionalism finally succumbed, in the period of economic prosperity after the end of the Second World War, the floodgates opened and fashion gradually took command over the entire domain of the consumer marketplace.

CONCLUSION

The social transition we have been discussing occurred in North America and the more industrialized parts of Europe in the 1920s. Frederick Lewis Allen provides a finely detailed retrospective of it for the United States in his famous bestseller *Only Yesterday* (1931). The opening chapter contrasts the beginning and end of the decade as reflected in the life of an ordinary citizen. Almost every detail would later be recognized as a landmark event in the constitution of a consumer society.

New forms of popular entertainment, new vehicles of mass communications, and new consumer products of immense popularity were being stitched together to form a new popular culture, a rich and coherent network of symbolic representations and behavioural cues, to replace the older cultures then fading away. Popular entertainment brought innovative musical styles, movies, and the "star system" that created famous personalities. The motion picture industry affected communications as well as entertainment; newspapers became easier to handle with the advent of the tabloid format; above all else the decade witnessed the arrival of radio broadcasting which subtly penetrated and blended with the mundane routines of domestic activity. Radio was more than a technological novelty providing efficient channels for advertising and popular entertainment; in one powerful stroke it integrated nuclear family units (once tightly bound to local communities but now isolated and dispersed) into a larger association unique in human history: a national consumer culture.

Finally, certain products that would soon dominate the consumer culture invaded the personal lives Allen describes. Automobiles were beginning to be sold on styling and "symbolic" values; the number of privately owned cars more than tripled during the decade. Cigarettes more than doubled in sales, and smoking in public by women was becoming acceptable. Cosmetics, new personal-care products, and much freer clothing fashions for women were also having a social impact. (A changing image for alcoholic products did not appear at this time in the United States because of Prohibition, but it would do so later.)

Lodged at the intersection of all these currents was national consumer advertising, which had just arrived as a recognized profession, an accepted partner with industry, and an inescapable presence in daily life. This was advertising's golden age, not merely because advertisers had grasped its almost unlimited "transformational" capabilities, but because society as a whole almost completely agreed with its key premise, that "the road to happiness was paved with more goods and services." Stephen Fox comments: "More than ever before or since, American culture and American advertising converged on a single point" (1984, 79). We would modify this judgment somewhat by pointing out that the next postwar decade (the 1950s) displayed much the same convergence of opinion.

The first stages of integration of advertising with the new technologies of communication, continuing innovations in industrial production, and new popular cultures oriented around consumer goods were in place by the end of the 1920s: the blending of commercial sponsorship, national personalities, and programming content in radio broadcasting; the general use of "famous personalities" (including movie stars) in advertising; the heavy emphasis in national advertising on certain key goods (automobiles, tobacco, personal-care products, later alcohol). Most important were the systematic studies of population statistics, opinion polling of media audiences (George Gallup got his start in the 1920s), and psychological research on consumer motivations that were explicitly intended to fuse through marketing and media the intentions of industry and the consumer into a single grand strategy for mutual benefit.

5

Advertising and the Development of Communications Media

Communication in pre-industrial societies was predominantly personal and oral in direct, face-to-face interactions in local markets, where barter and trade were the basis of economic activity; in places of worship, where ritual and sermons organized spiritual life; in courts and chambers, where officials held audiences; and in homes and communities, where the roots of cultural life were sunk deep in the soil of everyday social interactions. Communication—the transmission of ideas, feelings, attitudes, and experiences—was not mediated by technologies of communication.

However, as is the case today, communication flows were superintended by dominant institutions. Lines of authority and personal contact were well delineated, and ruling interests used whatever means lay at their disposal to transmit the versions of custom, belief, superstition, law, and power that suited them best. What distinguishes pre-industrial times from our own is that contact with social authority occurred through personal intermediaries. In modern society, direct and personal interaction is no longer the exclusive form of communication; it is now powerfully augmented and, to some extent, supplanted by interactions mediated by new technologies.

THE RISE OF MEDIATED COMMUNICATION AND COMMERCIALIZED MEDIA

During the last century, the process of exchanging ideas has become all but totally dependent upon mechanical and electronic infrastructures for symbolic reproduction and distribution. DeFleur (1970, 77) highlights this aspect in his "media diffusion curves" (Figure 5. 1), reminding us of the speed with which successive waves of communication technology have been invented and assimilated into modern life. (See also DeFleur and Ball Rokeach 1989.)

We will follow DeFleur in concentrating on the mass media, rather than other point-to-point communication technologies, such as the telegraph, telephone, telex, and computer, whose effects have been felt

FIGURE 5.1
The Diffusion Curves for Four Media with Ordinate Standardized

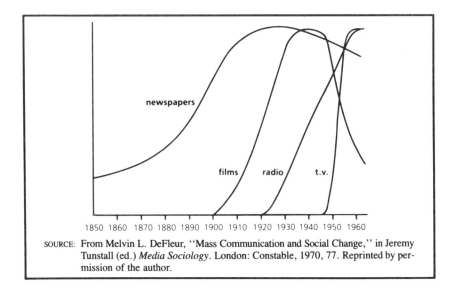

SOURCE: From Melvin L. DeFleur, "Mass Communication and Social Change," in Jeremy Tunstall (ed.) *Media Sociology*. London: Constable, 1970, 77. Reprinted by permission of the author.

mostly in the realm of business. The mass-consumer media are most closely related to the processes of cultural formation. We also follow Michael Real (1971), therefore, in preferring the designation " mass-mediated culture" to the more common "mass culture," for, whatever the nature of popular culture today, the instruments for transmitting it—the media—indisputably have a "mass" quality about them. What happens in and through them is dictated by audiences counted in the tens or hundreds of millions and by monetary transactions of similar dimensions. We have adapted this concept in our own phrase, "mediated communication."

There is a double mediation in the communication patterns of modern industrial society. First, during much of their daily lives, people are communicating through technologies rather than face to face. A technological means becomes the focus of the transmission and reception process, and the qualities of the technology and the forms in which it allows messages to be exchanged in these technological channels influence the patterns of communication. Innis (1951) and McLuhan (1964) have shown us that human experience and communication structures are influenced both by the perceptual and the social possibilities of a medium of interaction.

The second mediation is institutional. The panoply of communications organizations that create the technology, own or control the channels, and produce the messages also intervenes in the activities of human communication. These semi-autonomous organizations and the broader institutional framework in which they operate have become a major shaping force in the cultural life of modern society.

Taken together, both aspects have been active at the core of our cultural life. The spillover effects of this double mediation seep down into the farthest reaches of modern society, for the development of mass-mediated communication has been part of a historical process in which many of the other major institutions in our society—family life, religion, politics, business, education—have been realigned. Thus, communication technologies have a dual nature. **They are channels through which information and interpersonal contact can flow and mix, binding together an otherwise dispersed and disparate population. They are also part and parcel of the institutional structure in a capital-intensive industrial economy, putting power and authority at the service of particular groups for particular purposes.** This point should be kept firmly in mind throughout the remainder of our discussion.

Industrialism and the rise of mediated communication proceeded side by side. For example, the coming of mass media was facilitated by the effects industrialization eventually had on leisure time. As the length of the working day declined and the more puritanical aspects of the work ethic weakened, labour became less an end in itself and more a means of gaining access to life's necessities (and, later, luxuries). The time and energy no longer expended on work was available for other purposes, such as activities that contributed to the realization of personal goals.

The mass media seized upon this opportunity and began to reflect back their audiences' new interests and concerns as leisure-oriented consumers through popular films, radio programs, magazines, and newspapers. Their success (and later that of television) is proved by dramatic growth in audience sizes, which was the direct result of their quick adoption of communications forms and contents that focused on popular entertainments. The spheres of working life, business, and serious political and social issues were by and large relegated to well-segregated slots occupied by news and documentaries, except when they were refashioned to suit drama or comedy. Immense talent and resources were assigned to the task of making the style and substance of the mass media conform faithfully to the concept of "light entertainment." New cultural institutions arose to cater to the insatiable appetite of audiences for the media's products. Names like Beaverbrook, Hearst, Warner, and Disney became household words as the profile of communications as a social force became more distinct.

The prominence of mediated communication is very much bound

up with the social functions it serves. Light entertainments make few demands upon their audiences, and so can be amusing accompaniments to rest periods when the working day is done or therapeutic aids to recuperation from stress. No less significant is their simple filling of free time; contact with the mass media absorbs about half the daily time released by the reduction in hours of work over the last century. Thus, it is fair to say that one has replaced the other as a form of activity.

The adoption of mediated communication into the rhythm of daily life also implied the development of new industries which supplied the technologies that enabled every household to enter into the flow of mediated communication. The realm of culture itself was industrialized. Moreover, each successive medium became a consumer product to be sought after—in the case of television, before it was even clear what it was actually going to offer. Up to 3 percent of consumer spending was funnelled into communication and culture, and the modern living room took on the characteristics of a node on the communication networks. The industrial organizations playing a part in this cultural market—RCA, General Electric, Westinghouse, and so many others—found their fortunes rose with the importance of this new sector of the economy. The communication sector was becoming a distinctive and often autonomous actor in industrial society.

The rapid urbanization after 1900 was a factor in the development of mediated communication, as it was in the emergence of industrial production and distribution mechanisms. Commercial newspapers first flourished in centres where both business interests and readerships were concentrated. Radio and television were particularly appropriate for urban situations, for the transmission cost is the same regardless of the size of audience within the broadcast basin.

Ironically, spatial concentration of the population led to decreasing levels of interpersonal contact. The mass media very soon began to fill the gap with productions such as soap operas that recreated situations of everyday life. For urban populations, which are a concrete manifestation of the anonymity inherent in the concept of "audience," mediated communication gained a human face through their favourite stars.

But mediated communication is in itself a form of social organization, made up of the relations of media and audiences and the nature and influence of the messages that flow through these channels. Thus, the evolution of the print media, especially the newspaper through its contribution to informing and educating wider reaches of the public, into the so-called free press was considered one of the foundations of emerging political democracy. Advertising and the expansion of the commercial media were linked to the maintenance and growth of the market economy; it seems almost inconceivable that we could enjoy the benefits of industrial democracy without the activities of the commercial media.

Thus, the historical development of the commercial media deserves close attention. In what ways and to what degree has advertising shaped the growth of the mediated communication that is so important to the conduct of every aspect of contemporary life? In the sections that follow we will outline the development of the modern media and the institutional framework in which they operate, showing how advertising—through the rise of mediated communication—has had a fundamental impact on society as a whole. We will focus our efforts by exploring three thematic areas.

The first is the establishment of commercial media themselves. Toward the end of the nineteenth century, advertising had become the key to the operation of the media, as the largest generator of its revenue. Commercialization, which was also based on increasing readerships and lower costs, not only became accepted as the best economic basis for newspapers, but also as the best guarantee of freedom from government interference. From then onward, the idea of the commercial press and the "free press" became synonymous and would continue to govern the evolution of the mass media institutions under successive waves of technological innovation.

As a result, advertising considerations began to influence greatly the operations of media, particularly their orientation to content and programming and the organization of audiences in terms of social, spatial, and temporal qualities. The competition for audiences through programming became the *sine qua non* of all media. This is our second theme.

The process of development and change of audience patterns for different media became crucial to the communications system. The introduction of a new medium, which carved out its own relationship to an audience, implied changes in audiences for other media as well. Special-interest periodicals helped to create the mass audience base of the daily newspapers. Magazines, which cultivated the first mass nationwide audiences, increasingly lost them to broadcast media—first radio and then television.

Currently, newspapers address broadly based local readerships (far more stratified by social class in Britain than in North America), while most magazines seek national or regional readers defined quite precisely by interests, tastes, and social stratum. Radio, once a mighty national force, is now largely a local medium with audiences stratified by age; its continued high profile in daily life is a function of its concentration on music programming, which turns it into an accompanist to an almost unlimited range of other activities, irrespective of time or place. Television, in the hands of the networks, segregates its audiences rigidly in terms of time slots, but as a communications medium it is unsurpassed for its capacity to generate and hold the attention of audiences that are scaled in millions.

Our third theme is the very fact that the media are commercial, which makes them an important communicative genre in their own right, exploring the meanings of personal and social interactions as well as the meanings of goods in relation to those interactions. They confer a place of special importance to advertising's discourse about products. The average citizen now spends literally hours each day engaged in this discourse, not with friends, family, and neighbours, but through the mediated representations of posters, television, radio, and newspapers. Media have made commercial messages inescapable.

In expanding the discourse about goods, advertising accommodated itself to the communications environment. Advertising as communication evolved in response to the abilities of the audience to make sense of messages and in response to the ideas, styles, and forms that were being explored in other genres and other media. Within the proliferation of mediated communication a "dialogue of forms" occurred. Eventually the diffusion and intermingling of diverse currents of thought and action became synergistic, as ideas or styles arising in one medium or genre were transferred to others and adapted, refined, enhanced, or changed in form and emphasis.

For example, early prose styles for newspapers were modelled on letter writing, whereas later ones borrowed from novels and the periodical press. Radio absorbed performance modes directly from the theatre, the cinema, and recorded music. Television undoubtedly has been the greatest synthesizer, turning to its purposes features drawn from all previous media forms. Visually oriented formats in art, photography, film, and television expanded and enhance in the population as a whole the understanding of the communicative skills that are founded upon symbolic, dramatic, imagistic, and metaphorical construction.

Positioned at the hub of the commercialized media, advertising has been in a position to assimilate all these influences and to bring them together in new ways. In some senses, it can be regarded as the quintessential communications form of the modern era. Its noteworthy features in this context are its "condensing" of ideas, its skilful combination of language and imagery, its breadth of thematic and social references, and its accessibility to and acceptance by wide audiences that may even cross linguistic and cultural barriers. Its efficiency as a communicative form has, in turn, affected other media productions, including serious film, television programming for children, and visual art. Most notable has been the expansion of advertising's social role; it has become one of the bases for governmental, political, and corporate efforts at persuasive influence through communication.

In the following sections we will place the emergence of advertising and the debates about its social role within the historical matrix that led to the rise of mediated communication and the emergence of our commercialized media institutions. In addition to the publications cited in this account we lean heavily on the work of A. Smith (1979), James Curran (1977), and E. Turner (1952).

THE ORIGINS AND DEVELOPMENT OF COMMERCIAL MEDIA

Newspapers

The development of the printing press marked the beginning of the industrialization of communication processes. The invention of typography resulted in "the first uniformly repeatable commodity, the first assembly-line, and the first mass-production" (McLuhan 1962, 124).

With the invention of the printing press, modern society embarked on a long march that would usher communications into the marketplace as a product to be bought and sold rather than an activity, and as an important part of the production and consumption process. The early products of the press were frequently read in a group setting; the eighteenth-century newspaper was a common property read by a large number of coffee-house devotees or by cooperative readership groups. As prices fell and content changed, the newspaper gradually began to define a more private "individual" relationship to the reader. As specific readerships developed and were identified, the medium was segmented in order to cater to the range of interests within family units and social groups. All subsequent media developments have extended this trend toward communication as a privately owned and personally used household good. The "Walkman" is probably the best and most extreme example of fragmentation of the audience.

The emergence of the daily newspaper brought about an equally significant shift in the *forms* of communication, introducing a radical change in the style and organization of the written word as well as in the distribution and availability of knowledge about the world. In becoming an essential channel for the social dialogue of modern democracies, the news has assured itself a special place in the institutions that govern mediated communication. (Moreover, as news increasingly emphasized the timeliness of information, the first repeatable commodity also became the first disposable commodity; few things are as uninteresting as yesterday' s news.) The commercial press and the other businesses that sprang up around it are, therefore, prototypes for all the subsequent social transformations created by the industrialization of communication.

"The history of communications from the 1700s until our own century is largely the history of the Press" (Williams 1962, 22). It was by no means an untroubled history, for by the eighteenth century the press had ceased to be so carefully controlled as to be almost an organ of the state and had become a central feature of political factionalism. The repeal of the Licensing Act in 1695 had ended the broader phase of censorship control over the press in England, and the printing industries embarked on a period of growth linked to the expansion of newspapers. The Stamp Act of 1712 was moderately successful as a new form of control on the burgeoning press that continued in some form until the middle of the nineteenth century. It used market as opposed to political means to restrict circulations, imposing a duty of one pence per published page and an advertisement tax of one shilling per insertion (regardless of size) per issue. This effectively raised the price of publication and maintained the newspapers' dependence on sponsors and subscriptions from committed supporters. Advertising only defrayed a little of the cost of printing, so the coffee houses and other public forums for newspaper reading were crucial to maintaining the newspaper. These public places either provided newspapers free or rented them at very low cost. Circulations therefore rose more slowly than readerships as relatively few subscribers could regularly afford papers for their personal use. Political parties and factions within them based on coffee-house cliques became associated with particular newspapers. Subsidies to the press through various means became an important instrument for disseminating partisan views.

Papers were voraciously read and debated at the coffee houses. Improved transportation and mail service encouraged wider circulation, giving a provincial as well as metropolitan slant. Demand for up-to-date news increased constantly, since timeliness was crucial to political activity. Average circulations were one to two thousand copies with some of the larger papers reaching about twelve thousand. In spite of increases in advertising and stamp duties, by 1753, total circulation in Britain had tripled from the 1711 level of 2,250,000; by 1776 it had reached 12,230,000, and by 1811 it had doubled again.

During the nineteenth century, the expansion of the press in both Britain and North America was connected to the development of new technologies for printing, as well as the rise of new readerships and new reasons to publish. A hand press might produce 150 copies per hour, and typemaking and typesetting were still cumbersome processes. The development of the Koening cylinder printing method and of steam presses brought the printing rate up to over a thousand sheets per hour. By 1827, the *Times* was printing four thousand sheets on both sides daily.

Advertising volume increased dramatically with the growth in numbers of publications, in issue size, and in circulations and the appearance of a profusion of new products from manufacturers, especially after the repeal of the Stamp Act in Britain in 1856. In the United States, spending on advertising rose from $15 million in 1870, to $39 million in 1880, and to $71 million in 1890. By 1908, spending had reached over $140 million, with the lion's share going to the print media, particularly newspapers. Advertising revenue provided new capital and new profits for media businesses that were not used to large profit margins. The infusion of capital was invested in new print technologies that made daily circulations of over 100,000 (and up to one hundred printed pages per issue) possible for the first time.

From the advertisers' point of view, a problem with newspaper ads was the editorial restrictions imposed on style by the publishers. All ads at the time more or less resembled modern classifieds; the only variations permitted were in spelling, the use of repetition, and (on occasion) the use of bold type. Advertisements, which frequently were grouped together, dignifying the front page and set apart from the editorial content, were each only allowed to occupy a limited amount of space. In the late 1880s and early 1890s, Joseph Pulitzer and William Randolph Hearst introduced not only a new style of journalism but also a new look for advertising. These twin decisions marked the beginning of the modern commercial press.

When Pulitzer took over the New York *World* in 1883, he intended to make newspapers readable to new immigrants and to the lower middle classes by using simple and accessible language. He adopted anti-establishment stances, advocating curbs on business, defending unions, and agitating opinion on a whole range of domestic issues. The format of the newspaper included exciting headlines and display presentations in advertisements. Within a year, his paper was selling 100,000 copies daily, and within ten the total circulation of morning and evening editions was 374,000. These stylistic innovations opened up display advertising throughout the industry.

The creation of a press independent of political or party factions and of a specific circulation base of loyal subscriber-supporters, a press free to find its own niche purely in terms of its market success in winning and holding readers, was the final and most important step in the long process of commercializing the press. The commercial revolution in the daily newspaper was partly brought about by the development of advertising as a genre. The adoption of display ads and illustration techniques made possible by new print technology were part of the impetus for the expansion of advertising revenue.

Magazines

During the long maturation of the reading public in modern society, magazines carved out a special niche in mediated communication located somewhere between newspapers and books and borrowing ideas and writing styles from both (Peterson 1974). Magazines underwent several periods of development and transformation, during which they were influenced by—and, in turn, themselves influenced—other media.

Magazines were the first major competitors with newspapers for advertising, and they remain a significant part of the advertising marketplace today. Their own innovations in forms and styles reflected, in part, their search for a market niche, defined not only in terms of who their audience might be but also in terms of finding new ways to reach this audience. The Sunday periodical press in England was the first print medium to win substantial audiences for a popular press, achieving circulations of over 100,000, even under the disadvantages of the Stamp Act and advertising taxes (Williams 1961).

In Britain after the lifting of the advertising tax in 1856, a new range of magazines emerged to tap the potential reading audience as occurred in the United States, where no national newspapers existed to advertise the newly available branded goods in the 1880s. *Pickwick* and *Penny Magazine* in Britain and *Harper's* in the United States thrived on serial fiction and "light" matter lifted from digests of other literary sources. Stories taken from newspapers added breadth and the absence of copyright laws made these literary efforts cheap to produce. In the United States, low postal rates for printed matter under the Postal Act of 1879 helped to ensure national distributions, meaning that reading publics could be organized around interests and attitudes. Religious and farm journals were very successful, and company-sponsored journals like the Canadian *Massey's Illustrated*, published from 1882 by the Massey-Harris farm machinery company, were often well respected. Many of these journals were not dependent upon advertising (they often, however, accepted it when offered), but rather on circulation and various forms of subsidy.

During this time, magazines thrived without the need for advertising revenue, and many of them, such as the better literary and religious journals, viewed it as a matter of pride not to sully their pages with ads. "Quality" literary magazines like *Harper's, Atlantic,* and *Scribner's* were wholly dependent on circulation, and indeed were only persuaded by the famous ad-man, J. Walter Thompson, to accept advertising after long refusing to do so. (*Reader's Digest* held out until 1957.) The leading women's magazines, *Godey's* and *Peterson's*, maintained low-profile advertising policies for much of the latter half of the century; the *New York Ledger* (400,000 circulation) did not accept advertisements.

In the 1880s, other journals were specifically created for advertising. E.C. Allen launched the *People's Literary Companion* as a pulp magazine to advertise a soap powder for which he owned the marketing rights. He scattered his ads throughout sixteen pages of stories, fashions, and household hints, charging subscribers fifty cents a year; he quickly achieved a circulation of 500,000. The *Companion* was the first "mail-order journal," so named for the types of advertising it attracted and upon which its economic security was founded.

The most famous magazine success story of the times was that of

Cyrus Curtis. Curtis owned *Tribune and Farmer*, a somewhat successful weekly, from which he " spun off" *Ladies Home Journal*. The *Journal* began with a circulation of 50,000, and as a result of a huge advertising campaign on its behalf this shot up to 400,000, confirming Curtis's faith in advertising as the foundation of the magazine industry. By 1895, circulation was 750,000. Building on this model, Curtis launched the *Saturday Evening Post*, which by 1910 had a circulation of over 2 million.

The popularity of magazines was stimulated by faster linotype type-setting and the invention of halftone technology. A pioneer was the weekly *Canadian Illustrated News*, which combined these techniques with the new paper made from wood pulp, which took ink differently from rag paper and made illustrations of a far superior quality. Advertising rates for this journal were the highest in Canada, but its combination of superior illustration and longer lead time than the daily newspaper proved attractive to readers and advertisers alike.

Munsey's Journal, a light topical magazine filled with illustrations as well as illustrated ads, was one of the first to exploit the dynamic relation between advertising and magazines. In 1893, its price was reduced to ten cents a copy and one dollar (formerly three) for a year' s subscription. The result of this pricing strategy was a fantastic increase in circulation and a flood of ads. *McClure's* and *Cosmopolitan* followed suit, and the era of cheap general magazines had begun. By 1905, there were twenty magazines with circulations of over 100,000 in the United States with a combined audience of 5.5 million readers. Almost all included liberal amounts of advertising (some up to one hundred pages of it), using lots of display type and illustration. Much the same was happening in Britain, where *Tit-Bits, Pearson's Weekly,* and *Northcliffe's Answers* became the models for high-circulation, advertising-based periodicals.

The periodical press in the nineteenth century laid the groundwork for all subsequent developments in the commercialization of the mass media. The illustrated magazines, leading the way with innovations in photographic and colour reproduction techniques, altered the print media and advertising industry alike, because they demonstrated the economic vitality of cheap, high-circulation journals that relied on advertising revenue. It was soon quite apparent that their popularity with advertisers rested on their acceptance of a whole new range of display possibilities for the ads within their covers. They brought fame and honours to their owners, who developed print empires based on exporting the capital resources, together with the marketing concepts pioneered by these journals, into the newspaper domain. And, finally, the illustrated magazines established many of the methods of promotion and distribution that would serve well in the later evolution of all commercial media institutions.

THE COMMERCIALIZED PRINT MEDIA AT THE TURN OF THE CENTURY

At the end of the nineteenth century, a number of forces, each of which had been gaining momentum on its own track for some time, were beginning to coalesce: the upsurge in industrial productivity, and the recognition that disposing of its output required adequate domestic markets; the change from a rural to a predominantly urban population, creating "anonymity," mobility, and a widening distance from historical and cultural roots that prepared the ground for new patterns of everyday life, socialization, and consumption; the rapid growth of two print forms of mediated communication, newspapers and magazines, brought about, at least partially, by the ceaseless pace of technological innovation that offered the means of reaching a mass audience cheaply with a better quality product, including great improvements in graphics (halftone illustrations and rotogravure printing).

The fledgling advertising profession began to look beyond its original menial role of serving as brokers for media space (see Chapter 6), gaining recognition as an independent force along with manufacturers and the media. Later these three forces would be joined by consumers; later still, advertising began to regard itself as occupying the strategic point at which the others converged. At the turn of the century, the commercialization of newspapers that sought audience loyalty simply on the appeal of the paper's contents allowed advertising to assume a prominent role in the mass media.

As advertising became a major source of funds for the press, there was a reciprocal impact on the stance that newspapers and magazines assumed toward their audiences. Publishers began to regard their publications not so much as products to be sold to readers, but more as vehicles that organized audiences into clearly identifiable target groups that could be sold to advertisers; the audiences themselves became the "products" generated by the media industry. The selling of audiences to advertisers would later become an explicit and highly refined media marketing strategy. Our point here is that the framework for this approach existed by the end of the nineteenth century. As the mass media spectrum enlarged to include radio and television, of course, a regular reshuffling of the primary target audiences for each medium became part of the game. For example, major national daily newspapers were an important channel for national brand advertising until the 1950s, when it was attracted increasingly to television, and all but a few leading papers had to rely thereafter upon local and classified advertising.

Thus, competition from other media has repeatedly challenged the newspapers' pre-eminence as an advertising medium and forced them to make continual adjustments to the advertising market. For example, sectionalization, which became widespread during the 1960s, programs advertising into concentrated, topic-specific units; food preparation hints run with supermarket ads, market information with business ads, travel columns with package tour ads, and so forth. Sectionalization achieved for the newspapers the same results as segmentation did for magazines, namely the ability to address special audiences (theatregoers, sports fans, women interested in fashion) that advertisers wish to "target." As a by-product, multiple readership improved because detachable sections could be read simultaneously by different members of the family.

Many of the innovations in newspaper design, such as the liveliness of style that was the hallmark of the early mass-circulation dailies, the use of display and illustrated ads, photojournalism, and more recently, full-colour printing, were derived and modified from magazines. Weekend supplements and entertainment guides packaged information with the chatty journalistic style of magazines. Colour supplements and inserts have proved to be particularly useful; in Canada, these now account for 5.6 percent of all advertising revenue, about half the newspapers' total share of national advertising, reflecting the special importance attached by food and other retailers to attractive colour layouts.

THE IMPACT OF BROADCASTING

Newspapers and Radio

The newspaper competed for advertising with the periodical industry and a far more potent adversary—the broadcast media. In Britain, newspapers actively supported retention of the public domain monopoly of radio broadcasting and later fought the introduction of commercial television for obvious reasons. They were instrumental in the 1923 decision of the Sykes Committee that led to Britain's public broadcasting monopoly. The United States followed a different route. As commercial radio was being developed, a number of newspapers bought stations as a novel means of promoting their newspapers. By 1933, 28 percent of American radio stations were owned by newspapers—especially the big stations in large urban centres. Other newspapers protested the possible loss of revenue, but the pattern of cross-media ownership and the idea of radio as a commercial institution prevailed in public policy.

During the early Depression, newspaper advertising dropped 22 percent in North America while radio advertising rose slightly, due partly to the emergence of spot advertising to supplement network-based sponsored programming. Spot ads gave radio a regional and local reach in its advertising to supplement the national selling campaigns that came with networking. But the cost of radio advertising quickly rose as performers demanded a share of the benefits of their drawing abilities. At the same time, the proliferation of broadcasters resulting from radio's success meant that audiences, except for the most attractive network broadcasts, were little different in size from newspaper circulations in any given area.

Costs per thousand for local retailers remained satisfactory in newspapers, and it was mainly the national brand accounts, which were not in any event the mainstay of newspapers at this time, that shifted to radio during the 1930s. The actual range of products advertised on radio was limited. Food, drug, tobacco, and soap—the major product categories—formed "the backbone of American broadcast advertising, accounting for approximately two-thirds of the users in 1931" (Hettinger 1933, 128).

Radio began to compete in earnest with newspapers for the retail and local advertising trade after World War II, just at the time when newspapers were being forced to respond to the changes in the advertising market brought about by the introduction of television. However, the competitive pressures of television on newspapers were not as great as some have suggested. As Curran (1977) points out, the differences in the relationship of the two media to their audiences make them complementary. Television is a high quality "display" medium attractive for the mass marketing of consumer goods, while newspapers are a regional and local medium with excellent "information" properties. Television may have caused a shift of some types of consumer advertising away from newspapers, as it did in the case of mass-circulation magazines, but its real impact was in maintaining a competitive pressure on the rate structure for all media. It also increased the newspapers' reliance on retail and regional advertising, which has been increasing relative to the total market since the 1950s.

As we shall see, the degree of involvement by the advertising industry in the institutional development of the mass media was heightened enormously by the emergence of the broadcast media. But the ground had been thoroughly prepared by the industry's participation in the commercialization of the print media. Therefore, when radio came onto the scene, it turned out to be a fairly easy task to apply what had been learned to the new medium.

Magazines Narrow Their Focus

The 1920s witnessed the continued expansion of popular magazines, although nearly as many failed as were started. Total advertising expenditures were growing, but competition between media for the various markets was heating up. The national general-interest magazine was competing not so much with the newspaper, with its identifiable urban market very attractive to retailers, as with the new national radio networks. In some cases, national accounts were split between them or were shifted to the new sound medium as advertisers discovered spot advertising on a national basis.

Magazines responded to the challenge by offering new attractions to prospective advertisers. Women's magazines were at the forefront. A number of them set up departments with consumer panels and research services that they offered to interested advertisers. Thus, the magazines gradually became innovators of services desired by advertisers as well as contents. The use of audience research as opposed to circulation data became a widely accepted defensive measure against the encroachment by radio as an advertising medium.

But adoption of audience research by magazines had effects far beyond that of raising circulation figures. Readership studies discovered overlaps in readership patterns and magazines with few multiple readers. This knowledge allowed advertisers more tactical leeway in placing their ads, and those magazines that did not meet the advertisers' needs simply faded away. Daniel Starch and others pioneered in researching audiences—that is, who was reading what publications—but they soon went beyond the mere counting of readers; they asked about the readers' backgrounds and interests, thus helping to define the appeal of a particular magazine in terms of its audience.

Research oriented around the activities of the mass media has been a major force in welding together the social institutions that make up the consumer culture. Beginning in the 1930s, "social research served to unify business, advertising, the mass media, and through them, the further development of American culture." A continuous circle of mutual influence evolved, in which "researchers came to promote themselves to the media, the media promoted themselves to advertising agencies, agencies promoted themselves to business, business promoted itself to consumers, and consumers ultimately turned back to researchers for guidance" (Hurvitz 1985).

Magazines that survived the Great Depression began to use research to evaluate readers' reactions to features or new styles of presentation, and in many cases to measure response to and retention of ads themselves. The information gathered was important for setting editorial policy as well as for advertisers. Old formulas for success were cast aside and magazines developed new approaches. "Readership ratings came to be accepted as helpful 'feedback' which complemented readers' letters and editorial know how" (Barbour 1982, 134). This feedback helped editors to exploit their advantages in audience positioning, content, and style.

The introduction of television created frantic competition for the magazine industry during the 1950s, and the magazines both won and lost the battles. Many major national accounts, particularly branded foods and household goods, did shift to television. The product array advertised in a typical consumer magazine has narrowed dramatically over the last thirty years, with high concentrations of particular products in a few journals. A high proportion of the advertising space in *Maclean's*, a popular Canadian newsmagazine, is devoted to the alcohol industry. Many women' s magazines have personal-care and clothing advertising and little else. Successful magazines accentuated a special feature of their audiences, such as age, sex, income, region, and lifestyle grouping, to provide them with a firm advertising base. Not all group interests were represented by the magazines that survived, but the mass-circulation magazines reoriented their relationship to national advertising by narrowing their focus in terms of the products they could attract to their pages.

The specialist magazine market today shows clearly the dynamic relationship between magazine format and content and advertising. However, special-interest journals first developed during the nineteenth century (without carrying ads) for markets ranging from high-class literary or news journals, to religious, farm, hobby, and business magazines. Most were secure in their relationships and only expanded their reliance on advertising slowly. Many of them still cover more of their production costs from subscription revenue than from ads. Special-interest and "lifestyle" magazines were not created by advertisers.

The newer special-interest magazine's editorial focus is on a particular activity and product array, for example *Skiing, Tennis, Photography,* and *Computers.* Advertisers tend to think of these as reflecting a certain lifestyle with a direct connection to a product range. The more traditional special-interest magazines such as religious, business, or glamour magazines are less explicitly an advertiser's medium. The lifestyle magazine uses its editorial content to attract a narrow range of potential advertisers. In many cases, readers use them as "shopping guides" to assess products; advice to beginners is a regular feature inducting the reader into the special knowledge and skills of the activity. The lifestyle magazine blends advertising and editorial content until they are almost indistinguishable.

This more focused relationship is noticeable also in the "advertorial" sections, which first started appearing in business magazines like *Fortune* and are now spreading throughout specialty magazines. The advertorial is really an adaptation by magazines of the topic-specific newspaper section (women, sports, science) in which advertising and content can be prepackaged and inserted as a unit. A recent research study has demonstrated that when these sections are based on a single theme they improve the recall of ads by 30 percent.

Finally, the controlled-circulation magazine is probably the best illustration of the influence of advertising. Controlled-circulation magazines—distributed on a national, regional, and local basis—are delivered free of charge to those on a highly selective mailing list usually confined to more affluent sections of the city. If demographic and readership surveys prove that this "upscale" market segment can be efficiently reached by the magazine, then enough advertising can be solicited to cover all production costs.

The success of a magazine is dependent not only upon its ability to cultivate an audience in competition with other magazines, but in competition with other media as well. The special character of that audience—its spending habits, disposable income, openness to approaches through other media—are crucial factors in determining whether advertisers will use a particular magazine. Under these conditions, magazines are under pressure to orient themselves to audiences that advertisers particularly want, and these tend to lie predominantly on the wealthier end of the scale.

RADIO: TUNING IN THE COMMERCIAL INSTITUTION

The introduction of radio also marks an important point of departure for the advertising industries in North America and Britain. One of the most successful ventures ever undertaken by the advertising industry in North America was the selling of radio broadcasting as a commercial medium. Although the agencies and the commercial press were at similar stages of development, in Britain radio became initially a public sector monopoly. The agencies and advertisers had to wait beyond the introduction of television for the broadcasting industry to have a commercial component; in Britain, radio followed in television' s footsteps. Among the forces responsible for this was the strong resistance of the well-established newspaper sector, which was functioning as a national advertising system and felt threatened by radio. In many ways, advertising methods and approaches in Britain remained oriented to print until well into the 1950s, whereas advertisers in the United States eagerly explored the possibilities offered by other media. This may help to explain why in North America the agency system emerged as an important cultural force early in this century, while in Britain a similar impact was delayed.

Even in the United States both government officials and major industry spokespersons were seemingly reluctant to allow radio to turn itself into a commercial medium. General Sarnoff, head of RCA and an early visionary of the "music box" concept for radio, spoke out strongly against the commercialization of radio as late as 1924. The radio industry magazine, *Radio Broadcast Monthly*, railed against the dash of "advertising paprika," calling for governmental restrictions. Secretary of Commerce Hoover also wanted to preserve the dignity of radio, stating at the 1922 American Radio Conference that it was "inconceivable" to allow "so great a possibility for service . . . to be drowned in advertising chatter" (Briggs 1961, 7). The commercialization of radio was not the first or most obvious choice.

Early entry into the broadcasting market by retailers and producers of electronic equipment—who controlled up to 40 percent of the licensed stations in 1923—meant that broadcasting itself was initially a kind of promotional service for the hardware. In 1922, Station WEAF introduced the "toll" system for advertisers, enabling them to buy ten minutes of broadcasting time for one hundred dollars. But takers were few, even in New York; only $550 worth of radio time had been sold three months later.

Some early advertisers sponsored programs directly relevant to their products. Gillette hosted a talk on fashions in beards, and department stores backed programs on fashion, hoping to generate institutional goodwill and interest in their products. But for the most part, advertisers simply did not know what to do with radio. Only the development of regular weekly programs rather than one-time efforts led advertisers to see some merit in the new medium, although few programs—only 20 percent in 1927 and 36 percent by 1931—yet attracted sponsors.

The national advertisers and the agencies quickly became the best organized forces in the radio market, and their pressure helped NBC to emerge as the first national network of affiliated stations. Networks solved two major problems in broadcasting: they provided better quality programming, holding the interest of large audiences with the costs of production distributed across a number of stations; and their broader regional and national audiences helped to attract more advertisers into the medium, keeping rates down.

By the second half of the 1920s, national advertising on radio, although well mannered and "institutional" in nature, was catching on and becoming increasingly attractive to potential advertisers. As radio's audience grew, advertisers' interest followed. In the larger stations, the pattern typical today was already at work; programming was used to attract listeners who were then "sold" to advertisers (Barnouw 1978, 33). The Starch study of 18,024 radio homes for NBC did much to confirm the growing significance of radio listeners as potential markets for advertisers. Further audience research efforts detailed the rapid growth of the medium (17 million sets by 1932) and the interests and preferences of audiences to guide programming on the networks. The research shows how listening followed daily time curves, with evening audiences different in character and twice the size of daytime ones; how the programming mix of the networks was establishing different audience loyalties based on programming preferences; and, more importantly, how "program flow" from one show to the next could influence these loyalties.

Once programming sponsored by advertisers secured a firm foothold, and networking was a success, the full commercialization of the medium proceeded apace. Individual stations became dependent on the networks for material of sufficiently high quality to draw audiences, and on the fast-developing expertise of advertising agencies to secure a stable revenue base. National broadcasting and national advertisers nicely reinforced each other's interests. In 1922, only 6 percent of all radio stations were affiliated with networks; by 1937, this affiliation had risen to 46 percent, and by 1947 to 97 percent.

The growing evidence of radio's popularity and efficiency as an advertising medium persuaded some of the more adventurous advertisers and agencies to back it heavily. The Lord and Thomas agency helped Pepsodent to develop "Amos 'n' Andy," which became the most popular show on radio and quickly helped to triple Pepsodent sales. Albert Lasker, the agency's president, was convinced that a more focused and forceful selling message than the usual sponsorship mention or well-mannered invocation for products could be used on radio. The Lord and Thomas agency developed such ads for the American Tobacco Company. In the hands of the agencies, the style of national advertising on radio was changing and radio programming was changing with it.

Cecil Widdifield, an executive at Schwimmer and Scott Advertising, developed the idea of transcription, which allowed programs and ads to be recorded and distributed to various stations for replaying. Since the cost of talent was a growing concern, not having to pay for every performance was a considerable advantage, especially in network efforts. Mistakes, hesitations, miscues, and flubs could be minimized and program quality controlled. With transcripted programs now precisely pre-timed, it was possible to sell commercial spots between programs on individual or specific groups of stations to accommodate regional needs. Spot advertising became an important alternative to sponsorship.

From the late 1920s until the start of World War II, advertisers and their agencies controlled programming directly. Sponsors did much more than sponsor. They actually produced the shows, hiring performers, writers, directors, and musicians and leasing the facilities for production from the networks. The networks had virtually no control over the programming, and there is no indication that they wanted it.

The effect on programming was predictable: it became advertising by another name.

> In the sponsor-controlled hours, the sponsor was king. He decided on programming. If he decided to change programs, network assent was considered pro forma. The sponsor was assumed to hold a "franchise" on his time period or periods. Many programs were ad agency creations, designed to fulfill specific sponsor objectives. The director was likely to be an advertising agency staff employee. During dress rehearsal an official of the sponsoring company was often on hand in the sponsor's booth, prepared to order last minute changes. In Radio City—completed in 1933—every studio had a sponsor's booth. (Barnouw 1978, 33)

Even though substantial parts of the networks' schedules remained unsponsored, by 1935 7 percent of advertising expenditure was on radio, rising to a high of 15 percent during the wartime and postwar newsprint shortages.

During the war, government agencies in the United States requested network sponsors to encourage war services such as nursing campaigns and war bond announcements. Advertisers welcomed this opportunity to make their position more legitimate, since—with severe shortages of consumer durables due to war production—they had relatively little to sell. They formed the War Advertising Council to coordinate responses to requests for public-service messages and to produce these messages. Renamed the Advertising Council when the war ended, it determined the priority to be given to public-service announcements. General reputations and organizational images became an important aspect of advertising in postwar America. In other words, public relations and advertising began to merge.

Radio evolved differently in Britain, where government had controlled radio technology since its inception. Noting the unregulated situation in North America, and the rapid growth in the medium in the early 1920s, the British government appointed the Sykes Committee to recommend a radio broadcasting policy. The newspapers, which had not sought cross-media ties in owning and operating radio stations and were especially concerned about potential losses of advertising revenue, strongly lobbied both the Sykes Committee and its successor, the Crawford Committee, not to open up the airwaves to "advertising chatter."

The Crawford Committee's 1926 report led to the Broadcasting Act and the creation of a public monopoly—the British Broadcasting Corporation with a revenue base assured by an annual license fee on radio receivers. The BBC gave rise to an enormously influential tradition of public-interest broadcasting, but it soon became apparent that good intentions were not enough to elicit and retain audience interest; attractive and entertaining programming was required as well. In the 1930s, the BBC had to compete in many parts of the country with private commercial broadcasters beaming transmissions to Britain from the continent. The corporation launched an additional network for popular light entertainment, and eventually, in the face of a new surge of competition from offshore "pirate" stations in the 1960s, expanded to four. However, the Sound Broadcasting Act of 1972 at last created a structure of mixed public and private ownership, and thereafter independent commercial radio stations have competed with the BBC's four networks in the major urban markets.

In Canada, the commercial and public-interest streams converged in another way. Already by 1923 there were sixty-two licensed, privately owned stations, including one that was for a while part of the NBC network. From the outset, spillover of programming and advertising content from the United States was a major concern. In 1928, the Aird Commission recommended a system of license fees and a public broadcast monopoly on the British model. No action was taken, however, largely as a result of the clash over jurisdiction between federal and provincial governments.

The next official report in 1932 made very different recommendations. It proposed a dual system including both public and private broadcasters with revenues raised through both advertising and license fees. The Broadcasting Act of 1932 established a commission to oversee the radio system and in 1936 this became a dual system of commercial (private) and public-interest sectors all regulated under the auspices of the Canadian Broadcasting Corporation. The CBC thus was in the anomalous position of operating a single network of public stations and private affiliates across the country to compete with signals coming not only from the United States (over 80 percent of Canadians could receive such signals) but also from Canadian commercial stations—over which, in the public interest, it had a certain amount of regulatory control.

TELEVISION: SOLIDIFYING THE COMMERCIAL VISION

In 1936, the BBC undertook limited public broadcasting of television signals from Alexandra Palace as an extension of its public-service monopoly (Briggs 1961). This arrangement survived until the pressures of industry, advertising agencies, and a Conservative government majority in 1954 created a mixed broadcasting system with competing public and commercial elements. The new Independent Television Authority could allow spot advertising but not sponsored programming, so that advertisers could not gain a stranglehold on the production of programs, which the British authorities considered the major deficiency in the American commercialized broadcasting system.

In Canada, the Massey Report on the arts, in spite of many complaints from private broadcasters, suggested that Canada should have a national TV network under the CBC before commercial television was permitted. This rather confused situation was perpetuated in the Broadcasting Act of 1958. By that time, over 60 percent of Canadians could tune in to border stations in the United States; some Canadian advertisers preferred to use those facilities, and Canadian audiences had begun to develop their long infatuation with the products of American television. Finally, in 1968, although a new Act reaffirmed the concept of a single system made up of two different sectors, the public and private sectors in practice were split up and the responsibilities assigned to each were distinguished.

To the south there was little question that television would follow in the institutional mould of radio. American broadcasting began in 1939 on NBC from the New York World's Fair, with CBS soon following. By 1941, ten commercial television broadcast licenses had been issued. A moratorium on new station licenses was declared by the Federal Communication Commission (FCC) in 1948, so as to impose some order on the television sector, particularly with regard to channel allocation. The freeze lasted until 1952, by which time—although only sixty-three metropolitan areas were in the reception areas of television signals—television fever had been unleashed and the mass production of sets was underway. By 1957, television reached 97 percent of the continental United States and over 82 percent of homes owned a set.

The prewar structure of radio programming was transplanted to television. Advertisers still controlled programs, usually with one sponsor per show. In the 1945–55 period, two external factors influenced the relationships among broadcast organizations. First, the huge increase in available consumer goods led to commercials becoming an incessant part of the broadcast day. Second, the atmosphere of fear created by the Cold War and McCarthyism made sponsors tread cautiously in producing programs.

By the mid-1950s, the networks were becoming more and more uneasy about the control they had ceded to advertisers thirty years earlier. Most important was a legal issue: the networks were legally responsible for what they broadcast, though they had little say in it. Among other concerns was the lack of logic in programming; scheduling, in particular, was chaotic. The networks tried to implement the concept of "magazine programming," wherein they would take charge of content and offer spots separately to advertisers in order to gain flexibility in maintaining program flow, the holding of audiences from show to show. The advertiser was satisfied when the audience rating for his own program was high; the network wanted to maintain high ratings over as many programs as possible. But the idea fell flat. Advertisers obviously wanted to hold on to their considerable power. Why settle for a one-minute commercial when you already had a thirty-minute one?

Two things forced the situation to change: the discovery of fraud and deceit in the popular quiz shows, and the economics of program production. Production costs, even for soap operas and the game shows, were high, and talent was demanding a considerable payback on popular programs. It was difficult for one advertiser to produce an entire show and buy time for it from the networks as well. Production houses began to produce programs under contract to the networks or under network license, and then to sell spots on them to advertisers.

Although decision making seemed to be with the networks, advertisers still influenced programming as television was totally dependent on advertising for its operating revenue. What did advertisers buy with their dollars? The common-sense answer was that they bought time, either fifteen- or thirty- or sixty-second spots. But whose time did they buy? Advertisers did not purchase just "abstract time": they bought the time of particular audiences. Audiences were the currency of the advertising business and they became the currency for television programmers as well.

This becomes clear when we examine how advertising rates are set. Two factors determine the amount that advertisers will pay broadcasters. One is the actual number of people watching the ads. This aspect of audiences is known as cost-per-thousand, and it helps those who are paying to compare the audiences for particular media in numerical terms. In the past, before audiences were qualitatively differentiated, sheer size was the criterion. The larger the audience, the more the network could charge for advertising spots. The stress on numbers and audience share, which was what the polls reported, thus became essential to costing for the advertising industry. Its effect on programming was to create a conservative bias, with no risks and no controversy that would exclude, alienate, or miss parts of the audience. To appeal to larger numbers of people, programming, of course, must address itself to "common denominators" in cultural preferences—critics accused it of appealing to the "lowest" of common denominators. National network-sponsored programming simply could not afford to experiment with programming that only appealed to specialist or minority audience tastes.

The introduction of UHF (ultrahigh frequency), public sector educational broadcasting, cable, and then satellite began to fragment the audience. Moreover, as research into television audiences, their attitudes and preferences for products, lifestyles, and spending habits expanded it became clear to advertisers that there was a second important aspect of rates—the demographic characteristics of the audience. Advertisers became interested in buying audiences that consisted predominantly of people who were consumers, or potential consumers, of their products. Some kinds of audiences became more expensive than others. Programs had to be tailored to generate large numbers of the right viewers for the particular advertiser.

In the 1960s, for instance, CBS dropped a number of popular prime-time shows such as "The Beverly Hillbillies" and "Andy Griffith" because they attracted the wrong audience—elderly, low-income, and rural viewers. Advertisers had become keen on young, affluent urbanites who would be willing to try new products and keep using them for a long time once they became loyal to a brand. By 1970, this new audience logic of the television marketplace was throwing the network schedulers into turmoil.

Although advertisers made fewer decisions about which shows would be developed or cancelled, they continued to determine the criteria that programs had to satisfy. "They were helping create a dramaturgy reflecting the demographics of the supermarket. . . . The sponsor, from whom the money flowed, had left the sponsor's booth, but he had taken his influence along with him" (Barnouw 1978, 73). Far from freeing programming from advertiser control, the "magazine format" intensified it across the entire schedule.

> In practice, the networks, in their drive to sell every available advertising minute at the highest possible price, proved to be even less adventurous than the sponsors had. . . . Advertisers, in short, had proven to be more responsible and innovative as programmers than the networks. Network-originated programming now was set on a course to become ever more rigid and standardized, enslaved to ratings. . . . The magazine format programs turned out to be a formula designed first and last to accommodate advertising. At its worst the format amounted to little more than commercials in search of a program. (Bergreen 1978, 178)

Producers are also concerned with providing a conducive "environment" for the reception of commercials. Apparently this dictates a methodical blandness, so as not to upset or disturb the viewers as they are gently prepared for the ads.

Such was not always the case. In the early 1950s, the normal vehicle for drama presentation was the anthology series in which each week's show was different from the others. Many of television's finest moments were captured in the anthology series. However, because television was done live at this time, these self-contained plays featured indoor settings and tended to stress not physical confrontations but complex social and psychological issues without easy solutions. Meanwhile, the commercials offered happiness and salvation in one minute or less, which made them seem fraudulent.

The anthology series also often dealt with lower-class life and settings at odds with the sponsor's desire to encourage the audience to yearn for the glamorous, consumer-oriented lifestyles depicted in the ads. In the mid-1960s, the anthology series was replaced by a new format based on "episodes." As the major Hollywood studios started to produce for television, the restrictions on live performance disappeared and drama moved outdoors into glamorous settings with handsome heroes and heroines. The episodic series relied less on the creativity of writers, or on dialogue, and more on the filling out of an already established formula that walked a few flatly developed characters through an action-packed dilemma. Alas, these "dilemmas" were all too often the familiar ones of modern consumer life, featuring troubled personal relationships being rescued by a timely application of standard social values (Barnouw 1978).

The content, form, and concerns of commercials mimicked each other as well as the surrounding shows. The game shows of the 1950s, such as "Queen for a Day" and "The Price Is Right," explicitly emphasized consumerism; later, "Family Feud" and "The Dating Game" interwove social relations and the rewards of consumption more intricately.

Soap operas moved to the nighttime schedule and up the class ladder from the middle-class setting of "As the World Turns" to the American aristocracy of "Dallas," offering a new context for displaying the dramatization of consumption patterns and conventional status symbols.

The action adventures reflected ads more in terms of pace and excitement than thematic content. Once again, television blurred the distinction between programming and advertising, this time with respect to style — of character development, dialogue, music, and camera angles. Characters walked out of the programs and into the ads, even when the actors were left behind. Advertising uses television programming as a system of reference; returning the favour, programming uses advertising as its framework and, in some cases, its exemplar. "Sesame Street" adapted the pacing of advertising to the task of teaching preschoolers. Politicians took lessons from image counsellors expert in flogging whatever was set in front of them before they ventured forth to debate the nation's fate. Shot framing or cutting techniques pioneered in advertising to condense storytelling became stock tools of television dramas.

SHARING THE MARKET

Could the massive growth in print media circulations or the subsequent impact of radio and television on daily life have occurred without advertising? Advertising and the mass media marched hand in hand into the modern world. The massive increase in the number and technological sophistication of communication channels parallelled a similar expansion of messages directed toward consumers through advertisements.

Advertising expenditures grew steadily but slowly before the period of the commercial revolution in the press. The second half of the nineteenth century was a period of increasing numbers of new publications, and magazines and newspapers that previously had not accepted advertisements began to do so at this time. Also, a slow growth in new product types entered the advertising arena. The result was a moderate but steady growth in advertising volume up to the end of the century.

The beginning of the twentieth century was a major turning point for advertising. The revolution in the newspaper industry, which linked the increasing productivity of the press with income generated predominantly by advertising, coincided with a period of dramatic growth in advertising volume. The expansion of the magazine industry, too, in conjunction with a whole new range of products (especially branded consumer products), seemed to accentuate the growth of advertising. The first twenty-five years of this century was the period of advertising's most rapid growth.

Similar jumps in the volume of advertising can be connected with the introduction of radio in the late 1920s and television in the early 1950s.

The appearance of new media led inexorably to greater advertising volumes. The introduction of broadcasting media obviously produced competition for accounts among the media; but this competition only caused each medium to redouble its efforts to make its special qualities more attractive to advertisers by making the medium itself more attractive to audiences. The only period of declining investment in advertising came during the early Depression years of the 1930s when a number of major manufacturers reduced their volume irrespective of the availability of media.

The graphs in Figures 5.2, 5.3, and 5.4 chart total expenditures in advertising and the fortunes of the various media in the United States, Canada, and Britain in gaining and maintaining a share of that expenditure. (Note that these are ratio graphs, so that increases in dollar or pound

FIGURE 5.2
American Advertising Expenditure by Medium

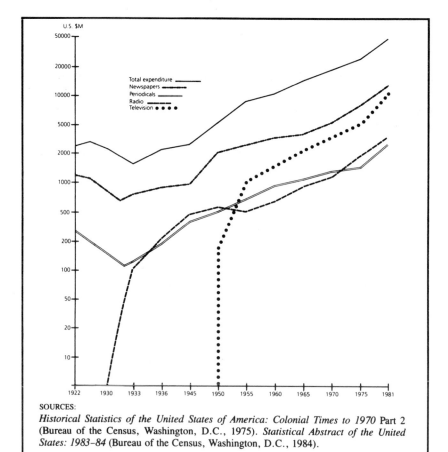

SOURCES:
Historical Statistics of the United States of America: Colonial Times to 1970 Part 2 (Bureau of the Census, Washington, D.C., 1975). *Statistical Abstract of the United States: 1983–84* (Bureau of the Census, Washington, D.C., 1984).

FIGURE 5.3
Canadian Advertising Expenditure by Medium

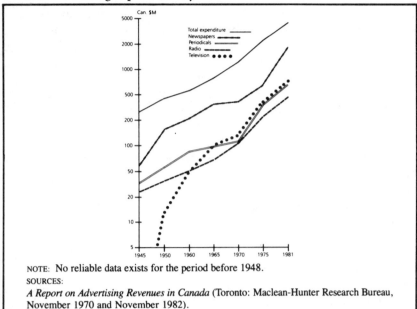

NOTE: No reliable data exists for the period before 1948.
SOURCES:
A Report on Advertising Revenues in Canada (Toronto: Maclean-Hunter Research Bureau, November 1970 and November 1982).

FIGURE 5.4
British Advertising Expenditure by Medium

NOTE:
Expenditure on radio advertising was insignificant for the period for which statistics are available.
SOURCES:
R.A. Critchley. *U.K. Advertising Statistics: A Review of the Principal Sources and Figures* (London: The Advertising Association, 1970). T.R. Nevett. *Advertising in Britain: A History* (London: Heinemann, 1982).

value in the 1960s and 1970s are many times greater than in earlier periods.) The graphs illustrate the consequences of divergent policies and institutions on advertising expenditure and how each new medium opened a new channel to audiences. Sometimes simply by adjusting the content and form of advertisements, audiences organized in a certain way by one medium could also be addressed by another. Advertisers, growing in number as nationally distributed branded products proliferated, faced an increasingly complex advertising environment. They shifted accounts from one medium to another as advantages presented themselves, creating competition among media for advertising revenue.

Advertising did not cause the expansion of mediated communication. As Raymond Williams (1961) points out, one can notice a general increase in circulations for the daily press long before it developed into the commercial press. Neither the spread of literacy to the working classes nor advertising created the "reading public"; it was already well established when the commercialization of the mass media began.

But the reorganization of the press, linking profitability indissolubly to advertising revenue, did help to make the newspapers affordable for the new lower-middle-class reading public, which was becoming much more involved in social and political issues. The Crimean and Boer wars in Britain, the Civil and Spanish-American wars in America, and World War I everywhere had a dramatic impact on the daily reading of newspapers, giving advertisers access to new consumers and publishers increasing profits as per-issue costs decreased with the new printing technologies and economies of scale.

Similar arguments can be made about the growth of radio and television. In Britain, where radio was noncommercial, the number of receiving sets increased rapidly during the 1920s; and postwar austerity only partially moderated the demand for television sets in the early 1950s before commercial television was introduced. Advertising did not create demand for these media, nor did its invisible subsidies support their difficult early years.

Even in the United States, the surge of radio buying preceded any large-scale advertising efforts. In 1924, over 1.5 million sets were sold, with annual sales rising to over six million by the time the Radio Act of 1927 defined advertising as in the "public interest, convenience, and necessity." Whatever changes in programming were made to encourage listening in the early phase had little to do with advertising, though subsequent growth in audiences may have had something to do with the influence of advertising on programming. However, it is impossible to pin this down, since no one can say with assurance how noncommercial broadcasting would have developed. Yet evidence from countries with noncommercial or only partially commercial broadcasting supports the view that the growth of mediated communication responds primarily to general social change within which advertising plays only a small part.

This is not to say that powerful reciprocal forces were not exerted by the successive revolutions in media technologies and advertising. In creating an institutional context and rationale that supported advertising, the press laid the groundwork for the commercialization of other media. Although competing media threatened to detract from print's share of the advertising pie, in the long run, the careful studies by Hettinger (1933) and Curran (1981) on the introduction of radio and television, respectively, show that by and large the advertising revenue garnered by them is not won at the expense of older forms. There was always one clear beneficiary—the advertising industry (especially the agencies).

What was most affected by the emergence of new means of communication was the "shape" of advertising or the design strategy rather than the volume. As new media brought new styles and approaches to the tasks of mass communications, advertisers adapted them to the special requirements of persuasion. The selling message was altered by the communications environment.

The influence of advertising on communications media has received more attention, as we have seen. It is unlikely that any of the means of mass communication could exist as they do without the money they derive from advertising. Wherever television and radio are not funded by government grants, they are almost entirely dependent upon ad revenue; newspapers depend on advertising for two-thirds of their revenue and magazines for about 60 percent. What advertisers get in return for their money is the right to insert their message in the particular medium. But this is not a totally passive insertion, since it occurs in an environment where media compete for advertising revenue. In what follows we are particularly concerned with how advertising influences the non-advertising content and operations of the media—that is, with the relationship between advertising and programming.

One view, often put forward by advertisers and the media themselves, is that advertising revenues merely make the programs possible. Watching the ads is the price we pay for getting the programming, but there is no direct connection between the money derived from advertisers and the programming it pays for—or more broadly, between the media's business interests and its production and distribution of content. Another view stresses that because advertising guarantees the profitability of the media enterprise, programming has become geared to the interests of advertisers.

Attempting to reconcile or choose between these two opposing points of view presents an intractable problem. The interlocking interests of media and advertising were constructed step-by-step, through quite deliberate, marketplace transactions and public policy decisions, yet to most people this development seems as natural and inevitable as the succession of seasons. Opinion polls in Canada, for example, reveal that most viewers of television feel insulted and demeaned by advertising, but accept it as a necessary part of the media system. "Nearly forty years of the present broadcasting system has conditioned a generation of citizens to find it normal. Most people find it difficult to think of other kinds of broadcasting systems and uses" (Skornia 1965, 44).

It is certainly true that, in television at least, the economic power and decision making that control the processes of communication tend to be separated from the editorial and creative activities that develop the content and programming. In both public and private networks, programming policy and strategy is regarded as proprietary information. As viewers, we experience these institutions mainly as communication providers, not as business organizations. For example, our knowledge of program decision making is normally limited to statements by media executives on a particular show's slippage in the ratings; what we do not see directly are the processes that make ratings the primary desideratum in the show's success or failure.

The difficulty is compounded by the fact that advertising itself is a service industry in the sense that it is dependent upon the activities of producers and providers of services. Advertising's subsidy to the media comes from the industrial sector, which reclaims it from the consumer. There is no direct market in commercialized media, as there is, for example, in the movie industry; we only buy it indirectly through a value-added payment on the price of the goods we consume. We have no way of seeing how our choice of goods is translated into advertising support for particular programs, magazines, or newspapers. In earlier periods in our own society or in countries where political parties control media directly, the connection between politics and the content and form of messages seems reasonably clear. But it is far more difficult to spotlight the relationship between business and communication where advertising interests and the logic of buying audiences are involved.

Behind the people who appear to us on the box, whose voices ride with us in the car, or whose words seem as familiar as the morning toast they accompany, is a large organization making decisions that shape editorial and program content. And behind that organization is an invisible institutional structure supported by tradition, money, and power, establishing the framework within which those decisions are made. These relations are "remote and impersonal" (Curran 1981); analysis of the influence of advertising on communications is contingent upon being able to peer through the murky waters where the many-faceted institutional determinants of programming lie.

It is, therefore, essential for us to separate the various organizational factors that impinge upon programming. We follow Murdock (1982) in distinguishing between allocative and operational control of media organizations. Allocative control can be defined as "power to define the overall goals and scope of the corporation and determine the general way it deploys its productive resources"; operational control as "decisions about the effective use of resources already allocated and the implementation of policies already decided upon at the allocative level" (Murdock 1982, 122). Advertising's influence tends to be concentrated at the allocative level; programmers are likely to have a good deal of autonomy over immediate production. However, media operations are still limited by the range of options defined by the goals of the organization and the resources allocated. As new forms of ownership and control emerged in the modern commercial media organizations, agencies began to distinguish between management and programming decision making.

Another media historian, James Curran (1981), urges that we also distinguish between influences that affect a single media organization and those that change the system or institutional arrangements for the media as a whole. For example, in the mixed broadcasting environment of Britain, decisions made concerning programming in the private sector can influence actions taken in the public sector, because these organizations compete for a common audience.

Similarly, because of the competition within and among media for advertising finance, actions by one organization (for example, the decision to accept comparative ads, fifteen-second spots, or advocacy campaigns) can influence the system as a whole by attracting or drawing revenues to a particular medium. Such actions alter the entire system. The same can be said of government policy (for example, the ban on cigarette advertising on television or regulations for alcohol ads).

Finally, possibilities for the direct influence of content keep changing. In earlier times, newspapers depended on advertising for less than half of their income, and the opportunities for advertisers to exert major influence was limited simply by the nature of the accounts. Most ads were classifieds, and only a few national brands and newspaper chains existed. Most papers served a very diverse collection of advertisers with small accounts. If pressure were exerted, the editor was in a position to ignore it because he or she risked losing only a small portion of income to maintain journalistic integrity.

By the 1860s, the British firm of Thomas Holloway was spending almost £40,000 year on advertising; by 1890, Sunlight and Pears were spending up to £100,000 each. In America, Lydia Pinkham was in the same league. It is reasonable to suppose that individual editors felt the presence of these large accounts in areas other than the balance sheet. Most of the magazines which at first refused all advertising, or just certain types, succumbed sooner or later.

The national branded products were generally produced by companies that also advertised other products. The potential threat of the angered advertiser was heightened when large advertising agencies started to work with several major accounts. At the same time, advertisers' interests were being diffused across a broader range of concerns. It was not the specific story that was a threat, but media editors' and programmers' preoccupation with issues that bore on advertisers' (and media owners') institutional interests—media and corporate regulation, news values, ideological issues in general, free enterprise and its prerogatives, and so forth. On such matters, business interests in the media and the rest of the corporate sector were in basic agreement. More directly, advertisers' interests lay less in specific contents and ideas than in the formats and stylistic techniques of media—layout, printing, program flow, orientation, and market strategy—which influenced the audiences gathered by the media and the markets that could be penetrated through them, their selling power, and the opportunities they gave to use advertising design and strategy to maximize advertising goals. Thus, the impact of advertising interests and practices spread generally through the whole media system.

6

Advertising and the Development of Agencies

As we have seen, the print media carved out a significant place in modern society before becoming dependent on advertising revenue. It is not unreasonable to suppose that they could have continued to develop with only a moderate dependence on advertising, relying upon mass circulation as the economic basis for expansion. Indeed, many of the mass-circulation print media were able to survive without any advertising well into the twentieth century (*Reader's Digest* is the best-known case). Advertising did not create mass circulation, nor was the development of the broadcasting media inconceivable without advertising. Radio in America, after all, was initially conceived as a public service using public airwaves in the public interest; little thought was given to the role it could play in promoting consumer goods until well after the networks were established. Special-interest publishing and broadcasting based on specific loyal audiences (which continues to work well for many small magazines, radio stations, and religious and educational television) could have been the model for the development of the media. Today, with cable and pay television services proliferating, the return to the idea of paying for special communication services (rather than have them subsidized by advertising) is an important trend, but it did not prevail at the outset, when, at least in North America, the advertising subsidy took root and helped to shape the growth of the modern communications industries.

What actually happened was that advertising became the crucial bridge between the activities of selling products and communication as both spheres expanded rapidly—a simple, but much overlooked aspect of its significance in modern society. A bridge is useful to the extent that something crosses it; in the case of advertising, what crossed was money, influence, and information.

The flow of money, reasonably straightforward at first, became exceedingly complex. In the late nineteenth century, producers began to allocate a proportion of their income to advertising. At first, the money went directly to the media; later it was channelled through advertising agencies, which took a proportion of the billing as their sales commission. Consumers pay this advertising subsidy to the media as part of the price of a product. The proportion varies across industries—manufacturers of cosmetics, personal-care products, and household goods allocate a high proportion of all expenses to advertising. For example, up to 50 percent of the cost of a perfume may be attributed to expenditures on advertising. Advertising now accounts for almost all revenue for the broadcast media (except in public networks such as the BBC), 75 percent for the newspaper industry, and anywhere from 60 to 100 percent of income for magazines. One of the major uses of this bridge, then, was to help allocate a proportion of the income accruing to industry from consumers to the development of media.

The media, in turn, adjusted to these new sources of revenue by setting up departments and services (such as market and circulation research) to accommodate their growing relationship with agencies and advertisers, thereby diverting funds from editorial, programming, and internal development efforts.

The history of advertising, therefore, is largely the history of the advertising agencies that served the needs of advertisers and media alike. In addition to the works cited, we have relied in our account on Sampson (1974), Presbrey (1968), Heighton and Cunningham (1976), Hotchkiss (1950), Seldin (1963), and Elliot (1962).

ADVERTISING AGENCIES: MANAGING THE FLOW OF SYMBOLS

In the earlier phases, advertising agents received special rates and arrangements (or kickbacks) for bringing a high volume of business. This was, of course, a hidden subsidy to the agencies themselves. The early agencies, then, developed primarily as buyers in bulk of media space that they then divided into smaller pieces and retailed to manufacturers, especially to the makers of patent medicines. Part of their pitch to manufacturers was based on circulation figures, but the quality of their "data"—and hence the value of their "product"—was highly suspect. (In fact, they lied to both sides in order to maximize their spread as intermediaries.) Eventually this led to an effort, spearheaded by Rowells and Ayers, to establish reliable circulation data.

As the agencies developed new skills, such as copywriting and artwork, and expertise in the arts of advertising, they also began to sell these as a service to advertisers. Today, these creative aspects are often billed separately, implying that the portion of the advertising budget that is not a direct subsidy to the media may be growing—in terms of our metaphor, this is the portion devoted to "bridge-building." In this sense, the consumer has subsidized not only changes in communications media, but the development of the agency sector as well. As we pointed out earlier, it is very difficult to ascertain whether this has resulted in increased efficiency and lower costs for the consumer, or the opposite.

The flow of information also went both ways across the bridge. Information flowed from producers to consumers not only through the ideas and images of the advertisements themselves, but also through the more general influence of the commercialized media in shaping audiences and favouring types and styles of programming that maximized the effectiveness of advertising. Information also travelled in the other direction—from the communication sector, consumers, and culture in general back to the industrialists. The agencies, in some cases assisted by the media, pioneered investigations into consumers' responses to media and products, first in terms of ascertaining reliable circulation figures and later in terms of audience and marketing research (Hurvitz 1984b and 1984a, 205–15). Ultimately, the skills, sensitivity, and knowledge about consumers acquired in the process of media research were used to help manufacturers appreciate and cater to the idiosyncrasies of the consumer. Audience and market research gradually came to play an important part in business strategy. "Perhaps primary among the influences that have affected the advertising business is the transfer of the public's role from that of a recipient of goods and services to that of a shaping force" (Harper, Harper, and Young 1963, 45).

The expansion of advertising created an institution that supported the "intelligence" function of industry; producers increasingly became interested in contact with consumers, but they ended up making it largely through advertising agencies. Industry gradually adjusted its marketing practices to the novel situation created by the consumer culture, and by and large it was the agencies who taught them how to do it. As the agencies worked increasingly in and with the mass media, they developed a sensitivity to communications processes that few industrial managers could match. Advertising agencies thought about products in terms of symbolic and communicative activities and they parlayed their concern for audiences into an obsession with the consumer.

The agencies employed an increasingly complex array of symbols and images drawn from a storehouse of cultural references, matching the intentions of producers and consumers and opening up the communications channels between mass production and mass consumption. Figure 6.1 shows advertising situated strategically between the spheres of industrial and cultural production. Producers must identify and communicate to markets (buyers or potential buyers) the particular features of or motivations for buying their goods. Potential customers and the reasons they have for buying particular kinds of goods can be located and studied through market research, providing the producer with knowledge about consumption and consumers. The tendency has been for the agencies to become more and more knowledgeable about markets and more involved in strategic decision making about them. The commercial media must be able to spot the types of programs and schedules that will attract the most advertising revenue by drawing audiences that advertisers wish to reach. They need to prove that their audiences are of an attractive size and quality in order to promote them to time/space buyers in the agencies. They therefore expand the activities of their own advertising departments and bend programming decisions to attract the most appropriate audience to satisfy advertisers' demands. Thus, programming and the production of culture become dominated by the needs of advertisers.

Between these two spheres is the advertising sector, made up of the agencies and the service companies that support their activities. On the organizational level, the agencies make the link by taking industrial accounts and creating campaigns for them that require buying media time to gain access to audiences. The basic activity of agencies, namely the design and execution of advertising campaigns, always involves some equivocation. There is almost never a perfect match between the potential market defined by the producers' interests in selling and the audience for a program or the readership of a paper. Matching audiences and markets through communication design, therefore, has become the

FIGURE 6.1
Position of Advertising in Relation to Cultural and Industrial Production

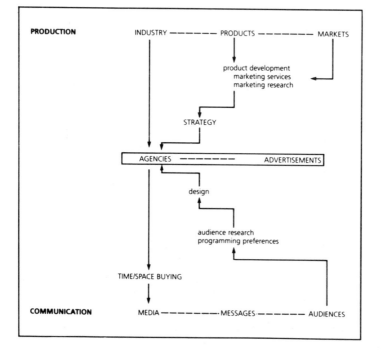

major mediation performed by the advertising sector, leading on a symbolic level to a communication output that fuses the meaning of products with the broader range of cultural references. The development of symbolic attributes for commodities was thus an outgrowth of this communication problem. The agencies discovered the ad campaign as the bridge to reconcile the different requirements of media audiences and consumer markets.

The first important activity of advertising was the reshaping of the institutional structure of media enterprises, the immediate effect of which was to change the relationship between media and their audiences. The buying and selling of audiences to advertisers became a dominant activity of the media. By the 1920s, print media were not only providing circulation guarantees or willingly submitting to circulation audits, but were actively devising ways to sell themselves to advertisers. Early on, they were touting their ostensible hold over their readers, as in this *McCall's* ad: "When a women shops . . . with imagination's aid she is looking far beyond the bright array of labels, the bins so neatly stacked, the price tags on the shelves. She has a picture in her mind, . . . a tantalizing vision that guides her purchase. *McCall's* editors know how to implant these mental pictures" (Pollay, n.d., 24).

The advertisers' agents were successful in getting the media to adapt their formats to advertising needs. Organizing the right audience in terms of demographic compositions and size was critical, but having the right effect was no less essential. Attention holding, audience flow, impact and timing, layout, style, readability, and a hundred other audience-oriented details all become major considerations in media decision making. The agencies communicated to the media what advertisers wanted from their audiences by moving their accounts, by making demands and suggestions, and by the example of their own campaigns.

On behalf of the major corporations, the agencies explored and systematized the best approaches to selling goods; they created formats and styles, undertook research, and speculated about what made effective advertising communication that elicited a response from the consumer. Their work—selling-as-communication—necessitated a sound knowledge of the materials (consumers and symbols) and of the media that they were using, and they gained a sensitivity to the difficulties of eliciting a consumer's response.

In attempting to fuse selling and communicating, advertising reached out into the world of culture for its sources and references, acquiring a special sensitivity to social trends, to styles, and to the creative dimensions of selling. The agencies never accepted the notion that products could sell themselves. They mocked the industrialist's obsession with the product as such and remained acutely aware that they addressed consumers as audiences of media and were not sales representatives on the road or in the stores. They observed, altered, and trans-ferred techniques, ideas, and images from one medium to another. They were soon leaders in specialized areas of communication, setting styles and patterns as well as reflecting them. As such, the trends, rhythms, and even the personnel of advertising had a wide influence on other forms of cultural production. Thus, advertising not only evolved as a unique cultural form with its own grammar and logic—where the relation be-tween consumption and popular culture was always the central theme—but also as a pattern for the whole communication field, affecting cultural activities ranging from fashion to election campaigns.

Advertising's appreciation of the concept of the audience promoted creative explorations not only of popular culture, but also in the field of social research. In pioneering statistical research on audiences, advertis-ing provided a new twist to the way in which institutions reflect the normative order; while their selling pitches were tied to accepted values and life images, they also began to explore and experiment with new variations, new "suggestive allusions," and new rhetorical styles as they tried to lace the motivation for purchase and the cultural context together.

Figuring out who the consumer was and how he or she could be best approached through media became a central facet of advertising practice. From the early writings of Professor Dill Scott, through the heyday of motivation research, right up to the current sophisticated statistical ac-counts of market segments, advertising agencies have attempted to use the understanding of consumers as a pragmatic feature of communicating with them. Social research helped advertising both to focus on a narrow range of normatively supported social imagery, and to make the connec-tion between a valued image and its market relevance more precise, thus transforming the communicative activities of selling.

Although the agencies' personnel worked for producers of goods and services, they themselves came from the communication sector and brought with them different approaches and skills. Some early indus-trialists wrote and planned their own campaigns, seeing little advantage in hiring the skills of an agency or specialist; in many cases, their copy and promotional ideas were excellent. The agencies, however, grew out of the publishing world, first offering the service of evaluating publications' circulations and coordinating the purchase of space in regional journals. As they developed, the agencies persuaded industrialists that the task of campaign design and execution was too complex for amateurs, and they began to offer an ever-widening range of communication services. (On U.S. radio in the 1930s, they undertook not only the production of advertising, but of programming as well.) In many cases, agency person-nel had moved to advertising from other communication activities, such as journalism, and later, radio or television production and direction. For them, the product was secondary to the task of selling it through their expertise in communication. In the constant dialogue with their clients, they brought their skills and concerns to the fore in marketing and advertising.

Debates have always raged in advertising about the best way to address the buyer; eventually it was agreed that this meant knowing about consumers and the media that were being used to reach them. In extending salesmanship, advertising had to change it. The army of drummers that the industry had used, mainly to persuade retailers to distribute their goods, was replaced with a barrage of messages designed to inform the consumer directly about the product (Joyce 1963, 21). Advertising changed the dynamic of selling by making it focus on the anticipation of purchase rather than on dialogue in the store. As the door-to-door sales representative was increasingly barred from the privacy of the home, the media were gaining access.

Advertising agents also learned that the relationship between an audience and a communication product was not like that between a consumer and most other products. Consumers treated buying a car as a long-term commitment, but their consumption of messages was different. Radios could be turned off and channels changed. Magazines could be browsed and dropped. Ideas and information disappeared or were forgotten. Attention had to be focused and held, and information had to be repeated. No upper limit existed to the pervasiveness of communication, but, likewise, there is no effective way to stop some very expensively produced information from being greeted with indifference.

The advertising profession was ever alert to the suspicion that its wares were a waste of money, since no one really knew whether advertisements had any effect. In this regard, the agencies played a crucial part. "By 1910, agencies and advertisers were already talking about 'marketing' and about integrating advertising with other marketing functions" (Joyce 1963, 22). Their chief tool was the marketing concept, a synthesis of what advertising agents were learning about communicative selling. The marketing concept is "a reaction to public needs and desires, sometimes even before those needs and desires have been stated. . . . It means listening to the public, primarily through research, and providing what it will buy, and buy again" (Harper, Harper, and Young 1963, 64). Advertising helped industry to integrate the marketing concept into its organization of production activities. Through research, strategy, and design the advertiser could take the consumers' everyday discourse about products and recycle it as the form, content, and logistics of communicative selling.

Indeed, in current American advertising practice it is not uncommon for "typical" consumers to speak directly to others like themselves. The marketing concept could not be more clearly demonstrated. Across the simulated backyard fence, a television actress advises her neighbour of the merits of a particular soap. The whole scene is reminiscent of an earlier era when people experimented with products, evaluated their merits, and shared their experiences directly with those close at hand. But the event is taking place on television during a specific type of programming designed to attract a specific audience segment (housewives). The script, actors, setting, even the colour balance have all been carefully chosen, vetted by research, modified, and vetted again. The same is true of the product. Both product and ad, seemingly so simple and straightforward, are the outcome of a strategy devised by one of the largest agencies in the world for a major corporation with one of the largest advertising budgets. It was advertising that made businesspeople interested in what the consumer had to say.

> Within the business sphere, we have had the development of marketing as an essential technique founded on the needs and desires of the public rather than the plant capacity of the manufacturer. During the course of this changing relation between business and the buying public, the advertising agency has become a bridge between the two. (Harper, Harper, and Young 1963, 70)

The two leading aspects of the historical mediation of advertising as a form of social communication are (1) the way it influenced cultural processes by shaping the generation of meaning in the consumer culture through its strategic position within the media, and (2) its impact on the production and distribution of goods through the marketing concept, which ultimately changed the nature of products and the way they appeared in the marketplace. These are illustrated in Figure 6. 1. The link between goods and symbols is created by advertising as a commercial institution working in association with powerful firms in different industries, and as a system of messages that infuses every aspect of our popular culture.

ADVERTISING IN THE NINETEENTH CENTURY

Until the latter part of the nineteenth century, manufacturers prepared their own advertising copy. Because publishers resisted requests for illustrations or alterations to the layout of the rigid, column-based format, the possibilities for creative expression lay only in the writing itself. Occasionally, a company might hire a writer or journalist to prepare the copy, but most often the task fell to the manufacturer.

Unlike newspapers, the picture magazines that abounded in the second half of the century could accept illustrations and graphic displays. Borrowing from the world of posters, illustrations began to creep into advertising, first showing the product's box or package and later demonstrating its qualities and uses. The well-known Pears bubbles poster was an innovation not just for using an academy artist to paint it, but also for the clever way it joined illustration and product (soap) with the title, showing that the illustration did not have to connect directly with the product's main selling point.

Indeed, many of the advertising styles and approaches that became the agencies' standard wares in the twentieth century had been explored earlier by individuals working alone. The agencies merely revised and systematized various practices, bringing the new psychology and statistics, as well as professional writers and artists, into the fold. Slogans, poetry, illustrations of enormous variety, layout, testimonials, coupons, contests, stars, naked women, and humour were already familiar ingredients in advertising. Once the volume of advertising began to expand and new formats won acceptance, the agencies assembled these basic materials into an integrated technical strategy using the new psychology and statistics, as well as professional writers and artists.

One of the first important services that agencies provided was the advertising directory listing newspapers that advertisers could use around the country, and, in some cases, in foreign countries. In the early nineteenth century, the firm of Lewis and Lowe published *The Advertiser's Guide to the Newspaper Press of the United Kingdom*, which was thirty-six pages long and included the average circulation, the average number of ads, the political character, and the price of each paper. Directories served the dual function of listing the agencies' wares as newspaper agents and providing circulation numbers for advertisers. One of the most comprehensive was the *Newspaper Press Directory* published in 1846 by Charles Mitchell, a thorough and well-organized man who had strong connections with regional newspaper editors. The directory was 474 pages long and included the usual list of newspapers and journals, circulations, affiliations, and price, but it also provided information for would-be advertisers "in their selection of journals as mediums more particularly suitable for their announcements" and other advice pertaining to the conduct of effective and legal advertising.

Mitchell's directory is the first instance of an agent attempting to justify his place in the scheme of publishing. Both publishers and advertisers suspected him of being an unnecessary parasite in the practice of advertising, but Mitchell argued that the provincial press would die without the agent. He attacked the notion that the advertising agent acted for the newspaper, stating that he rather assisted the advertiser to choose the best vehicle available. "The result of all this was important for the future—the advertising agent is a principal in his own independent line of business" (Hindley and Hindley 1972, 24).

Mitchell's directory shaped the practice of the slowly growing number of advertising agents. The 1856 edition included sections on libel laws, the changing newspaper, advertising taxes, and an essay on the philosophy of advertising dealing with copywriting, circulation, and market analysis. The directories reveal the extent to which the agencies were beginning to systematize the practice of advertising. Although only occasionally asked to provide copy or marketing advice, they were developing a full knowledge of their trade and offering advice in general terms. Mitchell, for example, noted that a lower-circulation paper read in the privacy of the home is a more useful advertising vehicle than a larger-circulation one read in pubs and beer shops, because the home reader browses and is more likely to return to the advertisements. By the 1890s, the shift from newspaper space sales to service in support of advertisers was well under way in England.

Volney Palmer, who set up his agency in Philadelphia in 1843, is generally considered to be the first independent advertising agent in North America. Like his British counterparts, he offered a list of selected journals in which he would arrange the placement of ads. His days were spent visiting businesses to persuade them of the benefits of his service. He offered free estimates, collecting a 25 percent commission on placements from the newspapers. An employee of Palmer's, S.M. Pettingill, left to open an office in Boston that became the largest of the thirty or so agencies operating during the 1860s. Pettingill offered his clients copywriting services in addition to the simple placement of their advertising inserts, which seems to have helped him to prosper.

The increasing number of newspapers was making the task of placing ads unaided too complex for the would-be advertiser. It was also changing the position of the agents. Newspapers lost interest in exclusive contracts with agents; in response, agents became independent brokers standing between the publishers and the advertisers, who bargained with the agents for the best deal on advertising space. As a space broker rather than a space seller, the agent's relationship with particular newspapers could be an advantage or a liability depending on the terms of the agreement.

George Rowell took space brokerage to its logical conclusion. He bought annual blocks of publishers' space, which he then resold to his clients at the rate of one hundred dollars for an inch per month in one hundred papers. Buying in bulk put Rowell in a position to bargain with the publishers for better prices, for he guaranteed payment irrespective of whether he collected his own payments. He also offered advertisers discounts for prompt payment.

Some agencies attempted to retain their special relationship with particular journals by brokering all the space in them on contract. J. Walter Thompson, for example, made breakthroughs in a number of literary magazines, including *Scribner's* and *Harper's*, which had refused to accept advertising until he persuaded the publishers that their journals would not be demeaned thereby. Thompson realized that such magazines, with their specialized and widespread circulations, would become an effective advertising medium to supplement the religious and farm newspapers and journals that he also serviced. By the end of the century, thirty important magazines were taking most of their advertising from him. "Thompson, more than any other agent, had developed the magazine field. This was a tremendous step forward for the entire advertising industry, because magazines were the first national medium" (Harper, Harper, and Young 1963, 79). The full significance of this step would be seen by the 1920s, when magazines became the major medium for national advertising, and the agency business itself a service predominantly for national branded and distributed products.

Rather than working in the interests of particular papers or journals, the major agents were directing advertisers to media suitable for their purposes and were thus beginning to have some influence over the press. But without information about actual circulations, they were in a precarious situation because they would always be perceived by the advertiser as favouring certain papers in their own interest. By the turn of the century, the untenable position of space broker had been abandoned for the more comfortable one of adviser to advertisers. Meanwhile, the American space broker was breaking the close attachment to the publisher by adopting the British idea of preparing directories with circulation and other information about each journal. In 1869, *Rowell's American Newspaper Directory* made many enemies among publishers who opined that his circulation figures and judgments were not up to scratch, but the importance to advertisers of such circulation estimates was drawing the agents closer to the advertisers. George Rowell was nothing if not enterprising; he sold ads in his directory to newspapers so that they could recommend themselves to potential advertisers. Another of Rowell's publishing endeavours blossomed eventually into the industry voice, *Printer's Ink*. As an entrepreneurial space broker, Rowell used his position between publishers and advertisers to advantage, but by 1895 there were four hundred like him in New York City alone.

With space brokering, the agent increased profits by buying space cheap and selling it dear. Another agent of the period, Ayer, took the final step away from the role of space broker. Ayer developed what he called the "open contract plus commission." This bound the agent and the advertiser for a period of time, usually a year, with the former taking a standard percentage of the billing as his commission; the agent no longer squeezed the advertiser to make a profit, but rather acted on the latter's behalf in finding the best group of journals for the advertiser's needs. The new arrangement helped to make Ayer the number one agency of the 1890s. The decision of the American newspaper publishers' association in 1893 to abide by their published rates and not to bargain with space brokers did much to make this system of billing work. The percentage commission tied the agencies' profits to the gross amount of billings they could win, and they would grow only to the degree that new sources of advertising could be channelled through the agencies rather than conducted directly with the newspapers. Local, retail, and classified advertising did not usually call for the use of an agency. For national advertising, however, working with an agency became a regular part of marketing. After the turn of the century, the policy of fixed commissions was gradually accepted by other agents and endorsed by the agencies' professional association. The standard 15 percent commission today remains the basic system for billing.

The advertising agency was becoming a viable service industry for advertisers instead of an adjunct of the printing industry. But changes outside the publishing world were also beginning to shape advertising. The new range of household products to be sold in national markets—soap, tobacco, bicycles, bootblacking, bread, beer—needed the agencies' services. Many of these products were branded and intended to be distributed on a national or broad regional scale. By the 1890s, over four thousand entrepreneurs wanted to advertise their goods and services beyond their own localities. New retail outlets for these national branded goods created new relationships between retailers and consumers; "the rise of national advertising abridged the autonomy of local merchants," because the shift of consumer preferences to national brands weakened the older stores which traditionally sold unbranded and often unpackaged items—crackers, pickles, candies kept in jars or barrels (Pope 1982, 25). In the large urban areas, new department stores like Wanamaker's in the United States and Selfridge's in England engaged in a large amount of advertising and were developing large internal advertising departments and accounts, finding in many cases that they could deal with publishers on their own in buying space. These retailers had good reason to appreciate the new opportunities of display advertising. Thus, although they did not need the agencies' space-buying services, they did want other kinds of assistance to produce the constant flow of copy necessary for the newspapers. Powers, who got his start as the first professional copywriter in North America for Wanamaker's in 1880, brought the simple and straightforward prose that became known as the "Powers style" to ad writing. He represented the new concern for communication skills being required by a whole new range of businesses entering into advertising without other connections to the communication industry. Ironically, although the department stores tended not to use the services of the agents, the new branded products they promoted depended on national campaigns devised and placed by the agencies.

Within the media, the cheap mail-order magazines for rural communities were being followed by national mass-circulation magazines largely dependent on the new nationally advertised products. These magazines, as Thompson realized, were perfectly suited to expand advertising's horizons. He was not alone. Ayer gave a $200,000 dollar line of credit against advertising space to Cyrus Curtis for the launching of his *Ladies' Home Journal.* Soon the agencies were able to supply a large amount of the advertising for such magazines. The most forward-thinking agencies were busy carving out strong relationships with the new media that were particularly suitable to their major clients, as well as encouraging media owners to develop new types of publications that could serve the agencies and the national products they represented. The agencies were to have a much more significant role in the development of consumer magazines (and, later, of radio and television programming) than they did in the earlier commercialization of the newspapers.

THE EARLY TWENTIETH CENTURY

Innovators in the print media and at the agencies realized the potential of systematic research. Curtis created a research department at *The Saturday Evening Post* around 1910. Probably the first example of an agency's market study demonstrating the relationship between circulations of particular journals and markets for particular products occurred in 1879. Ayer, attempting to challenge Rowell's hold on a threshing machine account, provided detailed market statistics on regional sales of threshing machines in order to make a case for a particular list of farm journals. Soon the agencies understood that knowledge of regional and sectoral fluctuations in markets and their relation to readerships for particular journals or papers was at the heart of advertising strategy.

With the rise of trade journals and consumer magazines as vehicles for national advertising, interest in marketing research among the agencies could only strengthen. Stanley Resor, who purchased the Thompson agency in 1916, was among the first to support research on consumer behaviour as well as on media. In 1912, he commissioned an original study of consumer markets entitled *Population and its Distribution,* and hired a number of noted social scientists, including J. B. Watson, the "father of behaviourism," to bring systematic scientific study to the advertising world. In most cases, the research conducted not only provided proprietary information that could guide strategy, but like the copy, art, and planning facilities offered at this time it could be sold as a service separately from commissions for ad campaigns. The agencies were becoming a progressive voice in the development of standardized methods for researching audiences and consumer behaviour.

The advertising business was being fundamentally reorganized. George Batten announced in 1891 that his agency would only take on service contracts that included all the functions of advertising for the firm. In 1899, Ayers undertook the whole process of designing advertising for the Uneeda Biscuit campaign, from choosing the name of the product to the supervision of merchandising promotions. At the Lord and

Thomas agency, Albert Lasker hired the copywriter J. E. Kennedy in order to provide the full service that the new kind of inexperienced advertiser was likely to accept. Lasker and Kennedy devised the philosophy of "reason why" advertising and its fundamental rationale that "the way to sell was to build consumer demand" (Harper, Harper, and Young 1963, 79). Copywriting and marketing rather than familiarity with the regional press was becoming the central aspect of agency business, and agencies were being freed of their ties to the press. By 1917, 95 percent of national advertising in the United States was being handled by agencies.

The founding in 1926, by advertisers, agencies, and media owners, of the Advertising Association with its mission to "promote public confidence in advertising and advertised goods through the correction or suppression of abuses" was itself a sign of the agencies' growing awareness of their key role in the marketing sphere. Industry-wide cooperation was essential to end the more outlandish and indefensible marketing practices if advertising were to achieve stability and promote business interests in general. This type of "public interest" advocacy proved how significant advertising was becoming in industry's overall strategies.

Of course, the harmony among agencies, media, and industry was ruptured at times, such as in the early 1920s when they parted company over the introduction of radio advertising, and again in the early 1950s over the beginnings of commercial television. But the unity was re-established, and the Advertising Association continues as an umbrella group for media, advertisers, and agencies with a wide variety of informational, supervisory, and lobbying functions.

The entrenchment of the marketing concept in industry and the advent of new technologies in communication meant that the agencies' continued success depended on providing a wide range of design, copy, and marketing advice to advertisers, particularly for national branded household products, food, and automobiles, and that they were working increasingly in media other than newspapers. The professional association and the agents themselves opened up research and auditing methods for magazines, radio, and finally television, uncovering and specifying the potential audience. Representing the part of advertising that was closely tied to national branded products, the agencies became advocates of the new national media. As they defended and redefined their niche in the expanding advertising world, the agencies had to create the kind of knowledge, skills, and services that would promote the interests of advertisers. Their survival hinged on this; many of the earlier space-brokering agencies that could not adjust to the new requirements fell by the wayside. On the other hand, there was abundant reward for innovative agencies that began to develop the full-service agency model. By 1925, such agencies accounted for the major share of national accounts.

COMMUNICATION STRATEGIES

Probably the earliest impact of the new service agencies was to make copy the central consideration of advertising design. By the early 1900s, these agencies realized that advertising of national brands was not just a matter of announcements, but rather of persuasion—using words to explain the advantages of one particular product or brand as opposed to others, and making a specific ad stand out from others in the increasingly cluttered columns of newspapers. Agencies had used those with literary talents before, but it now became standard practice to hire writers as regular staff. Although earlier examples of rhyme and rhythm abounded, the agency staff writers began to merge poetry and selling in unique ways.

The first and most obvious was in the slogan, which departed from earlier types of poetic writing in advertising by keeping the selling idea at the centre of the message. It borrowed heavily from newspaper headlines in striving for a tightly compacted unifying idea, and from poster advertising in its dramatic emphasis. Hardly literary, many were intriguing and innovative: "Good morning, have you used Pears soap today?" or "Don't be gulled by Yankee Bluff. Support John Bull with every puff" (doggerel invented to repel the American invasion of the British cigarette market at the turn of the century). Royal Baking Powder's "Absolutely pure," or Kodak's "Press the button; we do the rest," reveal the compression and purposiveness of language that was emerging as advertising's own signpost. Many of these slogans were developed for use with poster ads or illustrated magazines. In retrospect, in their suggestiveness and minimalist approach to language these slogans appear very modern.

The need for a carefully considered slogan at the core of an advertising campaign was becoming central to agency practice as a major factor in giving a clear identity to a branded product. More than language styles were changing. The concern for the stylistic integrity of branded products was leading to "personification" in the form of trade characters—Aunt Jemima, Lydia Pinkham, the Quaker Oats Quaker.

One noted copywriter in this style was Earnest Elmo Calkins, originator of some of the extraordinarily popular " Sunny Jim'" (character for a breakfast cereal) verses. Calkins advocated the integration of design elements, artistic qualities, and literary features into "that combination of text with design which produces a complete advertisement" (in Fox 1984, 63). In building his consumer magazine empire, Cyrus Curtis came to Calkins, after failing to find anyone else who could write the kind of copy he liked. Short and simple sentences in the "Powers' style" were also ideally suited to sloganizing; effective copy became the heart and soul of advertising campaigns, culminating in J. E. Kennedy's influential concept of advertising as "salesmanship in print," known as the "reason why" approach.

Getting the attention of the audience was just the first step in persuasion; advertising had to appeal rather than just attract, for if no desire were evoked the ad was not likely to be successful. An indispensable part of the "feedback loop" for refining the system of persuasive communications was new gimmicks that accompanied the novel copy styles such as coupons, one of the first ways in which advertisers could judge the effectiveness of their campaigns in terms of consumer response. The emergence of psychology as a scientific discipline was also influential. Rowell had predicted in the 1890s that advertising would eventually turn to psychology, and the publication in 1908 of the first systematic attempt by a social scientist to examine advertising, Professor Walter Dill Scott's *The Psychology of Advertising*, was to have a major impact on the profession.

Scott's operative concept was "the appeal," taking as his model hypnotic persuasion. Although he believed firmly in the appeal to rationality, he emphasized the importance of association. The product should be associated with pleasant experiences and ideas that the readers would associate with their own feelings and motives. He also stressed suggestion: "Man has been called the reasoning animal but he could with greater truthfulness be called the creature of suggestion" (cited in Pope 1982, 240–41). The two seemingly opposing tendencies of rationality and suggestiveness were not incompatible, for the whole point about reason-why advertising as a communicative strategy was that it was designed to persuade and to motivate.

The demand for reason-why advertising was closely connected with the needs of national advertisers to elicit demand for their new products. Especially in the realm of food, personal-care, and household products, the nature of the new item and the way it should be used were often unfamiliar. As we pointed out in Chapter 4, one cannot assume a "natural affinity" between the wants of individuals and the characteristics of goods. Breakfast foods, toothpaste, canned foods, polishes, and an endless series of previously unknown products had to be carefully introduced into daily patterns of life, and the methods and reasons for using them explained in detail.

Furthermore, the manufacturer of a branded product had to attract customers not only to a new type of product but also to the firm's label, differentiating the special qualities of the brand from its competitors. This "educational" function of advertising became especially prominent in the period of dramatic social change after World War I, when rising affluence, upward mobility, a marked destabilization of traditional values, and, in the United States, the quick assimilation of a large immigrant population were creating a potential market for new products. Ads often had an explicitly educational theme, with self-improvement messages designed to help "socialize" consumers—pitches for personal-care products such as razors for men and toothpaste for women—being added to the earlier campaigns for soap.

Fundamentally different problems in selling arose as a result of this broader "social" approach in the message system. Envy, class relations, and authority were a matrix in which to ground motivation for purchase; anxiety and an awareness of peer group reactions, especially fear of ostracism or social failure (recall the Brunswick toilet seat ad cited in Chapter 4), became core elements in the rationale for adopting a new lifestyle or consumption practice. Two good examples of fear-appeal advertising come from Listerine: "Even your best friend won't tell you," and "Often a bridesmaid, never a bride." In order to ensure a "realistic" setting for such messages and define the selling idea with precision, advertisers had to take a careful look at the subtly changing social positions of consumers.

Research also dispelled the notions of the "single type" of consumer and the undifferentiated audience, and highlighted the fact that persuasion involved more than reciting the merits of the product. In consumer magazines, for example, readership studies were beginning to point out basic facts about readers. It became abundantly clear to the advertisers that different approaches were reaching different segments of the population, and that their message formats had to be tailored appropriately; advertising effectiveness was a matter of correctly understanding specific situations. For example, marketing research was revealing that women bought 80 to 90 percent of all household goods. Since advertisers believed that women were subject to irrational impulses and did not want too much reasoning in ads, copy styles were altered accordingly. Other researchers revealed that the reading ability and vocabulary of consumers were not very high; this, too, affected the design of messages.

Different concepts of human motivation were beginning to filter into the advertising arena from psychology. After about 1925, people began to be thought of as animals impelled by drives and instincts, motivated largely by petty emotions, sexuality, anxiety, and a desire for upward mobility. Placing irrationality at the heart of the consumption and marketing process heralded a major transition in the agencies' approach. They did not abandon reason-why advertising completely, but restricted it mostly to introducing new products, and even here they increasingly grounded the reason for purchase in one of the consumer's supposed psychological traits rather than in the characteristics of the product.

The non-publishing environment of radio represented a real challenge, and some of today's more successful agencies got their start as innovators in radio advertising. First, the audience and the effectiveness of advertising had to be proved to potential advertisers, entailing an expansion of the agency's research function into listener surveys. A. C. Neilson was hired to do the first listener study by the J. Walter Thompson agency; Hooper ratings became very popular.

A variety of services for both the radio and magazine trades was developed in this period. The use of scientific methods in advertising pioneered by Stanley Resor at J. Walter Thompson was expanding rapidly during the 1930s and 1940s. Magazines had initiated product testing by consumers. Product and copy testing became common practice in the agencies. Knowing the consumers' mind meant interacting with them in as many ways as possible. (The systematic study of consumer preferences and marketing research in general was developed largely by the agencies with help from the magazine industry. Many of the women's magazines set up their own product-testing centres as consumption practice and decision making became a main feature of editorial concern; they also engaged in readership studies to establish their audiences, and created consumer panels to help advertisers, as well as to offer impartial advice to readers.)

A second relevant aspect of radio broadcasting was that advertisers stepped into the world of show business as producers of programming. Under the American network system, most of the major programs were produced by agencies who built studios, hired talent, and wrote scripts, thus broadening both their communication abilities and their understanding of the communications industry as they attempted to draw and hold an audience and to build a relationship between the advertisement and the program. People could not listen to selling messages all day, so the agencies began to explore styles of communication, the communication preferences of the audience, and the production values that would draw and hold them. Music, humour, stars, pathos, tragedy, excitement, and human relationships became familiar terrain for the advertising agency and opened up new ideas about how to improve advertising.

This much overlooked aspect was to have a dramatic and long-lasting effect on the skills and perspective that the agencies would apply thereafter in the service of their clients. Advertising on radio involved more than turning slogans into jingles. Radio was an enormously powerful communications medium, and its programming covered a wide range of human experiences. Probably the best illustration for the agencies' work in the 1930s is the development of soap opera. In the early years of radio, the major sponsored programs were clustered in the early evening prime-time period. Afternoon radio attracted few sponsored programs and consisted chiefly of music and household hints. Frank Hummert of the Blackett-Sample-Hummert agency decided to adapt the human interest appeal of the serial stories that ran in the daily newspapers to radio, inventing a drama called "Just Plain Bill," sponsored by Kolynos toothpaste, about a barber who had married out of his social class. Hummert pitched his appeal to the afternoon female audience. Its success created a deluge of imitators with far-reaching consequences.

The soap operas were written by the agencies and usually revolved around emotionally excruciating family dilemmas. The challenge was to develop product "tie-ins." (The term "soap opera" itself, of course, refers to the sponsorship of detergent manufacturers and testifies to the blending of advertising and programming.) A whole new domain of human interest and human interaction was being added to the agencies' repertoire as they experimented with story line, characterization, dramatic impact, and emotional tone and then applied what they had learned to the construction of ads. The close connection between programming and advertising not only implied that the programming was designed to suit advertisers' needs, but also—far more significant for the future—schooled the agencies in a whole new range of communication dynamics for ads. As a result, advertising became rooted in a distinctly human interest environment, and by 1938 radio had overtaken magazines in advertising revenue.

One important consequence was that products began to speak—to tell their own story. Although the full anthropomorphizing of goods had to await the use of animation on television (the Jolly Green Giant, the Michelin Man, the Pillsbury Dough Boy), radio took a preliminary step in dialogue; products, through advertisements, began to tell stories and the writing styles incorporated allusions to real social situations and a variety of settings.

The communicative impact of media advertising had its effects on other media. Improved techniques in art and the use of photography were important steps in the development of a new visual style. It was no longer sufficient merely to show the product; ads began to use pictures to illustrate abstract, scientific, or social qualities. Microphotography revealed germs in the sink; colour shots emphasized the glamour of car ownership. An entire "language" of illustration was being developed, much of it borrowed and adapted from the film world. Magazine ads with comic-strip formats were soon followed by images arranged in sequence like the story board of a film. The expansion of the narrative in copy and illustration was fitting the product into "lifelike" dilemmas.

An example of the merging of entertainment and advertising worlds was the use of testimonials. Radio and magazines not only helped to create the star system, but used it effectively in advertisements. The stars of radio could introduce the product within the programs, and as spot advertisements gained in popularity, famous names (especially film stars) lent their prestige to goods ranging from cosmetics to cigarettes, grounding the appeal not in some kind of argument about use, but in the associational field of prestige. When scientists and doctors testified on behalf of yeast, household cleansers, or margarine, the appeal was rooted in the apparently more substantial domain of expert authority, but the persuasive format (an association with a human figure "distant" from the ordinary person) was, in fact, identical.

During the 1930s, these creative explorations of the possibilities inherent in new media developed side by side with increasing knowledge through research about the audience. For example, experiments with styles, formats, visual appeals, and media vehicles for selling goods more directly to women were undertaken when research indicated the primacy of the female consumer and identified her as the reader of particular magazines (depending on social background and interest) and as the listener to daytime radio. Whatever the degree of validity of agency assumptions about women, it is clear that these assumptions changed the way the agencies practised advertising as they explored new forms for communicating with specific subpopulations of consumers.

After the heyday of radio advertising in the late 1940s, much of the experience and talent accumulated from radio production was turned to developing advertising modes suited for television in the 1950s and 1960s. Television was soon perceived as the "Cadillac" advertising medium for mass-marketed and branded national goods. It offered the display aspects of good graphics, the visual immediacy and excitement of film, music, and story lines, star testimonials, and the largest audiences ever drawn to a single medium. Its only limitation was the number of words one could squeeze into a thirty- or sixty-second segment. Television forced a further subdivision in the advertising market, and with its entrenchment as a national medium, both radio and mass consumer magazines would have to adapt to it.

As a medium of communication, television, like radio before it, offered new possibilities to advertising strategists. Encouraged by the agencies, early advertisers were enthusiastic about the size of its audiences and there was a vague but pervasive feeling that special powers resided in its visual representation and immediate attractiveness to most people. Products had been woven into a broad range of simulated and fictional settings since the turn of this century, but television simply could do everything so much better. Magazines had displayed goods amid Doric columns or Greek statues, thus positioning them within an associational matrix of images and styles; radio had opened up dialogue and social interaction as contexts within which appeals were made; television swept all earlier forms into its orbit and added others, ultimately offering the whole range of cultural reference systems to advertisers as aids in selling their wares.

Before the advent of edited videotape, television advertising consisted of two forms, either the filmed commercial or the "plug" for the sponsor by the host, a special advertising announcer, or a character within the show (Alfred Hitchcock and Johnny Carson found new sources of humour in this relation between media characters and advertising announcements). Filmed commercials were usually shot and edited by a camera crew and director borrowed from the cinema world, meaning the importation of a whole range of editing and cinematic techniques and concerns into the production of advertising. (Even today, there is a flow of personnel, ideas, and references between the cinema world and advertising, with some well-known directors working in both.) Shooting actors in ways that kept them credible, locating and arranging scenes, lighting effects, amusing story lines, and animation all became part of the advertising repertoire. Since television was best at simulating interpersonal communication either directly or as observed in drama, it seemed natural for television commercials to focus on these elements, and thus the testimonial and the minidrama became important elements of television advertising. Television offered a whole new range to the uses of people and dialogue that had been explored during the 1930s and 1940s. Visual and dramatic demonstrations—see-through toilets, the interiors of washing machines and stomachs, protective barriers on teeth and floors—all played an important part.

The early television years also led to refined research techniques within the agencies. Media research included circulation audits—specific viewer, listener, or readership studies—and early efforts to combine marketing and media research by establishing personal preferences in terms of products, pastimes, spending habits, and so forth; consumer research included demographic studies of users and product pretesting; advertising research included consumer panels, copy-testing sessions, split-half comparisons, and so forth. Each proved useful in helping the agencies understand the problem of advertising design in the context of a more detailed and accurate knowledge of consumers and audiences for media.

Pioneered by radio and magazines, the audience survey or "the ratings" became the basis of television program decision making. Sponsors bought and retained shows so long as the mass audience share was retained; when the ratings slipped, sponsors moved on to more favourable ground. Research became the basis upon which the links between agencies and networks were forged for national-brand product advertising.

Motivation research, or in-depth studies of consumers, elicited criticism both within and outside the industry, because it represented a way of thinking about the consumer that seemed to violate many people's sense of propriety. To Ernest Dichter, the major advocate of motivation research, the criticism implied that advertising was seeking to exploit the consumer's presumed unconscious and often irrational attachments to particular things. In fact, it was a natural extension of the application of modern psychological theory and methods to advertising. Motivation research borrowed at least two major premises from Freudian psychology: that people's real motives are hidden, and that they can be elicited through conversation and free association. The advertiser who wants to sell must appeal not to the limited set of motives identified in the 1930s, but to the specific insecurities, delusions, and attachments of the consumer.

Motivation research was really the logical outcome of the pursuit of the marketing concept, for it started the selling activity with the consumer and the consumer's personal situation. Motivation research, unlike the earlier applications of scientific methodology or distribution statistics, rooted the selling act within the human personality by directly applying psychological constructs to advertising. Human psychology was to be the basis of commercial strategies. The advertiser started with the general theory that the consumer's psyche was ruled by an irrational insecurity and a strong erotic undertone and proceeded from there.

The model assumed that the consumer did not make rational choices and was easily persuaded by images. Products had to be fitted into the consumer's deepest sense of self, defending it and giving it greater expression. As a receiver of communications, the consumer was depicted as immature and more interested in *how* something was said than in *what* was said. Research showed that many ads were little remembered and that consumers came away from exposure to them with only vague impressions: to achieve impact, an ad had to strike deep by being superficial.

Motivation research gave advertising a bad name and brought to a head the criticisms of Madison Avenue manipulation. Many practitioners themselves doubted the usefulness of such techniques, and others found the research results almost impossible to translate into design and communicational terms. Steps were taken by the industry and eventually by governments to limit experiments with subliminal messages. Still, by the late 1950s most major agencies had undertaken campaigns based on such research. Some, such as the McKann-Erickson agency, rose to prominence on the achievements of its researchers. A number of agencies were also pioneering the use of semantic differentials, consumer panels, experimental designs, and sophisticated attitude measurement techniques.

In a reaction against the increasing use of research techniques and their application in advertising design and testing, which, some people claimed, limited the creativity and effectiveness of ads, smaller agencies and independent consultants thrived on the fringes of the large outfits. Shops like Ogilvy and Mather introduced some of the newer, softer-sell advertising. Ogilvy states that he was concerned with establishing "the most favorable image, the most sharply defined personality" through imaginative design—such as his famous Hathaway eyepatch ad. His point was that the creative mind could understand the psychological makeup of the consumer as well as, or indeed better than, the researchers could; it was the grasping of some ineffable quality which brought dynamic appeal to a campaign that could make the difference. Ogilvy and Mather were enormously successful, becoming the third-largest agency in the United States by 1980. Eventually the most successful agencies offered a combination of both strategies.

In the 1960s, advertisers were faced with a confusing array of media, claiming different types of strengths in audience and impact. The agencies' task was to devise a strategy that selected the best medium or the most appropriate blend of media for the promotion of a particular brand at the lowest cost. Each medium had its distinct advantages, and various types of campaigns could use the media all together, in sequence, or in some ordered combination. The objective was to define the goals of a campaign, to set advertising's position within the overall marketing mix (which might also include public relations, display, offers, coupons, distribution, and dealership arrangements), and to use the media to buy access to the right audience at the right time. Sophisticated research methods aided the competitive stances that media managers adopted in promoting the unique audience features of their particular medium.

Radio, having lost the big national campaigns, had redefined its audience appeal on a station-by-station basis. Each station was directed toward an age and demographic segment, and fancy brochures promised that rates were adjusted to the desirability of the audience segment they commanded.

The mid-1960s was also a changeover period for the magazine world, as many of the mass-consumer magazines ran into trouble and the survivors addressed smaller readerships with highly desirable characteristics for particular products. The new special-interest lifestyle journals flourished, advertising a highly selective range of products.

The new research techniques were starting to provide more information than size alone about television audiences. As sponsorship gave way to spot advertising, research helped to guide the spot advertiser to the right audience. Highly intensive monitoring revealed that the public did not relate to television as a mass audience. In some regions, demographic groups were shown to be related to preferences for networks, programs, and products. Advertisers became as interested in the qualities of the audiences drawn to their spots as in their size. Les Brown (1972) describes television's scramble for programming that would hold the audiences that advertisers wanted when the networks realized that even programs with large ratings but the wrong audiences would have to be dropped.

Consumer research also divided products into different types (durables, domestic consumables, personal consumables) with life cycles of their own fitted into cyclical usage practices. No one group of consumers could be seen as "typical"; consumers fell into market segments with clustered social practices. Some were innovators, tempted with new products and gadgets; others were facing major buying decisions such as a first bank account, a first car, or a first home. People over fifty were poor general consumers but subject to appeals based on prestige and tradition. Sports-oriented men were heavy consumers of particular kinds of alcoholic beverages.

At present, the demographic variables are still measured, but the predominant focus of marketing and advertising research is on what we might call the "subjective" dimension of personal experience. The 1988 annual meeting of the Canadian Advertising Research Foundation featured a presentation by Dr. Jeffrey Durgee that gives a comprehensive account of what this focus on the subjective dimension of personal experience is all about. Durgee summarized his approach as follows: "The best advertising is based on consumers' subjective meanings." The key to understanding those meanings, Durgee said, is to be found in the notion of "structures," that is, "the ways consumers organize meaning to brands and products." He went on to describe these structures in the following way:

> *Life Context Structures* fit with the elements in life and can be determined by work questions, social questions and fantasy questions. . . . Products, like the lead in a movie, gain meaning due to plot/implied (what role does it play); settings (where, when); relationship between people; opposition (relevant conflicts); symbols (aspects of people's experience); moods and sequence of events.
>
> *Product Component Structures*—how people structure the components of a product. For example, with NyQuil, comment centred on the heavy dark liquid and the little cup, seen in terms of health and a communion cup or as narcosis and alcoholism.
>
> *Semiotic Structure.* Qualitative researchers have a set of questions to determine what the product is a "signal" of (causally related). The product can be either a cause or an effect of the referent. A product is a "sign" of something if both product and referent belong to the same cultural context, and a "symbol" of something, if arbitrarily or metaphorically linked to it.
>
> *Latent Structures*—found in consumer stories about first-time product use (causes of breakdown or performance beyond expectations); unusual, bizarre usage; odd ways of using; items that typify family, friends; exceptional events that the product was part of; and package/logo.
>
> *Semantic Structures.* Using a list of descriptive words and applying them to a product category and competing brands, a distinctive difference can emerge in how a product is viewed. (Marney 1988)

This approach has been given the name of "account planning" in England. According to one report, account planning "involves digging deep into the mind of the consumer in order to find a critical insight on which to build a powerful strategy." The key to this strategy is

> [l]istening to consumers. Listening and listening. Not just to what they say, but to what they mean. Listening for the expressions of need, of dissatisfaction, uncovering attitudes and behavior patterns. The planner's job is to immerse him or herself in the world of the consumer until the point of view of the consumer permeates the planner's thinking, and leads to the discovery of a critical insight on which to build a powerful strategy. (Bruce 1987)

This is an excellent statement of the two fundamental purposes of all advertising and marketing research: (1) to understand how consumers experience the meaning of products and how they formulate the intention to purchase; and (2) to construct persuasive communications strategies on the basis of that understanding that will reach the inner experiences of persons.

The flood of data that came to the agencies in the 1960s made advertisers think of consumers as organized collectivities that could be statistically described along two axes: media use and product preferences. Such revelations demanded a new orientation to advertising, and these research tools transformed the practice of advertising: "Such a conception calls for different communication and advertising objectives at different stages over time for a given product category and set of competing brands" (Sommers 1983, 8). Advertising was propelled beyond the marketing concept to the "marketing management concept." Effective advertising implied not only knowledge of the consumer, but also an organization that could coordinate media and marketing plans, accounting within this framework for the consumer's precise "social position'" and the possibilities of using different media to reach her or him. Marketing management theory specifies the role of advertising's place within the current institutional context: to understand the market segment and the audience segment, and to transform this understanding into a convincing campaign strategy.

The adjustment to market segmentation has meant that agencies have had to incorporate a new range of research, design, and management skills and to reorganize their delivery to accounts. The advertising "problem" could not be solved simply by promising to place the agency's two hottest copywriters onto the account. In the late 1960s and the 1970s, there were a number of failures, buyouts, and consolidations as the large agencies adjusted to the new demands made on them: of the ninety-two largest agencies in 1966, forty-one no longer existed by 1979.

The industry today includes both large, full-service agencies and small "boutiques" offering highly specialized research, media buying, or creative work, a sensible division in the heyday of market segmentation, with its sensitivity both to general consumption patterns (such as the attachment to automobiles) and to distinctive subsidiary "behavioural zones" (such as sports or popular music). Daniel Pope, using Boorstin's concept of "consumption communities," stresses "the attractiveness of the community, not just the desirability of the product," wherein "context rather than the product becomes, in a sense, the object of the consumers' desires" (Pope 1982, 280).

THE BONDING OF MEDIA AND ADVERTISING

As the preceding discussion indicates, we hold the view that an adequate appreciation of advertising's place in modern society arises out of a detailed examination of its historical evolution. This conviction is shared by others. Daniel Pope's *The Making of Modern Advertising* divides the history of advertising into three periods: the Gilded Age (about 1870–1890), the Progressive Era (1890–1920), and the Modern Era (1920–present).

The Gilded Age was the period of regional production and distribution when early industrial expansion led to increased advertising, largely in old-fashioned formats. The agencies acted as space brokers only, promoting the interest in advertising mainly on behalf of the print media. Growth in advertising was due to new products, proprietary medicines, department stores, and a very few national advertisers of branded goods; advertising played a very minor part in industrial production, and agency practice was in a rudimentary state of development.

The Progressive Era was the period of expanding mass production and the rise of national branded products. The broad institutional structure of advertising was established, with the service agencies moving to the centre of national campaigns. The business practices, ethics, and institutional structures of advertising were all put in place and regularized at this time, making it the formative period for the industry. Mass media advertising expanded dramatically and came to be regarded as a legitimate feature in the marketplace. Yet many remained unconvinced of either the necessity or desirability of product advertising on a large scale.

Pope's third phase, the Modern Era or "the era of market segmentation," stretches from the 1920s to the present. In this period, the marketplace began to move from production for mass consumption (that is, for an undifferentiated group of consumers) to one of production for consumption in a stratified marketplace increasingly defined by consumers organized into relatively well-defined subgroups. Pope suggests that by the end of the 1920s most of the important features of the modern advertising industry had already been established: the agencies' role in advertising, their strong links with various media, and their business practices (methods of payment and so forth). Thus, there remained only the need for advertisers to define market segments with increasing precision, and for agencies to learn how to address them. In this sense, the addition of new media and the changes in advertising approaches were of minimal consequence for the role of advertising or its eventual function in the contemporary marketplace.

Pope places comparatively little emphasis on the impact that agency practice, relations with the media, and marketing theory had on the evolution of the industry; however, he views its development as largely conditioned by the apparently irresistible wave of national product advertising itself. Once the agencies had responded to this wave by laying the foundations for their full-service capabilities, as they did in the 1920s, the institutional arrangements supporting modern advertising (according to this view) were in place. What happened thereafter was essentially the story of agency reaction to, and absorption of, the special features of later media revolutions.

However, there is more to the story of modern advertising than its institutional link to national manufacturing and the markets it developed. For us, no less important is the role that the agencies played in constructing the bridge between selling and communicating in contemporary society. Some other observers also have focused on a wider network of changes in seeking to assess advertising's social impact, among them Michael Schudson (1984). His interpretation isolates four important and interrelated dimensions: market forces, notably changes in the system of distribution; changes in methods of industrial production, especially the volume and types of goods; media forces and the way they adjust to advertising; the agencies and how they organize, promote, and redefine advertising practice.

Other authors—for example, Stephen Fox in *The Mirror Makers* (1984)—also identify innovations in advertising practice itself as the key factor in the industry's development. Fox argues that the influence of strong individuals within the business has taken advertising through periodic reconceptualizations of what constitutes good practice. He depicts its history as governed by alternating cycles of emphasis, shifting back and forth between "hard-sell" persuasive formats (reason why, unique selling point) and "soft-sell" suggestive ones (emotive or "creative," emphasizing design, lifestyles, and personal images). Although his biographical approach identifies the major advocates of these alternative positions and their arguments, it is less helpful in filtering out the essential differences between the creative approaches of the 1960s and those of the 1920s. Clearly both styles, the persuasive and the creative, have been a part of the repertoire of advertising for the past one hundred years, and they seem to come in and out of favour with different agencies at different times, for different classes of product, or with different types of audiences. But such cycles in themselves do not reveal the broader dimensions of change that make the two approaches so very compatible within the world of advertising. As one of our interviewees put the point:

> There has always been the distinction between two appeals: the rational and the emotional. They were separate. Either you had a rational product like a car or else you had an emotional one like cosmetics. We used to say, don't mix the two appeals. In the eighties you have to mix them.

The type of appeal used depends on circumstances. Fashion rules the industry, and approaches come in and out of fashion, with different agencies profiting depending on their orientation. But during the 1950s, for example, both heavily research-oriented agencies and those that stressed intuition and creativity thrived.

The idea that the industry just swings back and forth between two well-established poles leads to the belief that advertising has grown in sophistication over the years without really changing; for almost every type of ad today, there is some historical precedent. The alternation between persuasion and suggestion, so the story goes, is a struggle between the view of human beings as rational creatures and the view of them as emotional and creative.

Merle Curti found a smoother evolutionary development in the views of human nature held by advertisers, basing his study of changes in marketing outlook held by advertising practitioners on the contents of *Printer's Ink* for the period between 1890 and 1954. Curti sought to pinpoint the evolution of the dominant attitude in advertising thought. He divided the period into three phases.

During the first phase, The Rationalistic Image of Human Nature, advertisers tended to think of consumers essentially as rational and not easily persuaded by gimmicks. "Most experts who held to the informative purpose of advertising emphasized the basically rational, logical and sensible qualities of man without indicating further what these were" (Curti 1967, 338). They assumed that a person wanted to know first price, then function, craftsmanship, durability, and benefits—that is, all the reasons why one should buy—in order to make some estimation of the product's worth in terms of his or her own priorities. The rational view is reflected both by practitioners of reason-why advertising and by rationalistic academic psychology around the turn of the century.

In the second phase, The Irrational Conception of Human Nature, which lasted from about 1910 to 1930, "the dominant idea came to be that man is in actuality more irrational than rational. Merchandising techniques, techniques to appeal to various nonrational impulses, now received emphasis" (Curti 1967, 347). Human nature was viewed as malleable, not fixed. Advertising operated by suggestion, pictures, attention-gathering stimuli, and playing on human sympathy to persuade the consumer to desire the product. Campaigns were based on "appeals" and imputed motives, and sales would depend on how well the advertiser could take advantage of people's competitiveness, shame, desire for approval, or need for reward for achievement. Appeals to personal appearance, prestige, family, and home also were featured.

In the third phase, which emphasized the behavioural sciences and originated during the Great Depression and extended through the post-war years, the rational and irrational views of human nature were merged and modified. Advertisers began to talk more of satisfying consumer wants as opposed to creating them, and social science became a major influence introducing new research methods and techniques to the industry. Psychological conceptions of human nature were very influential in this period; the tension between rationalist and irrationalist notions was dealt with by accepting both. Advertisers learned from psychologists "that whatever decision we make, however purely rational it may seem, is deeply influenced by emotional forces, conscious, subconscious, or unconscious. Of special importance was the increasing recognition of symbols in evoking emotional responses" (Curti 1967, 354). Personality traits such as self-esteem, impulses for creative expression, and concerns for social relations that had been highlighted in the behavioural sciences, were explored minutely by marketers as bases for selling.

Curti linked variations in thinking about advertising to social and institutional ones. His analysis does not cover the contemporary period, but this has been addressed by Monte Sommers (1983), who traces the transition from psychological approaches to a broader marketing management approach, which trickled down into advertising practice from marketing theory. This strategy integrated advertising into a "global" marketing framework, brought new statistical methods to bear on decision-making tasks (including the concepts of product and consumer life cycles and the hierarchy of needs), and generally defined new goals and purposes for advertising around the concept of market segmentation. In this strategy, the main concern shifts from the consumer to the market, specifically the description of, and access to, segments or groups of buyers.

Thus, the understanding of the advertising industry is based on changes in its structure and relationships in the larger business sphere, and on changes in advertising thought and practice within the industry itself. The advertising industry is depicted as responding to shifts in the market or to broader conceptions of man and society. For the most part, it is not regarded as a "transformative institution" in its own right, or as a factor of significant proportions in modern society.

A comment by one of our interviewees illustrates this outlook: "After factoring out TV and media change, I honestly believe that North American commercial society has used advertising in 1910 the same as in 1980, except that advertising has adjusted as society has matured and the market has increased." However, we simply cannot discount variations in media when attempting to understand the changing qualities of advertising. For if we view advertising as primarily an extension of the industrial process of manufacture and distribution, and minimize its own interpretation of and contribution to mediated communication and its impact on modern popular culture, we run the risk of ignoring much of what happened in the twentieth century—the novel uses of visuals, dialogue, storytelling, film demonstration, characters, persuasive design, and marketing strategy.

Our own portrait places much greater emphasis than others on the close interconnections among advertising, the goods-producing sector, and media, and especially on advertising's connective or bridging function in relation to production and media. The advertising industry, led by its agencies, transferred knowledge about the media to producers, knowledge about audiences to media, and knowledge about consumers and how to reach them more effectively with marketing campaigns back and forth between producers and the media.

Advertising, especially the agencies, never responded just passively to changes in media, but in many cases became an active force in their development. Advertisers have been active lobbyists in the commercialization of the media and in reorganizing them to suit their own particular needs and orientations. It is impossible to write a history of the media in the modern world without giving significant attention to the role of advertising in shaping them, and at the heart of this story is the relationship between media and advertisers established by the agencies and the impact of this relationship on the concepts and practice of marketing thought. Advertising can never be thought of as simply an extension of what is happening in marketing or mass production or mass consumption; the key to its growing impact on society is what is happening in communications media.

Successive waves of innovation in magazine production, radio, and television are reflected in changes in advertising practices, from which resulted equally profound transformations in the way that advertisers thought about and approached consumers through the design of campaigns and marketing strategies. In order to map out these interconnections, we have constructed a historically based account that includes changes over time in the cultural determinants of consumption behaviour, the system of industrial production and distribution, the organization of the advertising business, the communicative models brought into the practice of advertising, and media technologies. Our account draws on the earlier work of Pope (1983) and Curti (1967), but emphasizes a broader set of factors.

The bonding of media and advertising, which is the principal force in these varied dimensions, developed in four stages during the twentieth century. Of course, reality is not so neatly demarcated as the dating of the stages presents it, and the latter phases of each, representing times of realignment and transformation, shade into their successors. Most importantly, the characteristics of each period do not disappear, but rather become subordinate components in a newer and more complex environment. For example, rationalistic-informative approaches dominant in the early stage are not so much subverted by the development during the 1920s of new ideas about the consumer and new media as they are channelled to specific media and product categories; classified ads do not disappear but are gradually restricted to personal and small retail selling in the major newspapers. The development of advertising is a process of "layering" techniques and strategies, culminating in a versatile, multi-dimensional armoury. Few ingredients have ever been simply discarded or forgotten; almost everything in the storeroom is subsequently dusted off, refitted, and returned to service in a more specialized niche.

Stage One: The Product-Oriented Approach (1890–1925)

The development of commercialized print media is closely related to our first stage, in which advertising is oriented toward the product. The service agencies, reaching beyond their earlier functions as space sellers, concentrate on copywriting and advertising design to sell the new national branded products. The agencies establish communication as the unifying element in the services they offer. They systematize and develop new styles of appeal, leaving behind the "announcements" of earlier periods in favour of a persuasive informational approach arguing the merits of the product (see Figure 6.2). The appeals are predominantly rationalistic in the sense that "reason why" demands an explanation of the motivation for using a product. The written text is the core of this explanation, although new technologies, first in magazines and then in newspapers, allow the increasing use of illustration and visual layout elements in the development of arguments about the qualities of the product. The agencies focus mainly on national campaigns and become particularly important to the consumer magazine industry. They extend their explorations of the stylistic elements of campaign design, merging visual and rhetorical devices and codifying these in agency practice.

Stage Two: Product Symbols (1925–1945)

The professionalization of the agencies now makes advertising capable of influencing public policy on the development of radio, and respond-

FIGURE 6.2
Stage One—The Product-Oriented Approach

ing positively and opportunistically to the national advertising possibilities of this new medium. Research into audiences for media broadens the marketing services offered by the agencies. The agencies move closer to the marketing concept, in which consumer disposition is a crucial element in advertising, even though knowledge about the consumer at this time is limited to very broad demographic or polling-based evidence. In this context, marketing thought begins to shift toward the nonrational or symbolic grounding of consumption based on the notion of appeals or motives, putting less emphasis on the product and its uses. More precisely, product-oriented advertising gradually is confined to particular media and types of goods.

The experience with media changes the practice of advertising. In magazines, photography and art allow for innovations in the associational dimension of argumentation. Products are presented less and less on the basis of a performance promise, and more on making them "resonate" with qualities desired by consumers—status, glamour, reduction of anxiety, happy families—as the social motivations for consumption (see Figure 6.3). In radio, institutional association is the early basis for sponsorship of programming, but during the 1930s experience with the role of dialogue, stars, and the development of characters allows the advertiser to assimilate much more about the social context of consumption as the basis of advertising strategy. "Tie-ins" between product and program, attention-getting devices, consistent and strong brand images, and testimonials knit together goods with the social, rather than the functional, basis of consumption.

Stage Three: Personalization (1945–1965)

The agencies transfer their knowledge of and contacts with the entertainment world made through radio and magazines to the new medium of television. Television quickly becomes the major medium for national-branded product campaigns, and, in many cases, the major source of income for the agencies. The new medium can combine design and cultural symbolism with characterization, story line, and dialogue. The communicative potential of television offers many new avenues as the personnel, stylistics of imagery, patterns of attention, and programming format are bent to advertising purposes. The agencies are also major players in the realignment of context orientations in older media, as both radio and magazines adjust to the loss of certain types of major national accounts by tailoring their subject matter and editorial slants to new target audiences (see Figure 6.4).

Both creative and research oriented professionals believe that knowing more about the consumer is central to effective advertising. Agencies once more expand advertising practice so as to include new types of

FIGURE 6.3

Stage Two—Product Symbols: Freed from the burden of utility, products engage consumers with more abstract qualities of goods.

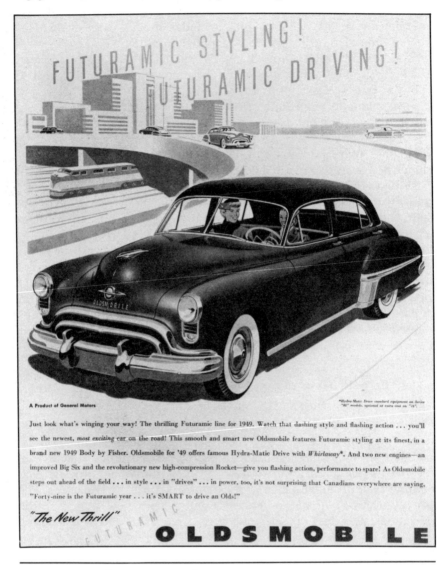

Source: Courtesy of General Motors of Canada.

FIGURE 6.4
Stage Three—Personalization: Objects carried cues fitting and proper to guide
the interior regions of the individual psyche.

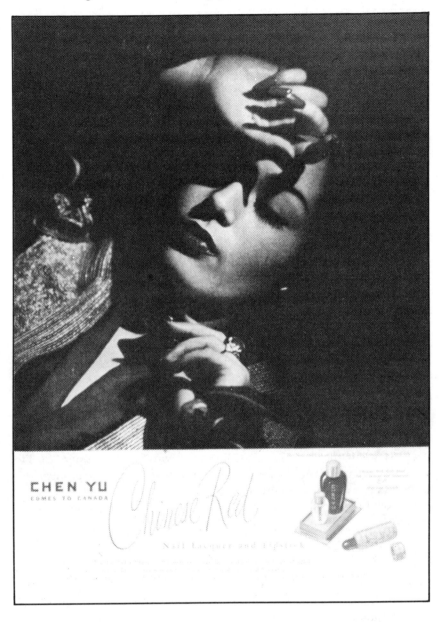

research, most notably the application of psychological concepts and techniques to studying consumers and what makes them buy. The advertiser seeks to gain access to the psychological makeup of consumers through personnel who are "in tune with the times" and who understand the ordinary consumer. Marketing strategy and advertising styles revolve around the idea of a prototypical mass consumer accessible through television—the quintessential mass medium—and characterized by a limited set of traits (interest in convenience, fascination with technology and science, desire for glamour).

Stage Four: Market Segmentation (1965–1985)

After about 1965, advertising practice adapts to the multi-media conditions of the present marketplace. Television itself is forced to target specific types of audiences desired by advertisers in order to compete with other media offering better access to local and specialized markets. Advertising is now seen as part of the marketing mix rather than as the main route to promoting consumption, and the agencies modify their routines accordingly, embracing marketing management, a philosophy that incorporates a whole new set of statistical and marketing research procedures into the preparation of advertising campaigns. These statistical packages concentrate not on personality but on activities of different subgroups of consumers, providing some analysis of their use of media, their consumption preferences, and their lifestyle attitudes. The breakouts of marketing research become the basis for decisions on design and media buying, allowing the agency to formulate marketing campaigns precisely targeted at particular groups of buyers (see Figure 6.5). There is no point in broadcasting expensive messages to those who, a bit of judicious investigation reveals, are bound and determined to remain indifferent to them.

As we mentioned, no phase supplants the foregoing ones, but rather each complements the others, adding variations and new operations to the existing repertoire. Posters, signs, and flyers—the classic means of publicity in early times—still flourish. Classified and local advertising still provide up to one-third of newspaper revenue. "Rationalist," test-oriented ads still frequently appear in the pages of newspapers and magazines, especially for certain types of consumer goods (stereo equipment, personal computers, more expensive automobile lines). The status-envy appeal formats of the 1930s, the testimonial pitches, and the celebrity appearance all persist for specific uses.

This is an "articulated" communication system, a collection of distinct yet interconnected parts, composed of products, persuasive strategies, and media channels whose unity is forged by the accumulated experience of the advertising agencies.

FIGURE 6.5
Stage Four—Market Segmentation: Products are positioned within the web of collective activities resonating with implicit consumption styles.

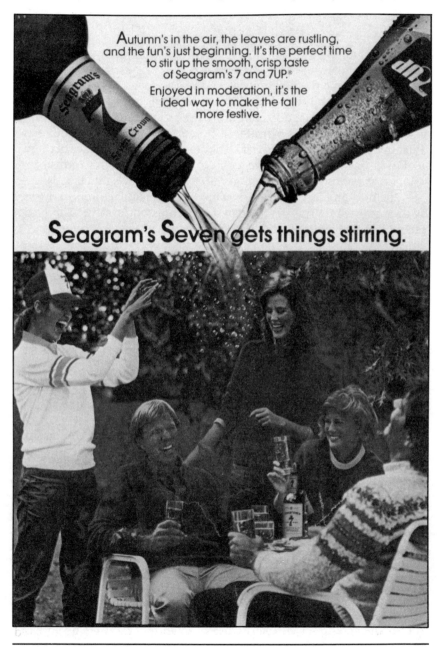

Source: Courtesy of Seagram Distillers Company, New York, New York.

7

The Modern Advertising Industry

From its origins in the nineteenth century, the advertising industry owes its survival to its ability to negotiate the relations between media outlets on the one hand and manufacturers needing to advertise on the other. We have referred to this as a bridging function between those other two domains. In maturing industrial societies, where marketplace activity of all kinds becomes ever more complex, the advertising industry developed as an institutional response to the economy's new needs.

The bridging function between media and manufacturers performed by the advertising industry, we have argued, is not passive. The bridge cannot simply be built and then forgotten, because it is a "switching" or transfer operation, rather than merely a crossover facility. Moreover, this operation grows in importance to the other partners with each passing decade, until it becomes indispensable to them. Eventually, the relations between media and advertisers are not just tied together by the advertising industry, but are defined by the role that it plays. Having achieved its own independence and economic power, the advertising industry does not passively reflect the interests of either of the other parties, but, so to speak, the compromises between them.

Because others' relations are defined through the advertising industry's workings, a purely institutional analysis is inadequate if we are to understand the role it plays in a modern market setting. Rather, we must look closely at the industry's internal mechanisms, and at the skills and knowledge that it has accumulated, because these arrangements and resources are what actually provide the substance of this role.

We saw in the previous chapter how shifting assumptions within the advertising industry could change the way linkages among persons and objects were portrayed. We shall now pursue this point in greater detail, showing how, like all institutions, the advertising business is shaped by its structural relationships with other institutions, its own internal interests, and by the assumptions and ideologies of its operating personnel.

ADVERTISING AGENCIES AND THE ECONOMY

Advertising agencies are hired by clients (firms that wish to advertise) to coordinate and direct the many types of activities that make up an advertising campaign. While a few advertisers create their own commercials and manage their own campaigns, the vast majority of business firms rely on advertising agencies that specialize in the promotion of goods and services and can draw upon the resources of skilled personnel and many years of accumulated experience. Agencies normally participate in the whole process of devising appropriate strategies for the particular good or service to be advertised—creating and testing various options, determining the potential effectiveness of the campaign, and buying space and time from various media outlets for the finished commercial messages.

Considered from another standpoint, the advertising agency for many years acted as an agent for the media in which the advertising messages finally were placed. Until the 1980s, in most cases the income to the agency from any particular client account was based upon the amount of money that the advertiser agreed to pay the media firms to display the finished message. Normally, this was 15 percent of the amount billed; if an advertiser, for example, paid $1 million to buy time or space, the income to the agency would be $150,000. In effect, therefore, hiring an agency cost an advertiser nothing, because, strictly speaking, this 15 percent came from the income of the media. If a company were to go directly to the media to buy space or time, it would have had to pay the full amount because the media save on clerical, administrative, and selling costs by dealing with a few agencies rather than with a plethora of advertisers, and find that the stable structure the agencies provide is well worth the commissions they are paid. In effect, therefore, there was no cost to the advertiser in hiring an agency.

The commission was, and has been, debated and criticized for many years, because the agency gets its cut regardless of the amount of creative work it does; if the same commercials are run for long periods of time, the agency will not have to do any additional work. Perhaps more important, because the agency's income is based upon media billings, it is in its interest to increase advertising expenditures and to push advertisers toward more expensive media.

On the other hand, the commission system is one way to price a creative product. Since the advertiser does not pay the agency by the hour, it can continue to push for high quality material rather than settle for the agency's first offering. The commission system forces the agency to assume a share of the risk involved; if the campaign is ineffective, the agency must withdraw it and devise another strategy, committing more resources for the same income (or perhaps losing the account). The agency has to make sure that the resources it expends on the account are adequately compensated in the size of the billings, so effective and cost-efficient advertising is beneficial to both advertiser and agency. The commission system, which has its origins in the space-brokering era of the late nineteenth century, remained pretty much intact until the 1980s. In the late 1970s, almost 70 percent of advertisers based their payments to agencies on a commission of media billings.

However, by the end of the 1980s the straight commission system, based upon 15 percent of media billings, no longer dominated financial relations between the agencies and clients. It is generally agreed that only about 30 percent of transactions are based upon some sort of commission. Most compensation systems are now negotiated on a client-by-client basis, with very few of them yielding as much as 15 percent. The traditional commission system was, in effect, nothing more than a cash flow situation. The agency would pay the media at 85 percent of the amount billed, and would then bill the client at 100 percent. It is this practice that is now being negotiated—to a reduced commission, a system of guaranteed profits, or a system of cost plus profit. According to a senior worldwide account executive,

> You really only have two kinds of systems—one generated on what it costs to make the advertising, the other on volume of placements. Then it's simply a matter of mechanics in terms of how much the client wants to pay for the services delivered. (Interview)

Based upon the services they provide their clients, advertising agencies have carved out for themselves a valuable position in the modern economy. They can be positioned along a continuum and distinguished by virtue of size and scale of operation. At the top are the giant global agencies that operate transnational accounts. In 1988, thirteen such companies had annual incomes of over $400 million each. The leader is Young & Rubicam, which had a worldwide gross income of $757.6 million on billings of over $5 billion, and which employed over 12,000 people worldwide. However, statistics such as these can be misleading, for many of the largest agencies are jointly owned by a much larger holding company. For instance, Omnicom is the holding company that includes BBDO Worldwide (#7) and DDB Needham Worldwide (#13), while Saatchi & Saatchi Co. PLC owns Saatchi and Saatchi Advertising Worldwide (#2) and Backer Spielvogel Bates Worldwide (#3).

A second category of agencies, not having the capability to operate internationally, deals largely with national accounts. The most well known of these middle-range agencies is Chiat/Day, which has its head office in California and receives over 95 percent of its income from the United States market. In 1988, this agency had a U.S. gross income of $62 million on billings of $500 million and employed 706 people. A third category of agencies deals largely with local advertising in the major metropolitan markets, while a fourth group deals with local advertising in the smaller markets.

THE 1980s: UPHEAVAL, CONCENTRATION, AND HORIZONTAL EXPANSION

"The ad-agency business is in the middle of the biggest turmoil we've ever seen" (*Newsweek* 4 August 1986, 41). This statement from advertising president Malcom MacDougall in 1986 reflects the tremendous changes that shook the advertising industry in the mid-1980s. *Advertising Age* dubbed this period the "Big Bang," occasioned as it was by a wave of business activity that saw some of the biggest giants in advertising merging with, or being taken over by, industry rivals.

While mergers have traditionally been a part of the industry landscape (there were two hundred acquisitions between 1977 and 1985), prior to the mid-1980s they tended to involve the taking over of small advertising companies, as well as the acquisition of companies that specialized in special and related commercial communications fields such as direct marketing, medical marketing, sales promotion, and public relations. These acquisitions had neither the pace nor the scope of more recent ones. For instance, the largest acquisition of 1982 was the purchase of the William Esty agency by Ted Bates. In 1986, in a celebrated two-week frenzy of merger activity, Saatchi and Saatchi Co. PLC purchased the Bates agency for $450 million. (Previous to this, BBDO International, Doyle Dane Bernbach, and Needham Harper Worldwide had joined under the holding company name of Omnicom.) In the ensuing period, there were numerous other mergers and acquisitions that culminated in WPP (a London-based communications company) buying J. Walter Thompson in 1987 and Ogilvy and Mather in 1989.

In the shift toward ever greater concentration of ownership, advertising agencies were moving to change one of the central assumptions of their industry—that one company could not represent competing brands. Before the 1980s, unlike other sectors in modern economies, the advertising industry could not rationalize its operations by having its member firms specialize in product types, due to a longstanding principle, agreed upon among agencies and their clients, that agencies would not handle the accounts of competing brands. Thus, agencies could not become experts on how to market one type of product (for example, automobiles), because at any one time they could represent only one of the manufacturers of that product. This forced the advertising agency to be a generalist, with its expertise spread across a range of product types. (Some industries—for example, travel, real estate, and theatre—use specialist agencies who handle competing accounts, but more in the capacity of a "listing function" than as something driven by creative content or differentiation.)

Some interesting consequences flowed from the principle of nonspecialization.

Unlike so many of the products they represent, advertising agencies cannot segment their market of clients to gain monopoly advantage. If a client is unhappy, it can pick up its business and go to another agency without losing a special expertise that only a few agencies can offer. (Shapiro 1981, 398–99)

Indeed, advertisers often require agencies to make speculative presentations before they are hired—a form of comparison shopping.

This is not to say that there was no impetus toward specialization within the advertising industry. Agencies tried, and still do, to make themselves indispensable to advertisers by devising special services that other agencies cannot offer (for example, unique research techniques); the hefty markup on such services accounts for a large percentage of the agencies' revenue. Agencies could also specialize by media and, most importantly, by target consumer, offering themselves as experts on advertising to children or to minorities. However, "mergermania" inevitably brought competing brands under the same roof for the first time, which prompted many clients to simply transfer their accounts to other agencies. In the aftermath of 1986 more than $500 million worth of advertising was reassigned by clients who suddenly found themselves partners (once removed) with their major rivals. For instance, American Honda switched $58 million in business from Needham to Rubin/Poster & Associates to avoid sharing agencies with Volkswagen and other automobile manufacturers.

Initial client reaction to the new agency mergers was very negative (Chrysler's Lee Iacocca asked agencies, "What's in this for me?"). Most advertisers have taken a wait-and-see attitude, described by one senior executive as one of "watching like hawks, for that first sign of self- rather than client-orientation by the agency" (Interview). Carl Spielvogel, a founder of Backer and Spielvogel (acquired by Saatchi & Saatchi), identifies three types of conflicts and suggests how each will determine the reaction of a client.

There are religious conflicts, like Coke and Pepsi, General Motors and Ford. This is sacred ground, where you don't walk with your shoes on. There are banana conflicts, where you mention a competitor's name and your client goes bananas. Again, tread very carefully. And then there are ultimate-wisdom conflicts; that is, it's a conflict if your client says it's a conflict. Already there's a relaxation of the definitions by advertisers because, it seems, the only agencies that don't have conflicts don't have clients. (*New York* 9 June 1986, 28)

In the immediate aftermath of the mergers, many non-merged agencies started to sell themselves to clients as an alternative to big bureaucratic agencies, with an emphasis on creativity, not the corporate bottom line. For their part, the new mega-agencies are very mindful of the need to assure their large clients that their valuable marketing secrets will be safe from competitors. There are two ways in which agencies try to honour this assurance. First, they create multiple networks under the umbrella of a holding company, so that different accounts can be assigned totally different institutional networks. Thus, Omnicom is made up of two freestanding networks (DDB Needham/BBDO), as is WPP (J. Walter Thompson/Ogilvy) and the older Interpublic Group (Lintas/ McCann Erickson). In this way, financial coordination exists alongside advertising independence. Second, agencies emphasize to employees the need for confidentiality. Most workers are required to sign a confidentiality statement upon joining and leaving an agency. As one creative director humorously put it, "We have an exit speech that says if you say anything there's a dead cat nailed to your door tomorrow" (Interview).

What was the impetus to this realignment of some of the major names in the advertising industry? From the analytical framework we have developed, it is clear that agencies survive and prosper based upon their mediation of the advertiser/media relation. While they are themselves freestanding economic actors motivated by financial considerations and providing returns for their investors, to accomplish this properly they also need to be able to fulfil their basic mediational function. In searching for the impetus to the upheavals of the 1980s, we should then look to either end of the partnership chain.

As advertising executives never tire of pointing out, advertising is a service industry, and there is little doubt that the initial impetus for the merger activity in the 1980s was prompted by the changing needs of clients, who were growing and expanding their activities to a global scale not previously seen. Companies that were already huge started to merge (R.J. Reynolds and Nabisco, and Phillip Morris/Kraft/General Foods) and to look upon the world as one market that could be sold products in much the same way (see the following section for further discussion of the trend toward globalization). These new giants were thus demanding that advertising agencies be able to offer the global services that they required. To be able to compete for clients at this level meant that agencies needed to be able to operate in the major global markets, which meant that they needed offices there. As a senior-level Saatchi executive put it: "We missed out on some big opportunities in the early 80s on some big assignments because we were just an English agency. We were determined to play the game in the big leagues and the big accounts now demand, at minimum, European capability" (Interview). The economic unification of Europe set for 1992 became a major impetus for the acquisitions needed to achieve European capability.

There are a number of strategies available to agencies for establishing the network of offices that the new global emphasis demands. An agency can (1) set up new offices in the markets in which there is a weakness, a very expensive and time-consuming option; (2) buy already existing individual national agencies in markets; or (3) buy a *network* of agencies that complement its existing strengths. This last option was exercised by numerous agencies in the mid-1980s. For example, Doyle Dane Bernbach (which had strengths in New York and Europe) combined with Needham Harper (which had strengths in Chicago and Asia) to form DDB/Needham as a freestanding network under the holding company of Omnicom (which also includes the BBDO International network and a third subsidiary that will combine the three firms' regional advertising, direct marketing, and public relations agencies).

At the same time as these changes were affecting the industry, there were also important developments taking place on the other side of the client/agency/media relation. Media companies, too, were accelerating the pace of concentration and consolidation, and the 1980s have seen the emergence not simply of giant national media conglomerates but, more importantly, *international* conglomerates. The major names in this global drive toward concentration are Time/Warner, Bertelsmann, Finninvest, Capital Cities/ABC, Thompson, News Corporation, Hachette Filipacchi Communications, and Maxwell Communication Corporation. These companies have cross-ownership in such media as magazines, newspapers, television, radio, cable, books, music, and film. Additionally, they are developing "media without boundaries" — for example, broadcast satellites — that will change the media landscape for international marketers and international advertising agencies. Many analysts within the media business speculate that in the near future five or six global media companies will dominate and control large segments of the available media outlets.

To operate in this world of giant clients and giant media, agencies, too, will have to be large if they are to serve client needs and deal with global media companies in an efficient manner. The mega-agencies, by combining their media buying into a consolidated package, gain what is referred to as "media clout." In part, the agency mergers were motivated by a concern to gain critical mass in media negotiations. As one media director put it: "You need to get the critical mass for when you are negotiating with the new media giants. You need a certain amount of volume to get their attention, otherwise you won't get as good a deal" (Interview). In many countries, rates are determined by volume and so it is important that agencies are able to deal with the new media giants on an equal footing. The mergers allow agencies to negotiate from a position of strength.

In a further extension of this desire to gain media clout, in 1988 some competing companies were seriously exploring the possibility of pooling their media buying. Omnicom and the Ogilvy Group created and share joint ownership of a third independent group that buys to the specifications of both companies. While such activity is, in part, spurred by agency desires to gain discounts from media, it is also driven by competitive fears that, as other merged companies put together efficient media operations that offer clients large discounts from media, major advertisers will consolidate all their accounts for their many different brands at one agency. Calling the new joint media-buying ventures "Big Bang II," *Advertising Age* reported, "[A] major fear among agencies that work for Procter & Gamble Co. is that Saatchi will put together an efficient media-buying operation for its units and that P & G will consolidate all its buying at Saatchi" (11 July 1988, 1).

In an important sense, then, the recent mergers were the agencies' response to events that were happening independently of them. As Neil Blackley, a British analyst, says: "Why go global? Why go for scale? Because the ad agency is the meat in the sandwich between giant consumer products companies and giant media companies. You either develop a niche position in the marketplace, as a creative boutique or whatever, or you develop internationally to handle conglomerating clients" (*NY Times Magazine* 2 July 1989, 38). Or as Martin Sorrel, head of WPP, reflected on the media mergers of 1989: "What's been happening in the last few weeks . . . just reinforces the changes taking place in the three circles of interest—clients, media and agencies. The poor old agencies need to respond to clients' needs and deal with the big media" (*NY Times Magazine* 2 July 1989, 38).

However, recent developments cannot be reduced solely to a view of advertising agencies as the "meat in the sandwich" that responds to what the bread is doing. There were also important developments taking place *within* the advertising industry that provided the impetus toward the mergers. Most importantly, the growth in the amount of money advertisers were putting up for directly advertising-related expenditures was slowing as promotions, tie-ins, and event marketing became increasingly important in the mid-1980s. This was especially bad news for public companies (those that offered shares to the public on the stock exchange), who were more vulnerable to short-term profit pressures. The only way agencies could generate more revenue was to attract new clients, and in a sluggish market the easiest way to achieve this was to merge with another agency and aggregate both companies' accounts.

Within this scenario, it was the British firms, Saatchi & Saatchi and WPP, that accelerated the merger frenzy with their own ravenous appetites for expansion. The Saatchi brothers, Maurice and Charles, along with Martin Sorrel (Sorrel, called "the third Saatchi" because of his financial dealings while still with Saatchi & Saatchi, now heads WPP) have transformed the global advertising business by treating advertising not simply as a service industry, but as a good *investment*. The Saatchis started off with a simple and modest ambition: to become the world's largest advertising agency (having achieved this goal, their new objective is to control 25 percent of global advertising expenditures). In 1975, the Saatchis went public, and soon many other agencies joined them on the stock market. To raise money for new acquisitions, these companies would simply issue new stock to investors. The subsequent acquisitions are explained in the following way by Preston Rabl, Sorrel's partner at WPP:

> Investors had overcome their suspicions of "people businesses" as they realized that the success of any investment is really determined by management—that is, people. There was then considerable interest in advertising and marketing stocks. In the main, these companies were not large and their management owned sizable proportions of their equity. Hence, there was too little equity to satisfy investor interest and these shares rose to levels where their prices were 20 to 30 times earnings—sometimes much higher. These companies were soon faced with the option of either making acquisitions or disappointing shareholders, as organic growth could not be sustained at the levels these ratios demanded. (*NY Times Magazine* 2 July 1989, 26)

The acquisitions, then, were not simply a business strategy: they were driven by the financial situation; there was thus a dynamic *internal* to the advertising business for the upheavals of the mid-1980s.

As American advertising growth rates were slowing at this time, those for the rest of the world were expanding. With the growing popularity of global marketing strategies, the creation of new consumer markets, and increasing media deregulation around the world, the United States share of global advertising expenditures is steadily decreasing to where it is now at or below 50 percent. The agencies have to be prepared in foreign markets where there has been growth in the advertising expenditures upon which they depend; in one sense, the mergers and acquisitions are prompted by a simple need to go where the money is.

An interesting consequence of the agency takeovers and mergers was that clients came to look upon the industry in a new way. As the prices that agencies fetched reached astronomical levels, and as some individuals made huge amounts of money (up to $100 million) on the sales, clients, beginning to suspect that perhaps they were paying too much for agencies' services, started to apply different criteria for working out adequate compensation. So passed the commission system, the three-martini lunches, and the country-club atmosphere that had characterized the image, if not the reality of the industry. Today, as a result of the mergers, advertising is now regarded as just another business in which the financial managers have wrested control from their creative colleagues. During WPP's takeover of Ogilvy & Mather, David Ogilvy, a representative of the old-style industry image in which creativity was king, was openly contemptuous of Martin Sorrel, a man who had never written an ad and had no desire to do so. (While the public image of agencies in the business community changed, it is doubtful that the general public was even aware of shifts within the industry.)

Subsequently, it appears that the "brand identity" cultivated by the agencies may erode as they become engulfed in further layers of financial bureaucracy. A 1989 survey reported that J. Walter Thompson and the Omnicon agencies had suffered a significant loss of brand identity among advertisers, while those that escaped the mergers achieved greater awareness scores. As *Advertising Age* commented on the future of the merged agencies: "Each of these agencies has been financially successful since the megamergers, but a weakening identity could signal long-term difficulties on the business front" (5 June 1989).

There is, of course, a limit to the extent of the mergers. There are only so many large agencies and only so many clients who want global services. The agency mergers may have reached their peak. By the end of the 1980s, a different type of transition was taking place as agencies started to ask themselves whether they were advertising companies or communications companies. Increasingly, the answer was the latter, and a new form of horizontal expansion began whereby agencies began acquiring ancillary services they had previously contracted out: promotions, public relations, direct marketing, market research, advertising production, and program production companies offered services that the agencies could now control directly. The global agencies are now realigning themselves as one-stop communications companies.

GLOBALIZATION

Clearly, by the end of the 1980s the advertising industry had gone through some startling changes. It had expanded and consolidated its global operations, and had emerged as a major cultural arbiter on the world scene. But we should be careful in how we evaluate the changes that took place, for very little in advertising is totally new. For instance, the Interpublic Group of Companies under the direction of Marion Harper had long ago pioneered the idea of international and multiple networks under one financial holding company. Indeed, examined historically we can see that the global expansion of the 1980s was the latest stage in an expansion that had begun as far back as 1899 when J. Walter Thompson opened an office in London. We can identify three distinct stages in this process.

The first period lasted from the turn of the century to the late 1950s and is characterized by American agencies opening foreign offices (first in Britain and Europe, and then the rest of the world) to serve *specific* clients who needed international marketing and advertising services. Before the 1960s, three agencies (J. Walter Thompson, McCann-Erickson, and Young & Rubicam) handled the bulk of international advertising for American firms. As one McCann executive put it:

> In general, McCann-Erickson has grown internationally in parallel to key international clients. Some of these (e.g., Esso, General Motors) we have served for over 50 years in various international markets. It has not been our strategy to open an office in a new country and then look for clients. We generally open offices to serve existing clients who have become active in these markets. (in Anderson 1984, 90–91)

This structure soon proved inadequate to meet the needs of the expanding consumer product manufacturers, who, starting in the 1950s especially, were exploring foreign markets that were not restricted to Europe. The advertising options open to these companies were limited. They could hire American affiliates in specific markets and local agencies in markets where there was, as yet, no international advertising presence. However, this led to major problems of coordination and accounting. As Noreen Janus explains:

> In short, the rapidly increasing number of U.S. corporations doing business internationally after the war and even into the 1960's were faced with a very difficult advertising problem: multiple agencies turning out campaigns of variable quality, with little or no control over the company and product image on a world scale, accounting problems associated with multiple agency relationships, and media and advertising statistics that varied across countries. (Janus 1980, 77)

Prompted by client needs, and sensing the opportunities and profits that awaited agencies able to offer international services, more American agencies began in the 1960s—the second period of global expansion—to establish overseas offices of one kind or another. While in the forty-five-year period between 1915 and 1960, American agencies had opened fifty overseas offices, in the 1960–70 decade alone they opened 196.

This second period is characterized by one of three types of relations between American agencies and their foreign offices: (1) "Branch agency," in which the overseas office is a subsidiary of the parent agency; (2) "Affiliate," in which the parent American agency has part ownership, with local interests, in an agency; or (3) "Associate," in which the American agency has no official equity but has a working arrangement with a local agency (Anderson 1984, 91). Eventually, American agencies came to dominate the advertising industry in countries all over the world—both developed and developing. As Janus notes: "One striking conclusion may be drawn from these data: U.S. control over the international advertising sector far exceeds its control over transnational industry itself; this is true at both the national and international levels" (Janus 1980, 82).

However, even within this scenario, not many agencies could offer services in every market within the world; they were strong in some regions and weak in others. With the emergence of manufacturing companies that sought to exploit to the limit the economies of scale offered by aggregating all possible global markets, a new rationalization was required.

The third period has already been examined in the previous section. It is characterized by the combination not simply of individual agencies but of systems of agencies, and is based upon serving the needs of corporations that are operating with a new philosophy of international marketing. The "guru" of this new philosophy is Harvard Business School Professor Theodore Levitt, who, in a provocative and influential 1983 article, announced that the age of the multinational corporation had given way to the age of the *global* corporation.

Whereas the multinational corporation adjusts its products and marketing techniques to suit the idiosyncrasies of individual countries (at high relative cost), the global corporation treats the entire world as if it were a single entity and sells the same things in the same way everywhere (at low relative cost). Levitt attributes the move toward global marketing to the fact that "the world's needs and desires have irrevocably homogenized" (under the influence of communications and travel). Citing examples from around the world of a curious mixture of traditional belief structures and western consumer goods, Levitt claims that

> [t]he products and methods of the industrialized world play a single tune for all the world, and all the world eagerly dances to it . . . Ancient differences in national tastes and preferences, in modes of doing business and the institutions of commerce, fall before the homogenizing modernity everybody experiences via the new technological facilitators. (1983, 30, 24)

The worldwide success of McDonald's, Coca-Cola and Pepsi-Cola, rock music, Hollywood movies, Revlon cosmetics, Sony televisions, and Levi jeans all seem to testify to the increasing homogenization of needs in the contemporary period.

Levitt conjoins the strategy of market segmentation with the seemingly contradictory one of globalization by claiming that a market segment in one country is seldom unique, and that similar groups can be found around the world due to the homogenization brought about by technology. Aggregating these different market segments into one on a global scale allows manufacturers to exploit economies of scale that large markets make possible (and, indeed, necessary if manufacturers are to compete successfully in the contemporary global marketplace).

According to Levitt, multinational corporations have been too "thoughtlessly accommodating" to local tastes and preferences, falsely presuming that "marketing means giving the customer what he says he wants rather than trying to understand exactly what he'd like." Global corporations, on the other hand, "never assume that the customer is a king who knows his own wishes" and constantly seek to standardize their offerings everywhere.

Levitt's analysis prompted advertising agencies (especially Saatchi & Saatchi) to rethink their role on a global scale. In 1983, the Saatchis took out a full two-page ad in the *Sunday Times,* the *New York Times,* and the *Observer* announcing "the opportunity for world brands" and their own preparedness for the new situation (see Figure 7.1).

> Most observers [the ad states] believe that the trend to pan-regional or global marketing will have a marked impact on the structure of advertising agencies ... because world brands require world agencies. Many expect to see the advertising industry moving in the same direction as accounting, banking, financial services, etc.—a polarization between worldwide networks servicing global corporations and strong local firms handling domestic clients in their own country.

These words have proved remarkably prophetic (or course, the Saatchis were in a key position to act to bring their own expansionist goals to fruition).

The third stage in the globalization process has also shifted the image of advertising—and especially international advertising—as a characteristic American institution. The key roles that WPP and Saatchi & Saatchi play in the new global industry have tinged the distinctly American flavour of advertising with a British accent. Indeed, in a situation in which global brands are developed at the outset, rather than developed for the American market first and then marketed abroad, and in which the thrust is toward integrated campaigns rather than "export" campaigns, the British agencies may have a special advantage. With their relatively small home market, and with international trade so critical to their economy, British manufacturers and agencies have had to take the rest of the world more seriously than have their American counterparts. In addition, London will have a privileged role within the European market because English is the international language. This, coupled with its financial position, will make London the communications centre of Europe, as well as give a key global edge to British agencies. Advertising may no longer be synonymous with Madison Avenue.

How will institutional changes in the industry affect the advertising that appears on television and in print around the world? Does global marketing also mean global advertising, in the sense that the same ads, produced in New York or London, will be seen all over the world? The precise nature of the new global advertising is still unclear. While global marketers would prefer to use one single message all over the world, existing national, cultural, and racial barriers will for a time prevent universal application, except for the largest and most adaptive world brands. Despite this, global advertising will still be characterized by an increasing degree of standardization and centralization in which the central campaign strategy will be devised at head office and distributed to branches around the world to adapt to local conditions.

There are three different ways, with many gradations between them, in which a local subsidiary of a foreign transnational advertising firm may put ads together. First, the central office sends an ad to be shown in its entirety (an extremely rare procedure, for even the most global ads require an audio dub into the appropriate language). Second, in what is known as the "prototype approach," the head office sends a broad selection of materials (films, videos, print), all developed according to the basic advertising strategy, from which the subsidiary chooses alternatives for the local campaign, blending the basic ingredients into a recipe for regional tastes. Third, in what is known as the "creative work plan," a general international advertising strategy is developed, which serves as a framework to guide the creation of various campaigns in local markets around the world. In general, there is a continuum from most centralized control to least. Different agencies work with variations of this continuum. McCann-Erickson, for instance, distinguishes between global brands, universal brand positioning, universal product positioning, and decentralized global products.

While the industry is currently in a state of flux, there is general agreement that the pressure within the new context will be toward more centralized campaigns, as these achieve greater economies and savings. This will be especially heightened as more and more products are developed initially as global products rather than as multinational ones adapted to global ones. What is clearly evident is a move toward more centralization of *planning*, if not execution. Richard Earle, senior vice-president/creative director at Saatchi and Saatchi, believes that

> [f]rom the marketing and advertising standpoint, most major marketing companies today are in a state of transition between country-localized and more broadly centralized forms of organization . . . The winning systems of the 1980's will be characterized by frequent communication among management personnel in different countries, a centralized brand and advertising management system, and centralized advertising production. (*Madison Avenue*, December 1984, 44)

A more likely intermediate scenario is that global markets will be seen as a collection of regional ones, and that separate regions will share similar advertising. Alternatively, Levitt's notion of homogenized market segments, particularly as they apply to metropolitan areas around the world, may lead to global advertising directed at specific segments within markets. As the Saatchi ad says (Figure 7.1):

> The most advanced manufacturers are recognizing that there are probably more social differences between Midtown Manhattan and the Bronx, two

FIGURE 7.1
Saatchi & Saatchi: A Global Strategy

Today, the most thoughtful companies are adopting a new approach to international marketing.

These companies are moving through the five basic stages in the life of a multinational corporation as seen in the chart below.

And as they pass through stages 4 and 5 the need for pan-regional and world marketing is emerging at the heart of their business strategy.

"The globalization of markets is at hand. With that, the multinational commercial world nears its end, and so does the multinational corporation.

The global corporation operates as if the entire world (or major regions of it) were a single entity; it sells the same things in the same way everywhere.

Corporations geared to this new reality can decimate competitors that still live in the disabling grip of old assumptions about how the world works."

PROFESSOR THEODORE LEVITT.
HARVARD UNIVERSITY

A New Approach

After the vicissitudes of the 1950s and 1960s, more companies are now reaching the status of having acquired 'critical mass' in various regions of the world. They are now starting to turn from primary concern about 'return on acquisition investment' and 'overhead recovery' towards getting to grips with long-term franchise building across each world region.

At the same time the progressive harmonization of 'headquarters' and 'local' management culture and style, evolving from more frequent two-way movement of personnel, is enhancing the likelihood of successful adoption and execution of pan-regional business strategies.

And meanwhile in Europe, management's strategic thinking is beginning to broaden to match the dimensions of the Common Market as legislative harmonization focuses attention on pan-European issues.

International Growth Priority

Companies have passed through the bygone age when many of them treated 'Overseas Division' as the poor cousin of the organisation, struggling to compete in foreign markets with strongly established indigenous competitors.

The international divisions of many companies are now beginning to 'come of age' and receive their rightful allocation of corporate resource, if only for the practical reason that corporate earnings growth in many multinationals is today often provided by non-domestic markets.

Business System Economics

The strategic value of pan-regional branding lies in the scale economies it affords across the company's business system – to help make the company the low-cost producer.

Where the economies arise will vary by product category, and may include research and development, materials purchasing, manufacturing, distribution and advertising.

The optimum business system for a European beer, for example, is markedly different to that for chewing gum, but the principle is the same. Secure, franchise-protected volumes at the regional scale can allow a company to *build a price/cost/value structure which will eventually put it out of reach of competition.*

Consumer Convergence

In the past, the successes in world branding have been few, and have been achieved by virtue of the sheer will and far-sighted commitment of managements who stayed consistently with a long-term vision for the business. Procter & Gamble is a company in this category that comes to mind.

In the future, the only winners in cross-country branding will be companies who have seen that social developments are making redundant the old idea that differences between nations are decisive in framing marketing strategy.

The most advanced manufacturers are recognising that there are probably more social differences between Midtown Manhattan and the Bronx, two sectors of the same city, than between Midtown Manhattan and the 7th Arrondissement of Paris. This means that when a manufacturer contemplates expansion of his business, consumer similarities in demography and habits rather than geographic proximity will increasingly affect his decisions.

Demographic Convergence

Trends of vast significance to consumer marketing, such as ageing populations, falling birth rates, and increased female employment are common to large segments of the modern industrial world.

Consumer convergence in demography, habits and culture is increasingly leading manufacturers to a consumer-driven rather than a geography-driven view of their marketing territory.

Decline of the Nuclear Family

Some of the most telling developments spring from the same source – the decline of the nuclear family. Observers have attributed this to various causes – the rapid pace of technological development; higher labour productivity which reduces hours of work; and other more metaphysical notions such as the emergence of a 'liberal' philosophy, which increasingly recognizes that a woman's role can exist outside the home.

DECLINE OF THE FAMILY UNIT

	UK		USA	
	1970	1980	1970	1980
OTHERS	29%	36%	29%	39%
MARRIED COUPLES	71%	64%	71%	61%

SOURCE C.S.O. US ANNUAL ABSTRACT OF STATISTICS

Whatever the causes, the effects in terms of household composition have been dramatic. There are now less children per household, and a declining proportion of households which conform to the two-adult-two-children pattern.

FIGURE 7.1 (continued)

sectors of the same city, than between Midtown Manhattan and the 7th Arrondissement of Paris. This means that when a manufacturer contemplates expansion of his business, consumer similarities in demography and habits rather than geographic proximity will increasingly affect his decisions.

The end result of the trend toward centralization of planning (and perhaps production) may well be the development of a new "international style" of advertising based largely on *visual* imagery, which by its very nature is less culturally specific than language. This, of course, is connected to the increasing penetration of television (and especially commercial television) into new areas and new markets, as well as to the development of global media, such as direct broadcast satellites, that will circumvent national boundaries, both geographic and cultural.

Ultimately, the issues we have examined in this section will frame the very important questions concerning the impact advertising's institutional structures will have culturally, politically, and economically, especially on countries who, while they are not part of the industrially developed western world, are now linked to it through information and culture. This is not a simple linkage either, mediated as it is by global corporations, global media, and the new global advertising agencies. The vital issues have to do with the role advertising plays in developing countries in terms of the formation and transformation of needs and values; the role of transnational advertising structures in addressing issues of poverty, cultural pluralism, and the rural/urban divide; the role of advertising in changing consumption patterns, especially as regards basic goods such as food, and the potential health issues these changes raise; the role of advertising in marketing products such as pharmaceutical drugs in countries where the infrastructure of consumer protection is also underdeveloped; the role of the agencies in influencing the development of particular types of commercial media systems; and, perhaps most generally and importantly, the role of the agencies in defining appropriate societal goals for economic development, and in creating conditions that favour luxury consumption at the expense of economic investment. (For more detailed discussions of these issues see Janus 1980; Sinclair 1987; Barnet and Muller 1974; and Anderson 1984.)

THE ADVERTISING AGENCY

While "[a]gencies like to refer to themselves as experts in marketing communications" (Varcoe 1981, 67), the creation of advertisements is more a process of negotiation both within the agency and in its relations with media and clients than it is a set of mechanical and technical routines. Advertising campaigns today (as opposed to the individual finished ad) do not originate in one person's genius or drive but in a complex process of intra- and interorganizational decision making and problem solving.

Most agencies arrange their physical layout around the work of four departments: creative, media, research, and account. Functional specialties (creative, media, copy, and so forth) rather than individual accounts are grouped together. It is the responsibility of the account department to coordinate activities within an agency and to manage the liaison between the agency and the client. The account department, therefore, must become familiar with the client's business in order to be able to integrate business and market information with research and creative materials to ensure the success of the advertising campaign.

While the account department runs the show as a whole, the creative department is an agency's heart and soul. On its strength or weakness the whole enterprise succeeds or fails. No formal qualifications are necessary for entry into creative work; one does not even need technical skills such as drawing so long as one is imaginative. In the past, copywriters dominated the field, but since the ascendancy of television, art directors have become increasingly important to the creative process as visual imagery replaced written text as the dominant mode of communication in national consumer product advertising.

Those who labour in creative departments believe quite firmly that their function is to persuade consumers to buy one brand over another on the strength of the advertising message. George Lois in a 1981 interview for "Sixty Minutes" on CBS compared advertising to poison gas:

> I've never worked on a product that was better than another. They hardly don't [sic] exist. So what I have to do is create an imagery about that product. I have to make it seem like a better product. . . . Advertising to me is poison gas. I put a commercial on the air, I spray it and I make people fall down. I make people say "I want that product." Not because the product is so much more wonderful than another product, but because they want to be involved in buying that product, they want to be involved in owning it, they want to be involved in knowing that they taste it, they want to be involved in going to the place. I make it fun. I make it a pleasure to be involved with something. That's my job.

According to another "creative," an ad campaign should be straightforward and "militaristic" in its strategy—and it should take up no more than half a page of typed prose:

> Then comes the magic and what art directors and writers make their money doing. . . . I make my living selling things. It's no different than any salesman. It's more interesting and exciting, less cold calls. All they're doing is using my brilliance and expertise to sell their products and I sell them that brilliance for as high a price as I can get. I get interested in it. I love looking at all the market figures. It's a puzzle, it's a game, it's the best game that I can play. If I felt I had it in me to live like a saint, I'd live like Ralph Nader. He's the person I most admire in the world, but I can't live that way. I have a family and want my sons to grow up and win Nobel prizes. I play this game and prove that I'm smarter than all the people who work on competing brands. (Interview)

The theme of advertising as a game, as a puzzle to be solved, is a recurring one. The constant challenge to come up with innovative ways to link communication and selling demands that such departments be fresh and exciting places populated by people slightly out of the ordinary. One employee said: "I get more ideas than other people—more and different. I have a different vision of the world, it's about four degrees different from everybody else. At seventy degrees you're crazy, but at four degrees—that's creative" (Interview). Many creative workers state that they would rather have been involved in other kinds of artistic endeavours, such as playwriting, composition, or film directing—but "the money" makes advertising irresistible (Shapiro 1981).

As we noted earlier, although agencies do not specialize in the type of product they handle, they can do so in other ways. In the creative realm, different agencies come to be known for particular approaches:

> Among creatives, agencies are also known by the style of the product that they turn out. Some agencies are known for their soft sell, others for their hard sell; some are said to be very good in conceptualizations, others distinguish themselves by the attention they give to execution of the idea or the quality of the production. (Shapiro 1981, 41)

Because the finished product is on public display, a good deal of concern is lavished on the quality of the advertisements that are finally produced. As one art director remarked: "What we do is a public thing. Everyone sees it on television. You know that everyone is seeing something that you did. A banker, no matter how successful, is never a star. His work doesn't get seen" (Interview). A creative director says,

> I like the idea of pleasing people. In the midst of all the junk on TV, the advertising is better than the shows. It's a matter of pride with me. Advertising is filled with people who want to do good work. This may be because it's a public business. If we do something terrible, we're going to be embarrassed. (Schudson 1984, 77)

Indeed, some of the industry's finished products create a good deal of embarrassment. One Canadian creative executive confessed,

> By and large 90% of TV ads are badly done. Words are put in people's mouths that people don't say. They praise the product. There's a lack of proportion and people's human integrity is attacked. I'm sickened by most of the ads I see and am ashamed to be in the business. (Interview)

In large part, this kind of reaction is an inevitable outcome of the uneasy alliance between the techniques of persuasive communication in general and the specific end (selling) to which those techniques are applied. Some contemporary television commercials attempt to deal with this dilemma by downplaying, and in some cases ignoring completely, the direct selling aspects of their messages.

The other departments in the agencies are much more representative of the business world in general. While the account department keeps the creatives and the clients talking to each other, the media department is the intermediary between the clients and the communications industry. It decides with the client what media time or space will be purchased and handles the negotiations for obtaining it. The media department uses the information provided by a number of media ratings companies to aid in deciding which channels to invest in, and to forge the vital linkages between audience segment and market segment with the most complete knowledge that money can buy.

A medium's audience is the naturally occurring groupings of readers, viewers, or listeners. These are the people to whom that medium gives advertisers access. The market segment is the target population at whom a particular commodity is aimed. It is the distinction between audience segment and market segment that necessitates the bridging function of the advertising agency. The history of the commercial media in western industrial societies is, in a sense, the playing out of this interaction between audience and market.

There has not been equal movement on both sides of the equation in the attempt to match audience with market segment, however. By and large, agencies have not encouraged their clients to change the market segment to match the audience segment available to them, but instead have tried to persuade the commercial media to change the audience segment to match the desired market segment.

Traditionally, the straightforward functions of the media department—buying space and time from media, and ensuring that the advertising is shown at the correct time and with the correct frequency—have been part of the taken-for-granted operation of the industry. However, recent events have led some experts to talk of a "crisis" for advertising agencies caused by agencies paying too much for inadequate space or time, and failing to monitor the media adequately to make sure the ads are shown. Herbert Zeltner (1984) suggests that agencies, under pressure to find ways to stretch the media dollar, may jump at what appear to be bargain rates only to later discover that the time or space purchased was inappropriate or ineffective. The deregulation of the communications industry reduced pressures on broadcasters to maintain and provide logs of the ads they broadcast, a problem that has been exacerbated by the agencies' practice of delegating the monitoring function to low-level and low-skilled personnel. As a result, many major advertisers have begun to ensure that their media activities are supervised in-house rather than left entirely to their agency (*Advertising Age* 1 October 1984). When things are progressing smoothly, the agency's service as negotiator between the needs of media and those of advertisers, like the contribution of all skilled negotiators, remains almost invisible; only when things start to go wrong do we become aware of the crucial role that the agency plays.

While it is the task of the creative department to come up with ideas for ads, it is left to the research department to evaluate how effective that advertising might be. Rarely does the department itself engage in the actual research: its function is normally to contract out such work and to interpret the results as they affect the overall strategy of the campaign. Various kinds of research are used at different stages of the evaluation process by agencies dealing with large national accounts. (The full range of procedures, of course, is carried out only for the major accounts.)

The first stage involves discussions among the creative department, the client, and the account team about the aims and direction of the campaign. Information about problems with past campaigns and past ads, about the market segment being targeted, about the views the target market holds about the product, and simple facts about the product itself are all vital at this point. Also important are general market information and knowledge about what rivals are trying to do; much of this information can be provided by the client or the agency itself.

Other kinds of knowledge can be gained from "focus group" discussions. In this research technique, a group leader guides representative consumers in talking about the particular brands or about products of a specific type. These sessions are videotaped and/or observed from behind one-way mirrors. The results usually do not show up in hard (factual) data, but in providing hints and hypotheses from which the creative team can set to work. More systematic methods (such as psychographic research) may also be used at this initial stage.

The general strategic purpose is to decide whether the campaign should be focused on consumers who already use this type of product but who are using a rival brand, or whether it should try to extend the overall market for the product type by aiming at non-users. Clients may also consider whether to switch from a "passive" campaign, stressing relaxation and leisurely enjoyment, to one with more excitement.

Once a problem has been defined, it is up to the creative team to devise various solutions. In television advertising, this normally involves the production of storyboards—a series of photographs or animated drawings—along with an accompanying soundtrack. Several storyboards will be presented to the client, who normally decides to test one or more of them. Again, focus groups may be used to review the storyboards, and their opinions become the basis for future decisions. Tests may also be conducted with larger groups of consumers, in shopping malls or in special studio settings, to get measures of "communication and recall," which indicate how likely consumers are to purchase the product advertised, or "intrusiveness and recall," which indicate how well an ad is remembered the next day. The results may lead the client to ask for modifications and fresh tests, or to authorize the production of one of the storyboards into a finished commercial.

Once the commerical has been produced, a battery of research instruments may be employed, including reruns of the communication/recall and intrusiveness/recall tests (and others) to measure physical reactions that are imperceptible to subjects. For example, Wesley procedures use galvanic skin devices to measure perspiration on the assumption that emotional responses that cause perspiration are related to what is happening in the commercial message. Other techniques track brainwaves or eye movement or analyze subjects' voices.

In addition to these somewhat "artificial context" tests, finished commercials may also be tried in a "real-market context." Test markets are picked in which the commercial is shown over the air. Results can then be evaluated by monitoring sales figures in those areas, though it is difficult to precisely pinpoint advertising's effect on buying. A preferred approach is day-after recall, as conducted by Burke Marketing Research. Telephone calls are made at random the day after the commercial is shown until two hundred people who saw the program containing the commercial have been reached. These respondents are then asked which ads, and what specifically about them, they can remember. If the test results are satisfactory, then the client will approve wider distribution of the commercial, but it is not unusual for a particular advertising strategy to be cancelled even at this late stage if the tests do not provide sufficiently strong support.

THE MEDIATION OF MEANING

The advertising industry is the repository for an unmatched collection of skills and knowledge accumulated and honed over almost a century. This "monopoly of knowledge" results from the unique position of the agencies in the marketplace. Media firms are experts in the programming and editorial matters that allow access to audiences. Producers of goods are experts in the design, formulation, movement, and marketing of commodities. Advertising agencies, on the other hand, are experts in coordinating the functions of these two areas: they specialize in mediated communication about selling. To be effective, the advertising industry must know both areas intimately enough to interpret the properties of each to the other, encouraging them to explore the limitless permutations of frameworks for consumer satisfaction.

We have already discussed the relationship between audience segments and market segments, and how the agencies have shifted the emphasis in importance toward the latter. In the final analysis, however, agencies have to use what the media marketplace offers at any one time and adapt their communication strategies accordingly.

For example, if an advertiser is interested in reaching adult males, almost certainly the best media buy is television sports programming. That decision will affect the nature of the advertising, for the agency will use those communication skills that best fit the medium. As Canadian creative executive Marty Myers explains,

> Different media work differently. Print is linear and it's a left-brain medium— it's linear, logical, rational, it goes a-b-c-d. Everything follows in sequence. If you have a long story to tell, if you have a success story, if you have facts, if you have news, the place to go, at least initially, if you need space to work in, is print. If you have a story that isn't a story, if you have to deal in clouds like perfumes and stuff (though that will work in magazines too with visuals

only), if you have an emotional story to tell, your best bet is probably the right-brain medium which is clearly television. It works a different way entirely. You don't have time to make a rational argument—you use a metaphor, something out of the other art forms. You do something out of music, out of film, out of drama—the really good creative people know a little bit about marketing and a lot about the arts. (Interview)

Good creative people know about selling and about communication, and they also know the limitations of each medium. Neither the media nor the client can duplicate such skills and knowledge, for they do not occupy the special vantage point that the agencies do.

The agency's intermediary role can be seen in changes such as the movement to shorter (thirty-second and, more recently, fifteen-second) television commercials. While advertisers like the lower price of the shorter spot, they want to get as much information, or as many "points," about their product as possible into the time for which they are paying so dearly. Agencies have to mediate this tension, based primarily on what they know about communication. As ad executive Denise Bruce says,

> Advertising can only do one thing in a thirty-second commercial. It can sell one thing about a product. Most advertisers think they can get the major benefit, the supplemental benefit, and more. If we try to jam them all in, it results in bad advertising. Advertising has to isolate the major benefit and promote it in a memorable, distinctive way and link it to the product. If it does that, it's achieved all it set out to do. (Interview)

The agencies are well positioned to manage the relations between access to audiences and the concern with selling goods, because at stake are essentially communications processes. Their expertise has been gained through practical experience within an evolving social and cultural context. Creative executive Brian Harrod explains,

> When they dropped from sixty to thirty seconds, TV suffered enormously. When it was sixty, we had time to have some fun, to amuse and intrigue—we forgot we're in showbiz, competing with Dallas and everything else. Sixty seconds allowed us to communicate a message, but made it easier to swallow and more enjoyable to look at. Now, with the thirty-second commercial, it's been much tougher, because once you've communicated what you have to communicate, you don't have much time to entertain. So TV has been a tough one. It took us a while to learn thirty seconds. At first we just condensed sixties. We used to tell a story with beginning, middle, and end. With thirty you have to just let it happen, and go more into visual tricks and try to intrigue, keep the product on the screen but keep you involved and excited. (Interview)

Remember also that, while the agencies have honed their skills through their experiences in making commercials, they are knowledgeable about programming as well, for until the beginning of the 1960s they were the major producers of sponsored shows.

The most important relationship affecting advertising content is the one between agency and client. Agencies are, after all, hired by clients, on whose behalf they presumably operate, and the client must give final approval to the options presented by the agency. Agencies naturally differ in how much they bend to accommodate the wishes of the client's representatives, but they tend to generate ideas with the prejudices of the client in mind. The result can be advertising that pleases one audience — the client — but that may not elicit the desired response in the target market.

Agencies have to please the client, but, for the sake of future accounts, they also have to ensure that their own reputations do not suffer. As one executive put it,

> We are judged by what goes up on the screen. If it's crappy, we look bad. The client does get what they want. You can't sell someone something they don't want. But if it doesn't work, you can't say: "We only did what you told us." That's not what they're paying us for. They're not paying us to tell them what they already know. (Shapiro 1981, 294)

Agencies are paid for their expertise in communication and there may be a good deal of anger, especially among creative people, when the client questions their professional judgment about the aesthetic aspects of their product. As one art director says, "To listen to the client in creative matters is death. We are the experts in that area. We listen to them in business matters, not creative" (Interview). Much of the tension during the creative process can be attributed to the ongoing evaluation by research. Ostensibly, the purpose of research is to evaluate the effectiveness of the advertising messages produced, but many people in the agencies say that its real purpose is to provide a rationale for decisions taken by representatives of the client company (they sometimes refer to it as "smokescreen" research):

> The truth is, much of that research is hocus-pocus. The reason most clients research advertising is not to find out if it's effective, but to conform to the system in their company, so if advertising doesn't work, they're off the hook. So they let the research make the decision and evade the responsibility. (Interview)

Not surprisingly, creative people are very antagonistic to the pressures that come from research. Many of them look back to the 1960s as the heyday of creative activity when research did not constrict creative possibilities. Advertising leaders such as Bill Bernbach, David Ogilvy, and Fairfax Cone are held in awe because of the stand they took on behalf of creativity. Their distrust of research came not from an inability to suffer criticism, but from a belief that research does not reveal much about how the consumer will actually perceive the ad. First, the sample of people who participate in the tests are not representative of the prospective consumers. Second, the tests measure the effects on the audience irrespective of context, setting, and the nature of perception:

> Where I come apart on some of this stuff is where they take a storyboard (you know it doesn't tell the story) and show it to a group of people and let them determine whether it should run or not—that is just plain stupid. The total effect of watching a piece of film in a theatre is one effect, on the TV it's another effect. If you get a piece of paper it's not the same. It's another phenomenon and you can't make the judgment. They do copy testing where they test word for word and phrase for phrase. The language doesn't work that way. You can't take a sentence and dismantle it. (Interview)

Third, testing measures only how well consumers can recall and identify aspects of a commercial, and this, according to creative people, says nothing about how effective that commercial is in moving people to buy. As David Banik of the Advertising Research Foundation says, "I've never seen scientific evidence linking high test scores with ultimate success in the marketplace. A lot of tests simply measure memorability. Does that have anything to do with sales persuasiveness? It might be true, but it hasn't been proven—not to me" (Schudson 1984, 82). The upshot of such pressure, however, is that ads are written to achieve test results rather than sales results.

The most strenuous objection to the intrusion of research into the creative process is that it simply does not work. There seems to be little connection between the amount of research resources expended and the effectiveness of ads as tools of "marketing communications." Brian Harrod remarks,

> I've seen research reach a zenith five years ago and it became impossible because it began to kill creative activity. Not focus groups but doing in-depth studies one-on-one with trained psychologists and eye camera where the eye is dilated—it was big money. And what happened was that time and again brave agencies and clients were not subjecting their ads to that and were beating the pants off the others. (Interview)

The one research technique that creative people deem useful is the least precise and predictive—the focus group. Almost everyone in the business agrees that the focus group is an invaluable tool that helps to generate ideas at the start of the construction process. Marty Myers comments: "We use it for input before we tackle the creative problem. Before we do, I like to go out and probe and do focus groups and interviews to find out what it is that the public appears to want, to feel what their state of mind is, how they're shopping, what they're doing" (Interview). The focus group is not a testing procedure, but rather a source of materials and ideas with which to work. Often phrases and words that participants come up with will be used in the actual copy. At the heart of the creative process is not just creative talent but an ability to reach people and, ultimately, an ability to understand people and their world. Without this, advertising easily could be just expressions of creative vanity, communication without end, art without purpose. Advertising can indeed be described as art with a purpose, namely, to make what happens in the marketplace interesting to consumers on a permanent basis. Advertising is neither exclusively selling nor exclusively communication—it is "marketing communication."

The relations—both external and internal—that the giant agencies who work on global campaigns have to mediate will become increasingly complex. Externally, for example, the advertising compaign will have to match up with the different ways in which company marketing and distribution structures are set up, and with the different ways in which brands are positioned in diverse markets. Internally, a new level of negotiation is added when local account executives and creative directors in offices around the world are included in the whole process. Appropriate corporate cultures will become important aspects of the situation for the mega-agencies.

CONCENTRATED COMMUNICATION

Thus far we have focused our attention on the construction process within the agency, but we have not discussed message production itself because for most national advertisers this activity is undertaken by other companies, not by the agency (albeit under the agency's supervision). At the production stage, the agency casts its net even more widely, drawing into its orbit production companies, studios, casting agencies, musicians, singers, and others. This part of the process involves the most painstaking attention to detail and execution, employing communication techniques and devices far superior to those used in the programming that surrounds it. (For a superb, blow-by-blow account of how a commercial is produced, see Michael Arlen's *Thirty Seconds* [1981].)

What, in this context, makes national advertising a form of "concentrated communication"? Paul Goodman remarked that the commercial form became the "only part of television at all which has fulfilled its potential," and Erik Barnouw (1978) thinks it should be regarded as "a new American art form." Awards are given annually within the industry for the best commercials, and there is a growing admiration for their aesthetic qualities among the population as a whole. Conversely, there is a growing despondency that network programming will never be able to raise itself from the depths of mediocrity to which it has sunk.

Why are many ads so good and all too many programs so bad? The basic answer can be found in the economic structures of commercial television. These involve a commodity—audiences' time—that is traded by both the networks and the producers of programs. The networks sell advertising time to agencies and producers fill the programming time so that audiences will watch. There are different purposes that are being fulfilled during the time under consideration, and different groups to whom it is being sold. If we look at the time periods in isolation, we can get a better understanding of why commercials and programs are so different.

When network executives decide their program schedules, what kinds of things concern them? What do they want the programs to do? The simple answer is that they want to get as many people to watch as possible—people looking at the set, paying attention to what is on. The more cheaply they can do this, the more money they make, because program costs must come from the revenue generated from advertisers. The creators of programs (and the networks and the buyers of these programs from independent producers) have no real interest in *communicating* a particular message, in making the audience think and react. They just want the audience to watch so that their time can be sold to advertisers.

Networks have no economic need for good quality programming that challenges and excites the audience. Simply attention-getting, as opposed to communicating interesting and thought-provoking material, is enough. The components of a set network formula are occasionally adjusted for particular programs, making commercial television a form of "recombinant culture" in which the same elements—sex, adventure, violence—are constantly rejuggled (Gitlin 1983).

Programs do not have to persuade viewers that they should watch television instead of doing something else. People do not turn on the television set to watch particular shows; they turn it on to watch television. Watching television is a habitual activity; regardless of what is being broadcast, the total television audience is remarkably stable. The networks know they can do little to affect the overall size of the total television audience. The challenge is only in making sure that people are watching your show and not somebody else's—as cheaply as possible.

Advertising time is a totally different story. To produce a half-hour of programming costs about $300,000, but the average cost for a thirty-second network commercial in 1984 was about $50,000, which represents $2 million for a half-hour of advertising time. A million-dollar commercial is no longer a rarity, and no expense is spared. What we see on the screen is the best possible performance and execution of the communications strategy. "Wretched excess" is the way one producer of commercials describes the process. The cinematography is state of the art; editing—coordinating visuals, voice, and music—is meticulously done to split-second timing.

The commercial, rather than the program, has become the focal point of the creative effort for three principal reasons. First, the basic purpose of the commercial is to *communicate* something, not just attract attention; it has to move us in some way, to make us think or react, to pull at our emotions, desires, and dreams, and ultimately to affect our behaviour after the time of viewing. This is much more difficult than simply attracting attention on permanent loan, so to speak. And since most ads are designed to be viewed more than once (unlike the programming), they have to be interesting enough to still engage the audience after multiple viewings.

Second, the severe time limit (usually thirty seconds) on the communicative act means that the ad must do its work quickly. Advertisers want to utilize every split second of their costly time. Commercial film editor Howie Lazarus notes,

> Nowadays, the basic new technique is your vignette commercial. In my opinion, it's a classic film approach—meaning that there's often no dialogue and the style emphasis is on the visual. The key thing to remember about the vignette commercials is that you can get so much more information into them. In fact, the vignettes more or less originated in response to the switch from 60 second to 30 second spots. They're a wonderful way to pack in information: all those scenes and emotions—cut, cut, cut. (in Arlen 1981, 180–82)

Third is the problem of "clutter" in the contemporary media, wherein the number of commercial messages—though not necessarily the time devoted to them—has multiplied in the past twenty years. One British executive was alarmed "that advertisers have allowed the editorial environment to become what it's become" (Interview). How can a particular ad stand out in the crowd of commercial messages broadcast together? The answer may also account for the fact that European advertising is generally regarded as artistically superior to North American advertising. An art director explains,

> The Europeans had no advertising for years. But when they did it was in the "magazine format"—that is, they would group all the commercials together. Each one would do something charming and then say the name of the product at the end. At that time the English agencies would get kids from North America to come over and teach them how to sell Tide—how to hit hard in selling. But as products reached the parity point there was the same need for charm here. While the Europeans had gone from the emotional thing into a use of the hard sell (but still with charm), very recently things have changed. We took some lessons from them. We in North America used to be conceited and think we knew it all but we learnt from them. TV was the reason, because they had been doing the magazine format with all the ads together and this was a later development here. They had 20 commercials altogether, so the question was how do you get them to remember you if you are #4? How to stand out and be memorable? If you adopt the hard sell approach the consumer might say, "Oh, who needs this, I'll go get a beer." In England and in Japan they learned to be subtle, entertaining, amusing. So

more emotion came to this country. We learnt from that. So you get attention
and interest and people remember the product. There's a great creative drive.
(Interview)

Such problems are compounded by the spread of the VCR and the remote
channel changer. Commercials have to be even better if they are not to be
"zapped" or "zipped" by the audience. Increasingly, they have to not
merely sell, but entertain.

Thus, it should not surprise us to discover that the agencies have
sought to employ the best talent they can find. They have gone not to the
producers of television programming, but to artists with experience in
filmmaking. The commercial has become an art form wherein communication, it would appear, has triumphed over crass selling.

> The medium is taken seriously enough to have attracted the interest of no less
> a talent than Richard Avedon, whose Brook Shields ads for Calvin Klein drew
> a great deal of attention a couple of years ago. And the latest batch of Avedon's
> Klein ads are perhaps more uninterested in actual advertising than any
> commercials ever before shown on American television. Technically they're
> fairly simple; in each, a young girl rambles on for thirty seconds, with the
> Calvin Klein logo briefly flashed about two thirds of the way through and in
> the final frame. But what's interesting about these ads is that they aspire to
> something like high art (Hirschberg 1983, 55)

Some directors have established themselves as experts in various commercial genres. Steve Horn (AT&T, Coca-Cola, General Electric, Kodak,
Miller) is the most sought-after director of ads that stress emotion and
feeling. Joe Sedelmaier is a master of offbeat comedy commercials (the
fast-talking Federal Express man, electrical applicances blowing up as
their warranties expire, disgruntled coffee drinkers hurling their coffee
makers out of the window). A host of other directors—Michael Cimino
(*The Deer Hunter*), Alan Parker (*Fame, Midnight Express*), Howard Zieff
(*Private Benjamin*), and Adrian Lyne (*Flashdance, Fatal Attraction*) flit
between movies and ads. Tony Scott, who directs modernist "Diet Pepsi"
ads and who also directed *The Hunger* and *Top Gun*, says: "I do thirty
seconds for the money and ninety minutes for the ego." His brother,
Ridley Scott, directed the innovative Chanel "Share the Fantasy" ads, as
well as such feature films as *Blade Runner* and *Alien*.

As the media environment becomes increasingly crowded, and as
communicating becomes more technically demanding, the producers of
commercials must search ever more widely and diligently for the best
talent they can find. Commercials must get attention and they must
communicate—quickly and in competition with countless other commercial messages. North American broadcasting today is an ironic scene:
the things people presumably want most—the shows—are produced as
cheaply as possible, just so that the screen will be filled and hold our
passive attention with its flickering images, while the things that people

often say they do not want—commercials—are produced with lavish care at great expense. Of course, it is important to point out that, while some ads may be the best things on television, other ads may be among the worst. Ads produced by local retailers and manufacturers for airing within their own home market, and even national ads that stress the "hard sell," are often viewed with great distaste by the television audience. Again, the quality of the final product is dependent, to a great extent, on the budgets available for production: the wider its market and the longer its running time, the higher the budget that is allocated for the production of an ad.

THE TWILIGHT OF ADVERTISING IN THE DEAL CULTURE?

The era described above may be ebbing to a close. In a 1988 article, Michael Gershman, director of a marketing company, writes that

> History will note that American advertising reached its watermark of influence from 1945 to 1985 . . . Not only is advertising now regarded as just another business in the United States; it is also a business in serious decline in terms of both profitability and influence within marketing circles and the larger business community . . . Three years of buyouts, mergers, mass firings, client conflicts, and shrinking revenues have removed much of the residual gloss from a world that was once synonymous with glamour. (1988, 23)

The major reason for this situation is the increasing importance of promotions to major advertisers—a shift that is itself related to a number of other real (and/or perceived) characteristics of the contemporary marketplace. We can attempt to understand these by again examining the changes taking place in the domain of clients, media, and agencies, and the reciprocal impacts of these changes on the overall situation.

The 1980s saw a movement by manufacturers to stress near-term business over long-term goals. The new emphasis took place in conjunction with mergers and takeovers of major manufacturers in "leveraged" situations (i.e., takeovers financed by borrowed money that the borrower must start to pay back immediately). In such a climate, immediate sales and profits are much more important than building long-term brand loyalty, and the best way to achieve instant results is through promotions—getting the product on prime supermarket shelves, and offering customers incentives (for example, coupons, premiums, sweepstakes, games, or bonus packs) to try the product. Unfortunately, image-based advertising is not good at getting people into stores with the express purpose of buying a particular product; its purpose is to build brand loyalty. As one media director put it: "Promotions destroy brand loyalty. Consumers have deal loyalty, not brand loyalty" (Interview). Consequently, by the end of the 1980s product managers were spending almost twice as much money on promotions as they were on advertising, which is one reason why agencies were starting to acquire promotions companies. We are no longer living simply in a consuming culture, but a more specific *deal culture*. In an age in which product parity has reached new heights, consumers are increasingly "waiting for the deal."

Another aspect of the deal culture is the proliferation of brands within one company. Gershman writes:

> Selling one product—a hamburger, for instance—lends itself to an advertising approach, because advertising can endow one product with a mystique. When R.J. Reynolds was selling only Camels, "I'd walk a mile for a Camel" was a great slogan, but now Reynolds has to market regular cigarettes, filters, recessed filters, longs, extra-longs, low-tars, ultra-low tars, and more. In such a marketplace, advertising can't do what it does best—convey images— because ad budgets can't handle the expense of advertising 20 or 30 brands." (1988, 29)

Similarly, while from 1947 to 1984 Procter and Gamble sold only one type of *Tide* laundry detergent, by 1989 there were four additional varieties; *Downy* fabric softener has added three different types since 1984. As brands proliferate (in 1989, there were 150 cereal brands that sold at least $1 million annually, compared to 84 in 1979), it becomes harder to differentiate within an increasingly crowded system, which is why promotions serve the manufacturer much better.

One possible consequence of the media clutter discussed in the previous section is that, because the overall environment is so "busy," individual messages are not as successful as they once were in building brand loyalty for one brand, especially as the fifteen-second spot becomes more predominant on television. Saatchi & Saatchi research director Penelope Queen comments: "People today have an acceptable brand 'set' rather than specific brand loyalties, particularly in categories like cereal, soda and cookies. The consumer is saying, 'That's the concept I want, and it looks like this package will fit that need'" (in Gershman 1988, 26). Consequently, the way a product is packaged has assumed a more prominent role in manufacturers' minds. Package design is also a threat to advertising's future development. Another way to break through the media clutter is through event marketing or tie-ins, in which a brand name is linked to a high-profile event (for example, in sports or film) or to another significant brand name (e.g., a Coke promotion at Little Caesar restaurants).

Finally, the changes that large companies went through in the 1980s may also have an impact upon the level of creativity exhibited in advertising. During this period of mergers, many commentators speculated about how the new giant bureaucratic structures would impact negatively upon the type of advertising produced. Greater sensitivity on the part of mega-companies to the pressure for efficiencies and financial savings will change the context within which creative work takes place. In the words of one media director: "Pressures have got down to the creative level because clients are not about to invest in a super production. They are looking to cut corners" (Interview). Additionally, much of advertising is now concentrated in promotions and events sponsorship, which inevitably produces a very stilted environment for creative advertising. Finally, during any period of change, when new corporate cultures and priorities have not been sufficiently identified, there is a certain loss of confidence and a tendency to play it safe and not take creative risks.

It is perhaps too early as yet to see the changes, if any, in the level of creativity in advertising. However, it is possible to anticipate that the new financial environment will, over time, change the resources that creative people have at their disposal. As one senior executive at a private company put it:

> In order for advertising to be continually effective, it has to enhance value. We have to understand the emotional and psychological needs of the consumers. That will cost money. Financial pressures may cut that first and this may lead to advertising that is more superficial and more clichéd. The knowledge isn't there; the training isn't there. It takes time in advertising agency cultures to think of creating ads in new ways. There will be very tangible differences in years to come. (Interview)

The American Association of Advertising Agencies reports that research as a percentage of total agency payroll expenditures—the largest area of decline—dropped by 2 percent between 1968 and 1988.

CONCLUSION

The modern advertising industry plays a special part in the social relations of modern society. By virtue of its presence in everyday life and of the economic dimensions of its activity, it appears to be an independent business institution, but it can be described more accurately as the point of intersection for the major institutional forces. The industry absorbs into itself information about the world of products, the world of media, the world of consumers, and the world of audiences. Perhaps no other institution in modern society reflects and holds within itself such complex relations.

Needless to say, its position and repository of skills and knowledge in persuasive communications do not vouchsafe the industry a scientific and all-powerful view of society and humanity that enables it to manipulate us at will. Yet we must clearly recognize that the advertising industry is one of the most important social, economic, and cultural institutions of our society because it is the intermediary through which so many currents of social change come together (see Figure 7.2). The direct influence of the advertising industry is by no means restricted to the marketing of products. In recent decades, it has also begun to act as negotiator for other institutional forces in the consumer culture. Some critics charge that the agencies have begun to spread their influence not only across the movement of commodities but also across the currents of ideas (through, for example, political advertising and advocacy advertising).

FIGURE 7.2
The Role of Advertising Agencies in the Twentieth Century

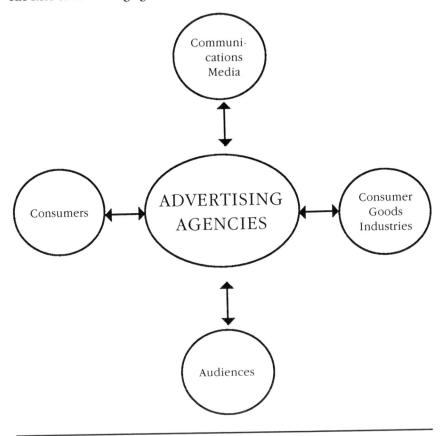

Modern advertising is important for the communicative power of the message forms it has devised, for the influence it exerts on other forms of cultural production, and for the ways in which it stratifies audiences in order to enhance its impact on the promotion of goods in everyday life. As an industry, advertising mediates between commodity production and cultural production; as a message form, it adopts, revises, and shapes other cultural message systems; most importantly, through research it appropriates the social structure of markets for goods and audiences for media, and recycles them as strategies targeted toward segments of the population. Thus, advertising is a communications activity through which social change is mediated—and wherein such change can be witnessed. This is not to say that advertising is the central determining factor of the consumer society; rather, we present it here as an indispensable interpretive key to understanding complex historical developments.

We focus on advertising, in large part, because as a communicative form it also seems to be an effective tool of socialization and persuasion. This, in turn, is tied to its institutional position, linking the major institutional forces of cultural and commodity production to the content and practice of discourse about commodities in the consumer culture.

Advertising is itself a "multiplexing" form that absorbs and fuses a variety of symbolic practices and discourses. The substance and images woven into advertising messages are appropriated and distilled from an unbounded range of cultural references. Advertising borrows its ideas, its language, and its visual representations from literature and design, from other media content and forms, from history and the future, and from its own experience; then it artfully recombines them around the theme of consumption. Through advertising, goods are knitted into the fabric of social life and cultural significance. The borrowed references are fused with products and returned to cultural discourse.

Advertising is also a message system about the performance characteristics and social meaning of goods. In everyday life, people talk about commodities—what they do and what they mean. Advertising uses consumer research to internalize this discourse and recycles it as the strategy, form, and content of advertisements.

Advertising has also become an accepted part of everyday life. Children sing jingles and dinner party guests talk about their favourite ads. The symbolic attributes of goods, as well as the characters, situations, imagery, and jokes of advertising discourse, are now ingredients of our cultural repertoire. Some spectacularly successful advertising campaigns (for example, the 1989 3-D Diet Coke ads that "premiered" on the Super Bowl telecast and the battery-driven rabbit that marched across other ads), themselves became media events and were reported as news.

Students of the history and development of the consumer culture are indebted to ads for the detailed records of cultural processes that they carry. In Part 3, we seek a method for examining those records and for reading in and through them the meaning of modern society's grand spectacle of people and products.

THE THEATRE OF CONSUMPTION

8

Two Approaches to the Study of Advertisements

Private companies who wish to know how the fortunes of specific products are, or might be, affected by the advertising lavished on their behalf have conducted many quantitative studies dealing with the effects of advertising on market behaviour, consumer choice, and social attitudes. Unfortunately for independent commentators who are interested primarily in advertising's more general social and cultural role in the modern world, most of these voluminous reports are kept confidential and are thus not a resource upon which they can draw.

Were this proprietary information available, our understanding of advertising would doubtless be greatly enhanced. However, its inaccessibility is not necessarily a damaging blow because, while the data normally assembled in such studies may be of great value to people whose happiness fluctuates with the movements of lines on sales charts, they are less germane to our own attempts to fathom the "systemic" penetration of our society and culture by advertising. Proprietary research necessarily is focused on very specific, pragmatic concerns, and so the data collected are fragmentary and bound by the impetus to discover either how to spark once more the interest of jaded consumers or how to enhance brand loyalty. Since these piecemeal studies are guided by such specific objectives, and although the researchers are usually well aware of what others are doing, the process as a whole certainly has no overall guidance and the patterns of their activities may become apparent only to those who observe them from a distance. Examining this immense amount of consumer research in detail, therefore, is likely to be of limited utility in understanding how advertising works its magic on the meaning of products in general, or for appreciating its powerful communications function. In other words, when we wish to study advertising as a system of social communication, the self-interested and conflicting actions of manufacturers become just one part of a larger totality.

The most fruitful direction for research is the analysis of the complete "set" of advertising messages themselves. Only this can give us a comprehensive perspective on advertising's cultural role. Academic researchers, therefore, have turned questions about the effects of advertising into questions about communication formats, messages, and meanings. By regarding the "texts" the advertising industry produces as a systematic expression of strategies and meanings, they have sought to uncover the commonalities in form and content and the points of departure occurring in this material over time that are not apparent at first glance—and that may never have been consciously intended by their creators. For such purposes, one must focus on messages themselves rather than on the reactions of consumers to them.

Two major methodologies have been employed in the study of advertising messages: semiology and content analysis. In this chapter, we evaluate their strengths and weaknesses in contributing to an understanding of advertising's place in modern society and culture. In the following chapter we describe our own approach, which attempts to combine the best features of the other two, and apply it to a sample of advertising material that spans the period from 1900 to the present. We then interpret this material against the background of the rise of mediated communication and the consumer culture.

SEMIOLOGY AND THE STUDY OF ADVERTISING

Semiology (or semiotics) is a method for examining textual material that emerged from linguistics and from literary and cultural analysis, rather than from the tradition of social science research. It can be used to study many kinds of social phenomena; anything in which meaning is thought to inhere can be investigated from this standpoint. The Swiss linguist Ferdinand De Saussure (1966), who was especially interested in the internal structures of linguistic systems, applied the term "semiology" to what he described as "the science of signs." From the outset, semiologists have concentrated on relationships among the parts of a message or communication system, for, they contend, it is only through the interaction of component parts that meaning is formed. The French theorist Roland Barthes (1973) was one of the first to study advertising from this perspective, applying semiotic tools to all aspects of popular culture, from Citroëns and wrestling matches to toys and soap powder commercials. Another precursor of the semiological study of advertising was the Canadian literary critic Marshall McLuhan. In *The Mechanical Bride* (1951), McLuhan anticipated much of the later interest in advertising from the perspective of its relationships to the media system and popular culture.

There are already many fine and detailed expositions of the methodology of semiology, for example, Barthes (1973), Guirand (1971), and Dyer (1982), and we need not duplicate them here. We shall confine ourselves to outlining the reasons why semiology is especially appropriate to the study of contemporary advertising and some of the basic concepts of the method (describing how, according to semiology, we derive meaning from advertising), and reviewing some of the major studies of advertising from this perspective.

The growing preponderance of visuals in ads has enhanced the ambiguity of meaning embedded in message structures. Earlier advertising usually states its message quite explicitly through the medium of written text (even if the most outrageous claims were made in the process), but starting in the mid-1920s visual representation became more common, and the relationship between text and visual image became complementary—that is, the text explained the visual. In the postwar period, and especially since the early 1960s, the functions of text moved away from explaining the visual and toward a more cryptic form, in which text appeared as a kind of "key" to the visual.

In all, the effect was to make the commercial message more ambiguous; a "reading" of it depended on relating elements in the ad's internal structure to each other, as well as drawing in references from the external world. "Decoding" what is happening in these more complicated message structures requires the use of a method—such as semiology—sensitive to these nuances. (Later we will return to these historical shifts in textual materials and imagery, and to the way consumers "read" them.)

Advertising design and content have also changed in tandem with the theory of market segmentation, which is rooted in the fragmentation of audiences and the specificity of messages. Daniel Pope (1982), as we have noted, dates the beginnings of this orientation in the 1920s. Market and audience research gives advertisers a vast amount of demographic and, later, "psychographic" data about the characteristics of the target audience. Advertising designed with this orientation in mind began to focus on the *benefits* accruing to the consumer in using the product, rather than on the characteristics of the product itself. This new emphasis led to an increase in narrative and dramatic forms that tell stories about consumers and their uses of products and a steady decline in the amount of textual information presented about products in national advertising campaigns. User-centred advertising draws upon the shared experiences, perceptions, and attitudes of the segmented audience, while product-centred advertising can rely only on product claims in its attempt to appeal to an undifferentiated mass market.

Advertising creator Tony Schwartz isolates the key point in this transition in his "resonance" theory of communication; at the core of advertising's purposes now is not the message itself as a communicator of meaning, but rather its *relationship* to the audience: "The meaning of our communication is what a listener or viewer *gets out* of his experience with the communicator's stimuli. The listener's or viewer's brain is an indispensable component of the total communication system. His life experiences, as well as his expectations of the stimuli he is receiving, interact with the communicator's output in determining the meaning of the communication" (Schwartz 1974, 25). The job of the advertiser is to know the world of the segmented audiences intimately, so that the stimuli created can evoke associations with whatever is "stored" in their memories and imaginations.

This means more than seeking to "reflect" the materials of everyday life. Advertising executive Jerry Goodis says: "Advertising doesn't always mirror how people are acting, but how they're dreaming. . . . In a sense, what we're doing is wrapping up your emotions and selling them back to you" (in Nelson 1983, 10).

Advertising indeed draws deeply from the predispositions, hopes, and concerns of its audiences, but it reformulates them to suit its own purposes, not reflecting meaning but rather *reconstituting* it. Looking at advertisements today is a bit like walking through a carnival hall of mirrors, where the elements of our ordinary lives are magnified and exaggerated but are still recognizable.

And this is why semiology is so appropriate, for it is about trying to answer some very basic questions concerning meaning: "How is meaning reconstituted both by advertisers and viewers of messages?" More simply: "How do ads work?" Semiology is the study of signs. Signs are things that have a meaning, that communicate messages to people. As such, almost anything can perform as a sign—an object, book, film, person, building, song, or ad. In other words, anything that has a meaning is a sign. Here we will confine our remarks to the advertisement as sign, and, more particularly, to the product in the ad. The question we wish to pose is: "How does the product come to have meaning?" This is not all advertising seeks to do, for it obviously seeks to give meaning to persons as well as to products, but the constitution of the meanings of persons in ads is part of the constitution of the meaning of products, and, in "strategic" terms, is subordinate. Even if one argues that advertising's most important social impact is on the way that people come to regard themselves, one must acknowledge that, from the standpoint of the advertisers, this takes second place behind the marketing of products.

Semiology originates in a discussion of signs, or more specifically, of a "system of signs." A sign within a system of meaning may be separated into two components: "the signifier" and "the signified." The signifier is the material vehicle of meaning; the signified actually "is" the meaning. The signifier is its "concrete" dimension; the signified is its "abstract" side. While we can separate the two for analytical purposes, in reality they are inseparable.

Roland Barthes gives the example of roses, which in most western cultures signify romantic or passionate love. The "meaning" of roses in our cultural setting is thus tied up with the idea of passion. In analytical terms, then, we have three elements in the communicative process: (1) the signifier—roses; (2) the signified—passion; (3) the sign—their unity as "passionified roses." One of semiology's most important points is the distinction between the signifier and the sign; they are not the same, although they appear to be the same. Nothing inherent in roses limits their meaning to passion alone. In another culture, or in another system of meaning, roses could signify something totally different, perhaps even the opposite of passion. The rose as signifier without the signified is empty of meaning. The rose as sign is full of meaning. In advertising, the creators of messages try to turn signifiers (goods), with which audiences may have little or no familiarity, into meaningful signs that, they hope, will prompt consumers to respond with appropriate behaviour.

Many aspects of our daily lives have a long and complex history within specific cultural processes, and it is often difficult to show how signs have arisen as meaningful constructions. For example, just how did roses come to have the meaning they do? It turns out to be easier to pose these questions about things that are explicitly designed to supply us with meanings, such as advertisements. Tony Schwartz identifies the explicit purpose of advertising as making products "resonate" with meaning for audiences. How, then, do ads communicate the meanings associated with products?

One of the best semiological analyses is Judith Williamson's *Decoding Advertisements* (1978). She uses ads from the French perfume manufacturer Chanel to illustrate her arguments. Her point of reference is seemingly a very simple ad: the face of a woman (the French fashion model/actress Catherine Deneuve) is shown with a picture of the product (a bottle of Chanel No. 5) in the corner of the image. To the question, What is the meaning of this ad? we might answer: It tells us that Chanel No. 5 is chic, sophisticated, and elegant; that by wearing it we would be adding something to our character which is the epitome of "Frenchness," specifically, glamour and flawless beauty.

Breaking this down in semiological terms, we have the signifier—the actual bottle of perfume; the signified—French chic, glamour, beauty, and sophistication (represented by Catherine Deneuve); their unity in the sign—"Chanel No. 5" *is* French chic, glamour, beauty, and sophistication.

Assuming that this is the meaning of the ad to us, the question becomes: How did we arrive at this conclusion? Nothing in the ad explicitly states this. The semiological approach, however, suggests that the meaning of an ad does not float on the surface just waiting to be internalized by the viewer, but is built up out of the ways that different signs are organized and related to each other, both within the ad and through external references to wider belief systems. More specifically, for advertising to create meaning, the reader or the viewer has to do some "work." Because the meaning is not lying there on the page, one has to make an effort to grasp it. There are three steps to the process.

First, the meaning of one sign is transferred to another. In Williamson's example, the meaning of "Catherine Deneuve" (herself a sign meaning French chic) is transferred to the product. No line of argument links the two, and the transferral depends on their juxtaposition within the structure of the ad. There are many ways this transfer can take place: between persons and objects as here; between social situations and objects; between objects and objects; and, finally, between feelings and objects.

Second, this transfer of significance is not completed within the ad: we must make the connection ourselves. For instance, nowhere is it stated that "Chanel No. 5" is like " Catherine Deneuve." This meaning does not exist until we complete the transfer. Beginning in the 1960s, advertisers started to see viewers explicitly as participants in the meaning-generation functions of ads. Marty Myers explains:

> Doyle Dane did things that other agencies said couldn't work. They worked because they treated people as if they had some brain and as though they had a sense of humour. They realized that people wouldn't mind a tickle, being challenged and being made to perform what the psychologists call closure— that is, give them "a" and "c" and they'll put the "b" in. Leave some holes in it. (Interview)

Williamson stresses that a sign is only capable of being transferred or of replacing something if it has a meaning in the first place for the reader or viewer. The transference requires our active participation: "There is a space, a gap left where the speaker should be; and one of the peculiar features of advertising is that we are drawn in to fill that gap, so that we become both listener and speaker, subject and object" (Williamson 1978, 13–14).

Meaning is not "received" in a unidirectional flow from elsewhere: the audience creates and re-creates it. It works not at us but through us. The ad is a mediator between creator and reader, standing at the confluence of the double symbolic process in the marketplace, where producers of goods attempt to construct one set of meanings, and where consumers use these meanings (along with meanings drawn from other sources) in the construction of their own lifestyles. This is the process of internal transference:

> We are given two signifiers and required to make a "signified" by exchanging them. The fact that we have to make this exchange, to do the linking work which is not *done* in the ad, but which is only made possible by its form, draws us into the transformational space between the units of the ad. Its meaning only exists in this space: the field of transaction; and it is here that we operate—we are this space. (Williamson 1978, 44)

Third, in order for the transfer to take place, the first object must already have a meaning to be transferred—it must already be significant to the audience. We must already know what Catherine Deneuve "stands for," what she means within the world of glamour, or there would be no significance to transfer.

In the same way, in Figure 8.1 we need to know the meaning of the persons and activities being represented and being transferred to the product. In this case the important value transfer is between the model, Margaux Hemingway, and the product. In the early 1970s, Hemingway was a fresh face in the world of fashion, representing a modern and flamboyant style. The transfers of meaning here work similarly to those just described, but their concrete value is different because Margaux Hemingway's meaning is "in opposition" to that of Catherine Deneuve. Even if we cannot identify the individual models in ads, however, we are usually able to deduce the reason for their presence by their "look," which indicates their position within the iconography of fashion.

Williamson calls these systems of meaning from which we draw the materials to complete the transfer "referent systems." They constitute the body of knowledge from which both advertisers and audiences draw their inspiration. In this context, mass-media advertising plays the role of mediator. If the audience is to "decode" the message adequately—that is, to make the transfer of meaning—advertisers have to tap the reservoirs of social and cultural knowledge maintained by audiences, and transform this material into the message ("encode" it), developing an appropriate format and shaping the content in order that the cycle of communication that runs from the audience's experiences and back again can be completed (Hall 1980).

In the era of market segmentation and the thirty- or fifteen-second commercial, this reliance on shared knowledge becomes even more important. The thirty-second ad allows little time to give information about anything. Advertisers pretty much have to use what already exists in the imaginations of the target audience:

> First, you work out who you are talking to—say men ages x to y, macho in attitude—demographic and psychographic information. We get this from research people and from the marketing people just digging around in the market. Then you know you are talking to these psychographics, attitudes about themselves—anything. I'll take anything I can get on that. The ideal target market is one person—tell me everything about them, their dreams, how they feel about the meals they eat, how they save, where they went to school. Tell me everything about them and I can sell them Hitler. So could you. But if we sold to one person it wouldn't be worthwhile so you have to find something that has a collective set of appeals. (Interview)

In the move from mass to segmented market, advertising strategy changed dramatically. Today, advertisers can draw upon the specialized

FIGURE 8.1
Referent Systems: Adrift in a sea of beautiful faces, the celebrity helps to fix the specific associations of the object.

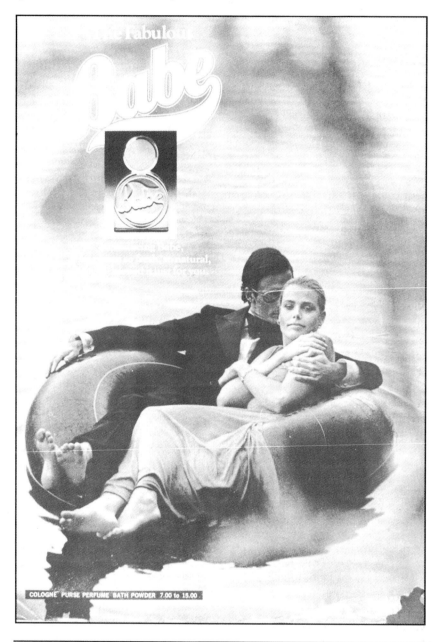

Source: Courtesy of Fabergé, Inc.

knowledge of fragmented audiences, so that the same product can be sold in different ways to different groups.

Codes

Since advertising works by appeal to "referent systems," it generates meaning through a process of connotation as well as denotation. Every message contains two levels of meaning: what it says explicitly on the surface and what it says implicitly below. In Figure 8.2, at the denotative (surface) level, the visuals tell us that "Sferoflex" eyewear is strong, reliable, and longlasting as actor and bodybuilder Lou Ferrigno attempts without success to break a pair of glasses. But at the connotative level, the ad tells us much more, for Lou Ferrigno is no ordinary bodybuilder: he played "The Incredible Hulk" in a popular TV series (alluded to in the text in the phrase "years of 'incredible' strength, comfort and beauty"). Ferrigno means more than just strength to his audience; he means extraordinary strength and this strength is transferred to the eyewear. At the same time, the positioning of the woman's hands and the pursing of her lips suggest the sexual attraction that Ferrigno and his strength carry.

At the connotative level, then, the ad implies that the use of "Sferoflex" glasses may make the wearer sexually attractive to women. Nowhere in the ad is this stated; we interpret it this way through internal and external transfers of significance. Moreover, this is not the only interpretation we could have made. If the same ad were viewed from a female rather than a male perspective, the eyewear could be connected to the beauty of the female model rather than to the strength of the male.

Connotation is a feature of all communication, not an invention of advertising. Propaganda relies heavily on it. Figure 8.3, from World War II, consists of two words and two symbols. At the denotative level, this message has almost no meaning: "I believe"—in what, who, or why is very unclear. At the connotative level, however, its message is unmistakable and powerful. The two symbols are familiar and powerful representations of two different systems of belief. The cross superimposed on the swastika is a strong statement that "I believe" the good of Christianity can triumph over the evil of fascism.

The connotative reading of the place of objects in particular had to be learned over time. While it seems from this example (and generally from the study of twentieth-century progaganda) that the connotative level has always been an important element in the reading of public statements, its transfer to product-based messages was not a natural one. Advertising had to teach an evolving consumer culture not just to enjoy visual stimuli, but to integrate visual and textual material, using goods as the linking mechanism to achieve an internal transfer of signficance. From about 1925 to 1945, the text duplicated the visual and told the des: Advertising muscles into the reservoir of popular cultural forms, often borrowing meaning from other idioms.

FIGURE 8.3
Visual Symbols: Imagery relies heavily on the implicit connotations associated with established social referents.

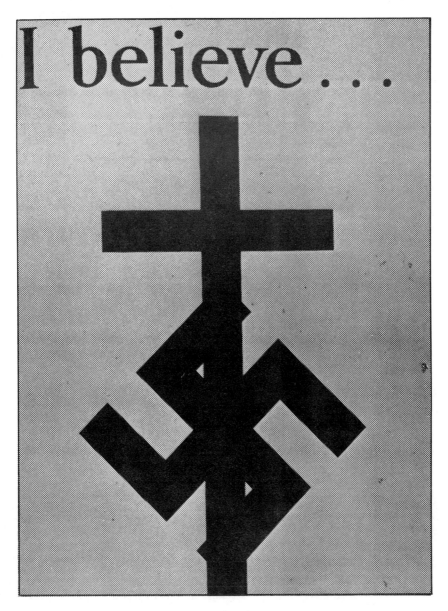

audience that what they saw resulted from using the product. In contemporary advertising, this ability to transfer is assumed because the audience is "advertising educated." For example, compare Figure 8.4, where the visual is described and its link with the product is made, to Figure 8.5.

Semiology highlights the way that we ourselves take part in the creation of meaning in messages, suggesting that we are not mere bystanders in the advertising process, but participants in creating a code that unites the designer and reader. If we are not adequately aware of the relevant referent system we will not be able to decode the message. As audiences are fragmented into smaller and smaller market segments, the operative codes for each target group become more specialized. Advertisers like working with narrowly defined groups rather than with diffuse, broadly based general audiences. The more narrowly one can define an audience and the more specialized the knowledge one can draw from, the more certain one can be of speaking to people in a language they will respond to.

While the production of messages and their reception by the audience may not always be perfectly symmetrical processes, each is incomplete without the other. If there is no common understanding, there can be no communication:

> I see advertising as such an imperfect way of selling things—there are so many failures. It's a coding process. I have a product to sell and an idea. I decide on something succinct to get your attention, then I encode it and put it into the medium. You see it and then decode it. I hope you get the same idea from the process that I started with. I hope you will make the choice and that the idea I as the advertising person had of what would cause you to buy that product has merit. (Interview)

While "there is no intelligible discourse without the operation of a code" (Hall 1980, 131), there is never just one code. In daily life, we use a great variety and multiplicity of codes: product codes, social codes, cultural codes, personal codes, and so forth. In Figure 8.6, we can see the operation of a subcultural code (sport). We must know why the names Jim Thorpe, Bob Mathias, and Rafer Johnson signify versatility. Although it is vaguely alluded to in the text, to obtain a "full" reading of the ad we have to know that these three are linked with the Olympic decathlon, which is made up of ten very different athletic activities. Without the information that they are all former Olympic champions of the decathlon, the transfers of significance are much diminished. This ad appeared in *Life's* special issue on the 1984 Olympics, and thus was intended for a specialized audience segment.

In Figure 8.7, taken from *Vogue*, one has to know that, in a certain cultural context, pickles and ice cream are conventionally associated with pregnancy in order for the opening, "As your family grows," to make

FIGURE 8.4
In older ads, text guided the interpretation of visual imagery, connecting it
with product use.

Source: Courtesy of Jergens Canada Inc.

FIGURE 8.5
The more cryptic language of contemporary ads is dependent upon the
audience's familiarity with visual decoding.

Source: Courtesy of Beecham Cosmetics Inc.

FIGURE 8.6

Subcultural Codes: Some ads rely on "skilled" knowledge of specialized domains of social life; here the athletes listed are all decathletes.

Versatility: To the names of Jim Thorpe, Bob Mathias and Rafer Johnson, add the name Plymouth Voyager.

Athletes run fast. Some run far. They can carry heavy objects over great distances. A few have the surpassing versatility to succeed at several disciplines.

Plymouth Voyager has that versatility. That's why it's called the "Magic Wagon." With an option, Voyager can seat up to seven in quiet sedan-like comfort. Or it can offer up to 125 cubic feet of carrying space.

Voyager is three feet shorter outside than a big station wagon, yet inside it has very nearly as much usable space. Front-wheel drive makes Voyager as easy to garage, handle like a car, yet as versatile as a wagon.

Now that's versatility. Or is Magic?

Source: Courtesy of Chrysler Canada Ltd.

FIGURE 8.7
Folkloric Codes: Advertising draws upon popular cultural knowledge, such as that surrounding pregnancy.

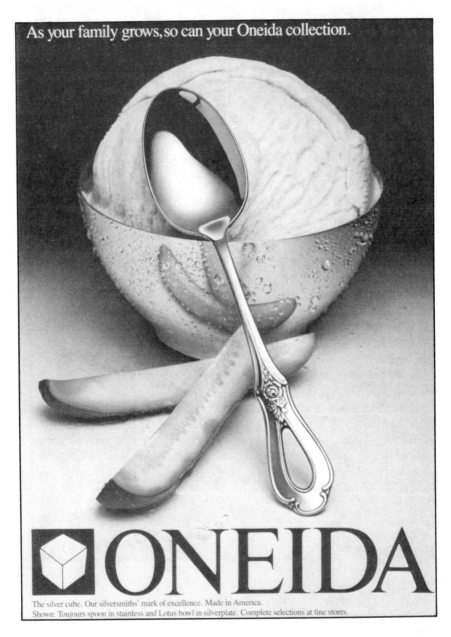

Source: Courtesy of Oneida Canada Ltd.

sense; the implicit reference has a much higher degree of relevance for a female audience. Similarly, in 1984 two ads appeared in different magazines for the cigarette brand Vantage. The one in the women's fashion magazine *Bazaar* featured an attractive woman holding a cigarette and leaning on a roll of fabric draped over a mannequin in an experimental dress design. The caption read, "Vantage. The taste of success." Clearly, this was supposed to represent a successful fashion designer. The other ad appeared in the male-oriented magazine *Sports Illustrated* and featured a young man dressed neatly in leisure clothes, holding a cigarette and leaning on the partly finished hull of the boat he is building. Although selling the same product, the two ads make reference to different notions of success and to divergent states of satisfaction or modes of desire.

In many semiological analyses, the argument becomes weak at this point. While the notion of code is insightful and imaginative in its conceptual outline, the applications to specific cases too often lapse into vague generalities. For instance, Judith Williamson's *Decoding Advertisements* starts promisingly by dissecting the codes of fashion that embrace both Catherine Deneuve and Margaux Hemingway as models yet differentiate each from the other. Later on, however, when the content of these "referent systems" is presented, her discussion abandons the sensual codes of the fashion world for the more abstract and "deeper" codes of ancient cultural traditions. These deeper codes are explained in terms of complex anthropological notions, fashioned from the realm of magic and alchemy and from broad sweeps of time, narrative, and history. Doubtless, Williamson's purpose here is to show how ads divorce these deeper sources of life and culture from the material and historical context that makes them truly meaningful, so that we are left with a hollow notion of things such as "nature" and "history." Such analysis and criticism is not incorrect, but it is just too broad. All of modern culture crawls with references to archaic impulses concerning the animals we love or fear, the idiosyncrasies of dining and dressing, sex roles, puberty and adolescence, marriage and courtship, power and domination. And most of modern culture remains rooted in the old oppositions: good and evil, sacred and profane, life and death. Certainly, one finds all this ancient baggage dumped helter-skelter into advertisements; but one finds it just about everywhere else, too. Although it is fascinating to unpack it, doing so does not tell one all that much about advertising.

Varda Leymore's *Hidden Myth* (1975) also seeks to transpose the notion of code into culture. Leymore tries to study modern advertising using the same type of structural analysis that anthropologists use to study the systems of myth in primitive societies. The codes of advertising are the same as the codes of myth, and reveal the "essential underlying unity of the symbolic function of the mind." In advertising are found the universal problems of life (good and evil, life and death, happiness and misery), as well as their promised resolution. Advertising is an anxiety-reducing institution, serving a function assigned to other institutions in pre-modern societies. Here, too, the approach is not so much wrong-headed as meagre in results. The rangefinder in the analytical lens is set to infinity, yielding a lack of resolution in the images.

As a method for the study of advertising, semiology suffers from a number of related weaknesses. First, it is heavily dependent upon the skill of the individual analyst. In the hands of someone like Roland Barthes or Judith Williamson, it is a creative tool that allows one to reach the deeper levels of meaning-construction in ads. A less skilful practitioner, however, can do little more than state the obvious in a complex and often pretentious manner. As a result, in these types of studies there is little chance to establish consistency or reliability—that is, a sufficient level of agreement among analysts on what is found in a message.

Second, because the semiological approach stresses individual readings of messages, it does not lend itself to quantification of results; it is impossible to base an overall sense of constructed meanings on the examination of a large number of messages. What insights may be extracted from this approach must remain impressionistic.

Third, semiology cannot be applied with equal success to all kinds of ads. For example, Williamson does not take a random sample of ads and then apply the semiological method to them, but seems to choose ads specifically to illustrate her points. Because such a procedure courts the danger of self-confirming results, the conclusions should, strictly speaking, be confined to those instances alone and not generalized to the entire range of advertising.

The Ritual of Gender Subordination

Notwithstanding its shortcomings, semiology has real strengths, above all its capacity to dissect and closely examine a cultural code, and its sensitivity to the nuances and oblique references in cultural systems.

In *Gender Advertisements* (1979), Erving Goffman points out that advertisements, considered as "pictures," are not viewed as unnatural and peculiar. This taken-for-granted aspect of advertising fascinates Goffman, for he believes that a close inspection of ads soon reveals much that is peculiar in their form and content. He turns his attention to gender representations—how males and females are shown—and the way in which the audience is expected to construct "gender meaning" from what appears in advertisements.

Goffman's key operative concept is "ceremony"—the actions or events that structure the meaning of social life. Ceremony, "display," and "ritual action" are codes that enable us to read social behaviour. Just as goods make "visible and stable the categories of culture" (Douglas and Isherwood 1978, 61), so, too, do ritual actions—the order in which one dons articles of clothing, the motions used in lighting a cigarette, the customary cocktail upon arriving home from work, the routes taken in journeys—give stability to daily life.

All such actions convey messages about people, including how they display their gender. Gender, of course, is one of the most important forms of codified behaviour in all societies, and every culture has accepted "routine" forms for communicating gender identity. A culture's social norms indicate how men and women are supposed to look, act, and relate to each other in a wide variety of social situations; the resultant ritualized behaviour "anchors" expectations, rewards, and punishments and stabilizes social intercourse. Not that ritual behaviour must always be taken seriously. Much of it is purely for the sake of keeping up appearances, and everybody knows it; therefore, it takes on the aura of a game in which the rules are arbitrary inventions designed expressly for creating and facilitating social interactions.

What is the origin of these gender displays? Goffman offers an intriguing answer. Rather than looking to our biological history and instinctual behaviour, as others have done, he suggests an answer based on a specific cultural relationship within the family—that of parent and child. In their customary dealings with others, Goffman says, men attempt to coerce females and subordinate males, and to create social distance from them by "application of the parent-child complex." In ritualistic terms, men regard females as equivalent to subordinate males and both as equivalent to children.

Goffman claims that we view advertisements in much the way that we view strangers in everyday life. During the course of each day, most of us see many people with whom we have no personal contact. To make sense of this world, we create, in effect, a "truncated" view of reality in which we lump things into broad general categories because we have no knowledge of their specific details. We view the representations of advertising in much the same manner, because advertising presents a world similar to the one that "a stranger to everyone around him really lives in. The realm is full of meaningful viewings of others, but each view is truncated and abstract" (Goffman 1979, 23).

A predominant theme in advertisements is an abstract representation of gender displays. Gender is "one of the most deeply seated traits of man. . . femininity and masculinity are in a sense the prototypes of essential expression—something that can be conveyed fleetingly in any social situation and yet something that strikes at the most basic characteristic of the individual" (Goffman 1979, 7). This is why gender is such a prominent feature in ads. Ads have to communicate quickly, at a glance (as in the world of strangers), and they require the participation of the audience to construct meaning. Therefore, advertisers are predisposed to rely on the repertoires of daily life for their materials. What better source to draw upon than an area of social behaviour in which ritual gestures are instantly recognizable, and which touches the very core of our definition as human beings?

In synthesizing these points, Goffman finds that advertisements are highly ritualized versions of the parent–child relationship, with women treated largely as children. For example, women's hands are usually portrayed just caressing or barely touching an object, as though they were not in full control of it, whereas men's hands are shown strongly grasping and manipulating objects (see Figure 8.8).

Persons on beds and floors are obviously positioned lower than those sitting or standing. People lying down are also in a poor position to defend themselves and thus are at the mercy of others. Lying down is also, of course, a "conventionalized expression of sexual availability." Goffman's sample of ads shows women and children on beds and floors much more than men are. In addition, he contends, women are shown "drifting away" mentally while under the physical "protection" of a male, as if his strength and alertness were enough for two. Women are also shown in a childish finger-to-mouth pose. Further, when men and women are shown in physical contact, the woman "snuggles" into the man in the same way that children solicit protection and comfort from their mothers. Goffman asks what such portrayals say about the relative social positions of men and women, and he highlights the question by suggesting that we try to imagine a reversal in the positions of the male and female models.

Ads are not merely accidental portrayals of these roles; they are deliberately posed creations. But why, then, do ads not look strange to us? Goffman maintains there is a strong relationship between advertisements and reality, or at least between advertisements and ritual displays. Advertisers do not create the reality of their world out of nothing—for the most part, they draw upon the same ritual resources as all of us and for the same end: to ensure that their "displays" are "read" in the correct way. "If anything, advertisers conventionalize our conventions, stylize what is already a stylization, make frivolous use of what is already something considerably cut off from contextual controls. Their hype is hyper-ritualization" (Goffman 1979, 84).

This does not mean that ads merely reflect reality. Although they draw their materials from everyday life, they select them carefully; much is included, but also much is omitted. By choosing only some things and by reintegrating them into the meaning system of advertising, ads *create new meanings.* This is Williamson's point as well. Thus, advertising enters into the routines of everyday life and produces meanings and categories that are not found elsewhere.

FIGURE 8.8
Gender Codes: Visual connotations of interpersonal relations are so familiar that the whole spectrum of gender relations can be called forth by the representation of hands.

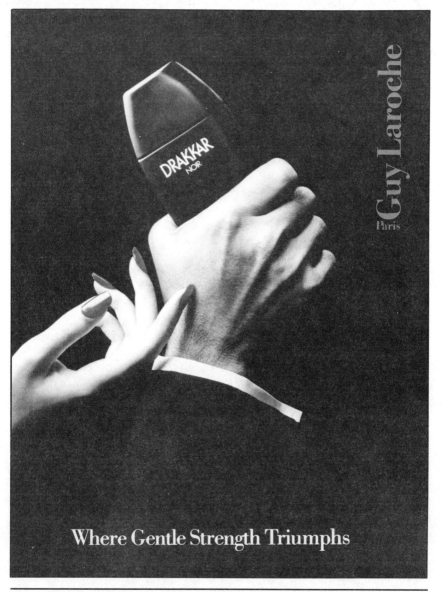

Goffman shows what the semiological approach can do in good hands. He forces us to reconsider the relationship between advertising and reality. He also uncovers the assumptions underlying the interpretive codes buried in advertisements, and the way advertising acts as an accomplice in perpetuating regressive forms of social relations. Ruled by its overriding imperative to communicate quickly, advertising first raids the ceremonial practices in our daily existence for its material, and then returns them to us in exaggerated forms, accentuating many of their least attractive features.

CONTENT ANALYSIS

The weaknesses of semiology as a method of studying advertising messages can be largely overcome by using content analysis, which is derived from a social science tradition rather than from linguistics and literary criticism. The issues of reliability, the size of the data base, and generalization from a sample to a larger universe are specifically taken into account in the content analysis design.

The unit for analysis in both methods is identical—the single ad. Semiology can admittedly do a better job on the single ad in isolation, because it is explicitly concerned with the "movement" of meaning within the text and between the text and the outside world. Content analysis can do little more than "unpack" the surface meaning of an ad in a rather obvious way; its strength stems from its ability to relate this information to the sample as a whole in a rigorous manner, and to detect patterns of similarities and differences.

"Content analysis is a research technique for the objective, systematic and quantitative description of the manifest content of communication" (Berelson 1952, 15). Four points in this classic definition require expansion.

First, "objective description" implies that there should be an acceptable level of agreement among different analysts about how to interpret the materials in question. Different researchers working with the same data, in other words, should arrive independently at the same descriptive classifications (or at least be within allowable parameters for variations). In part, content analysis attempts to deal with the variations that inevitably appear when observations by various researchers are compared by controlling the context within which those observations take place. Thus, "objectivity" refers not only to the interpretation but also to the control of observations.

Second, "systematic description" means that the same set of criteria should be applied to all the data under examination. The semiologist goes looking for descriptive categories within the material under examination itself, but the content analyst arrives at the data fully armed with the descriptive categories to be used, and can add no others later. This provides a basis for comparison and sorting within a data set. Content analysis is also systematic in that this data set is a preselected sample of ads, chosen by recognized randomizing procedures, rather than by picking out "ideal types" that best display the characteristics the researcher regards as being of special significance.

Third, the descriptive categories employed in content analysis can be tied to specific quantitative procedures, permitting a degree of precision in measurement. The semiologist may hazard a guess about the relative preponderance of certain imagery in advertising, as in "women are often shown mentally drifting from the scene," but the content analyst is able to make more definite statements: "In 82 percent of ads sampled, women were coded as exhibiting the characteristic 'mentally drifting from the scene.' " (Of course, the significance of this measurement can only be interpreted within the validity of the overall theoretical framework.)

Fourth, perhaps the most important point is that content analysis deliberately restricts itself to measuring the manifest or "surface" content of the message under study, for the simple reason that only in this respect can different investigators usually reach acceptable levels of agreement.

> The requirement of objectivity stipulates that only those symbols and combinations of symbols actually appearing in the message be recorded. In other words, at the *coding* stage of research, the stage at which specified words, themes, and the like are located in the text and placed into categories, one is limited to recording only those items which actually appear in the document. (Holsti 1969, 12)

There should be no "reading between the lines"; ideally, the account should be limited to what is apparent to everyone.

With these four points in mind, we shall review in detail the various elements of content analysis.

Theory

Although content analysis is considered an empirical approach, its starting point must always be theoretical. Just as in other scientific routines, the first step is to decide what to study; content analysis can only measure what one deems important to measure. The particular perspective from which one approaches the study of advertising or any other form of communication will generate the kinds of questions one asks.

For example, let us assume we are interested in the role advertising plays in gender socialization. On the basis of existing knowledge, we take as our starting point the idea that gender identity is not "given" by nature, but that males and females learn to behave differently through participation in social rituals. An important forum for learning gender identity in modern society is media presentations of sex role models, which are especially prominent in advertisements. The gender differences displayed in ads can be measured along many subsidiary dimensions; one that is easy to observe is occupational roles. Having adopted our theoretical perspective and arrived at this focal point for our research efforts, we are ready to design the study itself, from which we may derive some specific dimensions of interest and study. The concept we start with is systematic divergence in the presentation of occupational roles for males and females in advertising.

Constructing Categories

The next step is to break the concept down so that we have a working tool for the detailed study of particular advertisements. (Sometimes the term "operationalization" is used to describe how a concept is turned into working tools for empirical research by "splitting it up" into representative categories.) Occupational roles in advertising can be broken down in a number of ways. For our study, we might use the categories of occupational roles for females devised by J. Dominick and G. Rauch in their 1974 study of television commercials: (1) housewife/mother; (2) stewardess; (3) model; (4) celebrity/singer/dancer; (5) cook/maid/ servant; (6) secretary/clerical; (7) businesswoman; (8) teacher; (9) other (Dominick and Rauch 1974).

Two factors are of prime importance. First, we have to ensure that the categories we construct to measure the dimensions of the concept are exhaustive; that is, they must cover all the dimensions relevant to the concept that exist in the material under study. Often the difficulties encountered at this point are overcome by creating the category of "other" into which all problematic cases are fitted. Second, the categories must be mutually exclusive; that is, any occurrence should fit into only one category. For example, if we are trying to measure the racial/ ethnic typologies of characters appearing in commercials, and our categories are (1) Black, (2) European, (3) Caucasian, and (4) American, we will not get useful results.

Constructing categories is the most critical and time-consuming stage of content analysis, because in a very real sense the entire success of the enterprise depends on the coherence and appropriateness of the categories. Therefore, it is a good idea to pre-test the categories on a small sample of material and revise them, if necessary, to ensure that no major unexpected occurrences will complicate the coding stage later. We should then be confident that the categories adequately reflect the concerns inherent in our theoretical starting point, and that they fully tap the range of differentiations within our data set. The complete set of pretested categories is incorporated into a coding protocol, which tells the researchers what to look for in the material under investigation.

The refining and redefinition of categories at this preliminary stage also gives us the opportunity to guarantee the reliability of the coding protocol, that is, to check that the results will not be skewed by idiosyncratic readings. The usual procedure here is to compare the codings of one person with those of others, ensuring measures of consistency that will fall within certain accepted parameters.

Sampling

Now that we have developed our categories and tested the coding protocol, we must decide upon the "universe" that we want to study. We may be interested in the presentations of male and female roles in magazine ads from 1900 to 1984; if so, our universe will be "magazine ads from 1900 to 1984." Or we may be interested only in gender role presentations in magazines directed at a female audience in the year 1982. The universe would then be "magazines targeted for females in 1982." Defining the universe under analysis is important, because the generalizations we make on the basis of the study are applicable only to things within that specific universe.

Even when we have defined our universe, we will almost certainly not be able to examine every unit within it. For example, if we were interested in looking at role portrayals of men and women in prime-time television commercials over a span of one year, we would calculate the universe as follows: Prime time is 8:00 to 11:00 every evening, so the number of hours under study would be $3 \times 365 = 1,095$ hours for one network; on average at least twelve ads are shown every hour on network television, so our universe of ads for one year of prime-time television on one network would be $12 \times 1,095 = 13,140$.

It is unlikely that anyone would have the time, resources, and patience to analyze over 13,000 ads. Social scientists have devised sampling tables to help us select some fraction of our universe for actual study that will still let us have confidence in the generalizations we make about the whole. By using sampling tables, we can choose a smaller number of the items in the universe for actual study. In our example, 220 ads taken from the relevant time periods would safisfy the accepted conventions for sampling and reliability.

Coding

With a sample of the universe under consideration selected as our data base, we are in a position to start the actual analysis by applying the coding protocol to the ads in our sample. This can be done in a number of different ways in order to come up with data in a quantified form.

The most common is for the coder or coders to assign whatever is being measured to one of the categories that have been constructed. Theoretically, in our study of role presentations, the coder would assign the primary female character in each ad to *one* occupational category. If the categories have been well chosen, each applicable female character should fit into one of the existing categories. In practice, it is not this simple; many ads may have more than one primary female character. If we found this in a significant portion of our sample, we might want to adjust for it with multiple codings—a primary and secondary coding for the same set of categories. In this way, we can start to measure subsidiary themes in the data as well.

In some situations, we simply cannot choose one from a number of categories. For instance, to specify the racial types of people shown in ads in which more than one person or racial type appears, we would devise categories such as Black, Caucasian, Asian, Native Indian, Oriental, and so forth, and code each as either "absent" or "present." Here each category is treated as a separate variable that itself has two subcomponents (absent/present).

These two methods are coding at a "nominal" level of measurement, in that the categories are not ordered in any kind of way and no level of importance is attached to how they are constructed (they are just different from each other). In other situations, however, we may be more concerned with the *strength* of an item's presence within an ad (that is, its relative importance compared with other features), rather than just its appearance. In such cases, we can switch to an "ordinal" level of measurement. For example, we might be interested in the relative prominence of various themes—thriftiness, reliability, efficiency, patriotism— in automobile ads. To ascertain the strength of each theme, we could use a scale from 0 to 5, where 0 stands for "very weak" and 5 for "very strong." Patriotism used as a major selling point ("Buy an American-built car and support America") might warrant a 5 on the scale; used as a minor one ("an American tradition for over fifty years"), it might rate a 2. While this method yields a more precise measure of the presence of items in an ad, it has a major drawback in that it is difficult to achieve a high degree of reliability among different coders because the judgments are more subjective; this more interpretive task necessitates training sessions for groups of coders, in order to attain acceptable levels of intercoder reliability.

Analysis and Interpretation of Data

Depending on the size and complexity of the data set, the coding results may be analyzed by hand or run through computer routines. The researcher may then compare the numerical counts of the various categories under consideration; the process of giving statistical precision to unsystematic perceptions can be a very useful guideline for supporting hunches based on simple impressions.

Content analysis also allows the data to be reorganized along some different dimensions, especially if the data have been entered into a computer. We might have been coding each ad for many different things at the same time: specifying gender, occupations, and racial types, for example, or the type of television show or magazine the ad appeared in, the type of product it advertised and its price range, other themes present, and so forth. Then, by cross-tabulating two or more of the variables, we start to see significant differentiations and patterns within the data. For example, we can tell whether different types of magazines consistently portray male and female roles in divergent ways.

The main purpose of this final stage should be to shed some light on the theoretical starting point of the project, which really frames and guides the entire process. The extent to which the subsequent procedures address this issue directly, enabling us to understand it better, is the measure of the success or failure of any exercise in content analysis.

Strengths and Weaknesses of Content Analysis

The great strength of content analysis for the study of advertisements is its ability to supply some objective answers to the question, "What is going on in these ads?" In this context, the term "objective" implies no more than "satisfactory intercoder reliability." It allows us to treat qualitative data in quantitative terms, thus helping ground our analysis of images and words in something more than individual and impressionistic interpretation. When dealing with large amounts of data, patterns that otherwise are difficult or impossible to detect often show up in content analysis procedures.

However, content analysis has been dismissed by many writers as being totally inadequate for the measurement of meaning. They claim that meaning cannot be captured when communication is broken down into discrete categories of form and content, for meaning is dependent upon the place of any particular item within an entire system of language and image. Isolating any one element alters the meaning not only of that element itself, but also the meaning of the whole structure.

Colin Sumner maintains that content analysis puts too much emphasis on the "repeatability" of signs (that is, the number of times they occur), and too little on their significance for the audience. No matter how often something appears in the message system, if the reader or viewer cannot understand it, then the repetition is irrelevant: "It is not the significance of repetition that is important but the repetition of significance." Because content analysis does not pose questions about the meaning of items within a message, the repetitions it detects have no understandable context: "The absence of a theory of signs, signification and significance renders content analysis absurd because its key concept is left unsupported and that concept gives it no knowledge of its avowed object, the content!" (Sumner 1979, 69)

Sumner's point is that content analysis can say nothing about the audience's interpretation of the message because it has no theory of signification. But this is not necessarily a weakness, as long as one does not try to use it to demonstrate the effect on the audience. For, while content analysis cannot tell us anything about how audiences may be "reading" messages, it can tell us a good deal about what went into the construction of those messages. However, we also know that advertisers are on very familiar terms with their audiences, and that they expend a great deal of time and effort in learning how audiences decode messages. On this basis, we can say with some assurance that most aspects of modern advertising are meaningful to their intended audiences.

The real weakness in content analysis, especially for the study of advertising, lies in its restricted range of application. As we have seen, it can deal only with manifest content, that is, the surface or denotative level of messages. Modern advertising, especially in the age of market segmentation, works at important connotative levels of communication with multiple levels of meaning. Most ads today have a latent meaning that we are asked to "fill in" and thus participate in completing the message.

9

The Structure of Advertisements

We have examined two quite different methodologies that have been applied to the study of advertising. One is very interpretive, relying heavily on the skills of individual researchers, and asking primarily how meaning is constructed at different levels in a communicative act. The other is more systematic, primarily concerned with the manifest content of messages and usually leading to results that can be expressed in quantitative measurements. Researchers almost always choose one or the other approach, for they are regarded as incompatible.

This is unfortunate, for both offer valuable insights into advertisements. Can we, then, combine the strengths of the two approaches in a "middle-range" methodology? Can a method sensitive to the different, layered levels of meaning in advertising—considered as a text designed to be read by people in specific historical and cultural contexts—be combined with the more rigorous and systematic strategies of communication research? We think so.

A COMBINED SEMIOLOGICAL/CONTENT ANALYSIS APPROACH

We are firmly convinced that whatever methodology is adopted for the study of advertising must be rigorous and systematic while also being sensitive to the multiple levels of meaning and the multiple codes that ads employ. In other words, our "middle-range" option must try to combine both qualitative and quantitative strategies. It must devise categories that are reliable, exhaustive, and mutually exclusive, and at the same time take on more than just the surface level of messages.

As discussed in Chapter 8, "code" is one of the most important concepts in semiology. In discussing the attempts of Judith Williamson and Varda Leymore to specify the codes used by advertisers, we expressed dissatisfaction with the limited results the semiological approach alone obtains—a richness of detail with respect to only a few "ideal types" of ads. The method we propose offers a way to specify and measure quantitatively the different elements that make up the advertisers' codes as they are targeted to particular audience segments. If, indeed, advertisers do draw upon the frameworks of knowledge and expectations developed by their audiences, then advertisements directed at segmented audiences should reflect this differentiated appropriation.

One of the studies on which this book is based (Jhally 1984) was able to represent quite concretely the differentiated codes used by advertisers in their messages directed at male and female audiences. The data base for the study was television commercials broadcast during sports programming (male audience) and prime-time programming (regarded by advertisers as a female audience); one thousand network commercials were chosen as the sample (five hundred for each audience).

The results showed significant differences between the representation of persons in ads directed at the two audience segments, indicated by the gender of the consumer (the person buying or using the product) portrayed in them. In primetime ads, consumers were depicted as exclusively female 42 percent of the time and as exclusively male 15 percent of the time. In sports-time ads, consumers were depicted as exclusively male 51 percent of the time and exclusively female 1 percent of the time. The kinds of social groups shown in ads also varied greatly between the two audiences. While a person alone was depicted equally, the female-oriented prime-time ads showed many more couples and family scenes than did the male-oriented ads. The sports-time ads stressed male collective groups. In terms of the interpersonal relationships depicted, romantic love and togetherness were the most important for female audiences, while friendship and romantic love were most stressed in advertising for male audiences. Significant differences were also found in the lifestyles depicted in the two time periods. For example, an athletic "healthy" lifestyle was depicted in 18 percent of sports ads, compared with only 7 percent of prime-time ads, while a middle-class lifestyle was depicted in 19 percent of female-oriented ads, but only in 5 percent of male-oriented ads.

Such variables are not those usually associated with content analysis. They require a good deal of interpretation of and "reading into" the message under study. To give a more concrete example of the way this middle-range methodology operates in practical terms, let us turn to the subject of the values that are depicted in advertising. Values cannot be picked off the surface of the message and easily arranged into categories. Recognizing values depends on a process of interpretation and reintegration of the available information. The Jhally study broke down the predominant values depicted in advertising in four ways—values connected with activities, with personal relations, with general themes, and with products. The question posed was, What aspect of each of these four domains did advertisers attempt to utilize?

"Values associated with personal relations," for example, were further broken down into nine categories:

1. Beauty (culture, sophistication, grace, elegance)
2. Individuality
3. Ruggedness (macho, masculine, tough)
4. Family (family love, motherhood, warmth, tradition)
5. Romantic love (male/female romantic attraction)
6. Sorority
7. Fraternity
8. Friendship (male/female, mixed, non-sexual)
9. Sexuality (product will make you sexually attractive)

For each ad under consideration, one of these categories was chosen (if no personal relations values were present, "absent" was marked). The results were as follows:

	Percentage by Intended Audience	
	Female	*Male*
1. Beauty	18	5
2. Individuality	3	2
3. Ruggedness	4	19
4. Family	18	5
5. Romance	12	6
6. Sorority	3	1
7. Fraternity	1	13
8. Friendship	5	7
9. Sexuality	6	4
Absent	30	42
Total	100	104*

* Total does not come to 100 percent due to rounding.

We can see clearly some important differences. Beauty is stressed more for female than for male audiences, and the reverse is true for ruggedness and fraternity. Family relations and romance are more prominent in ads for a female audience.

The study in its entirety indicates that advertisers appeal to different audiences along different dimensions; in other words, divergent codes are in operation. The results give greater substance and concreteness to semiology's notion of code by blending its sophisticated interpretive sensitivity with the more specific, rigorous, and quantitatively oriented strategies that one finds in content analysis. Instead of looking to culture or nature or "mind," as the semiologists do, we have searched for concrete marketplace codes that can be broken down into subsidiary categories and compared with each other in terms of relative significance. We have thus captured with one approach both the enormous range of the reference systems and the depth of meaning that the world of advertising so tellingly uses.

The importance of audience code was the basis for a historical survey of magazine advertising, conducted by William Leiss and Stephen Kline. The remainder of this chapter will be devoted to a detailed look at this second study.

BACKGROUND TO THE STUDY

Few attempts have been made to use content analysis in advertising research to look at advertising in a wider historical context:

> The academic studies conducted thus far on the content of advertising have had a narrow topical focus and a brief time scope. Most have concentrated on the investigation of only one or two content factors for contemporary advertisements. . . . Content analysis of advertising is characterised by small studies investigating narrow topical areas of contemporary interest, occasionally providing longitudinal comparisons, but with no one study providing a multi-dimensional view of the advertising during a particular period or across time periods. (Lucki and Pollay 1981, 2)

We believe that the absence of a historical approach to the field of advertising messages detracts from our ability to understand the development of the consumer culture. In our own empirical study of advertising, therefore, we adopted a historical perspective. Our "middle range" methodology, adapting and combining what we regard as the major advantages of both semiology (sensitivity) and content analysis (systemization), sacrifices some of the distinctive interpretive strengths of each. Moreover, we did not set out to study a general "system of signs" in advertising but rather the field of commercial signs within the specific framework developed in the preceding chapters: the merger of advertising design and media practice as part of the internal development of the advertising industry.

METHODOLOGICAL OUTLINE

Our study was based upon the applications of a combined semiological/content analysis approach to a historical sample of magazine advertisements. The coding protocol attempted to reflect both reliability and sensitivity to the nature of advertising's communication. The protocol was devised and revised over a period of five years before a final version was ready.

The advertisements were coded by a team of four trained coders, all graduate students. Where the coders had difficulties or uncertainties in the use of the protocol, they brought their problems to the researchers for advice on making the allocation. Inter- and intra-coder reliability checks were made on a set of specified advertisements.

The sampling strategy was devised to provide conditions that would allow us to comment on certain features of the historical changes in advertising. Our intent was to describe the periodic shifts in emphasis that result from new communicative approaches, values, techniques, and so forth that were being developed or introduced into advertising. We knew that different media resulted in different relationships to audiences and had different emphases. How were we to compare 1920s magazine ads with 1960s television commercials along a historical spectrum? We had to take into account the fact that some differences were due to the development of new media rather than strictly to the historical development of advertising. For this reason, we decided to restrict our historical comparison to a single medium.

We also were faced with the practical problem that no historical material for constructing a sample existed other than in the print media. We chose magazine advertising as providing the best indicator of changes in advertising in general, in part, because it is heavily dominated by national advertising, and, in part, because it is a communication form open to influences from other media (newspapers, radio, film, television, photography). We felt that magazine advertising would allow us to construct a historical sample that would reflect the changes in the advertising industry in general and not confound those changes with differences among media. Our first assumption, then, was that broad changes within advertising will be manifest in national magazine advertising. Deviation from this assumption becomes the first limitation on the drawing of overall historical inferences.

We wanted to minimize the effects that changing management and editorial approaches in magazines might have had on our historical sample as the orientation to market segments changed. This factor was a significant concern, especially in the last fifty years. We resolved it by choosing two Canadian popular general-interest mass-circulation magazines (*Maclean's* and *Chatelaine*) that spanned the seventy or so years of history in which we were interested. We chose successful and surviving magazines rather than ones that fell by the wayside. *Maclean's*, which started out with an almost exclusively male readership in 1908, still had a predominantly male readership (though far less so) in 1984. *Chatelaine* since 1928 has consistently been directed at a female audience, with approximately 80 percent of its readership currently women. This limitation assured us that the overall market was covered, and also enabled us to make some comparisons between magazines directed at the broadly differentiated male and female audiences. We believe that our sample cast a reasonably wide net in terms of capturing the most significant trends in advertising.

We also wanted to ensure that trends in advertising within a given product category did not skew our interpretation of general trends. For example, appliance advertisements, significant proportions of which appeared in magazines in the early periods, moved to television during the 1950s. In order to minimize the effects of changes in the types of products that advertise in magazines, we selected products across a range that appeared consistently in magazines in significant proportions over the whole period.

To make this selection, we constructed profiles of the frequency of advertisements by product type in both of our magazines by randomly examining two copies of each magazine for each year. We developed profiles for each magazine based upon examination of 15,000 advertisements, noting for each the size of ad and the product type. Using these product profiles, we limited the products that we included in the final sample to smoking, automobile, clothing, food, personal-care, and alcoholic products, and corporate advertisements. All were present in reasonable proportions for most of the historical sample (alcohol was only introduced after the beginning of World War II). Based on these profiles, we were also able to estimate the proportion of all advertising in the magazines that our results reflected. In choosing these categories, we were assured of tapping more than 50 percent of the products advertised in magazines at any time (and, in most periods, much higher proportions).

A HISTORICAL STUDY OF ADVERTISING

The task of any content analysis is to "deconstruct" a set of ads into meaningful components or fields of representation and then to interpret the findings. In this study, we followed the course suggested by Leymore's (1975) semiological analysis, distinguishing between person, product, setting, and text. We noted the presence of each of these fields and the proportion of the total display area devoted to it for each ad. The historical trends are shown in Figure 9.1.

It is clear that the text has been declining in importance throughout the period under study; a word count illustrated more precisely the steady overall decline in copy. The emphasis on copywriting in advertising's early years shifted gradually to one on display and illustration. In many cases, the contemporary ads contain nothing more than a brand name, a slogan, and a few explanatory words—demonstrating a crucial change in the way advertising ideas are expressed within the ads, most particularly in the relationship between language and visual elements, in the information they convey. Textual information has been condensed, its actual content or emphasis changed, and the qualities and function of language transformed. As might be expected, the style, form, and content of visual representation also changed.

Changes in the proportion of textual and visual elements are not equally common in all ads. Advertisements for certain kinds of products, such as alcohol and tobacco, tended to use less text than others

FIGURE 9.1
Display Area Devoted to Each Field of Representation

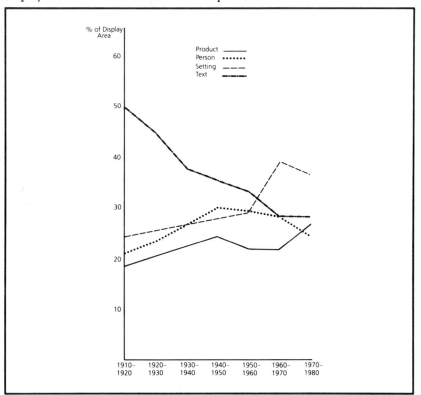

throughout the entire period, while automobile ads and corporate messages always used much more. Over time, product types became increasingly differentiated by the amount of text used. Detailed analysis
revealed that increasing "visualization" of selling messages in advertising design was one facet of the specialization of appeals around product
types. But the importance of the shift to visual representation in general
cannot be underestimated.

   **The shift away from text (the dominant field of representation before
the commercialization of media) is important because it indicates new
relationships are being forged between language and visual image within
the basic codes of advertising.** In the very earliest magazine ads, the
emphasis is clearly on the text and the information it conveys—mostly
about the product. The illustrations are primarily of the product or the
packaging that makes the product recognizable in the store. This is
inherent in display advertising.

   Through the 1920s and 1930s, we find increasingly frequent examples of ads in which the product is not the sole visual focus. In these ads, the text often explains the meaning of the illustration. Its metaphoric content, the identity of the characters, and the kind of relationship between the product and the abstract qualities represented in the visual, are stated as well as illustrated. In the earlier period especially, the text explains the reasons for consuming, the identity of the user, the appropriate context for use, or the benefits of the product, thus acting as the predominant field for providing the overall interpretation of the relationship between person and product. As such, the text closes off any ambiguity that might emerge from the new kinds and qualities of information provided in the illustration.

But with the increasing use of photo reproduction in society at large, and in magazine advertising in particular, the visual modality comes to be the predominant channel for expressing meaning in advertising. After the 1950s, the visual frequently stands on its own, undescribed and unexplained. The language of ads becomes condensed, allusive, conversational, or poetic. It is the visual that conveys the story, use, or reason for consumption. By today, the assumption is that the audience is capable of very complex visual decoding, that it can construct an understanding of the ad simply from a montage of visual signs for which the text often plays a minor explanatory or "sloganeering" role, helping only to draw attention to a key ideational element of the ad.

This complex transition to the visual representation of meaning in advertising design can be illustrated clearly in the changing representation of the user or "human persona." A more detailed analysis of the way people appear in ads helps to explain the changing relation between text and image, which parallels the overall decline of text. In Figure 9.2, we see that the proportion of ads with references to people — in semiological terms, the person code — increases dramatically during the 1920s.

Information about people is first introduced as textual description or as general information about (or testimonials from) "unseen" consumers and their experiences with the product. Among ads that use the person code, the proportion with visual representations of people reaches its peak during the 1930s; this is the period when textual information is being translated into visual codes. By the 1940s, the visual representation of people in ads begins to decline (Figure 9.1), as imagery takes over from the text as the predominant field. The "person code" has become primarily visual; at the same time, the emphasis upon people as a means of conveying ideas about the product, which had been a rising trend until about 1940, subsequently declined.

The same is true of the setting code, which also shifts from textual to visual modes of representation (Figure 9.3). At first, descriptions of the appropriate physical settings of product use dominated advertising, but after 1940 descriptions of what we might call the " social context" of use

FIGURE 9.2

Forms of Representation of People in Ads Using Person Code

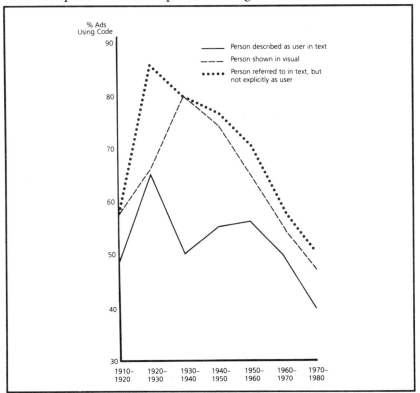

gains importance. More significantly, by the 1950s setting information is more often conveyed by illustration that tends to combine physical and social settings than by description. Moreover, the setting code becomes the predominant field of representation during the 1960s and thereafter (Figure 9.1).

In general, then, our approach recognizes that changes in advertising's use of the elemental codes (person, product, setting) is happening hand in hand with this transition in the mode (language/visual image) of representation. The development and expansion of visual forms of expression and communication prompted by artwork (some of the earlier inspirations were posters and period art styles) and photography has affected immensely the kinds of representations and information we find in advertising, and has had an equally powerful impact on the way we must "deconstruct" and interpret the changing meaning of the ads.

Figures 4.1 and 4.3 were presented to reflect the process whereby advertisers, especially during the 1920s and 1930s, targeted the consumer's understanding of and justification for changes in traditional role

FIGURE 9.3
Forms of Representation of Setting in Ads Using Setting Code

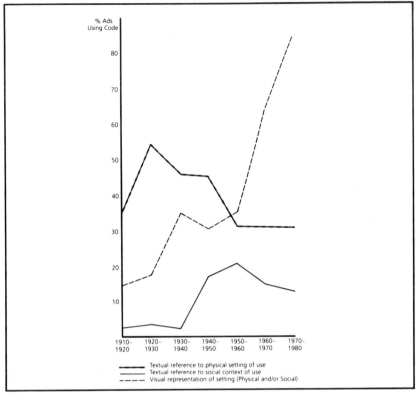

structures and behaviours. Advertising was not only "instructional" in the sense that it acquainted audiences with new kinds of products (processed foods, safety razors, deodorants) and the new social problems they were designed to solve, but also in that it taught the "grammatical skills" for decoding the ads themselves. In this period, many transitional ads use the text essentially to explain the image and its logic—to provide a key to the interpretation of the image. In Figure 9.4, the transfer of the metaphoric qualities of endurance from the person-image to the product must be fully explained in the text. In Figure 4.1, the gasoline additive lead is explained in the text through the metaphor of the relationship between cheese and macaroni. These transitional ads pave the way for forms that can leave out the explicit lesson by using the visual grammar with which ads are encoded and decoded. Thus, they provide us with important clues to the interpretation of later ads.

Present-day ads take for granted a great sophistication on the audience's part in making sense of visuals, text, and their relationship—the fact that we now have fifteen-second television formats without informa-

FIGURE 9.4
Metaphoric Readings of Product Qualities: The text helps the audience form a
metaphoric reading that links the product qualities with the visual sign.

tion loss reveals the kind of compression of meaning possible once the viewer is competent in reconstructing meaning from compressed formats. The development of communication in advertising itself is, therefore, deeply intertwined with the more general communicative competences of the audience.

As literacy and education were prerequisites for earlier forms of magazine advertising, decoding abilities are assumed in modern audiences who must make sense of modern articulations. The increased specificity and accessibility of advertising was underwritten by the successful adaptation of communicative techniques to the advertising genre; Figure 9.5 is an example of a transitional ad from the 1930s, in which microscopic inspection, foldaways, and image sequences accentuate the argument; Figure 9.6 uses a movie-like sequence of images to tell a story. These are but a few of the visual techniques that have expanded the communicative domains of advertising. One of the most important, and sometimes amusing, results of the application of these techniques is that it allows new points of view and forms of dialogue to emerge within the discourse of advertising. As seen in Figure 9.7, the introduction of the comic bubble even enables the product to "speak for itself."

We shall not detail and trace the development of all the communicative devices that are now part of the advertiser's repertoire. In this book, we can only trace on the broadest level how these devices have affected the representation of the relationship between people and products. Here we will simply reiterate the challenge that led us to combine the semiological/content analysis approaches in our study of advertising: changes in the referential content and ideas in advertising are closely interwoven with the transformation of modes of representation (in magazines, textual and visual modes) and with the development of formats for relating the different codes (persons, products, and settings). These concurrent changes lie at the heart of an analysis of communication in advertising.

BASIC ADVERTISING FORMATS

The above account provides the background for the interpretation of historical change in the general structure of representation in magazine advertising. In the following pages, we attempt to clarify the broad changes in advertising's patterns of representation through which people and products are brought into a "meaningful relationship." We will discuss representative ads that illustrate and highlight the framework for the interpretive task that all of us face when we try to make sense of ads. These ads are presented as ideal types to represent the prototypical formats within which the person–product relationship is constituted, and to help us chart the predominant patterns of meaning in various historical periods.

FIGURE 9.5
Borrowing from a scientific perspective, microscopic vision allowed consumers to view the product in new ways.

Chatelaine, February, 1933

Science shows
why Old Dutch Cleanser
costs less to use

OLD DUTCH LOOKS LIKE THIS
highly magnified under the microscope. The particles are flaky and flat-shaped, cover more surface, contact it completely, remove dirt with a smooth, clean sweep and do not scratch...as illustrated by this diagram.

... *because it goes further, cleans quicker doesn't scratch, cleans more things and brings Healthful Cleanliness*

GRIT LOOKS LIKE THIS
highly magnified under the microscope. Old Dutch contains no grit; avoid cleaners that do...the chunky, sharp-pointed particles scratch the surface leaving hiding places for dirt...as illustrated by this diagram.

The experience of hundreds of thousands of women is borne out by careful scientific tests of Old Dutch, proving conclusively that it is the most economical, safest and most efficient cleanser to use.

There's nothing else like Old Dutch Cleanser. Why? The microscope makes it clear. Notice that the particles of Old Dutch Cleanser are flaky and flat-shaped; that they lie flat on the surface and come in full contact with it whereas grit merely scratches the surface with sharp, hard points. That's why Old Dutch covers more surface, why it is more economical and efficient. It contains no harsh

grit or crude abrasives, no caustic or acids, and is therefore safe. It possesses a natural detergent energy that quickly removes both visible and invisible impurities, and therefore brings healthful cleanliness.

Old Dutch is ideal for every cleansing purpose — kitchen utensils and refrigerators, porcelain and enamel, linoleum and painted woodwork, silverware, china and glass. It's your greatest aid in preserving the health of your family, the spotless beauty of your home, the softness of lovely hands. For these reasons, women all over the country tell us that *Old Dutch is the only cleanser they need in their homes.*

This is the Old Dutch Rubber Cleaning Sponge. Convenient and practical. A little Old Dutch and this sponge does a quick, thorough cleaning job. An attractive bathroom and kitchen accessory. Send for it today. Mail 10c and the windmill panel from an Old Dutch Cleanser label for each sponge.
OLD DUTCH CLEANSER
Dept. 80; 64 Macaulay Ave., Toronto, Ontario.
Name_____
Address_____
City_____ Province_____

Old Dutch doesn't scratch. Convince yourself with this simple test. Sprinkle a little Old Dutch on the porcelain drainboard of your sink; place a smooth coin on it and rub gently. You'll neither feel nor hear the scratching of harsh, gritty particles. That's why Old Dutch is safe for all your cleaning.

Tested and Approved by
Chatelaine Institute
Chatelaine Magazine

MADE IN CANADA

FIGURE 9.6
Communicative techniques borrowed from other media expanded advertisers' ability to talk about products in new ways.

FIGURE 9.7
Through the use of comic-book formats, objects not only come alive but are given a more influential role in solving the consumer's personal problems.

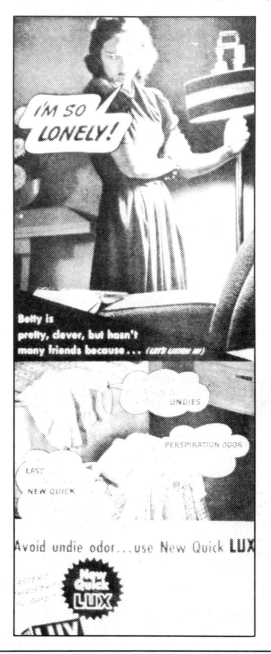

Source: Courtesy of Lever Detergents Limited.

The person–product relationship was forged within advertising's system of meaning into four basic communicative formats—crystallizations of the complex structure of advertising's multifaceted system of signs—which help us understand the basic patterns of integration between the semiological codes and the textual and visual modes of representation (Kline and Leiss, 1978).

The Product-Information Format

In the product-information ad, the product is the centre of attention and the focus of all elements in the ad is explaining the product and its utility. The brand name and frequently a picture of the package are prominent. The text is used primarily to describe the product and its benefits, characteristics, performance, or construction. Little other information is available and little reference is made to the user or the context of use of the product, except for instructions or special offers. The ad may contain visuals that emphasize the effectiveness of the product (for example, a microscopic view of a germ-free sink), or rational arguments pointing out the benefits of use, but it does not make extensive reference to the user. Those who believe that "rational" product information is what should be supplied to the modern economy often assume that this type of ad should constitute the whole field of advertising. An expansion of the earlier classified advertising format through more elaborate copywriting and illustration, the product-information ad was the dominant type around the turn of the century but has been declining steadily since then.

Several major variants of the product-information format differ primarily in the way they manifest the idea of the power of the product. The textually oriented ad (Figure 9.8) places greatest emphasis upon language—description of the product, promises, and argument. A second variant continues to rely heavily on text but also uses design and illustration to emphasize the features of the product and explain its advantages (Figure 9.9). In what might be called a demonstration ad, the ability of the product to achieve some end is visually illustrated, perhaps with the aid of scientific apparatus (Figure 9.10). Other variants and combinations exist, of course, and many modern ads give us elaborate visual representations of product benefits, but the central idea in this format remains the evaluation of a utilitarian matrix in which a product, its construction, its price, its utility, and its ability to perform certain deeds is considered. The product-information ad establishes a framework for understanding the product that stresses its singularity and its causal connection to a thoroughly pragmatic universe. We can represent this type of ad this way:

PRODUCT $\longleftrightarrow$ INFORMATION

FIGURE 9.8

The Product-Information Format: Heavy on text, illustration is primarily used to visualize the product and packaging.

THE COSMOPOLITAN.

The Larkin Soaps

The 30 Days Trial Begun

The Whole Family supplied with Laundry and Toilet Soaps for a year at Half Price. Sent Subject to Approval and Payment after Thirty Days' Trial.

IT IS WISE ECONOMY TO USE GOOD SOAP. Our soaps are sold entirely on their merits, with our guarantee of purity. THOUSANDS OF FAMILIES USE THEM, and have for many years, in every locality, many in your vicinity. Ask us for your neighbors' testimonials.

The Larkin Plan

saves you half the retail cost of your soaps, and doubles the purchasing value of this 50 per cent. saving in a premium bought for you below usual cost of making. One premium is **A White Enameled Steel, Brass-Trimmed, Bow-Foot Bed.** Metallic beds add beauty and cheerfulness to the chamber, while they convey a delightful feeling of cleanliness that invites repose. They harmonize perfectly with furniture of any wood or style. Brass top rod at head and foot, and heavy brass, gold-lacquered trimmings. Malleable castings that never break. Detachable ball-bearing casters. 4½ or 4 or 3½ feet wide. 6½ feet long. Head, 4½ feet. Foot, 3½ feet high. Corner posts, 1 inch in diameter. Very strong and will last a lifetime.

AFTER THIRTY DAYS' TRIAL if the purchaser finds all the Soaps, etc., of excellent quality and the premium entirely satisfactory and as represented, remit $10.00; if not, notify us goods are subject to our order. We make no charge for what you have used.

If you remit in advance, you will receive in addition a nice present for the lady of the house, and shipment day after order is received. Money refunded promptly if the BOX or PREMIUM disappoints. Safe delivery guaranteed. The transaction is not complete until you are satisfied.

☞ Many youths and maidens easily earn a Chautauqua Desk or other premium free by dividing the contents of a Combination Box among a few neighbors who readily pay the listed retail prices. This provides the $10.00 needful to pay our bill, and gives the young folk the premium as "a middleman's profit." The wide success of this plan confirms all our claims.

Booklet Handsomely Illustrating 15 Premiums sent on request.

THE LARKIN SOAP MFG. CO., Buffalo, N. Y.

Estab. 1875. Incor. 1892. Capital, $500,000.

☞ READ NOTES BELOW.

Our Great Combination Box.

Enough to last an Average Family one Full Year.

This List of Contents Changed as Desired.

100 BARS "SWEET HOME" SOAP	$5.00
For all laundry and household purposes it has no superior. Large Bars.	
10 BARS WHITE WOOLLEN SOAP	.70
A perfect soap for flannels.	
12 Pkgs. BORAXINE SOAP POWDER (full lbs.)	1.20
An unequalled laundry luxury.	
4 BARS HONOR BRIGHT SCOURING SOAP .	.20
1-4 DOZ. MODJESKA COMPLEXION SOAP .	.60
Perfume exquisite. A matchless beautifier.	
1-4 DOZ. OLD ENGLISH CASTILE SOAP .	.30
1-4 DOZ. CREME OATMEAL TOILET SOAP .	.25
1-4 DOZ. ELITE GLYCERINE TOILET SOAP .	.25
1-4 DOZ. LARKIN'S TAR SOAP	.30
Unequalled for washing the hair.	
1-4 DOZ. SULPHUR SOAP	.30
1 BOTTLE. 1 oz., MODJESKA PERFUME .	.30
Delicate, refined, popular, lasting.	
1 JAR. 2 ozs., MODJESKA COLD CREAM .	.25
Soothing. Cures chapped skin.	
1 BOTTLE MODJESKA TOOTH POWDER .	.25
Preserves the teeth, hardens the gums, sweetens the breath.	
1 STICK WITCH HAZEL SHAVING SOAP .	.10
THE CONTENTS, Bought at Retail, Cost .	$10.00
THE PREMIUM, worth at Retail . . .	10.00

All **$10.** for (You get the Premium) (you select, gratis.) **$20**

NOTE.—The Larkin Soap Mfg. Co., make our readers a wonderful offer. Not only do they give you a box of excellent laundry soap and toilet articles of value, but they also give each purchaser a valuable premium, and we personally know they carry out what they promise.—*The Independent, New York.*

When you write, please mention "The Cosmopolitan."

FIGURE 9.9

The Product-Information Format: A more subtle blending of text and illustration also enabled advertisers to refer to abstract features of product characteristics and design.

A car that *Bores* through the air... that *Floats* over bumps as if they weren't there. Get ready for the most surprising Ride of your Life!

NE . . . A ROUGH ROAD. Time . . . next nth. You're driving along in your old car ying to dodge the bumps.

bad enough for you . . . pity the passengers . . . you apologize . . . can't be helped.

denly a horn . . . you pull over. A strange car by. You catch sight of the man in the back s it possible . . . he was reading a newspaper! as an AIRFLOW De Soto. Today, every-wondering what it will be like. We cannot the complete story. But a few of the amaz-ts are here made public in advance.

Conquering the Air
the first problems that the pioneers of flying solve was . . . wind-resistance. The more could overcome it, the lighter they could their planes . . . the less power they would They studied the shapes of the fastest birds rels, albatrosses, condors . . . also the fastest . the Greenland shark . . . the blue whale.

tudy of aero-dynamic design became a . Today, aircraft builders have learned how flow" every inch of a plane's surface. You he results. Speeds better than 300 miles an Coast to coast in ten hours!

Ships, Trains Follow Suit
ally we have awakened to the fact that what rned about planes applies to other forms nsport. Airflow ships have clipped Trans-ic records. They're building new airflow to cross the continent in 50 hours!

The Motor Car must Catch Up
What about an airflow car? Manufacturers have toyed with the idea . . . a radiator here . . . a fender there. But that is not true aero-dynamic design. Look what happens when the typical car of today speeds through the air:—

At 60 miles an hour, it actually uses one half of its engine power fighting wind-resistance!

Why has no company produced a scientifically shaped car? For one thing, it requires a tremendous investment . . . for research and for manufacturing. Moreover . . . it means a complete departure from all the traditional ideas of automobile design.

De Soto has undertaken to pioneer the way because it enjoys the unequalled research and engineering facilities of Chrysler Motors. It believes that the public will not merely accept, but will enthusiastically welcome a car that is more modern, more comfortable . . . and safer than any low-priced car ever built.

Five Years of Research
Work on the new AIRFLOW De Soto began five years ago. Wind-tunnels, similar to those used by Governments and Aeronautical laboratories were installed.

Scores of models were made . . . thousands of drawings . . . then more than twelve months of gruelling secret tests over the worst roads that could be found. And now it is ready . . . a *new kind* of motor car . . . that will start a new era in the history of road travel.

Most Sensational Ride in Thirty Years!
The diagram above shows the seating arrangement in the car of today. The back seats are directly

over the back axle . . . the equivalent of travelling "steerage" on a ship. Not a single bump escapes you. No wonder that there are straps on the side for you to hold onto!

The design of the AIRFLOW De Soto (*above*), allows every passenger to sit "amidships." Add to this a revolutionary new method of weight distribution throughout the car and you have the reason why your first FLOATING RIDE will be a never-forgotten experience.

Sleep . . . at 80 Miles an Hour!
In an ordinary car, whether you know it or not, your nerves and muscles are tensed . . . waiting for the jolts. In the AIRFLOW De Soto you can relax utterly. Close your eyes and you will hardly know that you are moving. At 80 miles an hour . . . you can read the small print of a newspaper . . . write a letter . . . sleep comfortably. That's why there aren't any hand-straps to hold onto in *this* car. Nobody would ever use them!

No question about it . . . you'll gasp at De Soto's daring, new-day beauty. Its luxurious interiors will delight you. But the BIG sensation . . . the most significant motor car news of 1934 . . . will be the breath-taking AIRFLOW De Soto *Floating Ride*. Its importance is fundamental, not just a matter of new springs. It's a new way to BUILD a car!

Ride Three in Front . . . in Comfort
No more "crowding up" in the front seat. The new De Soto has settled that! Its front seat is eight inches wider. Plenty of room for three. Yet the car itself takes up no more room on the highway!

Make a Date with a Dealer
More people will want to ride in the AIRFLOW De Soto than in any other new car for years. Be one of the first.

COMING THE *AIRFLOW* DE SOTO

FIGURE 9.10
The Product-Information Format: Visualization was used to help demonstrate the utilities of the product in new, more effective ways.

SUDS-TEST *shows why* Chipso *washes your clothes with...*

Suds

not Chemicals

Now—from an actual photograph—you can see the amazing difference in soaps! A suds-testing machine reveals to you, for the first time, the sudsing power of five leading household soaps.

Here before your eyes is the explanation of Chipso's speedy cleansing. You can see *why* Chipso can wash as quickly as a "strong" soap ... *and more safely*. Chipso gives *more* suds. Millions of tiny soap-film hands reach into your clothes, surround the dirt—*lift* it out ... *safely*. Your hands stay nice ... colors stay fresh.

A soap that roughens your hands when you use it for dishes, is too strong for your clothes. It weakens them—wears them out before their time. Chipso washes with rich suds—it cannot hurt your skin.

Chipso gives more suds than ever! A new soap-making process has actually put an amazing amount of extra suds in Chipso. Rich, double-cream, active suds! Goodbye to weakened clothes. Goodbye to rough, red hands. Chipso's extra suds *lift* out even ground-in dirt—quickly, safely.

Put Chipso on your grocery list and learn the quick suds-way to wash clothes and dishes.

An Interesting Test

You *can* have speedy cleansing without "strong" soap. Chipso washes with more and richer SUDS! A new soap process has given Chipso an amazing amount of extra suds. These suds cleanse quickly, safely—everything from grimy little rompers to your finest linens.

In this remarkable test the same weight of Chipso and four other leading bar and package household soaps were compared for sudsing ability in a suds testing machine *under exactly the same conditions.* See the Chipso suds!

IMPORTANT—*Chipso dissolves completely in luke-warm water.* Compare the new Chipso Flakes for quick-dissolving with any soap you know—no matter what its form.

THE SAME RICH SOAP IN 2 FORMS

The Product-Image Format

In the product-image ad, brand name and package again play an important part, but the product is given special qualities by means of a symbolic relationship that it has to some more abstract and less pragmatic domain of significance than mere utility. The product becomes embedded or "situated" in a symbolic *context* that imparts meaning to the product beyond its constituent elements or benefits. Product-image ads, therefore, work by fusing two composite systems of signs, or two codes within the framework of a single message—the product code and a setting code. (It is not surprising that semiologists have been most ardent in recognizing this structure for interpretation in the field of advertising.) In generating the overall meaning of the ad, these codes are not necessarily synthesized by causal or logical linkages, but by association and juxtapostion or some narrative device. The symbolic association thus established brings the product into a meaningful relationship with abstract values and ideas signified by a natural or social setting such as a landscape, the workplace, the household, a cluster of artifacts of daily life, a historic moment, or a recognizable tradition or myth.

In order for the setting to be understood as a code rather than a locus of use, it must provide a frame of reference for interpreting the product's qualities. Each code implies a system of classification to which we are referred as the basis for interpreting the product's qualities. The fusion of product code and setting code, which formulates the basis of the product-image, depends largely on narrative techniques like metaphor, implied use, allusion, allegory, story line, and simple juxtaposition to expand the symbolic dimension of the interpretation. Without these means for drawing together codes, product-image ads would remain impenetrable. Figure 1.2 illustrates how a well-known myth can be the basis of a symbolic association in which the image of luxury and grandeur of the product is conjured. It is clear that the scene depicted is not the product in use. Moreover, without some knowledge of Cleopatra and her barge we could not make the required connection between the car and the abstract qualities being invoked.

The increasing use of art and photography encouraged the tendency to place the product within a symbolic rather than utilitarian setting because the communicative techniques involved in visual representation allowed for new ways of exploring the potentialities of products and their meaning in the human world. Visual representation, based on apprehended qualities, provides blurred and less clearly identifiable fields of reference. As depicted in advertising, settings are multidimensional and often provide ambiguous bases for the interpretation of the product image.

Typically, these settings are either "natural" or "social"; for example, in Figure 9.11 the superimposition of the cigarette package on a

FIGURE 9.11
The Product-Image Format: In the fluid and swirling world of images, the transfer of natural qualities to products does not seem strange.

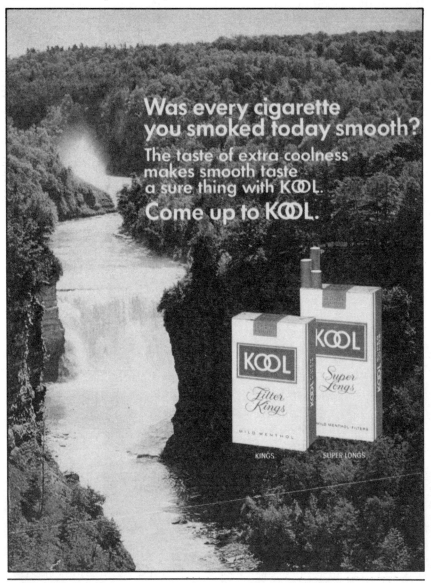

beautiful natural setting helps us not only to imagine a moment when we might use the product (the narrative), but, more importantly, to transfer the qualities of coolness and naturalness that we associate with this vista to the cigarette as well. Although users do appear in Figure 6.2, it is the representation of a social setting that helps us interpret the more abstract connection between the product and futurism. In Figure 9.12, the name of the line of silverware takes on the connotation of social standing illustrated and stylized in the drawing; in Figure 9.13, the can of soup seems to emerge directly out of the natural ingredient itself. The same interpretive logic is involved whether the abstract value is placed in a natural or a social context.

The logic of associative transfer of value is also the basis of some ads in which the human element is used as the symbolic context. In Figure 9.14, the person literally steps to the foreground and brings with her the essence of "trust" and "quality" associated with her profession. The similarity of the human and bottle shape helps us to transfer the abstract qualities to the product, creating the fusion necessary for the product image. In all these cases, the predominant interpretation results from the transfer of the abstract symbolic quality or value associated with a particular context to the product. We can represent the product image ad this way:

PRODUCT $\longleftrightarrow$ SETTING or CONTEXT $\longleftrightarrow$ SYMBOL

The Personalized Format

The direct relationship between a product and the human personality defines the primary framework of the personalized ad. Here the person code takes on an importance quite different from its use in the product-image ads, in which people sometimes appear as part of a social setting that transfers abstract symbolic qualities to products. In personalized ads, people are explicitly and directly interpreted in their relationship to the world of the product. Social admiration, pride of ownership, anxiety about lack of use, or satisfaction in consumption become important humanizing dimensions of the interpretation of products, as we note from the gazes of the people in Figure 9.15.

The framework of interpretation in the personalized ad presumes that "the way an individual or a culture identifies similarities and differences between persons and groups in their milieu is the foundation on which everyday social intercourse is based" (Forgas 1981). As cognitive psychologists point out, this process of social judgment assumes an "identity matrix"—a frame of reference for personality categories. This matrix is appropriated in the personalized ad to embrace social interac-

FIGURE 9.12
The Product-Image Format: Stylized illustration helps to crystallize the
particular social qualities that can be transferred to products.

Source: Courtesy of Oneida Canada Ltd.

FIGURE 9.13

The Product-Image Format: In the magical world of commodities, products
seemed to capture natural qualities and internalize them within the product
image.

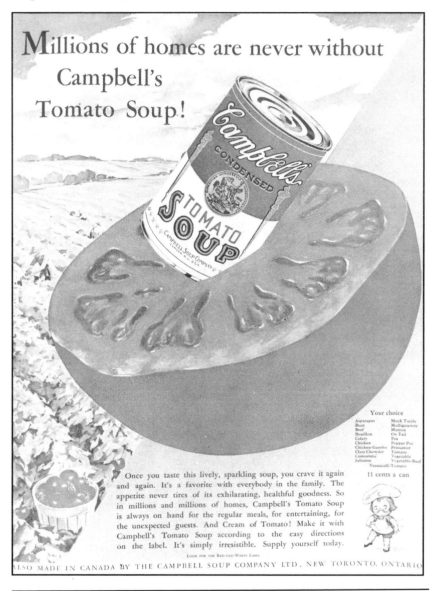

Source: Courtesy of Campbell's Soup Company Ltd.

FIGURE 9.14
The Product-Image Format: People appear, but as representations of abstract
qualities such as "trust" rather than as living individuals.

FIGURE 9.15

The Personalized Format: Pride in ownership and social admiration speak of a direct personal relationship to products.

Source: Courtesy of Ford Motor Co. of Canada Ltd.

tions around and through the product. The product does more than refer to the world of human interaction; it enters and acts in that world and resonates with its qualities. Sometimes, the product itself speaks as if it were a person saying things that humans can't. To quote one jewellery ad, "Yes, falling in love was pretty easy. But our diamond says we're going to make it last." The distinction between person and product codes becomes obscured. Even the characters that speak to us from ads become confused about the distinction: Candice Bergen testifies about her perfume, "Cie goes with all the things 1 love to do. Cie is me."

The way the relationship between the product and person is constructed varies greatly depending upon whether, for example, the person is a user, a consumer, or a typical representative of some personality type (smart, sophisticated) or group (homemakers, businesspeople). People may be shown simply as models, presenters, or testifiers, or in the course of their daily life. In all cases, the meaning of the ad is conveyed by the link between the attributes associated with the people in the advertisement and the relationship they embody between themselves and the product.

As the significance of the product becomes mediated by direct and personalized relationships, the separate worlds of people and products also merge. The cycle of consumption and satisfaction becomes an important thematic focus for exploring the relationship between people and products. Social interaction and judgment extends to and flows through the products people have or use. The product may even be personified, taking on human characteristics. In consequence, the dimensions of meaning that connect people and products are affective rather than associative or pragmatic. The emotions that engage people in human intercourse (love, anxiety, pride, belonging, friendship) also engage them with products.

The personalized format has a number of important variants. One is the testimonial in which the person's relationship to the product is based on experience with use or consumption (see Figure 9.16). Often, narrative devices are used to explicate the human dimension of the relationship between the persons testifying and the product in order to let them enter the scene with their particular qualities of credibility (see Figure 9.17). At other times, a person's role, or even just fame, provides the connection between the product and its recommendation. The scientist recommends the effectiveness of a cleanser, the starlet certifies her satisfaction with a soap, and the typical housewife tells us how pleased her husband is to have clean collars. A throng of characters display and tell us about their reactions to products. Early versions of this format often stressed the utility and effectiveness of the product, but more modern versions—which rely primarily on the visual image—stress the emotional experience of responding to products and being satisfied by them.

FIGURE 9.16

The Personalized Format: Testimonials are based upon experience with and use of products, often by celebrities.

FIGURE 9.17
The Personalized Format: Narratives help introduce expert testimonial while
personalizing the use.

In a second variant, the person is not present to "stand behind" the product so much as to "stand for" it (see Figure 9.18). The connection is made on symbolic grounds rather than through use or consumption. This is the basis of an ad image that has become famous all over the world, namely the Marlboro man; in this imagery the associative symbolic logic is very like the product-image ad, except that the symbolic reference stops at the world of social interactions and personality rather than referring onward to abstract values. The Marlboro Man *is* the product; in ads of this type, the person does not testify to or explain use, but conveys a range of attributes (here ruggedness, masculinity) to be associated with the product according to the personal prototype he or she represents. The person in these ads embodies a typified field of personal and psychological reference whose attributes can be transferred to the product by the convergence of these two fields of signification.

In the self-transformation ad, people change—make themselves better—through the possession or use of the product. In the most common self-transformation ad, consumers are invited to imagine themselves in some more idealized state (Figure 1.3). Figure 9.19 is an elaboration in the form of a "makeover" ad, typically associated with cosmetics and clothes. More subtle visual cues, like the mirror in Figure 9.20, are often used to imply the psychological nature of the transformation. The mirror helps to remind us of the relationship between the "antecedent" and "idealized" representations of human personalities that are at play in these ads. As the texts explain it: "Reflections of you. The way you want to be. To feel this season. Alive. Rejuvenated."

A fourth variant places the product at the very centre of social interaction—that is, within the stream of human relations. As Chevrolet once told us, its vehicle was, "More than a car—a member of the family." We see the product bring people into greater intimacy in Figure 9.21. In other advertisements, women get together to solve a personal problem, mother and father are in conflict over their son, or a person uses the power of a product to increase his or her own sexual attractiveness; in all ads of this type, the product is woven firmly into the web of human social interaction. Romance, friendship, social status, and the family provide the main social contexts for product use and association, although advertising draws on the whole gamut of social situations.

The common ground in all these variants is the "personalization" of the product image. The framework of interpretation is built specifically and directly around a relationship between people and products. The product no longer stands as an autonomous object independent of the human world, but rather is displayed as an integral part of the codification of human existence and interaction. We can represent the personalized ad this way:

PRODUCT ⟷ PERSON

FIGURE 9.18

The Personalized Format: Models stand for products and the connection between the two is so complete that they become interchangeable.

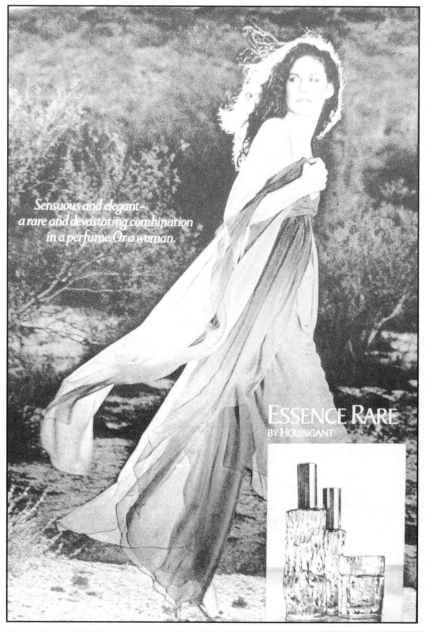

Source: Courtesy of Houbigant Inc.

FIGURE 9.19
The Personalized Format: Showing consumers before and after use emphasizes
the role products play in self-improvement.

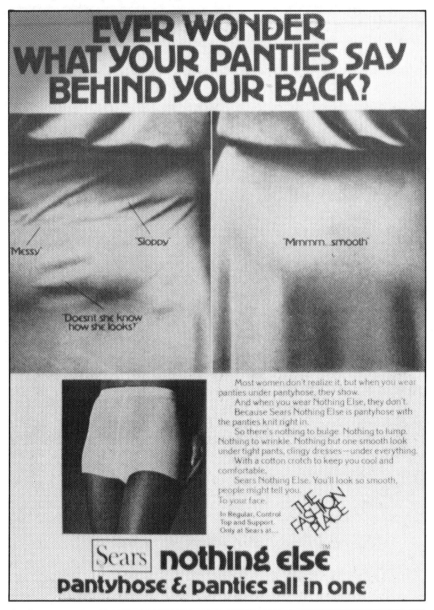

Source: Courtesy of Sears Canada Inc.

FIGURE 9.20
The Personalized Format: The mirror accentuates the fantasized completion of the self made possible by the world of products.

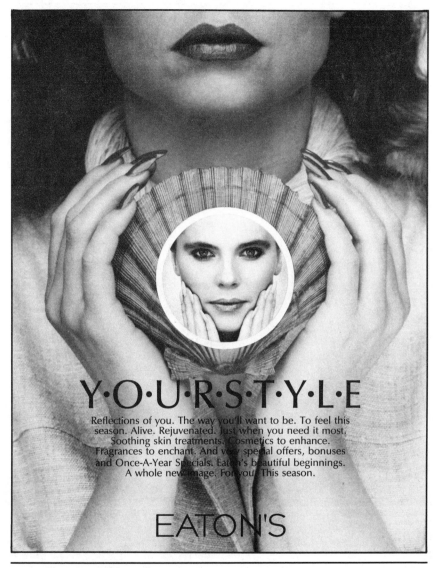

Source: Courtesy of Eaton's.

FIGURE 9.21
The Personalized Format: Situated at the centre of social interaction, products become intimate partners with use.

Source: Courtesy of Cointreau America, Inc.

The Lifestyle Format

In lifestyle ads, a more balanced relationship is established between the elemental codes of person, product, and setting by combining aspects of the product-image and personalized formats. The lifestyle format expands the identity matrix of the individual into a framework of judgment for social beings in a social context.

In most lifestyle advertising, the setting serves in the interpretation of the person code. Social psychology describes this as the use of "stereotypes" rather than "prototypes." A prototype is based on attributions about the personality or characteristics of a person (friendly, warm, intelligent). A stereotype is based on inferences about the relationship of the individual to the group or social context (class, status, race, ethnicity, role relations, group membership), and the notion of group identity is implicit in judgments about the individual. The lifestyle format, like the stereotype, implies that "situations are susceptive to classification in terms of different kinds of effects which they exert on the subject, that is, in terms of their significance for his well-being" (Forgas 1981). In one variant of lifestyle advertising, the idea of social identity is conveyed primarily through the display of the product in a social context; the people who are inserted into the scene remain undefined, providing only a vague reference to the person code (and therefore implicitly to use or consumption style). Often the occasion provides the unifying idea (Figure 6.4). More commonly, people, products, and settings of consumption are harmonized around a unified impression, as in the Dubonnet ad (Figure 1.4); no other information is really necessary because the ad provides a direct vision of a consumption style.

Early references to consumption style help to reveal the important dimensions of the lifestyle format. In Figure 9.22, a post–World-War-II ad for Coca-Cola, the text cues our understanding that consumption hinges around appropriate settings and occasions rather than strictly on satisfaction. Coke is being integrated into a consumption style, connoted by recognizable people in a known social situation, without emphasizing the act of consumption.

The other major variant of the lifestyle format synthesizes the component codes through a primary reference to an activity rather than directly to a consumption style. Here the activity invoked in text or image becomes the central cue for relating the person, product, and setting codes. In Figure 9.23 (cleverly captured within the shape of the product), sharing a friendly sporting activity is the basis of the connection with common use of the product. Lifestyle ads commonly depict a variety of leisure activities (entertaining, going out, holidaying, relaxing). Implicit in each of these activities, however, is the placing of the product within a consumption style by its link to an activity.

FIGURE 9.22
The Lifestyle Format: Immortalizing the trivial moments brings into relief the appropriate social occasions for consumption.

FIGURE 9.23
The Lifestyle Format: Reference to particular lifestyles is internalized within
the essential meaning of the product and reflected in its use.

In modern advertising, the allusion to consumption style is often very subtle. A romantic photograph can provide the basis of a story, however condensed and simplified. The minimal reference, "Last night," in Figure 9.24 suggests both product use and a significant moment in the story to help us interpret the photograph, which resonates with implied social dynamics. Such simple narratives are typical of the sophisticated way contemporary advertising blends visuals with text or "dialogue" to express consumption styles. For all the ambiguity and condensation we see in lifestyle ads, the modern reader seems to have little trouble understanding the implications of these scenes.

In the lifestyle ad, the dimension of consumption that provides the unifying framework of interpretation is action or behaviour appropriate to (or typical of) a social group or situation, rather than use, satisfaction, or utility. Lifestyle ads become most prominent after the 1950s, and, in part, reveal the accommodation of magazine advertising to television's powerful visual methods of storytelling and the matrix of consumption styles it portrays. We use the following interpretive framework to synthesize the person, product, and setting codes in the lifestyle ad:

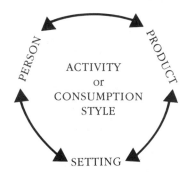

TRENDS IN ELEMENTAL CODES AND ADVERTISING FORMATS

One way to sketch the changing representation of the relationship between people and products implied in our analysis of formats is to trace the use of combinations of elemental codes (person, product, and setting) in the text and/or the visual portion of the ads. From Figure 9.25, we can see that the first phase of the period under study (1910–1930) is characterized by a declining emphasis on representing the product code in isolation (typical of the product-information format), and a corresponding increase in the appearance of the person and product codes together (indicative of either the product-image or personalized for-

FIGURE 9.24
The Lifestyle Format: The allusion to consumption style can be subtly nested in personal narratives and even in the breaking of social conventions.

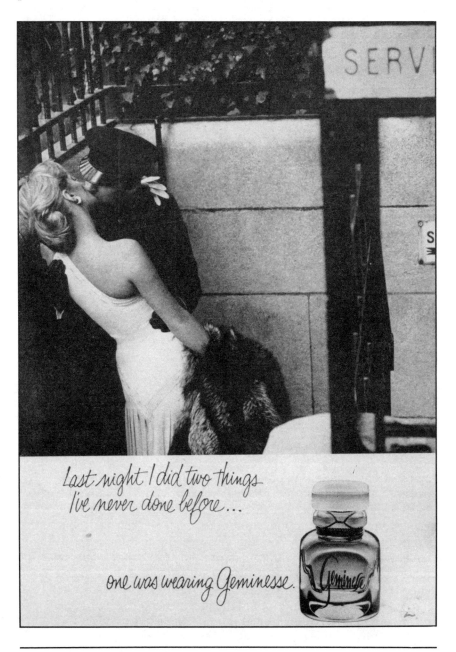

FIGURE 9.25
The Combination of Elemental Codes

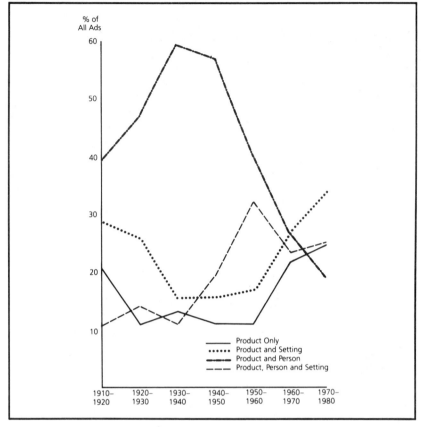

mats). In the 1920s and 1930s, use of the person and product codes together (reflecting, in this period, the product-image format more than the personalized format) is promoted to the seeming exclusion of other combinations. The setting-product code combination (in product-image formats that do not include representations of people) bottoms out in the 1930s; advertising of this type does not regain importance until the 1960s when the insertion of products into particular settings takes on a new significance (the lifestyle formats). Advertising that includes all three elemental codes remains infrequent until the 1940s and 1950s, when its dramatic increase offsets the decline of ads using only person and product codes. Advertising during the 1960s and 1970s is characterized by a rebound in the autonomous use of the product code, and by the continued growth in the combination of product and setting codes.

Broadly speaking, this analysis of code combinations identifies three important transitions. The 1920s consolidate the shift (already evident in

1910 when our study begins) away from the presentation of the product alone and toward its appearance in the human world. In the 1940s, the product-person code combination declines as styles that emphasize the product-person-setting ensemble gain popularity. During the 1960s, another transition is marked by the continuing decline of the product-person arrangement and the rise of both the product alone and product-setting combinations to the point where advertising today demonstrates a relatively balanced ratio among code combinations.

INTEGRATIVE CODES

The occurrence of combinations of elemental codes is only one indication of the fundamental changes in meaning, design, and style that frame our integrating interpretations and impressions of advertisements. To look at these changes more closely we must uncover the patterns in communicative form that bring together the meaning conveyed through these codes. These patterns allow us to understand the connections between components of the advertising message, and, therefore, to interpret the relationships between persons and products that advertising constructs. We might call these patterns "integrative codes." Integrative codes imply that systematic means are employed in the design of ads to unify the message conveyed across perceptual modalities (in magazines, textual and visual modes) and elemental codes. These regularities, in turn, suggest the integrative frameworks of interpretation which readers use to make sense out of an advertisement as a single message, but which may not correspond directly to them. We have designated the integrative codes that we found most important in advertising as style, appeal, and values.

Style

The analysis of stylistic trends in advertising provides one interesting way of examining how advertising messages "hang together." Detailed analyses of modern advertising stylistics are provided by Judith Williamson (1978) and Richard Pollay, in his historical study of American magazine advertisements (1983). We have already seen how advertising quickly picked up and explored stylistic ideas from other media and genres such as comic strips, film, art, fashion, photography, print design, and magazine layout. Throughout its history, advertising remained finely tuned to the expanding world of communication style, especially when it came to expressing ideas visually. From the time when advertisers employed famous painters to create posters, advertising style has been used to establish the identity of the product or company. More recently, stylistic coherence—common colours, design motifs, layout, moods—within an ad, or in a set of ads in a campaign, has become the rule rather than the exception. "Style" has become so much a part of advertising that its innovations are often credited as a major influence on modern arts and media practices.

Our very limited analysis confirms that advertising style responds to trends in other genres. Design and stylistic elements seem to be particularly important in the early part of the century and again after the 1950s (reflecting, no doubt, the influence of television on visual design in print advertising). Today, modern "boutique" agencies specialize in making the domain of communicative style one of the most important methods of product differentiation—as appears in our review of the ads themselves. This seems to be especially true of agencies outside the United States, for example, in Britain and Japan.

Most ads emphasize one particular style; Figure 9.26 shows fluctuations in preferred styles. Humour, in decline from the turn of the century, bounces back in the 1960s. The 1920s and 1930s show great use of narrative, probably under the influence of radio and film, with dialogue rather than third-party description becoming an especially important feature. This storytelling device is in decline by the 1940s and 1950s. Attempts to work with mood, using the emotive, rather than simply the documentary possibilities of illustration, rise dramatically during the 1920s, reminding us of the great impact that the introduction of new methods of photography and colour printing had on advertising. This emphasis on pleasing and composed visual images—on static rather than on dynamic elements—gradually declined through the modern period, although in fashion and personal care advertising, it remains an essential quality of style. The use of striking illustration coincided in the 1920s with a drop in the attention paid to such design elements as typography and layout, but design has regained importance over the years.

Appeal

"Appeal" is the term most frequently used by psychologists and advertisers to describe the basic motivational or persuasive technique used in an ad. In Chapter 6, we noted that the increasing systemization and professionalization of advertising led to appeal becoming, from the 1920s on, an important focus for practitioners' reflections on and pursuit of effectiveness in advertising.

Although most textbooks on advertising today still include a list of appeals, there are no agreed-upon categories to provide a typology for analysis, nor is there much consistency in the use of the concept. Andren, Ericsson, Ohlsson, and Tännsjö (1978) provided a protocol for analyzing appeals, which they used in their study of American advertising, but in it they mixed stylistic and psychological categories. Our own set of categories followed Lerbinger's (1978) more psychological definition of ap-

FIGURE 9.26
The Dominant Aspect of Advertising Style

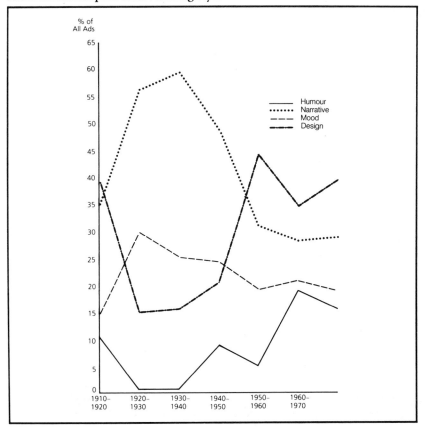

peal, which focuses on persuasive design, or what we will refer to as rhetorical form. Our categories account for the combined use of visual and textual fields of representation in advertising. Figure 9.27 illustrates our analysis of changes in the use of four types of appeal.

We use the term "rational appeal" to characterize ads in which reasoned argument based on product qualities, price, comparison with other products, description or demonstration of benefits, and utility are dominant preoccupations. Rational appeals decline fairly steadily, appearing in 27 percent of ads in the 1910-20 period, but only in 14 percent by the 1970s. Rational argument, of course, also occurs within ads where other types of appeal (such as worry appeal or expert appeal) are predominant, so this line does not capture all rational arguments used in ads. At the same time, our assessment of rational appeal was made irrespective of whether the argument appears in the text or the visual portion of an ad. For example, if the illustration depicts a person "before and after" using

FIGURE 9.27
The Rhetorical Form of Appeal

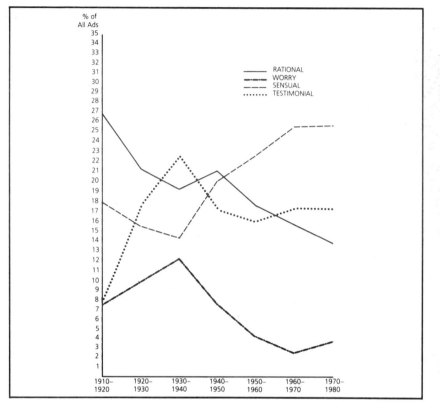

the product, we construed this as a visual demonstration of the benefits of using the product, and interpreted the ad as emphasizing rational argument. In other ads, the benefits of product use (sparkling dishes or clean sinks) are simply illustrated. Thus, one can shift from verbal to visual argument without losing the rational basis of the appeal. However, our study, like others (Pollay 1983, Marquez 1977), indicates a steady trend toward fewer stand-alone uses of rational forms of appeal in advertising.

Advertisers' assimilation of "irrationalist" assumptions about human motivation, which Curti (1967, see Chapter 6) found in industry literature after 1910, resulted in a new "psychological" orientation toward consumers. This turns up in the development of "worry" appeals based on anxiety and uncertainty, which peaked during the 1920s and 1930s. Thus, the worry appeal may reveal more than the general tenor of the times. An interesting contrast to the worry appeal is the relief appeal (not charted), which is based on the promise of satisfaction through the alleviation of a human problem or dilemma. While worry appeal dwells on the problem, relief appeal dwells on the solution. Relief may be promised not only from physical discomfort, but also from embarrassing social situations in family, romantic, and working life. Relief appeal proves remarkably popular, especially in medicinal advertising, and—after dropping off somewhat in the 1920s—reasonably durable.

Sensual appeal increases steadily after the 1930s. Through illustration or description, sensual appeal stresses the sensory qualities of a product, or the sensuality of the person or setting associated with it. In narratives, this appeal is primarily concerned with sensual experiences and the nature of pleasure derived in using products. Sensual appeal becomes the predominant appeal of the 1950s, particularly in those ads that stress the person code. Moreover, during the 1940s, sensuality is increasingly depicted in the context of human interpersonal relations. For a certain range of products, the romantic and loving relationship between man and woman becomes a metaphor for the interpretation of the consumer's newly eroticized attachment to the product. The romance metaphor successfully conveys the notion of a sensual bonding that is deeply rooted in human emotional responses as a new basis for the relationship to products.

Testimonial appeal is further broken down in Figure 9.28. Expert appeal is rational argument based not so much on the product's qualities and benefits, but on the qualifications of an expert or authority who recommends it. Expert appeal explicitly addresses the issue of the credibility of the claims offered in the ad by pointing to a source who bears some relation to these claims. During the 1930s, and again in the 1950s, the expert-appeal ad had a good deal of currency, with doctors, teachers, lawyers, scientists, and even knowledgeable laymen being used to certify goods.

"Star" and "popular" testimonials also peak in the 1930s and decline thereafter. These testimonial ads also stress the relation between a source and the claims presented, but they do so by emphasizing aspects of the relation between the testifier and the reader that are different from the case of expert appeals—fame, in the case of star testimonials, and "ordinary person" traits in the case of popular ones. Testimonial ads have usually employed testifiers who represent a social class "above" that of the ordinary person; this appeal to the audience's social aspirations was dominant except during the war years when conspicuous consumption was not politically acceptable.

In all testimonial ads, we note a trend toward humanizing the forms of argument and the presentation of claims. This trend is historically coincidental with the increasing popularity of photography, film, and radio. As these media—particularly radio, with its stress on the people who spoke about products—amplified the "star system" and cultivated

FIGURE 9.28
The Role Context of Testimonial Appeals

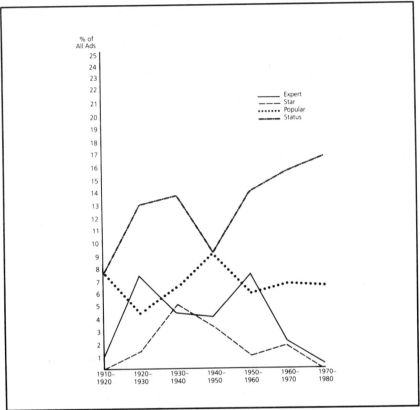

an interest in direct speech, magazine advertising assimilated their new emphases. But in the long run, the use of testimonials in magazine ads seems to have suffered as first radio and then television took over this rhetorical form of advertising, thus reflecting the complex relationship between appeal and the development of media. The product types usually associated with testimonials have shifted to the media—especially television—that are ultimately more suited to such an approach.

Values

A third aspect of integrative codes in advertising is the predominant value that the text and visual image of an ad articulate as the overall desired state of being. Advertising effects a "transfer of value" through communicative connections between what a culture conceives as desirable states of being and products (Leymore 1975; Nowak 1982). The analysis of value-charged references as unifying cognitions in ads has become a standard concern in advertising research, although once again there is no definitive list of categories.

Values, however, tend to provide a rather stable historical field of meaning (Pollay 1983). Advertising works within and reproduces the general normative order, responding to it and only slowly reflecting broader changes and ideological limitations in a society (Nowak 1982; Wernick 1984). Therefore, we do not expect advertising to show dramatic changes in values because advertisers want to work with potential states of being that are desirable, or at least acceptable, to a broad spectrum of the population (Fowles 1976; Sissors 1978).

So while changing technologies, institutional structures, practices of both media and industry, and the currents of artistic creativity have immediate and significant effects on advertising style and appeals, when values are at stake it is a different story. Advertising, especially in the modern period, seems to be a force for stability rather than change. Market research during the 1950s confirmed what long experience had already indicated: advertisers must root their messages in the existing normative order of our society. Although the values represented in ads may be slightly more diverse now and may no longer rely on crude generalizations and assumptions about the "typical consumer," the images of well-being articulated in advertising remain remarkably conventional. The artful blending of innovation in persuasive design with conservatism in values explains much of advertising's force and impact on modern life.

Still, some minor fluctuations in the degree of emphasis on leisure, beauty, romance, quality, or health point to changes in our society itself (see Figure 9.29). The rise of the value of progress in the 1950s and individualism in the 1960s and 1970s are good illustrations. We have no reason to believe that advertisers created these shifts in values; but, since advertisers stay tuned closely to the normative order, advertising as a system may well anticipate and amplify certain value changes that are in progress and deemed relevant for ads to particular segments of the population (for example, the youth subculture, the middle class, yuppies, or—now in the 1990s—environmental protection). The present stress on leisure values may be an instance in which advertising's orientation to particular markets promotes conditions that emphasize these values over others (such as family togetherness, tradition, or the work ethic).

THEMES

Our discussion so far has pursued the analysis of the advertising message through changes in the fields of representation (in magazines, the move

FIGURE 9.29
Values

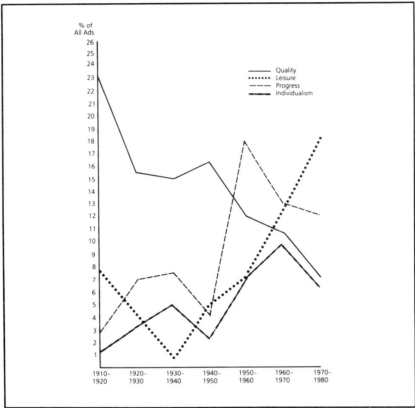

from the focus on text to illustration) and in the use of elemental codes. We also made comparisons within each field and elemental code. Examining the text of advertisements for themes that reflect the type of information or argument offered in them provided us with some important clues. We paid specific attention to the relationship between people and products. Even though the actual amount of text declines over the years, we found that we could note themes reliably because advertisers began to concentrate on a single, unified idea for the product, and to make less use of subsidiary themes (Pollay 1983). Our graphs (Figures 9.30a to 9.30c) present changes in the predominant themes in ads.

We noted a general decline in utility themes—the results of product use ("the cleanest kitchen") and the efficacy of the product ("deep-scouring action"). Mention of the processes of production and manufacture ("from the shops of skilled craftsmen") fades. Arguments about product effectiveness and utility, although still quite prevalent, have been declining steadily since the turn of the century.

FIGURE 9.30a: Product Utility Themes

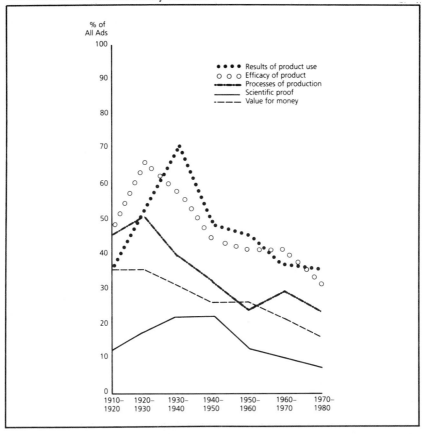

Meanwhile, the text has increasingly emphasized other types of relationships between people and products (see Figure 9.30b). The most general theme is satisfaction with or an emotional reaction to the use of the product ("never disappoints"), although this, too, decreases throughout the period. In contrast, descriptions of a direct personal relationship to a product ("a good friend in the kitchen") grow, peaking in the 1950s. By this time, products have taken their place in a scheme whose basic dimensions are framed by the individual human person. This so closely matches the growing importance of motivation research and the changes in advertising approach of the period that it hardly needs comment. The effects of this personal orientation are also revealed in a more verbalized "personification"—describing products as having essentially human characteristics ("the sexy young fragrance"). The product's ability to transform some aspect of the user—for example, personality or behaviour—increases during the 1930s and levels off in the 1950s.

Other themes also provide clues to changing relationships between

FIGURE 9.30b: Personalizing Themes

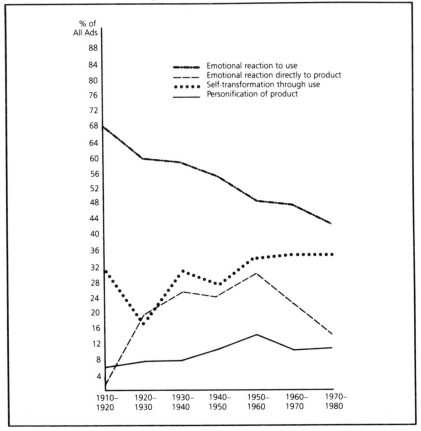

persons and objects (Figure 9.30c). The ability of the product to capture and render some aspect of nature as a quality of the product, which we have called "white magic" ("brings you the freshness of Springtime"), declines in the 1920s but recurs uncharacteristically for a brief season in the 1960s. "Black magic," defined as the ability of the product to increase the effectiveness of interpersonal relations, shows a fairly steady growth over a long period of time. These themes, rather than direct emotional reactions to the use of the product, increasingly define both the associative meaning of products and their direct utilitarian and emotive effects, offering new domains of satisfaction to be achieved in the postwar period.

People and Products

The analysis of themes helped to confirm our belief that the way advertising depicts the relationship between people and products has changed

FIGURE 9.30c
Other Themes

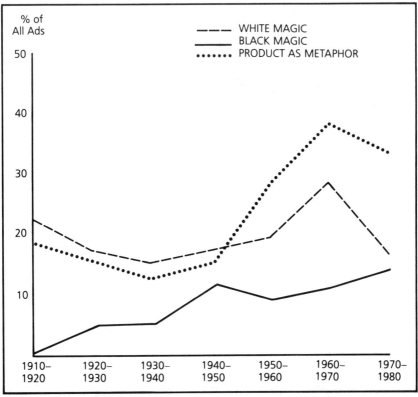

dramatically over the past century. We therefore turned our attention more directly to the ways advertisements present people and the nature of their experiences with goods—the person code in advertising.

We saw earlier in the chapter that the increasing amount of textual information about users during the 1920s, and thereafter the portrayal of persons through art and photography, led to the expansion of symbolic as opposed to utilitarian associations with goods. Figures 9.31a and 9.31b illustrate the manner of indicating use within the visual and textual changes. During the 1930s, a person may be shown more as a symbol of the product's inherent qualities than as a consumer. Another common approach is to show a consumer using the product in the visual and to state explicitly that this is so in the text—a testimonial. The consumer is most often depicted as a satisfied customer. Through the 1940s, the representation of use is increasingly implied in the illustration, while stated reference to use in the text is low. However, implied use is peaking in the text at this time.

FIGURE 9.31a
Representation of Use

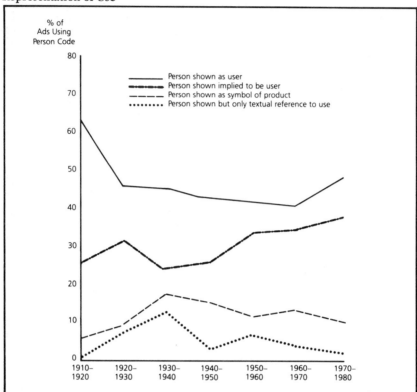

This tendency continues, with the illustration increasingly implying use while the text changes its allusions as well, from that of user and satisfied customer, as in the testimonial ad, to the implied use typical of the personalized and lifestyle ad formats. As we have seen, the emphasis on sensuality, on emotional reactions to products, and on social relations increases concurrently, peaking in the 1950s. The depiction of people in ads becomes concerned less with the person as a symbol of an abstract product quality and more with the experience and personal meaning of consumption. We see this as a new focal point within the person code. The people in ads undergo "cathexis" as the concentration of attention shifts to the direct involvement of people with products in settings of social intercourse and self-development.

Figure 9.32 illustrates a number of factors that also led us to conclude that the postwar period defines a new "emotional" relationship between people and products. The product is presented as a sensual thing experienced through consumption; the consumer knows the product through

FIGURE 9.31b
Interpretation of Use

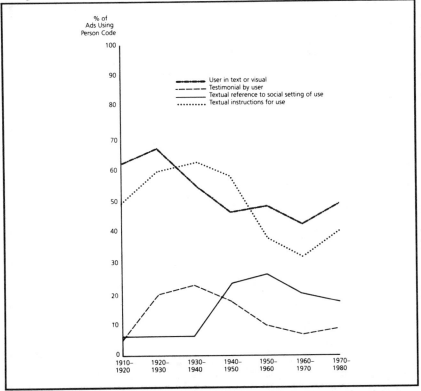

emotional reactions—primarily pleasure, happiness, and love (worry, relief, fear, and so forth play a lesser role)—not so much caused by direct use of the product but more as a general attribute of human experience associated with use. Romance, family, and parental love supply the context for human relations in which we respond to products. Especially during the immediate postwar period, human relations provide the metaphoric plane on which consumers are asked to interpret their "felt" response to products, and thus the relationship between people and products is "eroticized."

Although the number of ads depicting people is declining by the 1950s, in the ads that do so the actual proportion of the area devoted to the visual representation of people reaches its peak at this time. During the 1960s, the overall concern with the person code decreases as ads begin to emphasize the social settings of consumption. This is generally confirmed in other historical reviews, although some studies suggest that the importance of human representation in advertising declines after World

FIGURE 9.32
Relationship of People and Products

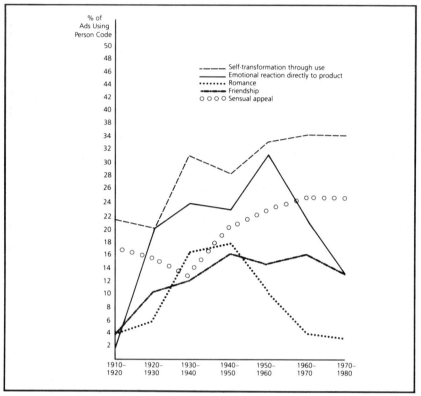

War II. This observation is only partially correct: first, it is textual references to people that diminish, and second, this decrease is part of the
changing emphasis in the relationship between people and products.
When the representation of persons is transferred from the text to the
visual field, it stresses the act of consumption rather than the result of use,
and thus focuses on the connections between people and products, not
on the people themselves. Further changes occur during the 1960s when
the lifestyle format comes to the fore, indicating new factors at play in the
modern period that emphasize the person's experience in social activities and situations.

TOWARD AN INTEGRATED HISTORICAL FRAMEWORK

In each culture there exists a main operator by which its representations are
transformed into reality. At times individuals and at times animals were
elevated to this role. In our culture, the mathematical-physical sciences, that

is the sciences of quantifiable and measureable objects, serve as the paradigm for all knowledge. We are spellbound by reverse animism which populates our universe with inanimate machines in the place of animated beings. (Moscovici 1981)

In advertising, we may indeed be spellbound by things, but we do not seem to be transfixed by the scientific world view. This century opened with rationalism and the objective characteristics of goods at the centre of advertising, implying a predominantly pragmatic relationship between persons and objects; but this mode of representation has systematically been eroded and replaced by one in which products have been "re-animized" and given meaning, transporting them from the rational-physical universe of things to the world of human social interaction. Perhaps the world of advertising has provided the counterweight to the scientific rationalism that rules elsewhere in modern culture.

The development of nonutilitarian representations of the world of objects in advertising can be detected first in the symbolic associations of the early years of this century; the field enlarges steadily as illustration and photography become prevalent in the 1930s, highlighting people in relation to products. The trend toward visually representing the symbolic domain continues in certain ads in the 1950s, but it now focuses on the consumer and the satisfaction of consumption. Beginning in the 1960s, the emphasis shifts from the consumer's experience to consumption styles and the activities and social context that link consumption with everyday life.

These shifts reflect not only the changing communicational environment in which advertisers work, but also the conceptual changes that were taking place in the practice of marketing and advertising (discussed in Chapter 6). The marketing concept was helping to draw attention away from the notion of "utility," which had emphasized the product and its effectiveness, toward that of "use," which was concerned primarily with the way the product enhanced the experience of satisfaction achieved through the act of consumption. Explorations in communicative form also contributed to the conditions in which a new emphasis emerged. For example, the shift from informational to symbolic presentation, typical of the product-image format, was no doubt enhanced by the possibilities revealed to advertising designers by the ability to illustrate the selling idea, as well as by the postulation of the "irrational" basis of consumption. The introduction of photography led to greater emphasis on people and settings, thus preparing the ground for new dimensions of symbolic reference. In this way, communication design became more than a passive reflection of the environment—it became a transformative activity.

Demonstrating the utility, construction, or effectiveness of a product is difficult to express visually. Use, on the other hand, seems to adapt well to illustration, especially when it is merely implied. As the emphasis moves from the efficacy of the product to the personal consequences of consumption, the advertising designer can explore the drama of consumer satisfaction rather than the prosaic facts of product effectiveness. Although the majority of early ads in which people appear either mention or show the person as a user, by the middle of the 1940s use is usually either implied or omitted. Even in ads from the 1920s and 1930s, in which use is explicit, the image of the person (or user) often also refers to the world of symbolic attributes beyond the realm of the product, or the mode and benefits of its use. Testimonial ads especially tend visually to stress the attributes associated with the user and not the act of use. The door is opened to more symbolic rather than rationalistic approaches to communication. The shift to product-image formats opens up advertising's discourse about products to include images of status, glamour, beauty, health, and respectable middle-class mores among the images of product quality.

The proliferation of representations of people in advertising creates its own problems. During the 1940s, advertising becomes so cluttered with pictures of typical people and beautiful people that the distinctive product image is almost lost. In the 1950s, some advertisers add distinctive features to their characterizations (the famous Hathaway eye patch, for instance), or attempt to sharpen the product image through greater attention to the setting.

Such changes in orientation are, of course, in part reactions to problems and conditions created within the institutional structures and the practice of advertising itself. The following description of the development of advertising as a series of emergent phases is our attempt to summarize the major adjustments in communicative formats in response to a multiplicity of problems facing the advertiser on the cultural, institutional, and practical levels.

Until the 1920s, the concern with the function, benefits, price, and construction of products dominated magazine advertising. We can best describe the implied relationship between people and products as utility. The central feature of the ads in this phase is the product itself. The question for the consumer is, What does this product do? In the 1880s, advertisers were highly restricted by the types of illustrations that were possible, but the commercialization of the media led to new possibilities in display and illustration, especially in magazine ads. Now a much better representation of the concrete "being" of the product was possible. The ads of the early twentieth century explored the nature of the product within these physical confines, as well as within the societal confines of the late industrial era. This exploration marked the final phase of what Pope (1972) terms "the Golden Era of advertising."

John Berger (1972) has commented generally on how oil painting increased the "tangibility" of artistic imagery, and on how photography extends this feature of visual representation in advertising. In the first two decades of this century, the ability to illustrate and photograph products caused the first cracks to appear in the strictly rational orientation of the product-information format toward utility. The concrete, tangible nature of the product became more important, and utility became associated with this. Sometimes the product was portrayed not just as a mere object for utilitarian functions, but as giving off emanations of another world of promise and potency. The product ascended a pedestal (often actually depicted in the ad); tangibility implied permanence and reverence, and the text expanded on these qualities made manifest in the visual.

The continuing development of the visual dimension of advertising and changes in advertising copy sped the transition to symbolic representations in the 1920s. Under the influence of the new media of film and radio, emphasis on what the product *did* diminished while the visuals increasingly explored what the product could *mean* for consumers—where it fitted within a world view expanded to encompass the whole of society and nature. This signalled a second phase in the developing relationship between people and products in which the product itself became more abstract—a value achieved in use rather than a thing valued in its own right. The product seemed to demand an answer to the question, What does it mean to use this product? The explicit depiction of the relationship between people and products became central; use began to replace utility as the most frequent means of showing the connections between people and goods.

Advertising in the period after 1945 faced a new challenge: the enterprise of turning war productivity to the purposes of the consumer market. New dimensions were added to discourses about uses. The key question became, What emotional reactions are consumers supposed to experience in consumption? Product quality and general consumer satisfaction were no longer sufficient. The product was being registered within a complex matrix of human emotional responses. The people in advertisements were not just experienced users of products; they had to convey an impression of the *nature* of the satisfaction they achieved. Advertising increasingly addressed questions like, How can I become happy through consumption?

The most recent phase of advertising can be recognized in the joint appearance of lifestyle ads and the highly segmented market of the 1960s and thereafter. Demographic research and market segmentation have become the operational matrix of advertising strategy. The concern has shifted to the identification of the consumer and the nature of the act of consumption within a social situation. The product has become a totem, a representation of a clan or group that we recognize by its activities and its members' shared enjoyment of the product. The response to consumption seems to be less concerned with the nature of satisfaction than with

FIGURE 9.33
Phases in the Development of Communicative Formats: A Historical Model

1910 — 1920 — 1930 — 1940 — 1950 — 1960 — 1970 — 1980			
INFORMATION	SYMBOLISM	PERSONALIZATION	LIFESTYLE
Utility	Personal Use	Gratification	Social Context

its social meaning—the way it integrates the individual into a consumption tribe. Meaning here focuses on questions like, Who is the person I become in the process of consumption? Who are the other consumers like me? What does the product mean in terms of the type of person I am and how I relate to others?

Figure 9.33 illustrates phases in the development of advertising's communicative formats. The sequence in this model is a broad interpretation of patterns in the development of advertising's communicative dimensions in a theoretically stable field in which data have been corrected for product and magazine type.

In fact, a more detailed analysis of codes found that both the type of product and magazine are related to changing qualities of advertising format. Certain products are sold consistently over long periods with the same approaches, as indicated by their orchestration of codes. For instance, across all periods we found that personal-care products were predominantly personalized, automobiles were given product-information treatments, and alcohol ads tended to be symbolic (concentrating on product image) or lifestyle in form (Kline 1983; Jhally, Kline, and Leiss 1985). The variation in advertising format for a product type seems to bear an inverse relationship to the increasing segmentation in marketing and media practice. For example, there was less variation in advertising presentations for particular product types in the 1960s than there was in the 1930s.

Advertising formats gradually narrowed as well, within the two magazines used in our study, in part because of the reduced range of products that advertise in their pages. But we also find that the advertising formats for the same product range differ noticeably between the two magazines, showing audience segmentation as well as market segmentation at work. Although in both magazines the product appears with identical emphasis, in the male-oriented magazine greater emphasis is put on the use of text and on the person code, while the female-oriented magazine shows greater stress on setting codes typical of the product image and lifestyle formats. Comparing the advertisements for the same products in the two magazines led us to the conclusion that the tendency was to narrow the form through which advertising addressed specialized audiences.

Increasing segmentation—noted in our review of advertising thought and practice—manifests itself in general trends in advertising formats as the constraint imposed by product type and audience orientation. This segmentation reached its highest level during the last twenty-five years, coincidental with the increasing emphasis on settings for consumption typical of lifestyle advertising. In this respect, the historical sequence of advertising formats is more like the overlaying process depicted in Figure 9.34, in which a new communicative approach or emphasis does not eliminate previous ones but rather allows more specific responses by the audience to the type of product. The accumulated experience and knowledge of the advertising industry as a whole, as distinct from trends within particular agencies, is reflected here. As advertisers come to believe that people buy cars based on their performance, cosmetics based on their image, and cigarettes based on how they feel about other cigarette smokers, these theories about consumers and how to persuade them become part of advertising communication.

If advertisers also believe (and they do) that women are less rational consumers than men, this will be revealed in the fact that the more rational forms of advertising occur less often for women's products and in women's magazines. Once again, careful analysis by product type and by magazine revealed that these results are "segmented." For example, analysis indicated that self-transformation ads, originally developed for the female audience, have been steadily gaining favour in the male-oriented magazine, whereas the "white magic" theme (imparting the virtues of nature to the product) and "black magic" (the product's power to captivate and allure) are highly concentrated in the female-oriented magazine. These differences are due, in part, to the concentration of these themes around personal-care products such as cosmetics, and, in part, to the increasing tendency of advertisers to address the male and

FIGURE 9.34
Phases in the Segmentation of Advertising Form: A Stratified Model

---

1900 — 1920 — 1930 — 1940 — 1950 — 1960 — 1970 — 1980

Information-Utility ————————————————— Cars/Technology
Corporate

Symbolism-Personal Use ——— Household/Durables
Food/Tobacco

Personalization-Gratification — Personal Care
Tobacco/Food

Lifestyle-Social Context
Alcohol/Food
Tobacco/Clothes

---

female audiences differently (Jhally, Kline, and Leiss 1985, table 1). The attempt to subsume audience and market segmentation into advertising's communicative strategy and design is an important part of the advertising system today.

Our study of advertising imagery shows a richly textured and artfully constructed set of messages whose common purpose is to bind together persons and products. The message formats evolve in a series of stages, as advertising practice is shaped by, and helps to shape, new possibilities provided by communications technologies. But society and culture are evolving as well, and we will now turn to the task of integrating the historical schemas presented above into the larger supporting framework.

10

Goods as Satisfiers

- *Think up the object according to its image,*
  not to its function
- *Render the reading of function ambiguous*
- *Tend towards a contradictory image: both*
  HARD and SOFT
- *Put dissimilar parts together*
- *Introduce an unexpected element (give a*
  feeling of suspense)
- *Make calm, poetic, introvert, mildly self-*
  mocking objects
- *Think of objects that are always different from*
  each other (differentiated series)
- *Give products mixed craft and computer-*
  world characteristics

("Rules of Design," *Domus*, 1984)

IMAGE AND METAPHOR

At first glance, what appears to distinguish the economies of modern western industrialized countries from others is the sheer number and variety of products. While this provides a convenient yardstick for those who like to measure the superiority of our standard of living by counting telephones, toilets, and television sets, another great difference, no less dramatic in scale, often goes unnoticed—the layers of images and symbols that surround us relating these products to our personal happiness and social success. Just because it fits so snugly and comfortably, our thick cloak of symbols seems to be a natural part of our being. The consumer society constructed this field of symbols and implanted it at the centre of marketplace activity, causing a profound transformation in social life. The nature of this transformation, the change in the social function of goods from being primarily satisfiers of wants to being primarily communicators of meanings, will be explored in this and the succeeding chapter.

Three forces are largely responsible: (1) the recognition of consumption as a legitimate sphere for individual self-realization; (2) the discovery by marketers and advertisers that the personal or psychological and interpersonal (or social) domains of the consumer, rather than the characteristics of goods, were the vital core of merchandising; (3) the revolutions in communications and mass-media technologies that made possible the rapid evolution of advertising formats, including the special significance of visual or iconic imagery.

Such developments became united in a social process that can be summarized in the following propositions. First, individuals should expect to achieve a significant measure of personal happiness and evidence of social success as a result of their involvement in consumption. Second, messages about achieving happiness and success will use "open-ended interpretive codes"—social cues for indicating to people how to decide what is socially acceptable at any given time, which do not rely on fixed or traditional cultural norms but rather encourage experimentation in achieving satisfaction. Third, the ability to transmit live visual representations of group action into domains of private life (especially the home) will offer guidance to people on how to integrate these particular commercial messages about goods into general patterns of behaviour.

These three propositions, in turn, are bound together by a single underlying theme: the most important feature of consumption activity is the *interpretation* of what "satisfaction" means in the lives of individuals. In the present chapter, we follow up the discussion of advertising formats in Chapter 9 in order to see how advertisers have integrated the psychological or " subjective" dimension into their portrayals of products. We seek to show that this innovation is rooted firmly in the understanding that, in the consumer marketplace, one's sense of satisfaction and well-being is based not on accumulated possessions but on subjective, shifting estimates of where one stands in relation to others and what values are most important.

Before turning to the structure of imagery in advertising, let us say a few words about the key terms used throughout this examination, namely image, icon, and symbol. *Image* (the root of the word "imagination") is the richest of the three, meaning either a verbal or visible representation, especially of a vivid or graphic character, suggestive of some thing, idea, or concept. Thus, imagery may be verbal—as it is most powerfully in poetry—or pictorial in nature. Modern advertising, of course, frequently utilizes pictorial and verbal forms simultaneously, and when we discuss the imagistic mode of communication in advertising, we are referring to printed messages or electronically transmitted audio and visual signals with both a verbal and a pictorial element.

Icon is interchangeable with the pictorial aspects of image; in common use it means a picture of a venerated figure in a religious setting. We use it to refer to pictorial representations of those secular values that have a special place or high status in our culture ("mother" and "father" in older times, "being modern" and "being sophisticated" today). Thus, the iconic mode of communication refers to ads wherein the pictorial or visual element is clearly predominant in the message as a whole, incorporating only a few words of written or spoken text in association with dramatic visual imagery.

By its very nature, verbal imagery is discursive while visual imagery is nondiscursive. Implicit in the former is an argument or a case for the association of the image with what it refers to, so that one could, if asked, spell out the relationship in a more extensive written text. In visual imagery, there is often an abrupt "imaginative leap" and a freer play of associations that is difficult to put into words. This is not a hard-and-fast rule, however, and many exceptions can be noted.

A *symbol* is a visible sign of something that is itself not apparent to the senses—it "stands for" something else. It invites comparison between the representation (the sign) and what it stands for. For example, an animal used as a brand symbol for a certain automobile model sets up a field of mental associations and possible analogies between the characteristics of the animal (both real and mythic) and those of the automobile (both physical and imputed).

Although symbolism can be expressed in verbal as well as iconic forms, modern advertising has strongly favoured the iconic. Among the reasons for this is that successful verbal imagery requires a reasonable degree of language skill in the reader or listener and a high level of attentiveness to subtleties in the message. But readers scan advertisements quickly and are therefore likely to miss sophisticated plays with words. Verbal imagery may thus be employed advantageously in short slogans, but in longer texts the result is unlikely to repay the creative effort. Also, the newer communications media—improved photography, film, and television—overwhelmingly favoured the iconic; radio, of course, is the exception, but even it contributed to the general trend by lessening the share of popular attention enjoyed by print media and by emphasizing brief, pithy slogans in its advertising style.

We suggested in Chapter 4 that the consumer society arises out of the ashes of traditional cultures, which are characterized by relatively fixed forms for the satisfaction of needs, and unleashes a grand experimentation with the individual's experience of both needs and the ways of satisfying them. The consumer society does not set up its own fixed models of behaviour to replace traditional ones but rather constructs, through marketing and advertising, successive waves of associations between persons, products, and images of well-being in an endless series of suggestions about the possible routes to happiness and success.

Modern advertising is so fascinated with the communicative tools of symbol, image, and icon because they are ideal for such constructions. They work by allusion, free association, suggestion, and analogy rather than by literal and logical rule. One possible interpretive scheme or specific instance of a correspondence between a product, a setting, and a type of person does not exclude another, or indeed many others. And this is the precise intention: that the whole ensemble of goods and messages should be as "versatile" as possible, should appeal simultaneously to the entire spectrum of personality types and lawful urges, including those half-formed, inarticulate yearnings that individuals can be brought to recognize and express only through the very play of such images.

An essential feature of the consumer society is its concern with what consumption activity *means* to individuals in a market-industrial economy that has eroded the guidelines for the sense of satisfaction and well-being laid out by traditional cultures. Into the gap step marketers and advertisers, who generate meaning by constructing schemas for well-being through associating images of persons, products, and settings. Such schemas are not necessarily imposed on naive and gullible consumers or accepted literally and uncritically; in fact, they would be less useful (not more so) to producers if they were, for then they could not open up so widely the sphere of consumption, as they now do, by tapping the infinitely varied play of potential meanings in the minds of individuals who are keenly attentive to what is happening in the marketplace.

The term "image" can have predominantly negative connotations, of course, when it is applied to what appears to be merely a manipulation of superficial features for purposes of misrepresentation, or when it is misleading in the weaker sense of conveying something beguiling or charming, not quite fraudulent but still not properly representative. In *The Image* (1962), Daniel Boorstin describes the "graphic revolution" in media technologies as being largely responsible for "the rise of image-thinking." For Boorstin, images are synthetic things, "pseudo-events," actions staged to serve a purpose and to make an impression. The best example is the politician's interview or "photo opportunity" carefully timed to make the evening television news. Boorstin's book is a lament rather than a criticism, however, because the public appears to be a willing participant in the fabrication and enjoyment of these illusions.

By the mid-1970s, articles in marketing and advertising journals showed that thinking about "image creation" and its legitimate offspring, "image management," was a serious business indeed. Images had been assigned a place of critical importance in the understanding of consumer behaviour, as the connecting link between the consumer's value systems and his or her preferences for products: "The majority of product classes are comprised of products which do not differ from each other in any significant way. Therefore, advertising functions to enhance physical attributes and their relative importance with respect to how the consumer sees him/herself, essentially providing psychological benefits through the image-creation process" (Reynolds and Gutman 1984, 27).

The metaphors of symbol, image, and icon work by analogy and allusion; they refer beyond themselves to something else; they invite comparison between two things which appear to be dissimilar but which, they suggest, have a shared meaning. It is our contention that **metaphor is the very heart of the basic communicative form used in modern advertising.**

As the message structures in ads become more subtle, a variety of techniques connect the various dimensions—text, visuals, slogan or headline, and, ideally, ad design itself—without calling attention to the "connective" techniques. Pollay and Mainprize (1984) have described some of these techniques, for example, presenting "puzzles" that require viewers or readers themselves to "construct the message and constitute the selling proposition." They also demonstrate how metaphor works in the composition of advertisements by putting people, activities, and scenes side by side with products and seeking to convert this contiguity into a meaningful relationship.

Paul Ricoeur (1977, 7) writes that "metaphor is the rhetorical process by which discourse unleashes the power that certain fictions have to redescribe reality." We would modify this superb statement only by emphasizing that the term "discourse" should refer to both verbal and pictorial communicative modes. Advertisements certainly are fictions, that is, imaginative creations or artful representations of possible worlds, and they strive mightily to redescribe reality, by taking familiar components of everyday life—recognizable people, indoor and outdoor settings, and social situations—and conjuring up scene after scene full of hypothetical interactions between these components and a product.

Figure 4. 1 nicely shows this communicative process in action. Here the basic rnessage that the sensible car owner will use gasoline with a lead additive is conveyed primarily through pictorial imagery, although the point is made in the written text as well. It is assumed that women should know something about the automobile, which is already well on its way toward achieving a special place among all goods in the consumer culture. The woman's hands call up unspoken references to the mother of the family in her traditional role as preparer of meals, a hoary symbol. The message structure is a metaphorical construction of elegant simplicity. Adding lead to gasoline (the unfamiliar act) has the same effect as adding cheese to macaroni (the familiar act). Reality is redescribed by a simple analogy between what would otherwise be considered by the intended readers (women who are just then becoming aware of what is entailed in automobile ownership and maintenance) operations that had nothing at all in common.

To summarize, a double symbolic process is at work in the consumer society. One facet of this process is the symbolism consciously employed by businesses in the manufacture and sale of products, including the

imagery used in advertising. Especially since the advent of market segmentation, marketers have through demographic statistics some prior
idea of the target audience for their messages, and know that a well-
conceived sales campaign drawing upon an almost unlimited stock of
traditional and innovative imagery can elicit new wants and consumption
styles. The other facet is the symbolic associations selectively employed
by consumers in admitting new wants and in constructing new lifestyles.
As mentioned earlier, up to 80 percent of new products introduced into
the marketplace fail to reach their profit objectives, with a high proportion of these then being withdrawn from the market—a pointed lesson
not only for entrepreneurs, but also for social commentators who agonize
over the "manipulation" of popular consciousness by advertisers. One
should not underestimate the elementary common sense of the general
population, just as one should not underestimate the degree to which
individuals are dependent upon social cues for guidance in how to
consume things.

THE ICONS OF THE MARKETPLACE

A high proportion of goods in the marketplace today appear cloaked in
layers of symbols and images conveyed by many means, including product design, packaging, store displays, fashion-trend changes, peer-group
pressures, and media-based advertising. Sometimes the schemas of association are complex and exquisitely composed, so that the idea of an
intended "message" is simply irrelevant. Around 1985, a window display
at Tiffany's in New York mounted a scene of urban decay in which two
mannequins—a male Bowery bum and a tattered bag lady—were posed
as the setting for a $50,000 gold-and-diamond necklace, which was
placed at the bag lady's feet. In this case, the window display, through the
incongruity of its elements, calls attention to itself by reversing our
normal associational fields.

More and more goods appear as mere receptacles for the generalized
play of meanings, as "fields" for human states of feeling that are projected
onto the physical and sensual substance of the object. The goods themselves almost seem to be mirrors that reflect back to us the blurry and
fleeting set of images cast over them.

"Modern goods are recognized as psychological things, as symbolic
of personal attributes and goals, as symbolic of social patterns and striv-
ings. In this sense, all commercial objects have a symbolic character . . ."
(Levy 1969, 410). On the immediate level, the introduction of symbolism
in presenting goods helped to influence specific consumer choices. On a
deeper level, another process was at work. Paradoxically, when utility is
rooted in the product's own characteristics satisfaction, too, is circum-
scribed since it is derived from allowing the product to carry out the

functions for which it was designed. When use is rooted in the consumer's psychological state, however, anything goes, for then something is useful only insofar as and so long as one believes this to be the case. But belief in the modern world is a flimsy affair, readily convertible as newer promises circulate. As goods are enveloped in symbols, the requirement to enlarge the scope and intensity of the total commercial effort in everyday life accompanies this transition in focal point from the object to the person.

The marketers' designs are not acts of unaided imagination. A considerable amount of consumer research established the importance of the symbolic attributes of goods in purchasing choices, both in general and with respect to specific frames of reference such as status, gender, and social class. Marketers seek to base the product image on a prior analysis of the interpretive predilections of the target audience. They may construct the image either for mass markets by using open codes of interpretation (symbols recognized by the average person everywhere), or for specific subgroups (such as teenagers) by using restricted codes.

Since consumption is, in part, a form of popular entertainment, the play of symbols in advertising generally is confined to the more superficial levels of psychological processes. But the price of superficiality is that the attention-getting power of most pitches decays rapidly and the turnover time gets shorter and shorter. Visual imagery is inherently better equipped than verbal expression—especially where vocabulary cannot be allowed to become too extensive or concept too subtle—to map and explore the surface features of changing events and to relate them quite arbitrarily to products through analogy and association, the potent inferential capacities of metaphor.

What results is a situation in which people are surrounded by things that are themselves "alive." The intensely personalized focus of the message and the incorporation of references to social settings and events provide the backdrop for the advertiser's imaginative task, which is to design the "package of stimuli so that it resonates with information already stored within an individual, and thereby induces the desired learning or behavioral effect" (Schwartz 1974, 24). Such information is not, except incidentally, the economist's information, which is composed of the product's characteristics, but rather the imagistic associations between the product and what is known about individuals and their expectations in life, including their feelings about status, peer-group influence, roles, social mobility, and changing lifestyles. This resonance between persons and things circulates freely through all of society's information channels, both interpersonal and institutional, including, of course, the mass media. In this context, the realm of needing becomes immersed within the domain of communication.

As a result, goods play a distinctive role in the human dialogue.

Considered as repositories of stored information in the broader sense, goods are an important means whereby consumers can communicate to others their relationships to complex sets of otherwise abstract social attributes (such as status), thus identifying themselves within social structures. This is the most general significance of what we referred to in Chapter 4 as the "transformational" mode in marketing and advertising. The most important function of product-related imagery is not to increase levels of consumer spending, but to transform the personal meaning of the everyday use of products as a whole.

"Corporate image"—and, at least in some countries, "national image"—advertising has become increasingly prominent in recent years, doubtless trading on the success of the product-image ad. Quasi-political messages promulgate the self-proclaimed qualities of the business or government entity itself, or its reflections on what is happening in society and politics. The major oil companies have spent considerable amounts of time and money on corporate-image advertising since 1973. Nationwide department-store chains have engaged in highly stylized "generic" campaigns, in part to protect their market share against invasion by specialized boutiques trading on the wave of market segmentation. Imagistic advertising is now also used by governments with broad political purposes in mind. In Canada, the federal government and that of the province of Quebec, in their competition with each other, have sought the loyalty of the population through intensive media campaigns in which the political messages themselves make no direct references to the actual sources of conflict. For example, the federal government has promoted "national unity" by emphasizing its commitment to "multiculturalism," showing scenes of vibrant and diverse ethnic communities but not referring specifically to the French-speaking population. In addition, governments of other Canadian provinces (notably Ontario and British Columbia) routinely use media advertising to promote "government policy," which is widely regarded as a poorly disguised exercise in self-promotion for the party in power.

Having discussed the growing preponderance of imagistic modes of communication in advertising that favour visual over verbal forms of expression, and having looked at some actual types, we wish to explore the special importance of iconic representation in presenting product-related imagery. Iconic representation, used alone or in conjunction with verbal text, is far more effective than text alone. Relative costs for advertising time and space reflect not only the potential "reach" of the mass media in the marketplace (the size and demographic features of the audience), but also the potential effectiveness of communications through these media in influencing consumption patterns. Among the various media, magazines and television emerged as prestige advertising vehicles because they are well-suited for transmitting both verbal and pictorial information. The intuitive understanding by advertisers that these two forms of communication could be highly effective was corroborated by findings reported in the psychological literature on the way people process information.

Given the highly selective way in which persons are known to survey their environments, it is the task of advertisements to break through the barriers to attention that people normally build. Design, layout, contrast, colour, striking and unusual imagery have all been shown to increase the likelihood and duration of visual scanning. Television has the special advantage of combining the dimensions of sound and picture together with movement and editing techniques to secure and enhance attention. Furthermore, research shows that iconic representation has a relatively greater impact on the "affective-opinion" components of attitude, that is, those aspects related to making decisions (Kline 1977). Iconic representation can be absorbed in a sort of "parallel process" without full conscious awareness, and thus it can register an impact without being translated into explicit verbal formulations.

Above and beyond the concern with attitudinal barriers, the advertiser's objective is to clearly differentiate its product's image from others by soldering the associational links between brand and image as fully as possible. The ad's impact, of course, will depend upon the degree of retention of these particular associations by the audience. When a visual image is used as a "memory peg" for the message, a person's retention of the ideas associated with the visual is significantly higher than it is if the verbal information is presented alone (Segall 1971; Sheehan 1972). A catchy tune or jingle has been employed as a memory peg for many years, but it appears that a visual image works even better.

Several other processes are also worth noting here. First, unusual or absurd images seem to enhance retention. Second, joining otherwise separate elements in a visual presentation appears to be advantageous; a complex of attributes is more easily recognized and remembered than a single one. Third, pictures elicit a greater number of free associations than do words.

The implications are obvious. Not only does visual imagery increase the attention paid to an ad, but it also can build strong associational links to a greater number of qualities, while at the same time retaining a high degree of ambiguity. The ambiguity that can be supported by visual imagery is significant, both for the ease with which symbolic qualities can be dispersed over a wide variety of product categories and types, and for the resultant indeterminancy of the associations. "Convenience" can be combined symbolically with images of "gourmet skill" for foods, "neatness" for household cleansers, and "casual lifestyle" for clothing. The openness of the product image to varying permutations and interpretations means that both advertisers and consumers can experiment freely with the meanings—which may be constructed differently by each, to be sure—in a particular ad campaign.

The consumer culture grants both marketers and shoppers wide latitude for such experimentation. The general tendency has been an almost uniform expansion of the boundaries of permissible symbolic reference. There are still forbidden zones established by legislation (restrictions on tobacco and alcohol ads), social taboos (forms of sexual expression), "good taste" (governed by industry codes), and unsuitable themes (those that are intrinsically inappropriate for selling goods, such as prejudice). Still, the borders of these zones are being scouted constantly for new material (as Tiffany's did with its bag lady image), and the prevailing rules are tested regularly by indirect or oblique references to currently prohibited images. Advertising's special love of humour comes in handy here, since humour defuses tension and serious disagreement; the waters can be tested, so to speak, by humorous or allegorical treatments when "straight" depictions would not do. A slightly ominous Russian commissar in a vodka ad, it is hoped, will add some allure to what is otherwise just another colourless liquid distilled from ordinary grain at a factory in the suburbs.

Thus, we take for granted the existence of an "image pool," without being able to specify how capacious it is or how varied are the entities it holds. From it, the advertiser must fish out something that will differentiate one brand from other products in the same use-type or the same subgroup of a use-type (such as a specific "class" of automobiles). Shampoos will be distinguished from conditioners, and Shampoo X-1 will be associated with "luxuriant beauty," X-2 with "youth and excitement," X-3 with "the natural look," and so forth. The effect is a broad range of divergent qualities associated with a certain product use-type. Uncertainty, defined as the range of possible alternative associations for a single product type, becomes a feature of the product image (as opposed to the brand image).

There are three key characteristics of the image pool. The first and most important is that it *redescribes reality*, stemming from its basic function in the service of marketing: the selling of well-being and happiness through the selling of goods. Since this is accomplished by selecting scenes from everyday life, the social reality in which we actually live is systematically redescribed to provide a suitable canvas on which the advertiser can work. This canvas is the basic level of redescription; on it is sketched a higher level, created by the nature of advertising's predominant communicative mode—metaphorical expression—wherein occurs the free play of associations drawn from the common image pool. The basic level is a function of advertising's commercial nature; the expressive aspect (the higher level) is not determined in detail by commercial considerations. The second element is *ambiguity,* which arises in the shift in emphasis from textual to pictorial information, the carefully constructed indeterminacy of the advertisement's open codes of interpretation, and the abstract quality of the product's symbolic attributes. The third is what we might call *fluidity.* Given the sheer number and variety of imagistic plays, we have no simple or straightforward paradigms for finally arriving at contentment or well-being. All that is certain is that new shows will be mounted, and that they will be preoccupied with involving our psychological energies in the theatre of consumption.

People must interpret both their needs and their experiences within the context of this elaborate and subtle message system. We can assume that they encounter much frustration and some anxiety in all this, but we also know that people find enjoyment in the stimulation of their desires by marketing techniques. There is a strong affinity between modern advertising's communicative modes and the social framework for the personal experience of satisfaction and well-being in a consumer culture. It is just this affinity that gives advertising its broad cultural and social significance.

Earlier in the chapter, we suggested that the predominant communicative forms in advertising—symbol, icon, and image, all unified in metaphorical expression—were oriented toward a single mode in human thinking and sensitivity: comparative judgment. Now we shall turn from individual to social judgment, that is, to how persons in social interactions form opinions about their economic well-being and "success," and how goods fulfil their role as "satisfiers" in this process; there, too, comparative judgment is the very heart of the matter.

RELATIVE STANDING

We have seen that in the consumer society the consumer, not the product, is the core of the message system about the sphere of consumption. Not the consumer as isolated individual, however; the act of consumption is always a social process. In selecting, using, and enjoying things, people look around to find out what others are doing. We can call this need for individuals to relate their tastes and choices to those of others the "intersubjective" aspect of consumption activity. It is bound up with a more general behavioural pattern that appears to be deeply rooted in the human personality—namely, the concern with "relative standing," the continual scanning of the social landscape to ascertain how others are doing and to compare one's own condition with theirs.

Traditional cultures established quite firm guidelines for intersubjective comparisons, presenting a limited set of role and behavioural models to guide tastes. The consumer society abolishes all such limits and creates an "open set" of intersubjective comparisons; advertising is one of the most important vehicles for presenting, suggesting, and re-flecting an unending series of possible comparative judgments.

A famous study of the processes of social comparisons is Thorstein Veblen's *The Theory of the Leisure Class*, first published in 1899. Veblen writes, "With the exception of the instinct of self-preservation, the pro-pensity for emulation is probably the strongest and most alert and persis-tent of the economic motives proper." Ownership of possessions—and the more the better—is commonly regarded as the basis for the drive to succeed, but Veblen contends that this view is superficial. It is not so much what one has as the relationship between what one has and what others (the more successful) have that is most relevant: "The motive that lies at the root of ownership is emulation. . . . The possession of wealth confers honor; it is an invidious distinction."

The fact that, in a developed market economy, all specific forms of wealth can be represented by a single standard—money, or what Veblen calls "the pecuniary standard"—dictates how the propensity for emula-tion is expressed in modern society. All tangible forms of wealth (grand houses, yachts, servants) are merely momentary signs of relative success and do not have any lasting significance. Unlike traditional societies where forms of wealth and social success, like the forms of satisfaction, tend to remain the same over long periods, a market society undermines fixed standards. Competition for social honour is freer, but victory is fleeting, since the criteria for success are always subject to redefinition.

An individual' s striving for a permanent place of distinction is like the pursuit of a mirage across the desert. The horizon of social honour recedes as one approaches it:

> But as fast as a person makes new acquisitions, and becomes accustomed to the resulting new standard of wealth, the new standard forthwith ceases to afford appreciably greater satisfaction than the earlier standard did. . . . So long as the comparison [with others] is distinctly unfavorable to himself the normal, average individual will live in chronic dissatisfaction with his pres-ent lot; and when he has reached what may be called the normal pecuniary standard of the community, or of his class in the community, this chronic dissatisfaction will give place to a restless striving to place a wider and everwidening pecuniary interval between himself and this average standard. (Veblen [1899] 1953, 38–39)

The need for conspicuous consumption is not confined to those at the higher income levels; its traces are found universally in the ordinary life patterns of almost everyone, excluding only the very poorest (who dis-play it as soon as they cease to be very poor). And it does not refer only to luxury goods, for the drive to consume is embedded in the very search for satisfaction itself, including the acquisition of what are commonly re-ferred to as the necessities of life. Virtually everything we use has what

Veblen calls a "ceremonial character": while what we consume serves the physiological maintenance of life, even at the level of immediate needs, it also places us at some known point in the set of social interactions whereby persons are judged as being more or less "successful."

In *The Joyless Economy* (1976), Tibor Scitovsky took up these themes in discussing people's changing preferences in consumption patterns. He sees a reciprocal relationship between changing preferences and changes in the sense of satisfaction stemming from particular activities. The dominant economic theory in his view "overlooks the possibility that the same influences that modify our tastes might also modify our ability to derive satisfaction from the things that cater to our tastes."

Were we to assume that our tastes—the kinds of things we choose to spend our money on—remained constant throughout our lives and were unaffected by the social changes (such as the images of new lifestyles) occurring around us, then we would become progressively more contented if our real income increased and we could afford to acquire more and more of the things we desired. In fact, when asked to rate themselves in attitudinal surveys—as "very happy," "fairly happy," "or not very happy"—proportions of the population in each category changed very little between 1946 and 1970 despite the dramatic and steady rise in real incomes in western nations after World War II (in the United States, average per capita real income rose by 62 percent between 1946 and 1970).

Why? Scitovsky sees four aspects to the answer. First, a significant proportion of the satisfaction in life that people experience is derived from status itself, that is, from the relative social rankings or interpersonal comparisons that are made at all income levels. Second, much satisfaction is derived from employment, but, once again, the degree of satisfaction is closely correlated to the income level and prestige of some jobs (especially the professions) as compared with others. Third, there is a strong correlation between satisfaction and genuine novelty; although we are accustomed to a steady stream of "new" goods, most of them are variations on the "collections of characteristics" that already exist, and, Scitovsky contends, the consumer society progressively reduces the amount of genuine novelty in our lives. Fourth, the admirable advantages in material comfort we have gained in the last generation—better housing, food, clothing, heating, and air conditioning—does not yield an enduring sense of satisfaction for us because comfort is like addiction: we quickly become accustomed to what is provided, take it for granted, and seek more; only when we are deprived of our customary gratifications do we even notice that we have them and are dependent on them. For example, those who grew up with outdoor toilets and at some point in their lives acquired indoor facilities appreciated the new comforts and valued them highly, whereas those who have had the indoor facilities all their lives regard them as nothing special. Central heating and air conditioning quickly become "normal" for indoor environments; most people are aware of them today only when the machinery breaks down.

Taken together, these four aspects of material progress "well explain why happiness should depend so much on one's ranking in society and so little on the absolute level of one's income" (Scitovsky 1976, 139). In *Social Limits to Growth* (1976), Fred Hirsch explores these themes further, arguing that a market economy produces two basic types of goods: those that provide for basic material necessities, and "positional goods." As the general wealth increases, the proportion of positional goods in total production becomes progressively larger.

Positional goods are the things that allow us to detect social status differences among individuals; their chief value lies in the fact that some persons have them and others do not. As we mentioned earlier, the valuations of things and activities are quite arbitrary. At one time, moving from central urban areas to the suburbs represented a positive status change for those who could afford it; at another, moving back from the suburbs to the centre of the city allowed the status rewards to be garnered.

Timing, degree of selectivity, and appropriate reference groups are what create positional goods in a consumer society. When only a relatively few persons have access to goods that are generally desired, such as country estates, the status benefits to them and the "social distance" between them and the rest of the population are enormous. A rising level of general affluence means that more people can strive for these symbols of success, and a few new entrants will be admitted to the select circles. The marketplace, however, also responds by subtly debasing and reinterpreting the success symbols; suburban housing developments where a few large trees have been left standing for the publicity pictures will be marketed as "country estates that everyone can afford." Meanwhile, the social elite has conjured up a new set of restricted-access status symbols for itself.

Hirsch is concerned, however, that this elaborate charade, which is something like an animal chasing its tail, requires considerable amounts of material resources to sustain it. A good example is the relationship between employment opportunities and educational qualifications. When relatively few people finished high school and even fewer went to university, higher education was widely perceived as the gateway to the professional careers monopolized by the elite, since entry to such professions required university degrees. Responding to popular demand, governments created more universities and more opportunities for entry, and more people now hold advanced degrees. Yet there remains in society as a whole roughly the same proportion of elite positions as before. What happened was that the social significance of advanced university degrees was diluted, with many who hold such degrees now filling low-status occupations while educational requirements for occupations shifted upward across the board. Society responded to the demand for fairer access to elite positions through university education with a shell-game trick.

In different ways, Scitovsky and Hirsch are both concerned with a similar feature of a competitive, market-oriented society that has generally reached a level of material affluence—namely, the great importance placed on the symbolic attributes of goods and the myriad ways in which rank and status are attached to them. Goods are not scarce in an affluent society; but the *status attributes* of goods are socially created scarcities, as they always have been.

Status or prestige is inherently scarce. There can never be enough for everyone because the whole point about attributes like prestige is that by their nature they must be distributed unevenly; only a few persons can be famous. The very idea of "everyone" being famous is a contradiction in terms, notwithstanding Andy Warhol's whimsical proposal that a way should be found to make everyone famous, in turn, for fifteen minutes.

Traditional societies customarily "solve" the issue by assigning prestige arbitrarily to those who inherit certain bloodlines or who do well in certain well-established forms of competition. The consumer society, in contrast, recognizes an open-ended set of competitive situations, but its need for status differentiation is no less acute. Therefore, to keep alive the game of relative standing it must fashion new socially created scarcities at every turn, new symbols of success to be striven for. It matters not at all *what* is chosen to mark status differences. The important point is that in the consumer society there can be no end to the process.

Is this a cause for concern? And if so, are marketing and advertising partly to blame? Tibor Scitovsky thinks there is cause for serious concern about today's economy, but he regards the source of the problem not as marketing and advertising, but mass production itself. Economies of scale dictate that the things that appeal to the widest group of purchasers can be produced most cheaply and efficiently, and therefore the lowest common denominator of taste tends to prevail. Thus, mass production caters to conformity (which Scitovsky labels somewhat provocatively as "mob rule") rather than to diversity and individuality. In this context, advertising's function is to secure agreement among the mob about what is to be mass produced; the vaunted "sovereignty" of consumers consists in choosing from among the limited range of goods that can be brought to market under these conditions. Advertising simply facilitates the process of agreement on which ones will be winners—and this is quite unimportant.

Fred Hirsch, on the other hand, tries to show that "getting ahead" for individuals is inherently wasteful and frustrating on the social level. Yet advertising is a major influence both in presenting this impulse in attractive terms and also in concealing its negative social effects: "To the extent that marketing and advertising appeal to individuals to isolate themselves from these group or social effects—to get ahead or to protect their positions—they are socially wasteful. They are then also socially immoral, . . . [for if] all are urged to get ahead, many are likely to have their expectations frustrated" (Hirsch 1976, 109).

Hirsch seems to believe that the socially useful qualities of goods may be separated from those that are wasteful and unnecessary. He then suggests that only the functional attributes of goods (their capacity to do things for us) are necessary and beneficial, whereas their symbolic attributes (how we experience using them and their effects on us as persons in social interactions) are frivolous and unimportant. However, it is abundantly clear that, for most persons, the functional and the symbolic attributes of goods are two sides of a single coin.

QUALITY OF LIFE

A market society systematically orients the individual's search to satisfy his or her needs toward its own core activity: the buying and selling of goods and services. Its decision mechanism is price-directed, and it compels individuals to earn cash incomes for goods acquisition and to make fine calculations about the marginal increments of contentment likely to be gained through allocating their resources in various ways. Economists have long argued that making such decisions depends upon adequate circulation of information about goods; we have suggested that the fully developed stage of the market society needs much more, particularly guidance on how the acquisition of things is supposed to lead to satisfaction.

The "free market's" great virtue is said to be its efficient allocation of resources, for supposedly in this way it makes available the best array of provisions to supply human wants. Discontent is readily apparent when provision for specific wants such as food, shelter, transportation, popular entertainment, and so forth is inadequate or nonexistent. But what about content? Most people do have a sense of overall satisfaction or dissatisfaction in their lives; furthermore, this sense cannot be correlated easily with their experience of particular wants and gratifications. Thus, the sense of satisfaction with life as a whole is a separate matter and must be investigated independently.

For a consumer society the key question is, To what extent are the types of wants generated in a market-oriented context satisfied by the types of goods produced there?

> The tendency of a market society [is] to give priority to those items that are directly price indexed, whereas life satisfaction is more closely linked to areas of life which are, if at all, only indirectly price indexed. The argument is

that a market's want-generating capacity is not at all irrelevant to the maximization of satisfaction; in fact, it may reduce satisfaction because it generates the wrong kinds of wants, wants that lead to decreased life satisfaction. (Lane 1978, 808)

What are, in fact, the ingredients of personal content in our society, and how are they related to consumer transactions? Is it possible that a mismatch between how persons usually experience contentment, and what the marketplace provides as the means for this experience, could lead to a decreasing rather than increasing sense of satisfaction even as social wealth rises?

As we shall see in a moment, quality-of-life studies report that the strongest foundations of satisfaction lie in the domain of interpersonal relations, a domain of nonmaterial goods. This leads us to wonder, since marketing and advertising are a product-generated discourse, whether the products they feature may be regarded only as a means by which individuals hope to attain other goals. This would be consistent with the fact that the consumer, not the product, has become the central focus of the advertising message itself. The second issue follows from the first. If what happens in the marketplace itself has little direct bearing on the deep sources of life satisfaction, too great an emphasis on the ambiguous associations between products and images of contentment may mislead consumers and actually diminish the possibilities for satisfaction.

A fully developed market society encourages individuals to express all their wants as wants for goods and services, that is, commodities. Yet "commodities themselves, and the income to purchase them, are only weakly related to the things that make people happy: autonomy, self-esteem, family felicity, tension-free leisure, friendships. This is a major defect in a want-satisfying mechanism" (Lane 1978, 815). This presumes, of course, that we have some well-founded ideas about what it is that makes people happy. Analysis of surveys in which sample populations were asked to rate the various aspects of their lives in terms of the degree of satisfaction yielded by them has given rise to "social indicators" of well-being and an overall measurement known as "quality of life."

Commonly used social indicators may be classified according to whether or not they provide a direct measure of an individual's reactions. Those based on reports from individuals about their own perceptions, feelings, and responses are referred to as "subjective indicators"; others, such as crime statistics, population densities, and employment rates, which count the occurrences of observed events are termed "objective indicators." In what follows, we shall concentrate on the former.

The case for the value of subjective measures of well-being is based on several points. First, there is a "desire on the part of the researcher for a realistic assessment of individual life experience" (Campbell, Converse, and Rodgers 1976) because the connection between what has been measured by the two different types of indicators (subjective and objective) is often mysterious. In addition, subjective indicators are regarded as particularly useful in helping to select from the almost limitless range of objective criteria (all the aspects of life that can be counted) the indicators that should be taken most seriously for social policy and planning purposes.

During the past twenty years, both single-item and multi-item scales have been used in extensive survey research on "subjective well-being" (Diener 1984, 542–75). For example, Dupuy's "General Well-Being Schedule" is a multi-item scale that seeks to assess seven different aspects: life satisfaction, health concerns, depressed mood, person–environment fit, coping, energy level, and stress.

Robert E. Lane (1978) looked at the findings of various studies to identify the most important elements in the composition of happiness: autonomy, or the feeling of having some control over the events affecting one's life; self-esteem, or the feeling of being respected for one's personal qualities; friendships; warm family relationships; and sufficient leisure time that is insulated from tension and stress. Other studies have grouped the elements of satisfaction into "social values" (love, family, friendships) and "material values" (economic security, success), reporting that the former outrank the latter by considerable margins. Certainly, no one claims that interpersonal factors are or can be the sole determinants of happiness; and it is also the case that, in our society, marketplace transactions and material values contribute a great deal to the life-satisfaction of many persons. Neither aspect should be ignored. The fascinating question is how they interact.

Norman Bradburn's (1969) investigation of national norms for mental health in the United States through periodic national surveys led to his interest in more general aspects of happiness and well-being. In his view of the psychology of well-being, two independent dimensions, one of "positive" feelings and one of "negative" feelings, react independently. In other words, most of us are at one and the same time satisfied by some aspects of our lives and dissatisfied by others; the two domains exist side by side, without balancing or cancelling each other out. Although the hypothesis is still controversial, subsequent research has added considerable support to it, as well as further refinements to the measures used in the surveys (Diener 1984, 547–49). It also appears to fit well with our own basic concept of the "fragmentation" that occurs in both the expressions of needs and the forms of satisfaction in a consumer society (see Chapter 4). Out of the attempt to match the dissociated "bits" of needs and satisfactions arise two parallel and disconnected series of feelings, one generally characterized by content and the other by discontent.

One of the earliest cross-national studies to use a self-evaluation approach was Hadley Cantril's *The Patterns of Human Concerns* (1965).

Cantril developed a single-item "self-anchoring striving scale" and individuals were asked to define, on the basis of their own assumptions, perceptions, goals, and values, where they believed they stood in relation to the two extreme points on the scale, which represented the "best possible" and the "worst possible" conditions of life. This study presents data from thirteen nations, including both rich and poor in terms of material conditions, and concludes that in all societies the sense of well-being is most strongly correlated with one's place in relation to the expectations generated by the social norms of the culture in which one lives.

Richard Easterlin (1974) re-analyzed Bradburn's and Cantril's data with a specific issue in mind: What can we conclude about the relation between income and happiness? In almost every case studied, and notwithstanding marked differences among types of societies, there is a very strong correlation between relative income and happiness within a particular country at a particular time. In other words, those with more income are, according to their own reports, more satisfied than those with less. But this correlation does not hold over a period of time in that increases (no matter how large or over what period) in real incomes spread throughout a population do not cause any greater proportion of that population to report themselves as being happier than they were earlier. Comparisons among countries also show a poor correlation between income and happiness in that no significantly higher proportion of people report themselves as being happy in countries with a relatively high material standard of living than in those with a lower standard. "In judging their happiness, people tend to compare their actual situation with a reference standard or norm, derived from their prior and ongoing social experience. . . . Over time, however, as economic conditions advance, so too does the social norm, since this is formed by the changing economic socialization experience of people'" (Easterlin 1974, 118–19). The horizon of satisfaction is a moving line, as Thorstein Veblen suggested long ago. Content is not measured by what one has, but by the ratio between what one has and what one thinks one ought to have in order to maintain self-esteem in the face of the normal consumption standards accepted by one's peers.

These cross-national and cross-cultural studies lend support to our premise of the strong interdependence among individuals in forming the sense of life-satisfaction associated with consumption behaviour. Whereas anthropological researches on primitive human societies had shown us just how important this interdependence was, its significance in modern society has long been downplayed, especially in reigning economic theory; recent research, however, has begun to restore this notion to its rightful place.

Finally, some of the research in this area has a direct bearing on the factor we have isolated as the heart of advertising's preoccupation with metaphorical expression, namely, comparative judgment: "A number of theories postulate that happiness results from a comparison between some standard and actual conditions." Such comparisons may occur either consciously or unconsciously, and the standard may be represented by one's contemporaries, one's past life, or one's aspirations. "Social comparison was the strongest predictor of satisfaction in most domains" (Diener 1984, 566–67).

Consumers in a developed market society are not left to wander alone and unaided amid heaps of goods, computing and recomputing to some decimal place the most advantageous fit between their yearnings and their purses. They do not—nor do they wish to—form their tastes and preferences in the private bliss of ratiocination and then descend upon innocent merchants to scrutinize their shelves with cold and wary eyes. Except when (as is too often the case even today) groups are pressed hard against the limit of deprivation by exploitation or an inhospitable environment, consuming is an elaborate social game, as it has always been in human cultures.

LIFESTYLES

In the late 1960s, sociologists started to write about "taste cultures," subgroups within a larger social setting formed by some well-defined features of their preferences as consumers. This was, in part, a reaction against the theory that modern industrial societies and the mass media of communication within them were responsible for creating "mass culture," a bland uniformity of popular taste that inevitably reduced all cultural domains (music, film, plastic arts, and so forth) to a lowest common denominator of quality. That theory is unfounded; although many of the attractive elements in traditional popular cultures had indeed been eroded, new syntheses continue to arise whereby different segments in the population affirm their commitment to distinctiveness and quality in contemporary popular culture.

In the 1970s, other sociologists developed a more wide-ranging theory—that of "cultural class" (Peterson & DiMaggio 1975; Lewis 1977). A cultural class is simply a component group within a modern society that has a "shared pattern of consumption." "Memberships" in cultural classes are voluntary and discretionary, based only on free choices made in everyday situations, and members may switch their allegiances from one class to another at any time. Taste cultures and cultural class are well illustrated in the phenomenon of popular music.

These new concepts were combined with ideas growing out of personality theory and attitude/opinion research, and given a more systematic expression in the notion of "lifestyles." Research teams based in advertising agencies, universities, and institutes created a series of "cluster analyses" in order to identify consumer typologies and to characterize different patterns of tastes and buying behaviour. Potential consumer markets are stratified according to a number of characteristics: (1) demographic—age, sex, income; (2) geographic—region, urban, rural; (3) psychographic—personality traits; (4) type of preferred benefit—taste, feel; (5) volume—heavy vs. light user. Marketers then combine this sophisticated approach to market segmentation with product differentiation, and product positioning and repositioning, in order to fit their product type and characteristics, and its relation to competing products, as closely as possible with the nature of the target market (McDaniel 1982, ch. 4). Various industries have adapted these general typologies to highly specific marketing domains, such as eating out, grocery shopping, and entertainment.

Among the more general studies, the one by Arnold Mitchell and his colleagues, sponsored by SRI International (formerly the Stanford Research Institute) and reported in Mitchell's *The Nine American Lifestyles* (1983), is perhaps the best known. They used the term "lifestyle" to describe "a unique way of life defined by its distinctive array of values, drives, beliefs, needs, dreams, and special points of view." They were looking for a scheme that would encompass individual, social, and marketplace dimensions of life, and that would be successful in predicting how a change in one dimension would affect the others, and also how the size and composition of social groups would change over time. To do this, they devised what they called the "VALS" (values and lifestyles) typology and arrived at a scheme made up of nine identifiable lifestyles (Mitchell 1983, 4).

Need-Driven Groups (11 %)
    Survivor lifestyle (4%)
    Sustainer lifestyle (7%)
Outer-Directed Groups (67%)
    Belonger lifestyle (35%)
    Emulator lifestyle (10%)
    Achiever lifestyle (22%)
Inner-Directed Groups (20%)
    I-Am-Me lifestyle (5%)
    Experiential lifestyle (7%)
    Societally conscious lifestyle (8%)
Combined Outer- and Inner-Directed Group
    Integrated lifestyle (2%)

The figures in parentheses give the proportion of the adult population in the United States that, it is claimed, falls into each of these categories on the basis of responses to the survey questionnaire completed by respondents in 1980. A rudimentary application of the typology was also made for France, Italy, Sweden, the United Kingdom, and West Germany.

The nature of each lifestyle is, for our purposes, sufficiently indicated by its name. (The detailed descriptions and the case study materials are quite illuminating, however, and we encourage the reader to peruse *The Nine American Lifestyles.*) As Mitchell indicates, the scheme combines elements from familiar conceptions of need- or drive-hierarchies (the most famous of which is Abraham Maslow's) and David Riesman's (1950) inner/outer-directed distinction. Its most challenging feature is that it attempts to describe both actual social groupings and a hierarchy of stages in personal self-development that culminates in psychological maturity. Except for those literally trapped in the most impoverished need-driven circumstances (such as poverty-stricken older persons), and for whom social constraints such as racial discrimination impose serious practical barriers, movement "upward" toward the integrated lifestyle is thought to be possible for anyone, and desirable from the viewpoint of developmental psychology.

Specific applications are sketched, for example, in personal life and in planning electoral campaigns, but the one that is most relevant for us is stated concisely by Mitchell himself: "Perhaps the most fundamental business use of lifestyle research lies in market segmentation." The typology can, it is claimed, assist business in the great task of "matching product to consumer" through precise design and targeting in advertising, as well as in product development, design, and packaging, not to mention its possible virtues in long-range strategic planning by businesses (Mitchell 1983, 165–72).

The application of lifestyle research to marketing is well-developed in Japan. One recent study by the Hakuhodo Institute of Life and Living (1982) uses the following market-segment categories (the names for the categories are as they appear in the English translation):

> Crystal Tribe (attracted to famous brands)
> My Home Tribe (family-oriented)
> Leisure Life Tribe
> Gourmandism Tribe
> Ordinary People Tribe
> Impulse Buyer Tribe

The preface to the research report notes that the term "consumer" in Japan is being replaced by the phrase "life designer," a change intended to take into account the high proportion of the population who formulate and express their wants autonomously, rather than merely by reacting to what happens to be featured in the marketplace at any time. This report is concerned especially with what is called "*hitonami* consciousness."

Hitonami translates literally as "aligning oneself with other people" and thus is roughly equivalent to "other-directed."

Hitonami, the internalization of the immensely powerful pressures enforcing social conformity in attitudes and behaviour, was deeply rooted in traditional Japanese society. (It is analogous to the practices of traditional western cultures that have died out in the modern consumer society.) After World War II, however, the social upheaval of the war and the postwar economic prosperity encouraged a new form of *hitonami* consciousness: "keeping up with the Satos," the social conformity of upward mobility and changing circumstances. Dominating Japanese society until the late 1970s, it is now giving way to newer trends.

The Hakuhodo survey sought responses to a questionnaire on ten major aspects of daily life. The results categorized the Japanese population into the following types:

The Good Old Japanese
The Silent Majority
The Confident Middle Class
The Style-Oriented Japanese
The Do-it-my-way Japanese
The Confident Theoreticians

In general, it appears that most Japanese now reject "keeping up with the Satos" in the sense of using material possessions to indicate social status. They buy products that "suit them in their style of life," and they place the highest value on "cultivating themselves and seeking self-fulfillment." These attitudes are represented most strongly among persons who fall into the do-it-my-way and the confident-theoretician categories who, although they are only a small proportion of the total population, have "sufficient confidence in themselves to act as innovators and trend setters in many aspects of Japanese daily life" (Hakuhodo Institute of Life and Living 1982).

Like the more general quality-of-life surveys, lifestyle research supplies convincing evidence on a couple of fairly simple but important points. First, most people are capable of formulating, in a consistent and comprehensive way, an interpretation of "satisfaction in life" in terms of broad goals and values; second, these formulations show an awareness of the relation between material or consumer goods and nonmaterial domains of well-being; third, individual judgments about present contentment, as well as aspirations, show the strong influence of changing tastes and norms in the surrounding social environment. What lifestyle research adds is evidence that many persons appear to express or communicate publicly both their value-orientations and their consumption preferences in discernible patterns.

11

Goods as Communicators

In a 1983 television commercial, a modestly dressed young couple stands before the automobile showroom window. As the narrator says, "Imagine yourself in an Oldsmobile Cutlass Ciera," the couple's image, reflected in the car's metallic paint, undergoes magical transformations: they are shown playing tennis at a club; getting into the car after their game; travelling through a neon-lighted city; being greeted by a doorman at a fancy hotel; and dining by candlelight in an elegant restaurant. The narrator comments, "No other car is a better reflection on you. Can you think of a better way to spend a night on the town?"

Another television advertisement of the same period, for a new tire called "Vector," shows the product in a series of interactions with people. The tire rolls by pedestrians and into a barbershop where it is greeted by name and its tread is examined; it continues down a snow-covered landscape and is saluted by passing skiers; it overtakes a cyclist in a sunny climate; and finally it rolls into an expensive home and is introduced by name by the butler to the master of the house.

In Uganda, the Batutsi still sing songs about their cows; in Kenya, the Masai have added industrial artifacts to their collection of ear ornaments.

THINGS COME ALIVE

Goods have meanings. Goods convey meanings. These elementary propositions help us to understand the consumer society and the role of advertising within it. A book entitled *The Meaning of Things* calls attention to "the ability of an object to convey meaning through its own inherent qualities" (Csikszentmihalyi and Rochberg-Halton 1981, 43). We have shown that, in a consumer culture, an object's qualities are a complex unity of two broad categories of characteristics—material and symbolic, or imputed. The communicative function nestles inside consumption behaviour in all human cultures at all times; objects serve the twin purposes of satisfying needs and conveying meanings.

In general, we agree with Mary Douglas and Baron Isherwood that "the essential function of consumption is its capacity to make sense. . . . Forget that commodities are good for eating, clothing, and shelter; forget their usefulness and try instead the idea that commodities are good for thinking; treat them as a nonverbal medium for the human creative faculty" (Douglas and Isherwood 1978, 62). We need only add that the role of advertising in modern industrial societies is to verbalize and to image the possible meanings of things, and to facilitate the exchanges of meanings occurring in social interactions.

Every aspect of contemporary life in market-industrial societies is permeated by the presence of objects. They range from what is wholly familiar (traditional foods) to what appears bizarre and slightly menacing, at least for now (synthetic blood); they may be very simple (buttons) or incredibly complex (guided missiles); they operate at speeds encompassing everything from the peddler's pushcart to the fastest computers.

It is extraordinary how quickly this situation arose and how easily humans adapted to it and learned to take it for granted, almost as if it were the "natural" condition of the species. One has to look back only two hundred years at the most to pre-industrial societies to realize the narrow range of things that were used in the normal routines of life, even for privileged classes, in comparison with the present day. Although the operative mechanisms in many devices are a mystery to most of us, they do not seem to inspire awe or terror, but rather indifference. After all, one cannot get too excited about the newest video game or electronic gadget, for one expects that next month or next year there will be something else yet more titillating.

We should not be misled by the sheer quantity of things around us and suppose that little remains to link us with older societies. The sphere of consumption in general, and how we use goods therein as communicators of meanings, are among the most dramatic instances of fundamental continuities and similarities among human cultures, from what we call "primitive societies" to our own. So common is the practice of investing material objects with richly textured layers of interpretive significance that it must be regarded as a basic feature of the human personality. Things are not merely passive adjuncts or decorative accompaniments, rather they "come alive" in the context of social interactions.

In an analysis of gift exchange and reciprocity among the New Zealand Maori, the anthropologist Marcel Mauss claimed that the very basis of exchanges of objects among persons was the idea that the object contains the "life-force" both of the person who made it and the natural materials used in its construction, as if the exchange of things were conceived by the Maori as the exchange of persons (Sahlins 1976, 215). In contrast, our modern industrial society fashions its objects through applications of its very rationalist science and technology, and it admits no obscurantist notions like life-force when it applies its rationalist technology to fashioning objects. Yet, at the same time, our marketing and advertising enterprise represents these products to us as if they were magically endowed with life; in television advertising products speak, move about spontaneously, and bring persons together. So much for rationality.

Human relations are mediated by things, which express, conceal, shield, or distort our motives and objectives. To have things serve us in this way we must make them seem as if they are alive or endowed with life-force. They serve thus as a "projective medium" into which we transfer the intricate webs of personal and social interactions.

We name our collective enterprise for producing things "the economy" and we often speak of it, too, as a living force. In times of business slowdown, we call for actions to "get the economy moving again," as if it were some huge, sluggish beast that inexplicably has stopped to rest. High government officials say that the purpose of public policy is to "stimulate the private sector," a phrase that perhaps ought to be dropped from the bureaucratic vocabulary on account of its noneconomic undertones. A constant refrain is the admonition to "let the market decide" among various options. Investors are said to "lack confidence" in the economy, as if it were some ne'er-do-well relative seeking a loan. Every commentator has a favourite nostrum for restoring the economy's "health."

Goods can act as communicators in social interactions because we breathe life into them. "Man needs goods for communicating with others and for making sense of what is going on around him. The two needs are but one, for communication can only be formed in a structured system of meanings. His overriding objective as a consumer, put at its most general, is a concern for information about the changing cultural scene." Goods are part of a "live information system"—not merely the messages or messengers in the system, but, in fact, the very structure of the message system itself. What is important is not the meanings attached to a particular thing or type of thing at any moment, but rather the relationships among an ensemble of goods (Douglas and Isherwood 1978, 95).

The above anthropological perspective on the function of goods in human cultures is significant for our understanding of contemporary life and helps us to appreciate the full extent of advertising's role in the consumer society. Note immediately that the phrase "live information system" denotes not bits and pieces of data about products, but rather the very activity of "making sense out of the cultural world around one," which, in turn, depends upon discovering a structured or patterned system of meanings in relation to which one can form one's tastes.

In the consumer society, we maintain, no institutions are more directly concerned with providing patterned systems of meaning for consumption activity than marketing and advertising. In the twentieth century, the evolution of cultural frames for goods (presented later in this chapter) reveals the broad outline of these patterns, and the influence of the "lifestyle" concept in the most recent period simply shows how explicit the patterning has become. Yet institutional strategies, no matter how influential, do not create or manipulate the patterns unilaterally: marketers and advertisers canvass the whole range of cultural symbols, past and present, and blend their borrowings with the characteristics of current goods and services in which, they hope, the symbolic meanings can be made to resonate. The resulting set designs are by no means always pleasing to us as consumers, but we do seem to be willing to return regularly to the theatre of consumption for the latest performances.

This is not merely a popular entertainment, however; these processes define, together with the forms of work and production, how our society reproduces itself over time. To recapitulate, advertising should be understood as a major cultural institution, not merely as just another of businesses' tax-deductible expenditures, because the world of goods that composes the manifest or surface level of its productions is itself one of the principal channels of social communication. Anthropological researches show us that this has always been so; what is new is the way we use this channel today. Sidney J. Levy contends that the anthropologist's perspective can "lead to a fuller understanding of why marketing managers do what they do and why consumers buy and consume as they do," because it interprets goods and services "not in themselves alone, but in their social symbolic role, as means of exchanging communications and furthering social processes" (Levy 1978, 568).

When traditional cultures, together with the guidance they provided individuals on how to consume, ceased to be viable, the longstanding "discourse through and about objects" could no longer be communicated in the old ways. The market-industrial society, which is unique not for its obsession with material objects, but for its capacity to transform the mix and characteristics in the world of objects quickly and regularly, opens new channels through which this discourse can flow. Yet **goods themselves remain the communicators, and it is through them that the discourse flows.**

Marketing and advertising are the major channels in the technological infrastructure for this communication process in the consumer society; other components are the residue of traditional cultures (especially outside North America), youth subcultures, the celebrity or "star" system, and the corporate business style as the pre-eminent model for career progress. In these and other components runs the "discourse through and about things" for the consumer society. Were marketing and advertising to be banned outright, for example, these other channels, or some newly designed ones, would have to be pressed into service to take up the slack. For, like our ancestors, we appear to be compelled to fashion our social interactions through goods.

The construction of social relations through goods is one of the strongest threads binding together human development from the earliest times to our own; all cultures shape into symbolic forms the materials of nature extracted from the environment. Marshall Sahlins emphasizes this theme in contrasting consumption practices of primitive societies with our own (Sahlins, 1976; 1972). He sees the most important difference not in levels of technology or types of objects but in the "site of symbolic production." He uses this term to refer to the social institutions most influential in reproducing and transmitting the behavioural norms that guide individuals in everyday life (for example, knowing what to eat and how to dress). In primitive societies, kinship is the privileged institution in this regard—today, it is the economy. Therefore, we should look upon the marketplace not just as a decision-making forum for employment, consumer expenditures, and capital formation, but much more broadly as a cultural system, as, in fact, the privileged institution for the reworking and transmission of the cultural symbols that shape our lives.

Now we can combine the theme of relative standing from the last chapter with the idea of goods as communicators into a unified conception of the marketplace as a cultural system. For the market-oriented discourse through and about things creates a powerful set of symbolic processes founded on an internal tension that simultaneously unifies and differentiates between persons. On the one hand, this discourse is a unifying force in society because it is anchored in one of the cornerstones of the human personality, namely, the propensity for using material objects as intermediaries in social interactions. The ensemble of goods thus serves as a general communication system in which everyone, at least potentially, can participate. On the other hand, the ensemble of goods is not a random assortment but a highly structured collection; material objects, having a certain permanence and being easily distinguishable from each other, serve ideally to mark social distinctions according to who possesses or controls any particular thing and who does not.

Such discriminations about social rank are grounded in what Thorstein Veblen ([1899] 1953) called an "invidious distinction," a judgment on a person's worth made largely in terms of whether or not that person appears to be willing to accept a given consumption standard as a behavioural norm. Even a casual glance will persuade us that the consumer society throws up invidious distinctions everywhere. We are constantly urged to compare the advantages of one brand over another, one class of goods over another, one marginal increment of satisfaction over another, one set of values over another, indeed one "lifestyle package" over another. Yet it is exceedingly difficult to pinpoint a rational basis for opting this way or that, which leaves most people with only a cheerful proclivity to play the game for its own sake.

And in truth, it is a fascinating, subtle, and exceedingly complex game, one that is hard to see clearly in our consumer society because of the sheer number and variety of goods and the worldwide scope of market transactions. We propose, therefore, to step back and examine how some earlier societies used goods as communicators in more tightly structured exchange relations, thereby glimpsing today's game better from a distance.

THE CONSUMER SOCIETY AS AN ANTHROPOLOGICAL TYPE

In a market society, all goods and services are "equivalent" in the sense that a common currency guarantees access to each of them on the same terms. In principle, no one who has the money to pay the asking price for anything is denied the right to acquire it, and distinctions among things are marked on the surface only by their relative prices. However, we do not normally carry our possessions around with price tags dangling from them, but instead rely upon the characteristics of the goods themselves — both their physical properties and the symbolic meanings imputed or ascribed to them — to "say things" about ourselves to others.

Communication is made possible, as Douglas and Isherwood have explained, by embedding behavioural signals within a structured or patterned system of meaning. We understand these signals because they are part of a set of events that has an internal coherence; a designer label on an article of clothing must conform to certain rules (for example, only certain names on the label will make sense) in order to communicate the desired signals. As individuals, we are dependent upon social institutions — such as, in a consumer society, marketing and advertising — to construct those patterns of meaning.

The formation and operation of such institutional patterning can be seen with great clarity in earlier societies because the "markers" for the patterns were specific physical objects, and because the rules of the game for consumption behaviour segregated activities on the basis of the objects involved. Earlier societies can show us not only dramatic instances of how goods serve as communicators, but also how ways of investing consumption activity with meaning persist to the present day.

Anthropologists have presented some primitive societies as made up of two dissimilar but related domains: the "subsistence economy" and the "prestige economy" (the latter is sometimes further subdivided, as we shall see). The subsistence economy produces — usually by the collective labour of extended family groups — all the basic necessities of existence for everyone, which make up the "consumption norm" for a particular society. An established redistribution mechanism for the goods produced in this domain is gift-giving managed by the tribal chief, and this "welfare" activity ensures that no constituent group's consumption level falls below an acceptable minimum.

The "prestige economy" is based in transactions within an entirely separate class of goods using specific media of exchange and often elaborate rules of conduct. It involves a restricted group of participants (usually only males). Possession or disposition of valued goods confers honour and prestige upon an individual and his kin group. The propensity for emulation, to use Veblen's phrase, that is embodied in the prestige economy is, in many cases, no trivial sideline in social affairs, but rather the very core of everyday life. In what is now New Zealand, "the desire for emulation was the industrial spur of the old Maori economy" (Firth 1959, 450).

The main elements in this dual economy of primitive societies may be summarized as follows: (1) each of the two economic domains has its own types of objects; (2) goods are classified in ranked, discontinuous, or incommensurable spheres of exchange; (3) social differentiation, including the assignment of prestige or honour, is accomplished through manipulations only of a specific class of goods; (4) these prestige goods reflect an artificially created scarcity that stems from the arbitrary ascription of symbolic significance to certain material objects. These somewhat abstract formulations can be fleshed out with illustrations drawn from anthropological studies, which are not only quite fascinating in themselves but also help to sharpen our perceptions of our own behaviour.

A dramatic instance of prestige competitions occurred among the Kwakiutl of British Columbia, who lived in a region of great natural abundance. "The Kwakiutl, even more than most peoples in the world, were obsessed with rank—indeed, in the midst of such plenty they created artificial shortages in the social system and their striving for high social position was an integral part of the economy" (Bohannan 1963, 254). Prestige was won by giving away vast quantities of ceremonial goods at potlatches. Competition was confined to two kinds of things: blankets and large pieces of engraved copper. The contest required potlatch rivals to offer up increasing numbers of blankets, until one participant ended this phase by tendering a copper piece; the competition ended in the destruction of copper pieces, the victory going to the person deemed to have destroyed the piece of greatest value. The rivalry was structured as a ritualized series of exchanges among designated objects which culminated in translating material values "into the purest value: reputation."

Related research on the economy of the Tiv, in what is now Nigeria, offers one of the best illustrations of how ranked and discontinuous spheres of exchange worked. The subsistence economy included food (yams, cereals, vegetables, seasonings, chickens, goats, sheep), household utensils (mortars, grindstones, calabashes, baskets, pots), and some tools. Exchange of these goods involved gift-giving and bartering. The prestige economy was complex, made up of two tiers. One segregated category of goods embraced slaves, cattle, ritual offices, a special type of cloth, medicines, and brass rods; exchanges took place only at cere-monial occasions, and within this category brass rods served as a medium of exchange. Above it stood another tier with a single "good": the exchange of rights in women.

Transactions that crossed the various domains were sometimes nec-essary, such as when a large amount of food was required for a feast and had to be paid for with brass rods, or when rods were used to purchase a wife. But the ranking of the three domains was all-important. The whole point was to avoid, so far as possible, exchanging high-category goods for lower-category ones; he who had to do so in order to fulfil a social obligation inevitably suffered a loss of prestige. Conversely, one strove to take advantage of another's social needs by converting lower-status goods into higher-status ones (Bohannan 1963, 248–53).

Richard Salisbury (1962) found that the Siane people in the New Guinea highlands also had three spheres of exchange that each dealt with a distinct assortment of goods. Goods in the subsistence sphere included everyday food items (sweet potatoes and other vegetables), tools, clothing, and housing. These goods were produced within each clan, maintaining both kinship relations and the basic consumption level enjoyed by everyone. Luxury goods encompassed tobacco, palm oil, pandanus nuts, salt, snakeskins for drums, stone for axe-blades, and palm wood for spears. These were produced or acquired through individual initiative, and exchanged on a reciprocal basis. They could be enjoyed privately or supplied to entertain visitors, for generosity toward one's guests was admired. Luxury goods formed an intermediary class allowing for the expression of individual differences in consumption style, unlike the subsistence goods, which exhibited little or no variation. Ceremonial goods were valuables exchanged by barter at public events, and included shells, ornamental axes, necklaces, plumes, headdresses, and pigs. Cere-monial exchanges occurred both within and between clans and a de-tailed accounting of comparative value was kept. An individual created strict return obligations to himself (and by association to his clan) by presenting ceremonial goods to others, and thereby gained a certain measure of prestige. Presenting such goods was also a vehicle of social mobility within the clan.

Very few transactions violated the boundaries set up between the three different types of goods, because they existed to supply a structured setting for social relations. The type of object clearly identified the sphere of activity and the accepted behavioural norms associated with it. "The more general rule is that commodities are used only in situations where the nexus of activity is clearly one of intra-clan help, inter-clan presentation, or exchange between trade friends; no commodity can be used in an ambiguous situation" (Salisbury 1962, 103). Not only were ceremonial goods never exchanged for food or luxuries, but persons who bartered between the subsistence and luxury spheres were banned from the trading for ceremonial goods.

The impact of the introduction of a new technology (steel rather than stone for axe-blades) on the closed, hierarchical spheres of exchange is of special interest. Production patterns in the subsistence domain remained the same, since women tended the crops and only men owned and used axes. The far greater efficiency and durability of the steel blades meant men had to spend significantly less time clearing the planting areas and building houses. The newly available time was absorbed exclusively into extending the domain of prestige competition, which was carried out both by fighting and by the peaceful exchange of the appropriate ceremonial objects.

Our primary motive in reviewing this anthropological literature is to emphasize the point made by Douglas and Isherwood that networks of social communication—including the world of goods as an information system—rely for their efficacy on structured situations. The discrete and hierarchically ordered spheres of exchanges in primitive societies show with great clarity the connection between social institutions (sex roles, group relations, relative standing, and so forth) and the use of goods as communicators. Richard Salisbury summarizes:

> The presence in non-monetary societies of discrete scales of value . . . is a simple mechanism insuring that subsistence goods are used to maintain a basic standard of life below which no one falls; that free-flowing power [prestige] is allocated peacefully, with a minimum of exploitation (or disturbance of the individual's right to subsistence) and in accordance with accepted standards; that the means for insuring flexibility in the society do not disrupt the formal allocation of statuses in the society or the means of gaining power. (Salisbury 1962, 204)

These discontinuous spheres of goods are a visible manifestation of the "deep structure" of human needs, showing that needs develop and emerge not haphazardly one after another in an undifferentiated series, but in clusters that reflect our efforts to delineate meaningful spheres of activity. The number of our wants and the number of objects available to minister to them is far less important than the nature of the boundaries erected to discriminate between the clusters and to create "structured situations" in society.

The physical and symbolic characteristics of the material tokens of prestige used to mark a person's standing relative to others must be capable of being clearly recognized as such, and they must be sufficiently complex to portray the necessary range of discriminations. So long as these conditions are satisfied, it matters little what is chosen; broken bits of seashells or beads of coloured glass will serve as well as mansions, antiques, or the top floors of downtown highrise buildings.

Which brings us back to the consumer society. After studying the social behaviour of the Siane, Richard Salisbury thought he discerned analogies between their three domains of activity and goods and the ways in which we regard at least some of the commodities we produce today. The one notable qualification is that we mix together what they strive so arduously to keep apart. In our range of automobile models, for example, one can discern a "subsistence nexus" in that all will convey passengers from place to place; a "luxury nexus" in all the available options and sophisticated gadgetry for greater comfort that most purchasers cannot resist; and a "ceremonial nexus" in the relative standing or prestige that certain makes and models signal.

In a consumer society, the most influential determinant of the status value of a commodity is its price, but marketing techniques allow many other factors to mitigate its impact. In automobile models, a "sporty" or "racing" package of imagery may be acquired at various points on the price scale. The terms "luxury" and "luxurious" often are employed indiscriminately in advertising copy for goods of undistinguished quality, in an attempt to persuade the consumer of modest means that even he or she can acquire something special and need not rest content with the ordinary things of life. Marketing strategies attempt to "punctuate" consumption activity by seeking to distinguish ordinary and special occasions, mimicking the spheres of goods in earlier societies.

Other ancient practices permeate consumption practices in modern society. The most noticeable is sex stereotyping. Many recent studies have documented its presence in advertisements and have raised questions about its impact on behaviour. In the context of our discussion here, sex stereotyping illustrates a basic point—that goods can serve as important communicators in human interactions when, and only when, they are embedded in what we have called structured situations.

How goods communicate meaning through the structured situation created by sex stereotyping is shown clearly, as we have seen, in Erving Goffman's *Gender Advertisements* (1979). Advertisements portray the physical carriage and gestures of male and female models and of specific parts of the body, such as hands, in ways that reflect and reinforce traditional patterns of sex-role expectations. Closely related is the notion that most objects themselves have a "gender identity." Marshall Sahlins (1976) quotes Stephen Baker's *Visual Persuasion*, which gives advertisers an overview of these distinctions. For example, trees, dogs, and trains are masculine; flowers, cats, and ships are feminine.

Sahlins uses this in discussing the more general point that a high proportion of consumption practices today are structured in ways similar to longstanding traditions in nonmarket societies. In the gender asymmetry of objects, feminine things tend to be "marked"—that is, exclusively identified—for female use, while masculine things are "unmarked" and may be used by anyone. Styles and types of clothing are, of course, heavily segregated in terms of gender. But **cultures overlap numerous layers of structured sets of meanings in the same objects.** There are other determinants besides gender. We also differentiate ceremonial clothing from working clothing, the former (tuxedos) being marked for exclusive occasions, the latter (off-the-rack suits) being unmarked (Sahlins 1976, ch. 4).

Our food preferences also continue to carry cultural baggage. In North America, we not only separate animals generally deemed fit to eat (cows and pigs) from those that are not (dogs and horses), but also construct a status hierarchy placing beef above pork and, within this, some flesh parts (steak) above others (organs). Sidney J. Levy conducted in-depth interviews with six consumers concerning their attitudes toward cooking and eating—which he called their "stories" or "myths":

> The little myths show how the basic vocabulary of cooking and eating is used to express identities by males and females, the young and the mature, and people in low, middle, and high status positions. General modeling by age, sex, and social status is a familiar one to marketers; here the analysis observes how specific symbolic distinctions are being made among specific foods, ways of preparing them, and in some of the ideas they represent, such as family unity/dispersion, naiveté/sophistication, routine/festivity, sickness/ health, grossness/subtlety, conformity/deviation, sacred/profane, etc. (Levy 1981, 60)

Levy thinks that structured differentiations like these condition personal experience in the consumption process, and that marketers can facilitate what he calls the "dialogue" between marketers and consumers if they are aware of this.

Finally, the economist Albert O. Hirschman (1982) has identified some discrete domains in today's world of goods by analyzing how we ordinarily derive benefits from them. He distinguishes between the goods we consume (consumer nondurables) and the goods we use (consumer durables). The goods we consume include all those things whose composition we destroy or alter in deriving benefits from them (food and drink, fuel, personal-care products, and most clothing). Other things we use over long periods without greatly changing their material composition; Hirschman further subdivides this category into things in continuous use (housing, refrigerators), in sporadic use (cars, dish- washers), and occasional use (pianos, cameras). We derive immediate, sensuous, and clearly identifiable pleasure from nondurables—the taste and smell of food, the feel of clothing, and so forth. But we find most durables, although largely indispensable, provide little lasting satisfac- tion; after our initial pleasure when we acquire them, they become part of the taken-for-granted routine of everyday life. As Tibor Scitovsky pointed out (see Chapter 10), they are the comforts we depend on and assume will be supplied one way or another, but usually we are aware of them only when they are absent.

In the pre-1950 period, before the consumer society really blossomed, people spent most of their incomes on nondurables, that is, on the kinds of goods that yield immediate and sensuous pleasure. Experience with the consumption of nondurables thus set the standard for the sense of satisfaction. When the balance of consumer expenditures tipped in favour of durables, it was inevitable that people evaluated these new goods according to established expectations for satisfaction; although durables are useful and beneficial, they do not give rise to the same kinds of pleasure, and therefore may be the source of some vague but very real disappointment. This conjecture is Hirschman's contribution to explaining why surveys fail to show a rising proportion of general happiness in contemporary society. Disappointment "arises typically because new types of purchases are undertaken with the kinds of expectations that consumers have come to associate with more traditional purchases" (Hirschman 1982, 45). The suggestion that there is a "lag effect" inherent in the individual's search for satisfaction fits well with the conclusions we reached in Chapter 10 concerning the way people compartmentalize their positive and negative feelings, and with our surmise that there must be a deeply rooted ambiguity in personal experience in the marketplace. In part, then, this ambiguity is a response to changes in the types of goods themselves; different types of goods reflect different structures of meaning, and changes in them affect the kinds of gratifications that can be derived from consumption.

The issue of consumer disappointment forces us to ask: **Are persons misled in any significant measure by the symbolic meanings woven into the world of goods?** We have offered numerous illustrations, drawn both from earlier societies and our own, of situations in which material objects are the prestige tokens that "stand for" social distinctions and that facilitate the flow of messages between persons. Do these communications processes always serve worthy purposes? Or do they also distort and blur our perceptions of social events?

FETISHISM: DISTORTED COMMUNICATION IN THE WORLD OF GOODS

The objects we acquire, display, or simply admire are a powerful medium for the circulation of messages about ourselves to others, and for learning the forms of expression for social interactions (the status symbols, clothing styles, and so forth) that appear to be sanctioned at any one time. This ensemble can be said to represent, in Marshall Sahlins's (1976) words, "man speaking to man through the medium of things." Presumably, most of us, most of the time, strive to convey our intentions and perceptions truthfully; but evasions, outright lies, and honest mistakes are not unknown. More important, the subjective bias with which we all operate inevitably colours our reading of events. So we must ask, Is the discourse through and about things spoken with forked tongues?

In considering this question, we will continue to look chiefly at the place of objects in social interactions, and pay little attention to the role they might play in the psychological development of individuals. (For an excellent discussion of this point, see Part I of *The Meaning of Things* by Csikszentmihalyi and Rochberg-Halton [1981].) There are stages in childhood where a fixation on particular objects seems to be both a necessary and a normal process that, so far as we know, occurs universally. However, in some cases, an abnormal fixation on objects can occur in which, for example, a male cannot perform sexually under normal conditions, and seeks to use what psychoanalytic theory terms a "fetish object," such as a woman's shoe, as a catalyst to reaching orgasm.

The notion of fetish, as we shall see, is helpful for investigating to what extent the discourse through and about objects contains elements of distortion and misrepresentation. The Portuguese coined the terms "fetish" and "fetishism" as a result of the European encounter with African societies beginning in the fifteenth century. They were describing the widespread practice they observed of addressing or employing material objects in order to effect a change in the condition or behaviour of another. Traditional ceremonies involving fetishes persist to the present. Of special interest are practices that blend old fetishisms with other elements in response to pressures exerted by twentieth-century market forces operating on a global scale. The anthropologist Michael Taussig tells of Bolivian tin miners who have called upon a mixture of folklore and Christian doctrine to construct a representation of what has happened to traditional ways of life, particularly in the domain of producing goods. The tin miners' mythic structure explains that the people have been seduced away from their traditional agricultural pursuits by the promise of great wealth in the mines. But the mine owner is actually the devil who has deluded the workers. To protect themselves from the dangers of the mines, the miners adapted peasant sacrifice rituals to their new situation, seeking to propitiate the devil-owner with gifts and ceremonies, chewing coca together and offering it to the icon that represents the devil-owner.

> His body is sculptured from mineral. The hands, face, and legs are made from clay. Often, bright pieces of metal or light bulbs from the miners' helmets form his eyes. The teeth may be of glass or crystal sharpened like nails, and the mouth gapes, awaiting offerings of coca and cigarettes. The hands stretch out for liquor. In the Siglo XX mine the icon has an enormous erect penis. The spirit can also appear as an apparition: a blond, bearded, red-faced

gringo wearing a cowboy hat, resembling the technicians and administrators. . . . He can also take the form of a succubus, offering riches in exchange for one's soul or life. (Taussig 1980, 143)

Thus, materials from older fetishistic practices were adapted and transformed to provide a workable representation of what the introduction of wage labour meant for the relationship between humans and the material world. The personification (the devil) of the agent behind these changes is anchored in the concept of "seduction" when, lured by material wealth, people accept the rules of the game in a market economy founded on working for wages and producing tin for world markets.

What prompts cultures to create such representations is the need to supply a coherent account (however implausible it may appear to outside observers) of changes that have a major impact on established ways. Social relations oriented around longstanding modes of production and exchange—subsistence agriculture, extended family or kinship groups, barter—began to dissolve as private capitalists and market economics took control. But what is *visible and tangible* about these changes? It is not capital-investment decisions, international stock-exchange fluctuations, or profit targets set by multinational corporations for their operations in foreign countries. It is loss of access to land, cash wages determined and paid by strangers, radically different types and conditions of work, and the breakdown of kinship groups. For the indigenous peoples of Bolivia, just as for the peoples of Europe a century earlier, structures of life and experience familiar to countless generations suddenly disintegrated before their very eyes. It is hardly surprising that they should suspect the devil of having a hand in it.

The objects of the material world and the activities needed to sustain life no longer make sense by the accepted standards of judgment. The establishment of a market economy unravels and discards not only specific things, habitual routines, and norms but also the integument holding them together, the sense of a collective identity and fate. At first, no new means for binding together the experience of the material world is proffered. It appears only as an "immense and astonishing collection of goods."

The preceding phrase is from the opening sentence of Karl Marx's *Capital.* In reading the many tomes on political economy published in his day, Marx noticed something peculiar about how social commentators described the emerging market society and its advantages. They seemed to regard the domain of material production, when governed exclusively by the rules of "free markets," as something beyond human control, obeying only its own inherent principles, almost as if the economy possessed a "life of its own." (The reader may recall our own examples of this in contemporary discourse earlier in this chapter.) Marx saw in this philosophy an analogy between the propensities of religion and the new way of thinking about a market economy that had been developing since the eighteenth century. In religious thought,

> the products of the human brain appear as autonomous figures endowed with a life of their own, which enter into relations both with each other and with the human race. . . . [So] it is in the world of commodities or goods with the products of men's hands. I call this the fetishism which attaches itself to the products of labor as soon as they are produced as commodities, and is therefore inseparable from the production of commodities. (Marx [1867] 1976, 165).

This is a remarkable statement, especially considering when it was penned; except for some perceptive comments on related topics made around the turn of the twentieth century by Thorstein Veblen and Georg Simmel, two of the founders of modern sociology, about a hundred years passed before the fetishism/market economy theme was seriously taken up again. What connects Marx's notion with our earlier discussion of fetishism is that he, too, encountered the idea by reading a book (in his case, one published in the eighteenth century) about European voyages to then unfamiliar places. He detected a similarity between the fetishistic practices in African societies, where certain material objects were regarded as embodying forces that could affect human behaviour, and the way the political economists of his own day described the operations of a market economy as an independent force in society, steered by its own mechanisms (the so-called laws of supply and demand) that compelled all sensible men and women to act in accordance with its dictates. Those who protested against poverty or degraded working conditions were told that there was a "natural" level for wages, determined by the marketplace itself, and that neither labour unions nor legislation could interfere with its mysterious ways. Any notion of tampering with the wild, roller-coaster ride of the business cycle in the nineteenth century was resisted just as strenuously.

Marx argued that this conception of the economy and its "laws" was regressive, because it left most people at the mercy of unmastered forces. But his argument also contains a particular point of special relevance for this chapter, namely that **the misrepresentation about production and consumption in a market economy is embodied in material objects themselves.** And should such a fundamental misrepresentation be found to exist, it necessarily would call into question the power of goods to serve as meaningful communicators of personal intentions, motives, and objectives.

To live according to the principles of a market economy is to be immersed in buying and selling transactions every day, where everything one has (especially one's mental skills and physical energies) and everything one wants or needs has a price. In other words, as a market-industrial economy expands, more and more elements of both the natural environment and human qualities are drawn into the orbit of exchanged things, into the realm of commodities. Everything has some use to someone (or so it is hoped), and likewise everything has a price at which it can be acquired.

When elements of nature and humanity are ever-increasingly absorbed into the market's orbit, becoming exchanged things, they begin to appear to us as objects, or at least as *objectified forms*. Fewer and fewer aspects of our environment and ourselves remain "outside" the domain of buying and selling. By and large, in earlier times individuals were expected to adjust their behaviour to role requirements, and, in the early phases of our modern economy, occupational structures dictated the behavioural standards to which people were expected to conform. More recently, however, we are commonly told to "market" ourselves, to regard our qualifications and experiences as components that we can "repackage" in various ways to suit the demands of changing employment patterns.

The process of converting more and more elements of natural environments and human qualities into objectified forms—commodities—constitutes the very essence of an expanding market-industrial economy. This busy enterprise has yielded abundant fruit, which is why the social wealth produced by it appears, in Marx's words, as an "immense and astonishing collection of goods." This is what strikes us immediately, overwhelmingly, as we look about us and consider just how much *more* there is now than at any other time. So strong is this impression that it is easy not to notice that what is missing, what does not appear immediately to us, what remains hidden beneath the surface in the vast world of goods, is any adequate representation of the *social* character of production and consumption activity.

With the progressive specialization of labour, most of us work at a narrow range of tasks, and in industrialized nations today the majority of the labour force has no direct involvement in the production of any material objects, although upon reflection we know that we work in an integrated production system and that what we do is connected somehow with the overall economic result. For the most part, we encounter objects as users and consumers; since in these settings we usually have specific aims in mind (the accomplishment of certain tasks or the gratification of particular wants), the social processes through which these objects came to be produced as appropriate for consumption remain in the background.

In our political rhetoric, we worry a good deal about the condition of our economy as a whole, but this is a rather abstract and distant concern. The point is that we tend to allow the economy itself, as the sphere in which the world of goods is produced and consumed, to represent what binds us together as a society. Goods themselves do provide some of the major lines of communication for our system of social relations. But the lines are buried, so that we sometimes run the risk of focusing too much interest on the surface attractions of things and too little on their more important communicative functions: "If things attract our attention excessively, there is not enough psychic energy left to cultivate the interaction with the rest of the world" (Csikszentmihalyi and Rochberg-Halton 1981, 53).

This point may become clearer if we recall the "double symbolic process." On one side, businesses incorporate their understanding of consumer preferences (and how they might be changed) into the physical and symbolic characteristics of the product, though the design and marketing strategies are not necessarily visible or obvious to consumers (nor are they meant to be). Meanwhile, consumers construct their own self-images and preference patterns out of an enormous array of symbolic associations and behavioural codes that manufacturers are not always able to anticipate or decode. Thus, what we get is not the whole story.

Marx did not see the consumer society emerge, but he did spot the first forms of this peculiar feature in a market economy, remarking that the objectified forms for what is produced and consumed there have an "enigmatic" or "mysterious" character; although marketed goods have a richly textured social composition, involving coordinated production, distribution, and consumption on a global scale, their social character is not immediately apparent. Thus, commodities are "sensuous things which are at the same time supra-sensible or social"—a combination of features that we can see, touch, and smell, on the one hand, and of the complex but hidden social relations orchestrated by the market economy on the other.

Commodities are, therefore, a unity of what is revealed and what is concealed in the processes of production and consumption. Goods reveal or "show" to our senses their capacities to be satisfiers or stimulators of particular wants and communicators of behavioural codes. At the same time, they draw a veil across their own origins: products appear and disappear before consumers' eyes as if by spontaneous generation, and it is an astute shopper indeed who has much idea about what most things are composed of and what kinds of people made them.

Marx called the fetishism of commodities a disguise whereby the appearance of things in the marketplace masks the story of who fashioned them, and under what conditions. Is it important for us to hear this story? Are we, in being deprived of it, experiencing a systematic distortion of communication within the world of goods itself?

The story matters not because we would necessarily act differently once we heard it, but because it draws attention to some otherwise unnoticed aspects of a market economy, including the role of advertising in it. Although goods serve as communicators of social meanings, they do not do so in straightforward or unambiguous ways. Goods are communicators in a market-industrial society, just as they have always been in human cultures; but precisely what they communicate—and, equally as noteworthy, fail to communicate—is something that can be determined only by close analysis.

Commodities tell us a great deal about themselves, at least insofar as their surface features are concerned, especially in advertisements. But, unlike goods in earlier societies, they do not bear the signatures of their makers whose motives we might assess because we know who they are, nor do they tell us how we should behave with them as they do in societies with closed spheres of exchange. Recall that among the Siane people in New Guinea "no commodity can be used in an ambiguous situation" (Salisbury 1962, 103). In contrast, a market economy revels in ambiguities that flow from the double symbolic process, and under their sway the discourse through and about objects must be, in some important measure, systematically distorted—a passage through a carnival hall of mirrors.

The distortion arises primarily on account of what is omitted at the surface level of representations about needs and commodities. Neither the conditions of production, nor the manufacturer's marketing strategies, nor the subtle ploys of the ad agency's "creative" department is meant to attract our attention as the object presents itself to us. On the other hand, although most people seem willing at least on occasion to indulge their fantasies in stores, market researchers can find no simple correlations between personality traits and ordered arrays of consumer preferences. Like producers, consumers too draw a veil across the sources of their enterprise.

A market society is a masked ball. Here we bring our needs to dance with their satisfiers (goods) in close embrace to the melodies of an unseen orchestra. The costumes serve products well, for they hide the fact that so many of them are just ordinary chemical compounds tarted up in fancy packages; our disguises are equally advantageous, shielding from others' gaze our many disappointments—as consumers—in our partners' performances.

There are distorted patterns of communication imprinted on the collection of goods circulating in a market-industrial society because some important aspects of producing and consuming activities generally remain out of view. The discourse through and about objects is carried on from behind elaborate masks; advertisers and marketers fashion huge numbers of masks, and in selecting some, consumers allow themselves to be persuaded that they can serve their needs. At social events, conversations are customarily limited to polite remarks about superficial matters, and discourse in the marketplace generally confines itself to the surface qualities of objects and our possible reasons for being interested in them.

In fashioning masks for goods, marketers and advertisers use all the available media of communication to move back and forth across the interface between the production and consumption spheres, restlessly creating and refurbishing zones of encounter between needs and products. As we indicated in Chapter 10, advertising mirrors the identifying sign of the consumer society—the unending play with new possibilities for satisfaction. This sign is reflected concretely in the general characteristics of goods themselves—changing qualities, styles, materials, and modes of appeal. As represented in advertisements, goods are active, potent ingredients in social interactions; they are bearers of powers that can affect us and assist us in affecting others. In advertising, we encounter a lush and entertaining realm of fetishes.

Certainly our fetishes do not serve us in the same way as those used in primitive societies. Another important point is that in modern society goods themselves are not fetishes, except in unusual or abnormal circumstances. Rather, through marketing and advertising goods are fitted with masks that "show" the possible relations between things on the one hand and human wants and emotions on the other. These masks are our fetishes. They make things come alive, make them able to act—almost literally—as participants in social interactions. They encipher goods in codes that we can read and act upon.

This perspective enables us to understand two interrelated features of the consumer society: the ambiguous sense of satisfaction experienced by individuals, and the role that marketing and advertising plays in its formation.

Distorted communication is a structural component of the world of goods itself. In a market-industrial society, the domain of communication is indeed systematically misleading because it makes so few direct references to many essential aspects of our producing and consuming activities. Any direct connection between goods and the enduring sources of contentment in life is concealed; the happiness surveys report that people regard earlier generations (which had a noticeably lower material standard of living) as being more contented, but also that most would not wish to live as people did in those times.

Certainly, advertising seeks to link goods with images of happiness and content by designing masks for things that display such linkages. Sometimes the designs are actually false or misleading, but this is not one of their inherent features. Legislation and industry guidelines (at least in western societies) have tended to reduce considerably the extent of overtly untruthful or deceptive practices. While the masks are meant to influence consumer behaviour, it is certain that they do not and cannot control it. Thus, we do not contend that modern society's realm of fetishes is generally harmful or manipulative in general. The vital issues about advertising today are specific ones, such as the wisdom of promoting alcohol and tobacco products, stereotyping, and directing messages at children. We shall return to these points in the following chapter.

CULTURAL FRAMES FOR GOODS

In earlier societies, individuals became acquainted with the meanings carried by objects through culture and customs. In a consumer society, needs and commodities must be introduced by some other means. Marketing and advertising become the chief matchmakers. Toward the end of the nineteenth century, the burgeoning array of new goods that began to emerge from mass-production techniques presented businesses with the challenge of "binding" products to culturally sanctioned formats for the satisfaction of needs. Marketers and advertisers had to start constructing props for the ball—sets of masks for goods—using whatever media technologies and persuasive or "appeal" formats were available to them. But partners at the masked ball need melodies, not words, for dancing; they also need instruction in the new steps. The music and the choreography for any dance comes from its cultural frame of reference.

First, the ground had to be cleared, ground that had been occupied by traditional social collectivities rooted in pre-modern economic conditions and formed by regional, religious, ethnic, linguistic, craft, and other local customs. The objects that circulated therein reflected these determinations: the distinctive dress and cuisine of ethnic communities, the closed associations of skilled craftsmen, the special kinds of things provided for feasts and celebrations. The coming of the market-industrial system changed all this.

Where the division of labour, mass migrations from rural to urban areas, sustained technological innovation, and the erosion of traditional customs had rent the fabric of social collectivities, mass marketing began to feel its way, gradually stitching together a new type of human association.

In the first phase of mass marketing, before the emergence of the consumer society, familiar objects were replaced by industrial articles promoted largely on the basis of their own "abstract" qualities: their utility, advanced technology, low cost, and efficiency. Thereafter, marketing and advertising strategies sought with ever greater self-awareness to fill the void left by the disappearance of traditional cultures by creating a sense of social solidarity in messages about the relations between persons and things. Whereas the new system of commodity production emptied the world of the traditional material elements in the lives of groups, the new system of mass marketing sought to refill that world with its own form and content.

The consumer society brings into being a distinctive way of life based on a notion that individuals can regard their affiliation with social groups as a fluid milieu of temporary associations that are based on styles of appearance and behaviour as well as on choices of activities. No one is bound permanently to particular circumstances originating in accidents of birth or fortune; on the contrary, everyone can participate in an eternal process whereby groupings are dissolved and regenerated.

The distinctive content of the consumer society is that these temporary associations, based purely on the arbitrary wills of their members, revolve around structured sets of products and messages about them. "Flapper," "zoot suiter," "soul," "hippy," and "punk" are just a few of the exhibitionist styles that the more cautious majority have skirted apprehensively on their way to department stores and supermarkets; after a decent interval, fragments of such styles, suitably muted and sanitized, filter unrecognized into the consumption practices of more respectable folk. Marketers and advertisers are responsible not for imposing behaviour patterns on unsuspecting people, but rather for ensuring that (lest the audience fall asleep) sufficiently entertaining new productions are mounted in the theatre of consumption, that (lest the audience stay away) the program is changed often, and that (lest the audience be offended) the theatregoers become broad-minded enough at least to tolerate, if they cannot enjoy, the extravagances that are paraded before their senses.

In much national product advertising, goods stand in an indeterminate relation to the personal activities, interactions, and self-transformations associated with them. There are no "causal" connections between the persons and the things represented; rather, the product simply is associated with a highly stylized set of visual images. The product image serves as an emblem for a social grouping; consider the Coca-Cola ad that portrayed a multi-racial, multi-ethnic group of young people singing sweetly about "harmony" in the world. We call this the magical representation of social collectivities.

In such a format, the product appears as a sign or indicator for a collectivity that is defined by its appearance and activities—the devotees of punk music and rock video, the beer-drinking sports fans, the fitness and healthy living set—and constituted as a social series by means of the various products with which it is associated. This mode of presentation has assumed the leading role only through a long developmental process that began about a hundred years ago. The principal stages of development are sketched in Table 11.1, which is based on the stages in advertising practice we developed in Chapter 6 and illustrated by our historical study of magazine advertising in Chapter 9.

TABLE 11.1
Evolution of Cultural Frames for Goods in Relation to the Development of
Media, Marketing, and Advertising

MEDIA FOR ADVERTISING*	NEWSPAPERS/ MAGAZINES	RADIO	TELEVISION	
MARKETING STRATEGY	RATIONAL	NON-RATIONAL	BEHAVIOURIST	SEGMENTATION
ADVERTISING STRATEGY	UTILITY	PRODUCT SYMBOLS	PERSONAL-IZATION	LIFESTYLE
PERIOD	1890 1900 1910	1920 1930 1940	1950 1960	1970 1980
ELEMENTS IN ADS	product qualities/ price/use	product qualities symbolic attributes	product person prototype	product activity (person/ setting)
METAPHORIC-EMOTIVE THEMES IN ADS	quality, useful, descriptive	status, family, health, white magic, social authority	glamour, romance, sensuality, black magic, self-trans-formation	leisure, health, groups, friendship
CULTURAL FRAMES FOR GOODS	IDOLATRY product is abstracted from process of production, presented as pure use value	ICONOLOGY products are embodiments of attributes, configured in social judg-ment	NARCISSISM products are personalized, satisfaction is judged in interpersonal terms	TOTEMISM product is emblem of group-related consumption practice

* Pre-1890: Posters and billboards.

The cultural frame for goods supplies the general design principles for fashioning the masks for goods that highlight what is distinctive and unique about each period. This does not mean that a single cultural frame overshadows everything else that is happening at that time, or supplants completely what came before. Different marketing/advertising strategies overlie one another, and all continue to play some part in the total sales effort down to the present day. In other words, we cannot segregate events neatly into separate piles, since human action is not a well-ordered phenomenon. But using cultural frames of reference can help us to mark where the edges of behavioural patterns (that in themselves remain rather indistinct) rub up against one another. We have called the four cultural frames for goods idolatry, iconology, narcissism, and totemism.

Phase One: Idolatry

We name the period 1890–1925 the idolatrous phase of the market-industrial society because advertising messages at this time carried a strong tone of veneration about products. What generated this tone was the industrial system's newly discovered sense of power and accomplishment, dating from about 1875, when it recognized that its great capacities could be applied to the mass production of consumer goods. There followed a great outpouring of mechanical devices, cleverly answering or anticipating the requirements of every conceivable task and occasion in domestic life, so bountiful that some people surely must have feared being buried under an avalanche of objects.

The overt selling strategy can be described as "rational" because its discourse was saturated with descriptive narratives about products and their many qualities, about the great range of their potential uses and benefits, about their common-sense advantages in saving time, energy, and money. But it must also be characterized as a quasi-logical discourse because the surface appearance of the text—dispassionate, informative, elaborately reasoned—concealed vital qualitative differences between quite sensible products and uses on the one hand, and simply fraudulent and sometimes even dangerous ones on the other. The patent-medicine advertising of earlier times was notorious for systematically confusing real and imaginary ailments, and even more so for making utterly unfounded claims about the efficacy of products. Until about 1905, narcotic-based elixirs containing opium and cocaine were widely touted in baby products such as colic cures and teething remedies and in products said to relieve " female distress"; this may remind us why some restrictions on the creative imaginations of producers and marketers are thought to be necessary.

Whether the uses were exotic or prosaic, the discourse through and about objects was anchored in the object itself and its image. By calling this "the idolatrous phase," we do not mean to suggest that the discourse was generally false or misleading, for the great majority of goods had some sensible quotient of genuine utility, and the lavish descriptions of their qualities contained an unmistakable undertone of equally genuine pride in their manufacture; rather, we wish to highlight the fact that the "veneration of the object" has inherent limitations.

While offering a coherent design principle for messages about the relationships between persons and things, and while celebrating enthusiastically the technological innovations of the day, the focus on the object was a backward-looking practice in many respects and thus an inadequate medium for the newly emerging consumer society. The uses with which products were largely associated originated in traditional patterns of activity, artisanal values, and established stereotypes for per-

FIGURE 11.1
The industrial system's newly discovered sense of power was manifested in a strong tone of veneration of the product.

FIGURE 11.2
The overt selling strategy was rational because its discourse was saturated with descriptive narratives about products and their many qualities.

"THE ONEITA"

PAT. APR. 25 TH 1893.

L IEUT. PEARY, of the U.S. Navy, is the most experienced of all living men in Arctic exploration. Before embarking on his present expedition, and after a thorough investigation of the subject, he equipped his force with a supply of Oneita Combination Suits in a suitable weight. The advantage of these garments, from a purely scientific and practical point of view, the distinguished explorer found to be, that, while retaining the heat of the body, they do not encumber the movements of active men. In short, they liberate man from the "curse of clothes," leaving him as free for unhampered agility as the leopard in his velvet skin.

SEND FOR ILLUSTRATED BOOKLET.

ONEITA KNITTING MILLS,

Address Dept. F.   Office: No. 1 Greene Street, New York.

FIGURE 11.3
Advertising manifested a quasi-logical discourse that systematically confused
real and imaginary claims.

sonal roles. The messages about the new products extolled their capacity for helping people do better and more quickly the tasks they were accustomed to doing. By and large, they did not seek to upset the culturally grounded interpretations (for example, sex-role distinctions) either for familiar undertakings or for the types of objects ordinarily associated with them. This severely limited the scope of the consumer market with respect not only to the range of goods supplied, but more importantly to the far richer range of meanings that could be attached to goods once traditional roles and activity patterns were challenged.

Phase Two: Iconology

Icons are symbols, and between 1925 and 1945—the initial phase of the consumer society—the utilitarian aspects of goods were increasingly subordinated to a network of abstract, or symbolic, qualities and values. The masks for goods were no longer copied directly from the manifest appearances of product characteristics or from allegations about pressing personal needs. This marked the transition point at which the earlier denotative discourse, reflecting the quite specific attributions of qualities to things, became subordinated to a far more expansive connotative discourse, rooted in suggestion, metaphor, analogy, and inference.

In the iconistic phase, the focal point swung away from the object as an independent entity and toward the person as the intended user, but the process stopped halfway. Although the qualities of goods referred to in advertisements were generally cast in more abstract and suggestive terms, these qualities were still bound tightly to the things themselves: automobiles were expressions of a modern outlook, soaps of family integrity and caring, shoes of sobriety or status. (This theme is epitomized in the mode of representation that we have named "white magic," wherein the product appears to capture or control some potent but largely unspecified force of nature.) On the other hand, the persons who appeared in ads were not yet autonomous individuals; they were often mere exemplars of reigning social values carrying the burden of society's commitment to family structure, status differentiation, and hierarchical authority.

Iconology was a system of meanings, not a representation of feelings. Its inherent limitation was that the reigning social values that were supposed to link the attributes of things (freshness, goodness) with the interests of persons as consumers were too domineering and overwhelmed all other elements in the message format, causing both products and persons to appear "frozen" in space and time. The advertisement's communicative power was checked and held in equilibrium, hovering uncertainly between the poles of person and product.

FIGURE 11.4
Utilitarian aspects were subordinated to symbolic qualities and values.

Source: Courtesy of Camco Inc.

FIGURE 11.5
The persons who appeared in ads were mere exemplars of reigning social values.

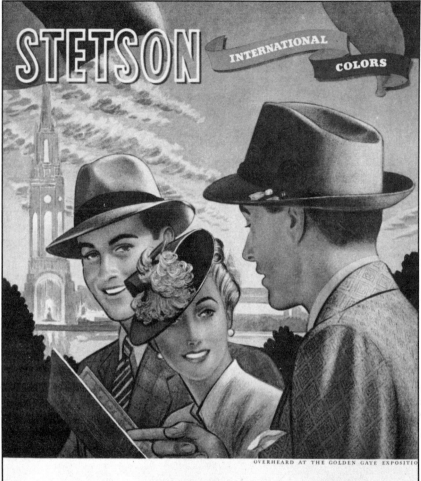

FIGURE 11.6
Products and persons were abstract, appearing "frozen" in space and time.

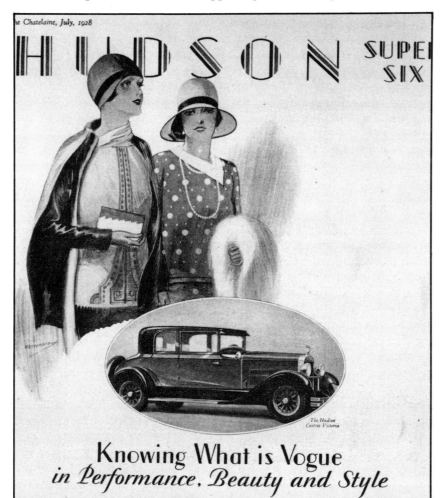

The Chatelaine, July, 1928

HUDSON SUPER SIX

Knowing What is Vogue
in Performance, Beauty and Style

This is the real joy and satisfaction of car ownership.

Hudson leadership of mode is but another expression of the value that has been the first principle of Hudson manufacture since the beginning.

The resources, which in a moderate-priced car attained the highest mechanical possibilities of the day, have been

brilliantly employed to create and lead a new vogue in beauty, comfort and luxurious appointment.

The wealth of quality detail you see, feel and touch—and every refinement that surrounds you—is typical and expressive of the quality that Hudson gives where character must guarantee the unseen values.

Phase Three: Narcissism

Whatever its ultimate shortcomings, the iconistic era opened the way toward cultural frames for goods that were more satisfactory in the consumer society. As the focal point shifted closer to the person, it brought emotion, which had been absent earlier, clearly into view. To make the discourse through and about objects truly come alive required greater psychological depth in the portrayal of the person, the creation of a domain where the meaning of things could resonate in response to an individual's changing emotional states. Having been admitted to the innermost recesses of the psyche, the product reciprocated by placing its powers at the individual's disposal. In the narcissistic phase (from about 1945 to 1965), consumers were encouraged to consider what the product could do for them, personally and selfishly. A prominent theme in advertisements in this phase is images of control over other people's judgments exerted with the product's assistance; we have labelled this "black magic."

During this period, objects were released from bondage to authoritative symbols. For the first time in the consumer society, things entered the sphere of ordinary human experience, and the means of entry was the metaphor of "personality." The most striking example is what has been called the "mirror ad," wherein the human face (almost always a woman's face) dominates the scene and stares out from the medium at the viewer-consumer. Like the product-symbol ad of the preceding era, this format too has a domineering tone; the difference is that this tone is carried not by abstract values but by the authoritative gaze of the human persona. (The literal meaning of the word "persona" is "actor's mask.") Despite the fact that the model in the ads is stylized, rather distant, not easily recognized as a "real" person—appearing as a kind of "imaginary other"—there is enough emotional force in the gaze to create a bond of identification between the viewer and the ad persona.

Persons were shown in social interactions as well. Romance was for the 1950s an effective way of communicating suggestions about erotic relationships without giving too much offence; images of warm family relationships were also prominent. Products seemed to bask in the glow of interpersonal attachments, as it were, showing for the first time in a market-oriented system that objects not only carried cues for public behaviour, but also were fitting and proper as guides in the interior regions of individual psychology.

The personalization format, too, had its own limitation, but one that was easily overcome. The range of imagery used for displaying the product in relation to interpersonal dynamics was too narrow, too conventional. But meanwhile industrial society had been changing rapidly; steadily rising real incomes during this phase opened the way to the far

FIGURE 11.7
Released from the bondage of symbols, things entered more intimately into the
spheres of ordinary human experience.

FIGURE 11.8
Tone was sometimes carried through a persona—stylized, rather distant—appearing as a kind of "imaginary other."

oooh, that lavender feeling...

FIGURE 11.8 continued

FIGURE 11.9
The meaning of things could resonate in response to an individual's changing emotional state.

Source: Courtesy of CIL Inc.

FIGURE 11.10
Objects secretly promise mystical powers of control and enchantment.

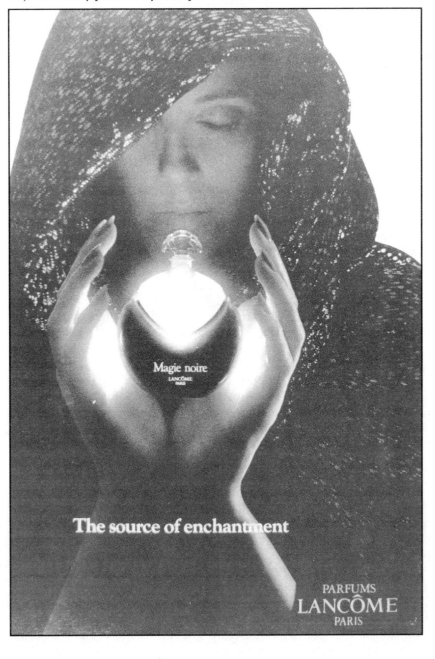

freer experimentation with "styles" of life and consumption that was to become a hallmark of the succeeding period.

Phase Four: Totemism

In primitive societies, totems are representations of animals or other natural objects identified with a particular subgroup, such as a clan. Totemic artifacts as a whole constitute a code, that is, a system of social meanings. The things represented as totems are thought to stand in some intrinsic relation to each other, and, as emblems for interrelationships, they can be "read" for what they signify about social interactions among those who are divided by and grouped under them.

Marshall Sahlins has applied the concept of totemism to contemporary society. Traditional totemism constructs a "vast and dynamic scheme of thought" by its " systematic arrangement of meaningful differences" in representations of natural objects. The market-industrial society seeks to do something similar using manufactured goods: "The goods stand as an object code for the signification and valuation of persons and occasions, functions, and situations" (Sahlins 1976, 178). Earlier in this chapter, we illustrated this point with examples of how choices among types of clothing and food are made.

During the present totemistic phase, the identifying features of the three preceding periods are recalled and synthesized. The product-related images are gradually freed from serving only the narrowly utilitarian qualities of the thing itself (idolatry), abstract and authoritative symbols (iconology), or a too restrictive array of interpersonal relations (narcissism). Here utility, symbolism, and personalization are mixed and remixed under the sign of the group. Consumption is meant to be a spectacle, a public enterprise. Product-related images fulfil their totemic potential in becoming emblems for social collectivities, principally by means of their associations with lifestyles.

Lifestyle patterns, like the older "totemic operators," incorporate social differentiation and testify to the existence of subgroups through symbolic displays. Today's totems (product images) themselves are the badges of group membership, which also entails self-administered codes of authority for dress, appearance, popular entertainment, customary places of assembly, behaviour rituals, and role stereotyping (for example, "macho" versus "non-macho" subgroups).

With this final stage in the sequence of cultural frames for goods, we are able to pull together the principal strands of argument from earlier chapters. Toward the end of Chapter 10, we tracked issues about the formation of the sense of satisfaction and well-being in the consumer society, and arrived by diverse paths at the concept of lifestyle; however, our discussion remained largely at the level of general notions, such as

FIGURE 11.11
Things must be "read" for what they signify about social interactions among those who are divided by and grouped under them.

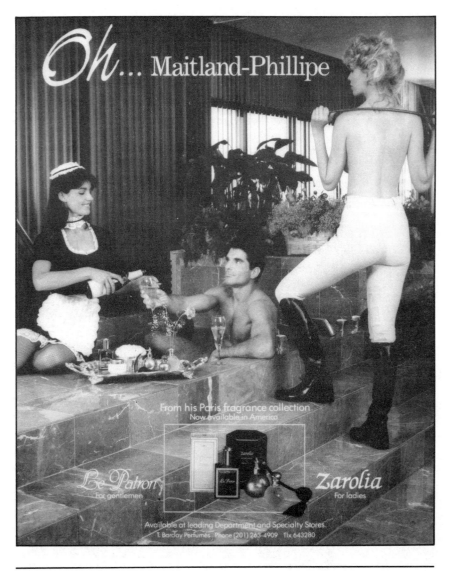

Source: Courtesy of T. Barclay Perfumes.

FIGURE 11.12
Utility, symbolism, and personalization mix. Consumption is a public spectacle as product images fulfil their totemic potential by means of their association with lifestyles.

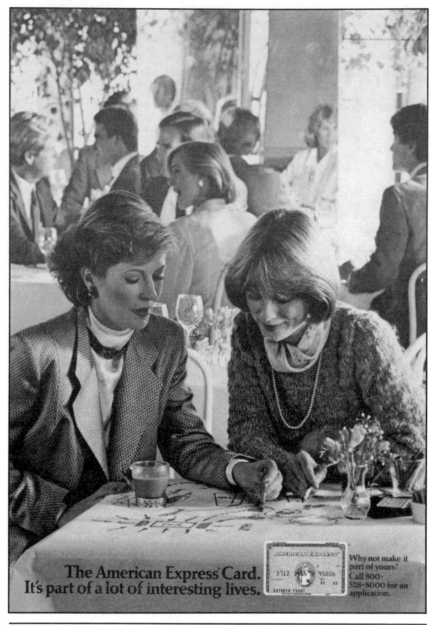

Source: Courtesy of American Express.

FIGURE 11.13
Totemic distinctions can be conveyed through the abstracted stylizations
associated with patterns of modern life.

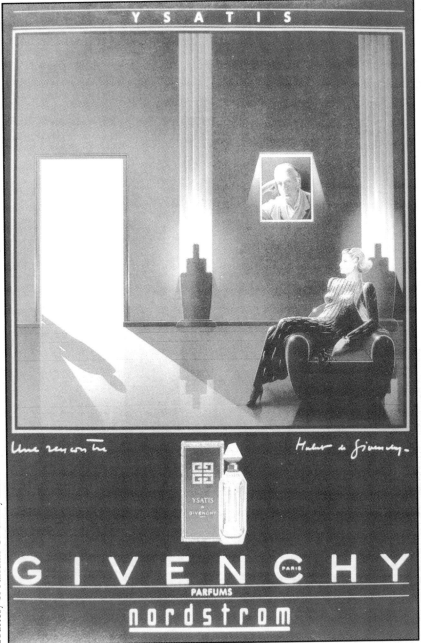

relative standing. We noted that the concept of lifestyle had begun to play a prominent role in marketing and advertising forums.

The present chapter led us to the same place by far different routes. Here we paid close attention to the tangible features in the landscape of the consumer society, namely, goods themselves. The masks they now wear, reflecting design techniques perfected over almost a century of marketing/advertising strategies, bear the emblems of ever-shifting lifestyle patterns. The existence of such patterns means that there is a wonderfully orchestrated play of social behaviour oriented around consumption practices today—our masked ball. Given its prominence in our lives, we should concern ourselves with how the spectacle is staged.

We may think of marketing as the host, and advertising as the master of ceremonies and conductor. Their staging for the spectacle of consumption often is brilliant, so much so that it can distract us from our duty to ensure that we do not sacrifice or neglect other important values and goals just because we have become enraptured by the dance.

PART 4

IN THE HEAT OF CONTROVERSY— ADVERTISING, CULTURE, AND POLITICS

12

Issues in Social Policy

In the eighteenth century, Samuel Johnson remarked that advertising was so "near to perfection" that no further improvements in it could be imagined. The dramatic innovations in advertising practice since that time have proved him wrong, keeping advertising's productions in the public eye and prompting never-ending debate and controversy about its social role. In Chapters 2 and 3, we observed that most of the debate today is a rehashing of longstanding postures based on uncertain ideological premises. On the one side, advertisements are sneered at for being banal and denounced as manipulative; on the other, they are downplayed as being inconsequential to consumer choice, or, paradoxically, extolled as the mainstay of the free marketplace and democracy itself. Yet, widespread disquiet with these accounts of the place of advertising remains. On occasion, there arises popular support for the restriction of some aspects of advertising practice, sometimes from the public gallery, and at other times from government or the industry.

The 1980s witnessed a broad drift toward the "business perspective" in the United States, including the deregulation of advertising and media industries, and increasing commercialization of broadcasting systems in other western countries such as Britain and France. And yet advertising remains a point of friction among a number of controversial social policy debates of the decade (Singer 1986). Some of the questions often asked are:

- Should there be limits to political advertising expenditure?
- Can networks refuse, for reasons of taste, controversial condom commercials?
- How far should governments go in the advocacy of their own social programs, including taxes that have not been ratified by Parliament?
- Should children's "program-length toy commercials" be allowed?
- Should we ban tobacco and alcohol advertising?
- Are certain images of erotica in ads offensive?
- Should we regulate the advertising of services by professionals such as lawyers and dentists?

Indeed, the courts in Canada have even been called upon to determine whether street solicitations of prostitutes, the language of shop signs, and

351

the displays of street vendors are matters that fall under constitutional guarantees for the freedom of speech.

A cursory glance at all of these issues reminds us that the uncertainties about the social role and mandate of advertising continue into the 1990s, and that we still have little understanding of how, within a free and democratic society, we may define reasonable limits to marketing's social communication. Yet it is clear, too, that a satisfactory response to each of the above questions depends upon a conception of advertising different from the view, established in economics, that advertising is simply the distribution of information about products available in the market that enables consumers to make rational choices. Indeed, advertising does, to varying degrees and with limited success, fulfil the economists' informational function. But that is certainly not all it does. Increasingly, our conception of advertising has to accommodate both the unintended social consequences of marketing communication, and the broader cultural effects of our particular market communication system.

The historical evidence indicates that advertising provided more product information—relating to a product's characteristics and particularly its utilitarian features—at the beginning of this century than it does now. History thus helps to remind us that product characteristics and utilities no longer appear as the central discursive focus of marketing communication. Consumer studies, too, confirm that consumers do not look to advertising solely to evaluate the performance, durability, and effectiveness of products.

The simple point is that advertising today communicates more about the social context in which products are used than about the products themselves. The primary field of content in modern advertising is contemporary culture itself, and advertising is a contested discourse precisely for this reason. Advertising is more than a mechanism for communicating product information to individuals: it is a cultural system, a social discourse whose unifying theme is the meaning of consumption.

Advertising professionals often react to suggestions of a connection between this type of "larger" social issue and their own creative activities on behalf of their clients with a mixture of contempt, wariness, and surprise. As one of our interviewees said: "I think advertising can play a role in helping to integrate people, though not a very substantial role. But I don't think advertising should be saddled with the various social problems." But we cannot continue to talk about advertising as if it were still nothing but "salesmanship in print." Nor as a form of persuasive communication is advertising exclusively concerned with merchandising concerns; it now impinges upon many dimensions of politics, education, and society. To talk about advertising demands that we deal with a wide array of promotional communication activities that have been mobilized, by those who have access to the mass media, to extend various channels of influence over social life. Most major corporations, and now many government and noncommercial organizations, engage in acts of strategic communication based upon marketing models.

THE POLICY TRADITION

Advertisers, media, and ad agencies have struggled hard to define and articulate what their larger social role might be. As the Libertad campaign recently declared, this means locating the arguments about advertising in debates on freedom of commercial speech (see Figure 12.1). But it is also the case that the advertising sector has sought to do so through codes of conduct they consider appropriate to their business. Indeed, industry self-regulation emerged quite early on in this century, when the extravagant claims in patent-medicine ads threatened to arouse a backlash against all advertising. "Truth in advertising" was one of the first professional rallying cries to help advertisers organize their initial programs for self-regulation.

The formulation of self-regulation codes helped advertisers to articulate the industry's perspective on advertising's role, and also helped to legitimize advertising by promoting a sense of professionalism among the majority of practitioners. Indeed, their own stand against extravagant claims, unfair competition, and misleading communication became absorbed into advertisers' working practice. Among the arguments about commercial free speech, one never hears an ad executive claim that misrepresentation is an inherent part of the freedom of commercial speech. Advertisers were not averse to government attempts to establish monitoring and regulatory structures that receive complaints about "unfair and deceptive" advertisements, because they quickly recognized that such mechanisms work in the interests of the industry as a whole by exposing the few "bad apples" before they taint the whole barrel.

In most western countries, there exist formalized regulatory activities, beyond legislation and the law courts, that are designed to supervise the advertising and media industries. These include guidelines established by the industry associations; pre-clearing and review panels (especially for food and drugs); watchdog groups (Media Watch); standards councils; complaints procedures; codes of ethics; and formal regulatory agencies like the U.S. Federal Communications Commission (FCC) and the Canadian Radio-television and Telecommunications Commission (CRTC). The profusion of regulatory agencies led one of our Canadian industry sources to comment: "We are the most regulated business in the world. The lawyers check every word that goes out of here. Health and Welfare Canada has an enormous staff checking what we write. The Canadian Broadcasting Corporation has a whole department of taste." To advertisers, who feel that their trade is just a business like any

FIGURE 12.1
To forestall regulation, advertisers have narrowed the discussion of advertising to issues linked to freedom of expression.

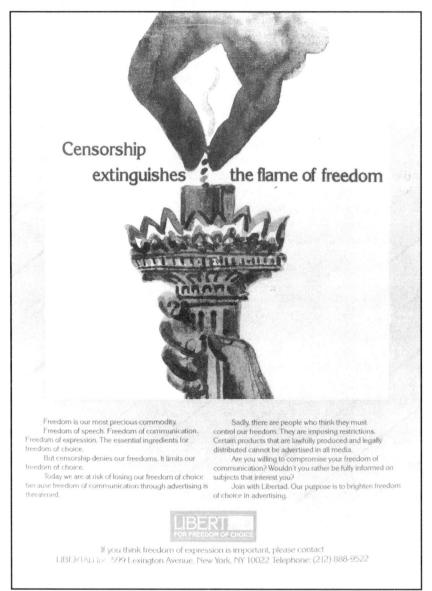

other in the marketplace, the elaborate systems of guidelines and regulations appear cumbersome and restraining. Yet the irony of all this regulation is that the advertising business is very little influenced by regulations. As another of our interviewees stated: "I've never been very affected by regulations. We're self policing."

The advertising industry has always responded emphatically, and often deftly, to issues of special concern that threaten its autonomy, by urging self-regulatory mechanisms as the best means of controlling the potential for abuses. But the industry's attempts at self-regulation, beyond the rather simple issues of "truth in advertising" and "fair business practice," have not always been effective or long-lasting. In the 1980s, the FCC and Federal Trade Commission (FTC) in the United States, after many years of lobbying and submissions by the advertising industry, began the process of deregulating commercial television and advertising in the hope that market forces and industry self-regulation would eliminate the need for regulation, particularly in the controversial area of children's advertising. They did so without much appreciation of how the industry would react, and in the face of some clear warnings that self-regulation was not likely to be successful.

Yet the deregulation did not bring about a reduction in the intensity of debates about advertising. As Armstrong and Brucks (1988, 111) recently noted in their review of children's advertising policy:

> Self-regulation alone cannot deal effectively with the complex problems of children's advertising. . . . Neither government regulation, consumer education for children and parents, advertiser and media efforts, nor self-regulation can work alone. But if all of the parties could work together—under a delicate blend of checks, balances and compromise—then these issues may finally be resolved.

Such cooperation rarely occurs. More often bitter critics, who accuse advertising of all manner of evil, are ranged against self-appointed advertising spokespersons set to defend unwaveringly their right to regulate themselves. In this context, one should keep in mind Kottman's (1969) view that "competitive selling is a kind of game played in the marketplace. Though there is a need for rules, there is also a need for sportsmanship and social responsibility within the context of the present culture, which is far from perfect and has created advertising as we know it."

The fact that advertising does not fit within neat policy categories helps to explain why there is so little consensus on how to regulate it. Because it stands at the intersection of industry and culture, advertising can (and has) come under attack from diverse perspectives. At the same time, and perhaps as a result, comparatively little critical attention has been paid to the cultural and institutional nexus within which advertising works. It is easier, of course, simply to lay blame for everything that is going wrong with our market-driven society at the feet of advertising. But the result is a chaotic litany of unrelated complaints that fails to provide a framework in which to set policy.

The absence of guidelines has made it difficult for both supporters and opponents of advertising interests. Because so many different social issues are bound up with advertising one way or another, the rights or restrictions applicable in some cases do not appear to be relevant in others. This was evident when Canada's Department of National Health and Welfare banned tobacco advertising from all media in 1989. In presenting its reasons for going to court over the legislated ban, Bob Foss of the Association of Canadian Advertisers (ACA) asked: "What will be next? We know there are many places people would like to see [an ad ban]. Numerous products have been targets, like tobacco and children's toys and alcoholic beverages. . . . We're afraid it could come about if a precedent is set." The clear implication behind Foss's question is that there is a unitary principle for advertising's role and impacts that extends to all forms of advertising, in all media, and for all purposes. But should advertisements for hazardous products like cigarettes not be regulated differently from those for milk? Should television not be more restrictive in the way it advertises beer than it does cookies? Are not children less able than adults to understand the purposes and messages of advertising? To suggest that the protective mantle of free speech covers all cases equally is to overlook the very significant practical differences between the social issues involved in each of them.

Such differences arise precisely because, as we emphasized in earlier chapters, advertising is not just about the goods it displays; it also communicates much about the meaning and desirability of those particular goods, the social context in which consumption takes place, and the use and purposes of products and their production. In short, advertising orients people to goods, provides images of users, and conveys a mood, tempo, and stylistic that can be associated with various consumption patterns and images of well-being. The policy debates about advertising should now assimilate this understanding and recognize that the increasing sophistication of marketing communication demands a new way of thinking about the consequences of the unique combination of economic and cultural forces at work in our society.

Advertising is the apex of a cultural subsystem, a distinctive pattern of social communication that continues to alter our society in a number of important ways: it has transformed the institutional framework for market society, enhancing the power of large-scale corporate entities who undertake strategic marketing communications; it has created a highly concentrated and increasingly narrowly owned group of agencies that are experts in the new practices and forms of persuasive communications and the audience research upon which they are based; it has radically reordered the economics and audience bases of communications media; and it has changed many of the forms and practices of socialization in our society generally, including the television commercial itself, programming formats such as the rock video or children's television, as well as the entire spectrum of social, governmental, and political marketing. If we are to assess the controversies surrounding advertising, we can do so only by understanding the full scale and cultural significance of all this communications activity.

Through a cultural–historical analysis of advertising, we have attempted to show how the emergence of advertising forms within mediated communication (the commercial media) radically changed the cultural discourse of modern industrial societies, and how these forms came to assume a privileged place in that discourse. In the course of this chapter, we shall outline the implications of these developments for the emerging social policy questions that have confronted advertising. In doing so, we will explore the implications of our rethinking of advertising's role for the broader questions of social policy that arise in market society.

The central thrust of our analysis has been a "structural" approach. Advertising impinges directly upon some very sensitive and important areas of life, and this forces policy makers to think very carefully about its proper place within a democratic society. The uniqueness of advertising agencies, and the regulatory issues confronting them, is that they have emerged as the point of mediation between the industrial, cultural, and communications sectors of society. Accordingly, advertising has encountered three different sets of social policy considerations—those connected with business, media, and social relations. Each of these has its own mandate, organizational focus, and traditions of regulation. Each has its associated groups advocating their interests, which define the debates over the following contested terrains: teachers and parents vs. toy manufacturers, tobacco companies vs. government and anti-smoking advocates, television stations vs. anti-stereotyping groups, and so forth. The policy debates about advertising evolved historically, both as the broader climate of opinion changed and in response to particular changes in the advertising industry. The aforementioned conflicts exist as a record of the various attempts to make advertising take responsibility for some of its perceived social and cultural impacts.

THE BUSINESS OF HONESTY

Advertising is subject to the constraints our society imposes on all economic activities under the aegis of "fair business practice." Thus, like any other business sector, advertising must respond to the perceived need to make the marketplace function efficiently and fairly, a matter that goes beyond the issue of accurate information about products provided by advertising.

Advertising has generally been accorded a place of honour among economic activities, because we believe that it aids consumer choice and generally supports competitiveness in the marketplace. For this reason, it has been indirectly subsidized through the tax system. The most obvious acknowledgment of advertising's legitimate place in the industrial firmament is the fact that it is generally allowed as a fully tax-deductible expense of doing business. However, in 1976 Canada's notorious Bill C-58 denied this tax benefit to Canadian advertisers who placed advertising in "foreign" magazines distributed in Canada; it took an occasion such as this, when tax law was used to make cultural policy, to bring the issue of advertising's key role in the sphere of cultural production to public attention.

Although the principles of *caveat emptor* and freedom of commercial speech have been articulated throughout the history of business, the ravages of unrestrained industrialism created a climate of opinion, in the early part of this century, in which restrictions on advertising appeared necessary to ensure the maintenance of fair business practice. Indeed, concerns about honest business communication date back to the medieval period, when merchants and shopkeepers were threatened with the rack for shortening the standard measure of bread or diluting beer, on the grounds that consumers deserved some assurance about the measure they were buying. With the advent of industrial production and the resulting proliferation of new products in the market, the relationship between the claims of producers and the actual quality, price, and quantity of goods became a matter of ongoing interest for both consumers and competitors.

Advertisers and the neophyte agencies themselves became concerned during the opening decades of this century about the secondary threat that exploitative advertisers posed to the industry as a whole. Reasoning that the deceptions of a few (particularly the extravagant claims in patent-medicine ads) were detrimental to the credibility and legitimacy of the rest, advertisers and agencies developed codes of ethics, promoting them as vehicles for self-regulation, and also urged governments to legislate in those areas where the worst infractions were occurring. In 1924, in Wembley, England, the Associated Advertising Clubs of the World adopted the "Wembley code of ethics," which reads, in part, as follows:

We pledge ourselves:
(1) To dedicate our efforts to the cause of better business and social service;
(2) To seek the truth and to live it;

(3) To tell the Advertising story simply and without exaggeration and to avoid even a tendency to mislead;
(4) To refrain from unfair competitive criticism;
(5) To promote a better international understanding based upon a recognition of our mutual responsibility and our interdependence;
(6) To conserve for ourselves and for posterity ideals of conduct and standards of Advertising practice born of the belief that truthful advertising builds both character and good business. (Turner 1952, 184)

For all their overblown rhetoric, advertisers and agencies shared consumers' concerns with the matters of truthful product claims, unfair or deceptive business practices, competitive advertising, and false pricing, and they saw distinct benefits for themselves in the enactment of legal sanctions against gross abuses of rogue marketers or fringe sectors of the economy. Ad agencies have long since accepted the longstanding business concerns about fair and competitive practices that became entrenched in both legislated and industry generated guidelines and procedures (Greyser 1972).

"Fairness" in advertising became part of American industrial law as early as 1914, as a component of the codification of competitive business practice, with the formation of the Federal Trade Commission. In the United States, the notions of unfair and deceptive advertising were further articulated in the Wheeler-Lea amendment (1938) to the FTC Act. In Canada shortly thereafter, the Combines and Monopolies Act was extended to include advertising; and the Department of Consumer and Corporate Affairs was later given jurisdiction over complaints about misleading and deceptive advertisements.

The relationship between these trade restrictions and the First Amendment to the American Constitution were contested in the courts over a number of years, leading to the landmark "Virginia Citizens Consumer Council Inc." decision, which appears to have entrenched the constitutional rights of commercial speech. As Ashman (1979, 23) noted: "On May 24, 1976, the Supreme Court of the United States handed down what well may be the most important document in the recent history of advertising in this country. . . . While still subject to regulation on a variety of grounds under administrative law, advertising that tells what is available and at what price is also in the public interest for a variety of reasons, including the fact that it is indispensable to the operation of a free enterprise marketplace."

The legitimacy and survival of advertising may well have rested on the advertising industry's acceptance of some limitations on commercial speech. Restrictions against falsifying a product, or misleading the consumer about its characteristics and price, have, in fact, not proven onerous to the industry. As Brian Philcox (1989), president of the Association of Canadian Advertisers, acknowledged in his public defence of the newly won constitutional protection for commercial free speech in Canada: "Commercial free speech simply means the right to inform the consumer of what's for sale. It is also the right of the consumer to be informed. At no time does an advertiser have license to misinform. Let's not forget that advertising, along with all the other facets of marketing communication, is a deeply rooted part of our cultural heritage." Accepting these limitations was thought to make good business sense, because advertisers also believe that consumers base decisions about products on rational performance criteria. Philcox goes on to suggest that "advertising must be the most vulnerable business activity in existence. If the product doesn't live up to the copy writer's promise, then the consumer will trash it. That product will die, and deservedly so."

As Alan Rae of the Canadian Advertising Foundation (CAF) has stated, all policy for advertising—both regulation and self-regulation—is presented "as ways of attaining one or two common goals—to protect the consumer and ethical business against false, misleading or even unfair advertising" (*Marketing* 1986). The acceptance of honest advertising and its interpretation as the absence of deception or false beliefs brought about a significant reduction in truly misleading advertisements; those that do occur are adequately reported and dealt with by the available complaints mechanisms. Most potential offenders are eliminated by the various official and unofficial pre-release review processes. The complaints wing of the National Advertising Review Council in the United States, for example, receives only about two hundred complaints a year concerning misleading advertisements. Correction of offending ads that slip through the net is usually swift. For example, when a Canadian government agency showed a young man riding in the back of a pickup truck in one of its ads (an illegal act under the transportation laws), the spot was quickly withdrawn and re-edited. Rae concludes: "The fact that in recent years complaints received by CAF deal more with social issues, indicates that the battle against deceptive advertising is increasingly successful."

But the definitions of deception and unfairness in advertising turn out to have been more controversial than was imagined at the time when advertising was more textual than visual. The nature of "dishonesty" had to be worked out in the changing context of social communication, particularly where performance and pricing claims for products became infrequent. The broader, still contentious issues concerning what is being suggested or implied by modern advertising imagery form the basis for many of the recent critiques of advertising practices. For example, it has been repeatedly suggested that cigarette and alcohol advertising encourage young people to take up these habits, because the advertising designs are "youth oriented" in their choice of models, stylistic devices, and references to the symbols of youth subcultures.

The case of advertising for alcoholic products is particularly instructive, for it may be one of the longest-running battlegrounds of advertising regulation. In the wake of prohibition attitudes in the 1920s, the Canadian government had restricted all advertising for alcoholic beverages. During the Second World War (after December 1942), however, the spirit beverage producers were allowed, like many other advertisers, to engage in corporate and public service advertisements under the War Time Alcoholic Beverage Order. This order was rescinded in 1947, and thereafter broadcast ads for beer and wine were permitted provided that they were acceptable to the provincial governments. Under pressure from manufacturers and broadcasters, in November 1963 the Canadian government issued "General Guidelines" for the advertising of beer and wine, which, among other things, stated that the ads could not present drinking as a necessary part of social activity or as a status symbol. They also could not show their product, except incidentally during the manufacturing process, and could include no family scenes, minors, glasses, bottles, or people engaged in consumption of alcohol. A pouring sound could not be used as a sound effect.

These guidelines were adjusted slightly over the next two decades to allow the showing of bottles and "pouring" sound effects. Moreover, in 1972 (following the U.S. broadcasting ban on spirit alcohol advertising) advertisers reached a voluntary agreement with broadcasters to restrict the advertisement of distilled spirit products to print media (mainly magazines). A preliminary evaluation of the results of the guidelines on distilled spirit advertising revealed that advertisers, however constrained they felt, committed few infractions; the study also indicated that the range of social imagery, social relations, settings, and values in such advertising was narrower than it was for other product categories (Leiss and Kline, unpublished).

The problems inherent in self-regulation were illustrated in 1986 when the CRTC invited broadcast and advertising groups to draft a new self-regulatory code on alcohol advertising guidelines (CRTC 1986)—an attempt that failed. The difficulties arose precisely because the regulators, rather than requiring advertisers to publicize the possible harm done by their product (in proportion to the amount of product advertising carried in the media), have instead chosen the path of attempting to define and control the presentation formats of the product ads themselves, determining, for example, what social imagery (party scenes, appearance of being "high") could be communicated. In 1986, the CRTC was reconsidering its guidelines for regulating beer and wine advertisements, which include the highly controversial limitation on the advertisers' ability to show people actually consuming alcoholic products. In support of their arguments that the industry should be self-regulated, the Association of Canadian Advertisers and the Institute of Canadian Advertising once again argued that excessive meddling by regulators has led to the preponderance of lifestyle advertising that many critics find offensive in TV beer and wine commercials: "Advertisers should be allowed to show 'slice of life' scenes with consumption of these beverages as they happen under normal, real life, appropriate conditions." (*Marketing* 1986).

This statement is particularly interesting for its seeming acknowledgment that there is an important distortion in the imagery of life provided in beer commercials, in the sense that beer advertisers do not depict life "realistically"—that is to say, they do not situate their product in "normal, real life" situations. In Canada, there has been a double response to this bias in advertising's depiction of beer consumption. The brewers have tried to counter this bad publicity by launching a public education campaign which highlights moderation in drinking (Figure 12.2). Meanwhile, the CAB, fully aware of the income broadcasters receive from beer advertising, have undertaken the production of television public-service ads that focus on drinking and driving.

Sometimes advertisers attribute such distortion to the restrictions imposed by the guidelines themselves and forced upon the beer and wine advertisers, which led to their preference for lifestyle-image approaches. Of course, the claim that the guideline forces this particular format by restricting images of product consumption is specious. If the guidelines stated that beer and wine or any other ads should always be honest and faithful representations of reality, showing alcohol being consumed under "normal, real life appropriate conditions," advertisers would be even more upset at this restriction of their depiction of social relations to what was "realistic." This should serve only to remind us that the fictive, not the descriptive, depiction of life has become the central "truth" to which advertising aspires; from the advertiser's perspective, "imaginary" lifestyle depictions do not violate truth and honesty claims.

Arguments about the implications of advertising design are much more difficult to resolve. The fact is that advertisers count on viewers' abilities to construct, from the symbolic clues they provide in the ad, an interpretation of the promise of their products. Generally speaking, advertisers would like to imply that such interpretations are subjective, that is, the responsibility of the viewer alone. Ashman (1979) remarks, with regard to the issue of the limits of communication formats in advertising, that "there is a difference between false advertising and the advertising which may be considered as misleading upon the application of value judgments." Most of modern advertising communication falls into this latter category, making few falsifiable claims but invoking many

FIGURE 12.2
In response to criticism of their industry's advertising, brewers promote a different perspective on drinking from their branded campaigns.

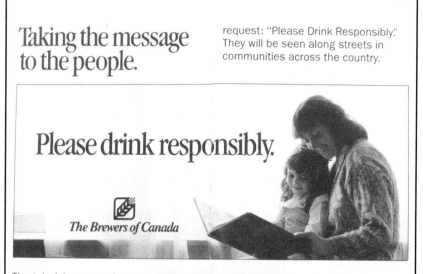

Taking the message to the people.

request: "Please Drink Responsibly."
They will be seen along streets in communities across the country.

The television campaign has reached Canadians, literally from coast to coast, and has done an effective job of changing people's attitudes. However, to ensure that the Responsible Use message reaches people when and where it's most crucial, the Brewers have extended the campaign to include outdoor boards and posters. The outdoor boards feature scenes from the TV commercials, and the simple

In addition, posters with the same message can be seen in distribution outlets for alcoholic beverages everywhere. Together with the TV campaign, these public service messages are reaching Canadians wherever they go.

Source: Courtesy of the Brewers Association of Canada.

value judgments. The problem of modern advertising policy is that the ground upon which the issue of dishonesty first rested has shifted, from the matter of overt verbalized deceptions (the advertiser lying about the qualities, price, or effectiveness of the product) to the implied claims or the potential inferences and interpretations that a viewer or reader is led to make as a result of the complex language and imagery used in advertisements. Does an ad that alludes, in overblown and poetic language, to sensuous or sexual attributes imply that erotic gratification is a consequence of that product's use? Does an image that shows a "housewife" using a product imply that working women do not? Does a picture that shows a partially dressed woman struggling to be free of a man in a car imply rape or sexual domination?

Attempts to operationalize honesty, in the context of modern visual media, imply an interpretive response on the part of the recipient of the message, as well as something about the intention of the advertising designer. The advertisers have been adamant in arguing that any attempts to regulate communication formats would be a violation of their freedom of speech. During the 1970s, the FTC did attempt to expand the purview of the honest advertising edict by opening up the matter of substantiation of product claims, and by attempting to develop trade regulation rules concerning disclosure of information and inferred claims in advertisements. But as influential advertising creator Tony Schwartz (1974) pointed out, advertisers can only run afoul of regulatory agencies or industry codes if they make overt claims about their products that cannot be substantiated; an ad that does not involve a claim cannot be false or deceptive in this sense. Thus Schwartz advised advertisers to make no claims at all about the product, but rather to use imagery and symbols to create a message that resonated with "social" truths for the target audience. Our own historical analysis of advertising messages shows that the industry was doing this well before Schwartz offered his advice. The language of implication and creative allusion supplanted product claims as the standard practice in advertising. The decline in "hard" information and the concomitant rise of imagery and lifestyle advertising as a mode of communication has likewise promoted more ambiguity in advertising and made most guidelines for deceptive and misleading advertising of little consequence to advertising practitioners.

Advertising firms have found that their intermediary role between goods-producing industries and the mass media allows them a certain amount of flexibility in heading off potentially damaging limitations imposed by any broader implications of the edict of honesty. Advertising would be highly restricted indeed had it been mandated to discuss only scientifically proven selling points for products. Yet in response to the call for honesty, the advertising industry opted to change the terms of the debate by drastically reducing the number of overtly questionable claims made in commercial messages, and by using the communicative opportunities of the new visual media of photography and television to invoke attributes of products that could not be inferred directly from the message. The controversy, when analyzed in this way, reminds us that **all mediated communication subsumes a relationship between a designer of messages and their interpretation by audiences.** Advertisers admit of no case for dishonesty when the deception lies in the eye of the beholder; the consumer is assumed to be a person fully capable of rational evaluation of messages. But there are, clearly, cases in which doubts exist about the capacity of receivers of information to understand and evaluate messages.

The longstanding rationale for regulatory codes for children's advertising, for example, is based on the principle that children are incapable of identifying advertising as commercial persuasion, and moreover do not have the experience and conceptual abilities to evaluate advertisements (Roberts 1983). In other words, children as viewers have neither the ability to understand the persuasive intent of advertising nor the level of conceptual and experiential maturity needed to evaluate commercial messages rationally. This argument has been at the heart of repeated attempts to restrict or ban advertising to children. In 1978, FTC staff proclaimed:

> It is both unfair and deceptive, within the meaning of Section 5 of the FTC act, to address advertising for any product to young children who are still too young to understand the selling purpose of, or otherwise comprehend or evaluate, the advertising. If it is unfair and deceptive to seek to bypass the defenses which adults are presumed to have when they are aware that advertising is being directed at them, then it is unfair and deceptive to advertise to children in whom these defenses do not yet even exist.

This FTC (1978) paper articulated the widely accepted notion that children's advertising had to be restricted because of the special vulnerability of children.

This principle was recently confirmed as providing reasonable grounds for limiting broadcast advertising for children in Quebec, where a ban on advertising directed at children under age 13 has been in place since 1976. The ban was upheld recently in the Canadian Supreme Court (1989) ruling as a reasonable limitation on commercial speech, because it accords with consumer protection legislation that strives to "protect a group that is most vulnerable to commercial manipulation." The court goes on to state that "in sum, the evidence sustains the reasonableness of the legislature's conclusion that a ban on commercial advertising directed to children was the minimal impairment of free expression consistent with the pressing and substantial goal of protecting children against manipulation through such advertising."

The concept of the capacity to "defend oneself" against the persuasive force of advertising has been a particular concern with respect to children; but it also underwrites restrictions and pre-clearance procedures for advertising in which highly scientific or specialized or professional knowledge is required, most notably food and drugs, prescription pharmaceuticals, and medical and professional services. The implicit reasoning behind the arguments for the regulation of advertising in these product domains has to do not only with the special risks involved in the products' uses, but also with the possible inability of consumers to apply informed judgments in evaluating the characteristics, quality, or utility of the product or service. It is argued that the average consumer should not be expected to have the knowledge and training sufficient to make informed choices with respect to specialized medical procedures, prescription drugs, lawyers, or toxic substances. Such reasoning has resulted in restrictions on professional advertising and elaborate regulatory processes that attempt to vet products before they are brought to the market, as well as the FTC's attempts to define trade regulation rules for such areas during the 1970s. In other cases, the same reasoning has led to restrictions being placed on the distribution of the aforementioned products in the market (age limitations) or on their use (product warnings or guidance). In most cases, product-specific regulations were formulated to control what advertisers claim about those products and services.

Attempts at defining grounds for the restraint of commercial speech have typically treated issues of fairness and honesty as general principles for regulating many aspects of the advertising business. The advertising industry itself has, for the most part, accepted the criteria of fairness and honesty when they are narrowly defined, but it has also resisted broader interpretations of these principles for fear that they may become entrenched in regulatory processes. By and large, the industry has been successful, such that, as of 1989 at least, regulation of advertising remained narrowly based on the issue of false or misleading communication.

FAIR'S FARE

There were, of course, concerns expressed about the advertising business other than that of misleading and deceptive advertising. For example, in the past one of the important restrictions was on comparative advertising, or "knocking copy." Since the early years of the agencies it had been argued that attacks on competitive products, or even the mention of them in advertisements, were prone to abuse and generally lowered the tone of advertising. For many years, comparative advertising was avoided primarily through advertiser self-restraint, in spite of the fact that even advertising's staunchest defenders had to admit that such restrictions tend to dampen business competitiveness. In the 1970s, the issue was hotly contested after the FTC instigated a new ruling on comparative advertising; a series of well-known soft drink campaigns helped to focus the debate about comparative advertising, and some modifications to industry codes have made comparative advertising subject only to truth claims tests and libel laws. Comparative advertising is now a part of the North American scene, although knocking copy is more often suggestive and humorous than seriously comparative in the way the FTC hoped to make it.

The belief that advertising leads to greater efficiency in markets makes it a tempting lever of economic management. As Brenda Andrachuk (in Kohut, 1988) of the Association of Canadian Advertisers states: "If you assume ads help drive sales, that means your sales drop" when advertising is limited or pre-empted. Recently, the introduction of more extensive advertising practices into socialist economies, such as China and the Soviet Union, has raised the question of whether advertising is a means of encouraging the spread of markets and the inflation of demand, as well as promoting greater efficiency in the marketplace. The results of socialist experiments with capitalism are not yet clear. In all likelihood, no definitive answer to the question of advertising's contribution to efficiency or "demand inflation" in particular product sectors can be given, because there are so many other determinants of marketing and consumer trends.

Advertising has long been considered a tool for exciting and dampening specific sectors by creating demand for a particular range of products; this idea has had particular allure in socialist economies (Hanson 1974). The reverse logic has been used as a rationale for sectoral bans in western economies on advertising for products that create particular health or social risks, as in the cases of spirit alcohol or tobacco. When such bans are threatened or put into place, advertisers are quick to protest the innocence of their craft in creating or stimulating demand. One professional told the CRTC that most of the research studies he had seen did not show a link between advertising spending and increased consumption. For example, beer advertising was designed for brand switching: "Marketers can only promote a brand that fulfills a consumer demand in a manner that is superior to the competition . . . . The sole objective of advertising is to gain brand share at the expense of the competition" (*Marketing* 1987). This issue lies at the centre of disputes concerning products whose consequences are or can be harmful to health and socially costly (for example, tobacco, alcohol, or drugs).

TOBACCO PRODUCT MARKETING

During the last few years, tobacco advertising has provoked intense controversy, with many groups calling for either further restrictions on it or a total ban. Until recently in North America, restrictions on the content and placement of tobacco advertising—for example, its exclusion from radio and television—were the result of voluntary agreements between governments and the industry. However, there is now considerable discussion in the United States about legislating a complete prohibition against tobacco advertising. In Canada, such a prohibition came into effect at the beginning of 1989, a noteworthy event, since—at least in western societies—it is highly unusual for a government to institute a total ban on the advertising of a product that can be sold legally.

The federal government's Bill C-51 became law on June 28, 1988, through the Tobacco Products Control Act, "an act to prohibit the advertising and promotion and respecting the labelling and monitoring of tobacco products." Section 3 defines the purposes of the Act as follows:

(a) to protect the health of Canadians in the light of conclusive evidence implicating tobacco use in the incidence of numerous debilitating and fatal diseases;

(b) to protect young persons and others, to the extent that is reasonable in a free and democratic society, from inducements to use tobacco products and consequent dependence on them; and

(c) to enhance public awareness of the hazards of tobacco use by ensuring the effective communication of pertinent information to consumers of tobacco products.

Section 4 states: "No person shall advertise any tobacco product offered for sale in Canada"; this includes advertisements by anyone in Canada that are placed in foreign publications or broadcasts for the purpose of promoting tobacco products specifically in Canada, but Section 4 also contains a blanket exemption for the contents of foreign media distributed in Canada.

The ban became effective January 1, 1989, for magazines and newspapers, while the prevailing voluntary ban on broadcasting ads became mandatory on the same date. Outdoor ads are banned as of January 1, 1991, with a provision for gradually reducing expenditures on the same beginning in 1989. Retail signs are banned as of January 1, 1993, but only brand-name store signs in existence at the beginning of 1988 can continue until that date. Promotional sponsorships of cultural or sporting events were also banned as of the beginning of 1989, excluding contractual arrangements that were in place on the date (January 25, 1988) when the final version of Bill C-51 was introduced in the House of Commons. However, no product logos or cigarette depictions are allowed in publicity for events, and monetary expenditures for the same are frozen at 1987 levels. Other provisions in the Tobacco Products Control Act include bans on free distribution of product samples; on rebates, contests, prizes, etc.; and on use of cigarette trademarks or brand names on nontobacco goods such as clothing.

Section 9 of the Act requires a health-effects warning (to be defined by regulation), including a list of toxic constituents in the products and the smoke produced by burning them, and gives authority for the requirement of an informational insert for product packages. Thus, the passage of the Tobacco Products Control Act marks the first time in Canada that the health-hazard warnings appearing on tobacco packages have the force of law. The new set of warnings, which now must be placed prominently on the front of tobacco packages, appeared toward the end of 1989, replacing voluntary practices in effect since 1971, under which a single English/French text ("Warning: Health and Welfare Canada advises that danger to health increases with amount smoked—avoid inhaling") appeared, in small print, on the side panel of cigarette packages.

Section 9(3) of the Act states: "This section does not affect any obligation of a distributor, at common law or under any Act of Parliament or of a provincial legislature, to warn purchasers of tobacco products of the health effects of those products." Thus, the Act attempts to prevent tobacco firms from using the hazard-warning requirement as a defence against civil liability claims. Finally, the Tobacco Products Control Act contains elaborate stipulations on reporting by manufacturers to the Minister of National Health and Welfare on such matters as sales, product constituents (including prescriptions on testing methods), and controlled expenditures (e.g., for sponsorships).

Almost immediately upon passage of the Act, Canadian tobacco manufacturers—Rothmans, Benson & Hedges, RJR-Macdonald, and Imperial Tobacco—filed lawsuits against the federal government, claiming, among other things, that the prohibition on advertising and promotion in the Act is a violation of the Charter of Rights and Freedoms in the Canadian constitution, which contains protections for freedom of speech and expression similar to those guaranteed in the First Amendment to the U.S. constitution. The first of the tobacco cases opened in Quebec Superior Court in October 1989 and at the time of writing was still under way.

Advertising is sometimes called "commercial free speech," in order to distinguish it from "political speech," which encompasses all comments on social and political issues made by individuals and organizations. Thus, the two main issues to be decided by the courts are: (1) whether commercial speech is entitled to exactly the same kind of protection, as a fundamental freedom, as is political speech; and (2) if not, what restrictions on commercial speech are "reasonable" in a "free and democratic society." Earlier in this chapter, we referred to the 1988 decision by the Supreme Court of Canada upholding a Quebec law that forbids advertising directly to children, on the grounds that children, being more at risk from influence by the persuasive techniques of advertisers, are entitled to special protection. In other words, the government could restrict or ban commercial speech directed at this particular audience, because children could be presumed to be incapable of "discounting" the persuasive force of advertising messages. (Here, as in the case of tobacco advertising, it is important to note that the prohibitions apply only to Canadian promotional productions, and that Canadian audiences continue to be exposed to such advertising in the U.S. media, both print and electronic, that reach them.)

In the case of tobacco product advertising, the federal government's legislation is based on its understanding of the very serious health risks incurred by users of tobacco products. The government's position may be stated as follows: Even though the effects of advertising and other promotional activities cannot be identified with precision—because human behaviour is complex, and there are so many influences (such as peer approval) on a person's attitudes and behaviour—advertising must be presumed to have *some* persuasive effect on consumers. These presumed effects are helping to encourage persons to begin using tobacco products; encouraging them to continue doing so, even when tobacco users become aware of the associated health risks; and, finally, promoting the erroneous belief that switching to brands that are lower in tar and nicotine content will significantly reduce those health risks. Due to such effects, consumption of tobacco products and the consequent health risks are higher than they would be if people were not exposed to promotional activities (including advertising) on behalf of tobacco products.

In responding to the government's position, the tobacco industry has made three basic points. First, selling tobacco products remains a legal activity, and it is therefore unfair and unwarranted to ban outright promotional activities on their behalf. Second, there are many other products, such as alcoholic beverages and motor vehicles (especially off-road vehicles and motorcycles), whose use and misuse give rise to serious health risks, and yet the government has not imposed a total advertising and promotion ban on these product groups. Third, it is not the intention of tobacco-product marketing to attempt to persuade non-users to begin using their products; rather, tobacco-product advertising is aimed at encouraging existing smokers to switch brands, either among competing manufacturers or among product lines by the same manufacturer. From this perspective, the government's prohibition will not, therefore, have the desired effect in lowering health risks.

PERSUASIVE DISCONTENTS

Concern with unfair business practices also gave rise to a debate about persuasive techniques that appear to violate the assumption of rational communication. The impetus for this issue was the identification of formats or techniques of communication that gave advertising an unfair advantage as a means of persuasive communication. In the 1950s, as advertisers changed their formats with the advent of TV, a growing sense of power began to accrue to advertising agencies. Since then, agencies increasingly competed in the market based on their special abilities to break through clutter and utilize effective powers of persuasion—that is, their ability to psychologically grab the audience. Accompanying this sense of power, critics perceived the need for ethical standards for communication practice that could define restraints on the use of new media formats. Probably the greatest impetus for the suggestion of limitations on advertising's range of communication practices was the emerging belief that advertising provided excessive advantage to the corporate sphere. Vance Packard's famous attack on the depth-psychology techniques being adapted to marketing strategy, *The Hidden Persuaders* (1957), created a widespread desire to define the boundaries of honest persuasion, and hence the limits on the formats that advertisers should be permitted to use. So, for example, although it has never been shown conclusively that subliminal messages (assuming their use in real campaigns) inserted in ads can affect product choices, fears about the subversion of personal autonomy resulted in quick government action; there are laws against using subliminal advertising in a number of jurisdictions, and, although the industry, in the words of one of our interviewees, regards the issue as the "UFO of business," this particular limitation on expression gained widespread industry support.

Because public media are regarded as being vital to democratic discourse, the accumulation of influence by advertisers within commercial media systems has also raised the spectre of unfairness in the performance of the media, who must be concerned about sponsor reactions when they treat "controversial" issues. The case has been made that large advertiser accounts can distort media impartiality (based on the threat to withdraw sponsorship) and narrow the treatment of controversial issues like smoking, alcoholism, health, pollution, or similar public issues. Through their implicit pressure on the media, large advertisers can use ads like the one shown in Figure 12.3 to influence the discussion of public issues. Likewise, corporate advocacy forces public interest groups as well to enter the debate about social policy and social behaviour through the gateway of advertising (see Figure 12.4). Yet through the resources available to them to buy time and space in media, large corporations appear to have considerable potential to constrain or skew public debate.

Advocacy advertising—the selling of ideas, ideological viewpoints, or corporate images—has been around for a long time (Marchand 1987). The U.S. Federal Communications Commission had attempted to control

FIGURE 12.3

In the 1970s, oil companies began to intensively use advertising to respond to the public discussion of the energy and environmental crisis.

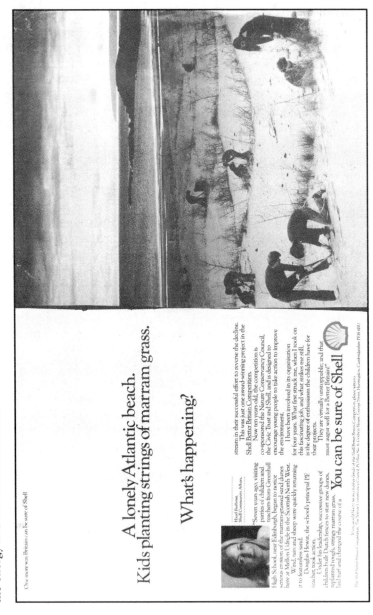

FIGURE 12.4

Advocacy campaigns in the commercial media have increasingly become an important means of influencing social discussion for corporate, government, and public-interest groups.

Source: Courtesy of Non-Smokers Rights Association.

such messages with its "Fairness Doctrine," which, in effect, put a limitation on broadcasters when it came to controversial and advocacy advertising. But during the 1980s the fairness criterion was dropped, making the exercise of advocacy a matter of broadcaster self-restraint. Indeed, in Canada, where such a doctrine never existed, most advocacy advertising was already being channelled either into sectoral business associations (such as the Insurance Bureau of Canada and the Pulp and Paper Association), or through arm's-length advocacy groups (e.g., the Citizens' Coalition), as a way of getting around media objections to particular corporations or political organizations undertaking controversial advocacy campaigns.

The belief that too much influence was accumulating within the advertising industry was also responsible for the Ontario provincial government's establishment, in 1973, of a legislative committee (*Foreign Ownership and the Advertising Industry* 1973) to investigate the degree of foreign ownership and control of the advertising industry in Canada. Some Canadians were alarmed by the growing degree of American participation in the Canadian industry. Could the larger, better financed, and more experienced American agencies with corporate headquarters in the United States force smaller local ones out of business? And how effectively could these foreign agencies reflect Canadian cultural values in their advertising? Although the committee's report was indicative of a particularly sensitive period of national development in Canada, the issue of foreign ownership has recently been taken up on a worldwide basis, with the growing realization that mergers and buyouts are increasingly narrowing the range of agencies who control a major share of global advertising business, and who therefore dominate advertising everywhere, including in developing economies (*Marketing* 1986).

Related concerns about competitive business practice arise from the issue of concentrated ownership and control in the advertising and communications industries. As in any industry, increasing concentration of ownership and a rash of mergers and buyouts have led industry insiders and outsiders alike to wonder whether the current situation creates anticompetitive and oligopolistic conditions in the advertising business itself. Of special concern from the clients' point of view is the fact that, after mergers, many account managers find the same agency handling both themselves and their competitors, leading to fears about industrial espionage and indifferent service. Can the same agency effectively service different clients who are competitors in the same market sector? There is concern, too, that a highly concentrated advertising industry that focuses exclusively on major branded goods sectors could be less innovative, less creative, and less responsive to public concerns and to social change (Black 1989).

The larger of the recent mergers compel questions, as well, about the power that the super-agencies command when they span commercial, political, advocacy, and public-relations activities. Although it is often argued that the unregulated market is the best guarantee of competitive advertising, it is interesting to note that broadcast advertising itself has been a strongly regulated market in most western countries. The end of advertiser sponsorship led to a highly regulated TV system in which the number and length of advertisements per hour are subject to regulator approval. Such rules made advertising time a limited resource in a restricted communications market, which has helped to keep TV-spot advertising a very expensive form. (It was this fact that led the U.S. Justice Department to file suit against the National Association of Broadcasters, on the grounds that the Television Code limitations on advertising were a restraint of trade.)

CHILDREN'S ADVERTISING

Eliminating restrictions on the amount of commercial time has been a particularly important policy issue affecting children's advertising. In 1974, the FCC limited Saturday morning network television to nine-and-one-half minutes of advertising per broadcast hour. In 1980, after intensive hearings, the FCC reversed this ruling, reasoning in its suspension of the guidelines that market forces and industry self-regulation would prevent the "overcommercialization" of media. The regulatory agency assumed that both the limited demand for children's advertising and self-regulatory codes established for children's broadcasting would suffice to restrain children's advertisers.

Contrary to this expectation, expenditure on children's marketing increased dramatically between 1982 and 1987 in the United States, particularly among toy advertisers, who not only became the leading children's advertisers but also used the *de facto* deregulation implied by the suspension of children's guidelines to launch product-based animated programs, dubbed the "30-minute commercial." The controversy subsequently led the U.S. Court of Appeals to reverse and remand to the FCC its order eliminating commercial time guidelines in 1987. In doing so, the court questioned why "the commission has suddenly embraced what had theretofore been an unthinkable bureaucratic conclusion" that the market did, in fact, operate to restrain the commercial content of children's television.

The mechanism of deregulating commercial time proved ironic in its effects on children's programming, for it was associated with the general industry deregulation taking place in the 1980s. The net result was the production of new opportunities for children's merchandising, which decreased the role of network broadcasters in children's advertising while increasing the intensity of marketing communication initiatives. By using syndications of television stations in impromptu networks, toy marketing consortia were able to both compete with network children's programming and to short-circuit the broadcaster-based guidelines for the self-regulation of children's advertising that had been developed independently of the FCC. For example, the broadcast industry codes restricted the use of children's TV heroes in the advertisement and required that children's advertisements not take advantage of children's inability to distinguish fantasy and reality, or programming from advertising. Many of the advertisements for character toys, however, use scenes from the animated TV series interspersed with images of children playing with their character toys—in one ad, for example, a young boy is shrunk, climbs into a toy plane, and flies off into a GI Joe program (Kline 1988). By reorganizing the economic basis of communications, toy marketers have been able to circumvent the system of self-regulation set up by network broadcasters.

The syndicates encouraged the production of low-cost tied-in children's programs, which were subsidized by the toy manufacturers (Englehart 1986). The result was network revenue losses from children's programming. Explaining his own network's threats to withdraw from children's network production because they could not compete, NBC executive Brandon Tartikoff explained in 1988: "For the last three years we have not made the kinds of profits that we did five or six years ago. . . . The shrinking profits are due to the boom in recent years of children's shows sold in syndication to independent TV stations" (in Boyer 1988).

The effect of the dispute over commercial time was to throw the *de facto* self-regulation of advertising—particularly children's advertising—into a state of conflict and contestation in which it is neither regulated nor governed by an effective system of self-regulation. The overcommercialization of children's television, however, does not appear to hinge on whether market or nonmarket methods are used to define limits to children's advertising. Attempts to restrain commercialization by permitting more advertising merely underline the uncertainty surrounding the regulation of advertising markets in today's complex media environment. The rise of cable and satellite television, and the popularity of VCRs, "zapping," and syndicates have recently challenged network television's dominance of the home entertainment market by chipping away at audience sizes for most prime-time network programs. The array of marketing communication options available in commercialized media confirms the futility of policies or regulatory programs that operate with a very narrow understanding of how the highly complex cultural marketplace works.

MEDIATED PRACTICES

Another tradition of restrictions on advertising arises from the fact that advertising, as a form of communication, is subject to all the rules, rights, and expectations that govern our communication systems, particularly the media. Advertisers have been active in advocating their cultural rights of free expression, comparing themselves when under the threat of censorship to the arts and to the news media. But because advertising emerged at a time of great uncertainty about the cultural role of the media, special concerns about community standards and values have been raised and acknowledged by advertisers. As Canadian Advertising Foundation Chairman Frank Philcox has stated: "Commercial free speech does not come without constraints . . . Corporations must operate within the ethical standards of honesty and good taste our society demands [of public communications]." Thus, like all public expressions of opinion, advertising is also subject to legislated limits to public discourse, including sedition, libel, slander, and copyright restrictions (varying by country), and to other laws and regulatory frameworks that govern the media in general. There are very few instances worldwide in which advertisements have violated these general principles.

The controversy over advertising's communicative practices has centred around the industry's special obligations to respect community standards and values, to uphold national interests, and to support the development of national identity. These provisions are often buried in the wording of national broadcasting legislation—as in the case of the proposed Canadian Broadcasting Act—and by implication, might be extended to all aspects of broadcast enterprise, including advertising. In general, the Act assigns, through its licensing procedures, the monitoring and maintenance of community standards generally to its regulatory agency (CRTC). In the specific case of female personal hygiene products, for example, the CRTC turns these requirements into a specific set of guidelines. Similarly, until recently Canadian broadcasters refused condom ads on the grounds that they were obliged to avoid advertising that was controversial or in bad taste. In many cases, broadcasters use community standards to reject controversial advocacy advertising. It is not in any broadcaster's interest to deeply offend community standards or public taste, and most advertisers respect such provisions as ultimately working in their own interest—although they are sometimes chastened for adopting such a mainstream and bland view of life.

A closer review of social policy disputes reveals, however, that the social concerns expressed by the critics of advertising have gone well beyond the narrow confines of honesty and good taste that industry spokespersons acknowledge. The industry has been recently accused of being insensitive to how its images "degrade or objectify women," or diminish particular racial and ethnic groups with unrealistic and limited images of their social life. The feminist accusations have been the most vociferous. In the 1970s, a common criticism arose about the limited depiction of women as housewives, mothers, and sex objects (Courtenoy and Whipple 1983). Most of advertising was directed toward women as consumers in the home and therefore ignored women in the workplace. Gaye Tuchman (1979) argued that such representations are demeaning and offensive to women because they convey their opposite, the "symbolic annihilation of working women." Critics were also concerned with what was considered an excess of overtly eroticized images, postures, and interaction rituals of women in advertising, all of which represent women's subservience to men (Goffman 1979). Others criticized the use of underage models posing in a sexual way, pornographic scenes of implied rape, bondage, and the objectification of women. Advertising as a whole stood accused of reinforcing a biased and predominantly male view of life and male fantasies in its representation of women, and more generally of setting white, middle-class community standards.

The problem of community standards and values within the social representation of advertising remains a controversial matter because it remains impossible to ascertain objectively what these standards are. Advertisers wonder why, among so many communication practices that treat life similarly, their industry is singled out. They also point out that matters such as pornographic representation should be covered by appropriate legislation dealing with all relevant instances, not just advertising-related ones. The advertisers maintain that many of the ads criticized by activists and watchdog groups do not, in fact, violate community standards but rather the personal, somewhat prudish, and highly politicized taste of the critics. The advertisers maintain that the admittedly erotic or ambiguous images of women used in many campaigns are similar to arts and fashion photography and do not violate community standards. They claim that, according to their own research findings, many women like and respond positively to the images in these advertisements. Truly offensive ads, they contend, would receive complaints and be quickly withdrawn. Despite the serious consideration given to this issue, new guidelines and self-regulation appear to have failed to change advertising practice; public policy seems to be at a loss as to how to deal with problems like gender imagery beyond monitoring and chastening advertisers (CRTC 1989).

Likewise, it seems far simpler for critics to focus on the representations of contested social relations as they appear in advertising than to confront the deeply rooted afflictions in our society that lie at their source. Advertising is particularly vulnerable as a system of social imagery because it is so prominent and intrusive, and because its condensed format implies greater simplification and typification in its representations, which leaves advertisers open to accusations of distorting real social conditions and denying the authentic experiences of ordinary people.

Advertisers often reject the criticisms of offended social groups with the idea that advertising must respond to social changes in values and taste only if and when they affect the market. Thus, when the rising numbers of working women created new niches in the market for cars, advertisers began to show women driving cars rather than draping themselves over them, and the evidence does confirm that the depiction of women in nontraditional roles has increased in recent years; in fact, critics have begun to express concerns about the psychological burden that the new superwoman image—the "yuppie" housewife who works, is a brilliant mother, and is also glamorous—places on modern women's expectations of themselves.

Because they are governed by the marketing concept, most advertisers claim that, at worst, they are reflecting partial images of reality. Advertising may not accurately depict society as a whole, but neither is it a total distortion, for its reflected images represent fragments of the population, market clusters, or lifestyle images that exist among significant components of the market. Advertisers often claim they are simply responding to consumer demand in their advertising. It is for this reason that Michael Ray (1982, 482) believes that effective targeting can eliminate most of advertising's offences:

> [The] underlying mission that is central to the questions of society and the future . . . is to produce communication campaigns in marketing that get to the right people with the right message at the right time. . . . If this kind of communication was accomplished, advertising could be one of the most pleasurable, effective, and moral forms of communication. . . . If such efficient communication is achieved, most of the problems of advertising and marketing communication and society disappear.

The dynamics of "addressing the market" also underscore the disputes of ethnic and racial stereotypes. For a long time, images of blacks were not used in mainstream mass-marketing campaigns, because blacks were not considered a significant group within appeals to the mass market and because few advertisers targeted this group. As the consumer power of blacks was independently recognized by marketing, however, there appeared more frequent depictions of blacks among group scenes; black stars were used in more ads; and, in the narrow-banded media of radio and magazines, predominantly black advertising venues were set up. Agencies now exist that specialize in the black market segment and more black family "sitcoms" are featured in the network schedules.

Attempts by the advertising industry to address a specific market segment do not, of course, excuse it from the consequences of doing so through public media. In a perfect world, all advertisements would be directed only toward willing targets, but the growth of "zapping," and numerous complaints about junk-mail advertising and automated telephone sales—the most targeted forms of advertising—remind us that advertising remains a deeply intrusive act. Consumers are not always given the opportunity to seek out or choose the advertising information they want. By virtue of their power of dispersal throughout media, advertisers avoid this most important condition of being in the marketplace: that audiences would choose them in preference to other cultural activities. So although advertisers hate to be "saddled with the problems of society," their selective and limited depiction of social groups and ideologies continues to draw criticism. Advertising is chastened for reinforcing racial, ethnic, and sexual stereotypes; for disrupting the normal socialization process; for perpetuating environmentally inappropriate behaviour; and generally for promoting goals, values, and imagery that oppress, objectify, or dehumanize people.

Our own research has confirmed that advertising is a form of communication that adopts a very limited perspective on our society and the way people aspire, act, and interact in it. In reflecting an image of life governed by merchandising objectives, advertising has inherited all our cultural uncertainties about the consequences of consumerism, about cultural diversity, and about the role that social inequality plays in modern life. Although they are under no legal obligation to provide a view of life that authentically reflects the situations and conditions in society, advertisers should not be surprised by the number of people who find fault with a public discourse of social life solely determined by marketing criteria.

The above debates about representation serve to provide a clearer sense of both the unresolved issues in our system of advertising communication and our general discomfort with censorship when it borders on matters of depicting social life. Our society seems unable to attack the issue of social representation directly, precisely because it is both a highly controversial and deeply rooted social problem. Conceiving of communication as a marketplace, we are content to let consumers' preferences be the best judge of cultural preference. So why are the same criteria not extended to advertising representation?

This question reminds us that it is not simply the representation of a group in the advertisements, but the relationship of advertising to the media system as a whole that is truly at stake when a group is excluded from marketing's view. And this perhaps explains why advertising fails to provide any sense of social diversity and change. In the current commercial arrangements for media, targeted programming formats and alternative images survive only when that audience is of interest to a sufficient group of advertisers. For example, since the 1970s representations of women outside the home setting or the domestic relationship have become increasingly common; but the recent collapse of a women's issues magazine like *Ms.* points to another effect of advertising: despite its half-million readers—largely upscale working women—*Ms.* failed to establish an adequate advertiser base. Advertisers appear to have a bias toward domesticated media (if not imagery), which raises the concern about the relationship between market targeting by advertisers and the ability of alternative or nonmainstream commercial media to survive.

Because advertising is the economic fulcrum of the commercial media system, its influence on media markets has also been a matter of public policy debate. To the degree that commercialized media adopt a biased view in their productions, marketing dynamics appear to be one of the causes of this bias. For example, sensationalism and a general show-business quality in TV news coverage, excessive violence and sex in programming, and a marked degree of triviality and banality overall, have often been connected with the commercial logic of programming. In the late 1950s, concern with the potential abuses of the sponsorship system of advertiser involvement in programming came to a head with allegations that the chairman of Revlon (the sponsors of *The $64,000 Question*) was fixing the show. This, and other factors, resulted in general agreement that, in spot advertising—in which advertiser involvement in program production is restricted— an arm's-length relationship between the networks and advertisers is in the interests of both.

However, in the atmosphere of deregulation that arose in the United States during the 1980s, one major exception to the arm's-length policy surfaced in the area of children's toy advertising. The longstanding rule that children's TV programs should not feature products or identities associated with advertiser product lines was rescinded. The development of "program-length commercials" became a central element in children's toy marketing, producing, over an eight-year period, up to fifty new series, each of which "starred" a toy. Co-production arrangements and character licensing provided toy manufacturers a means of controlling the television exposure to their products. The change was particularly poignant because, in the past, children (especially young ones who had trouble remembering brand attributes and names) had not been seen as a viable market—that is, until their rising allowances and their increasing influence over family decisions made it worthwhile to advertise to them (McNeil 1987). Until well into the 1970s, children's programming was concentrated in the "holes" in the daily TV schedules (TV remains the predominant commercial media for children), and it was characterized by oft-repeated low-cost cartoons and family serials. Networks felt little compulsion to develop attractive or high-quality, children-oriented programming when low-cost repeats sufficed. As children's media mogul Cy

Schneider (1987) put it, the interest of the media lay in "keeping the costs down, the audience up and the regulators out."

Recently, as a result of deregulation and character marketing, new program producers are in the perilous position of depending directly on advertising and licensing interests to profile their new character toys. The commercialization of programming has frustrated and confused the policy debate about children's advertising, which until recently had focused upon specific questions about the capacity of children to establish a rational and informed basis upon which to judge and evaluate an advertiser's claims. Now the debate must also address the inability of children to differentiate between fantasy and reality in ads, and, more generally, between the purposes of programming and advertising as television forms.

While children's program-length commercials have been the subject of intense debate in recent years, neither the FTC nor the FCC has resolved the regulatory issues that have been raised for the communications industry. This is because most regulatory structures have been more interested in content than in the institutional and economic relationship between advertising and media sectors. This limitation is particularly relevant in the case of Canadian advertising policy because the Canadian Broadcasting Act does not include cable transmissions. So although guidelines preventing program-length commercials and an advertising code preventing abuses of the child's capacity of imagination are still in place, Canadian children regularly see, through cable TV services, both American children's advertisements and the program-length commercials, because only Canadian-produced advertising and broadcasting are subject to national advertising codes. The growth of cable and satellite broadcast "spillage" make a mockery of national guidelines and codes; thus, transnational spillage becomes an ever more important issue in a highly globalized media context. In Scandinavia, for instance, satellite broadcasting circumvents more regulated social milieus. Similar concerns have arisen in the wake of recent Canadian attempts to ban cigarette advertising in all media; when over 60 percent of the magazines read by Canadians are foreign, it is difficult to understand how a ban can achieve the goals of reducing Canadians' exposure to cigarette promotions unless foreign media are subjected to the same policy.

Advertising throws back at us deep and unresolved tensions about the representation of social life in media. Attacking advertising for its biased view, and for its undoubted contribution to perpetuating regressive social practices, is one thing; but actually seeking to modify or eliminate practices enshrined in public attitudes, behaviour, and institutional structures by reforming advertising representation alone is another. Actions directed at correcting social problems, in domains where advertising is only a bit player in a much grander drama, will inevitably prove frustrating and inept. There may be good reasons for limiting certain sorts of persuasive techniques, for controlling stereotyped representations, or for regulating economic demand, but these are policy matters that cannot be addressed solely by controlling advertisements. Where social policy demands it, advertising policy should be seen rather as an integral part of more general economic, communications, and social initiatives. Questions about the economic function of advertising are not easily resolved, but one thing is clear: we cannot criticize advertising independently of the social context in which it performs; the focus should be, not on advertising practices, but on the specific set of institutional relationships through which advertising is tied to the social issues that concern us most.

SOME QUESTIONS—AND A DECEPTIVELY MODEST PROPOSAL

We have three questions about the role advertising plays in modern consumer societies. First, we take it for granted that the discourse through and about objects exists in all societies as a fundamental part of social relations. We wish to ask whether this discourse in modern consumer societies is fully open to collective participation (and therefore shaped by the public will), or whether it is too greatly dominated by advertising and thus under the sway of particular (corporate) interests. Note that, in formulating our question in this way, we do not intend to hold the advertising industry responsible for dominating this discourse; its privileged position is the result of larger institutional developments during the century.

We answer that the discourse about goods today is too narrowly controlled by commercial interests, and that it should be framed more broadly. We can imagine a discourse about satisfaction and the meaning of products that is under the direct influence of the corporate sphere to a lesser degree—a more democratically determined discourse in which commercial interests have a reduced but still prominent role. The logic of this argument could lead to tighter limitations on the amount of advertising, or even to its outright banning, but these are not our only options.

We need to achieve a fuller range of influences in the discussion and evaluation of goods and their role in our lives. Just as we do not believe that the party in power should control the political dialogue in a democratic society, we do not believe that any single institution should control the public discourse about goods. We have sought to safeguard democracy through such means as the autonomy of the press, but we have not sufficiently secured the workings of democracy in the marketplace.

The rise of mediated communication and its close affiliation with advertising has meant that for some time now the most visible public discourse on consumption has been orchestrated through the media.

(Interpersonal influence and individual evaluation are still important aspects of consumer behaviour; however, they tend to be confined to private actions.) Possibly, then, it is to the media that we must turn to open other avenues to expand this discourse.

Consumerist magazines, such as *Consumer Reports, Canadian Consumer,* and the British *Which?* are the best models for such alternative channels. Moderately successful consumerist programs, as well, run on both Canadian and British television. These magazines and programs are inherently sceptical and often rigorous; products and their utility are examined critically and tested carefully. Alternative channels could, if expanded, provide both a noncommercial voice for the discussion of goods and an opportunity for manufacturers of new products to present their goods to the public. Support and amplification of the outlook represented by the consumer movement in the discourse on products is one way of counteracting the distortion that now leaves that discourse largely under the sway of commercial interests.

The second question arises out of the institutional relationship between the media and advertising. As we have seen, the media work within broad parameters established primarily to serve the needs of advertisers who wish to create and gain access to particular kinds of audiences. Has the commercialization of the media optimized the quality and potential uses of these media themselves? There is no doubt that advertising influences the performance of media, not only in the exercise of direct control over content, but also in the avoidance of controversial subjects, banal program formats, stereotyping of audience segments, and ownership concentration in media industries—broader issues that should draw more attention.

The question of how well the media function under largely commercialized conditions is related to a number of our most cherished beliefs about democracy. With media output controlled by the audience logic of advertising, there is no real marketplace for ideas—that is, no public forum where widely different types of social actors can buy and sell information, opinion, and images that express their interests. One serious consequence flowing from advertising's predominance in the media marketplace is that the combination of economic and audience logistics has led to a high degree of concentrated ownership and control in the media industries, prompting many commentators to ask whether diversity of views, quality of programming, and attention to minority interests or special audience needs have been sacrificed in the mad scramble for large or "upscale" audiences (Curran 1977; Murdock 1982; Compaigne 1979). Certainly, the transition from small and politically committed audiences for newspapers to massive general-interest ones was a by-product of commercialization. The light entertainment bias and other programming rigidities are all based on the competition for audiences within and among media; this affects public broadcasters, as well, because they must compete for audiences in order to justify receiving government funds.

Since the connection between media and advertising is so firmly established, is it feasible to try to sever the link between programming decision making and the audience considerations of advertisers? One of the simplest ways of doing so in the broadcast media (without banning advertising itself) would be the formation of "advertising magazines," which would occupy a certain period in the program schedule, such as an hour in the morning and an hour in the evening, to be occupied solely by advertising. All commercial networks would allocate the same slots. The concept is rather like the advertising inserts in a newspaper, which exist as separate entities to be perused by interested consumers who are looking for particular types of goods. In a sense, the magazine would function like a catalogue, and it would be possible to index it as well.

Magazine-format advertising would continue the funding of media by advertisers, but also ensure that advertising considerations were not the basis of programming decision making. Since it is conceivable that the overall ratings of networks, stations, and magazines might contribute to advertisers' decisions as to which networks were most desirable, it would be possible to make the magazines an industry-wide effort. For revenue considerations, the key indicator, of course, would be the audience composition and size for the magazine, which would respond directly to the quality of the advertising and information offered in the segment. Consumers thinking about a purchase and interested in finding out more about products would be the main audiences for magazine-format advertising, and the advertising styles themselves would have to respond to a higher level of assumed interest in the products.

Magazine-format advertising would work differently for the print media. A possible model would be the publication of *Advertisers,* with the revenues channelled into subsidizing printing costs through publishers' holding companies for each of the magazine and newspaper trades. In other words, advertising revenue could be channelled into publishing in general—particularly into the material and technological expenses of printing—without directly influencing editorial content. As a result, print-media revenues would more accurately reflect the relationship between circulations and editorial expenditure, and the general costs of printing would be kept down for several types of publications.

The separation of publishing and printing would help to create market conditions for print media that were not distorted by the advertising orientation. For example, the fate of the *London Daily Herald*—which ceased publishing with a daily circulation of three million because it could not draw enough advertising—would be less likely to occur. The advertising subsidy would be more evenly distributed across the publishing industry, rather than accruing to those publications whose audiences meet the needs of advertisers. The magazine-format *Advertisers* could function either as separately distributed material (advertising digests), or, under certain conditions, as detachable inserts. Inserts would provide advertisers with advantageous targeting mechanisms that might prove attractive; after all, retail and local advertising, which provide about 70 percent of newspaper advertising revenue, is well suited to the insert and digest formats (the 30 percent that is derived from classifieds might be allowed to persist in the newspapers).

The third question—and the most difficult one for public policy—is concerned with the broad significance of advertising as an enormously versatile and attractive genre of social communication, and with its overall relation to culture and society. How does advertising itself affect the development of personal identity and the social aspects of consumption? We have traced the historical process in which the meaning of goods and the nature of the satisfactions to be derived through them have been systematically reformulated by economic institutions. These transformations were, in part, responses to changes in social composition such as the blurring of class distinctions, but more directly they were an internal response by the advertising industry to the problem of selling goods in the environment of mediated communication. Both factors gave rise to a great increase in the number of portrayals of human relationships in advertisements. The systematic emphases and obsessions in these portrayals show clearly that advertising is less at ease with depicting some types of human relationships or consumption patterns than others.

Various considerations in advertising practice were responsible for the bias in ad content. For example, the reduction in rational appeals, the amount and quality of information about production, and the utility of the product are all related to changes in the way advertising communicates through the media. No matter what gave rise to the bias, however, there are calls to supplement current restrictions on misleading advertising content and inference (implied claims) with restrictions on "irrational" advertising, lifestyle advertising (for beer and cigarettes especially), and stereotyping; matters of advertising's "rhetorical forms" and appeal approaches may, as a result, become part of a regulatory policy agenda. A Swedish research team, for example, has called for the elimination of irrational styles of advertising (Andren et al. 1978).

The case of stereotypic representation of people in advertising is especially instructive. We usually understand discrimination in this respect as involving the underrepresentation of a particular category of people or groups—for example, not enough working women or blacks in middle-class occupations. Two factors are responsible for the attention given to advertising stereotypes: (1) advertising is so visible that people have come to regard criticism of it as an effective way to address the broader social problem of inequality; and (2) advertising is such a compressed form of communication that its dramas, characterizations, and role structures are both clearer and more "typical" than what is shown during programming time.

Identifying stereotypical misrepresentation in advertisements is relatively easy to do, but attempting to remedy the situation is harder than would appear at first glance. Perhaps one could require matching representations to social statistics. Would advertisers be allocated proportional characterizations—one child-minding ethnic father, three yuppie lawyers, and two working businesswomen? Such a directive would not really solve the problems of stereotypical misrepresentation, because, of course, it would only perpetuate whatever inequities still exist in society. The problem lies not so much in the relationship that advertising content bears to reality, as in the reasons that advertising uses condensed codes of characterization and in the reasons for targeting particular audiences. In other words, stereotyping in advertising cannot be solved by treating it as a matter of inaccurate representation. We need instead to understand the mediational position of the industry. Advertising personnel are no more sexist or racist than people in other areas. They are merely concerned with *communication that will sell products.* Operating in a cluttered environment with severe time restrictions and targeting to segmented audiences, advertisers draw upon generalized representations of social groupings to enhance communication. As Erving Goffman (1979, 84) has said of advertisers, "their hype is hyper-ritualization." However, ads are not only about selling, for they operate in a social context and have social effects. Thus, we must try to sift out the aspects of advertising practice that have potentially negative social effects and seek to address them as precisely as possible.

The questions of greatest societal import that advertising raises are best summed up in disputes about the industry's role in the socialization of children. The issues—which emerge in clear relief because the audience is still in a process of formation and occupies an uncertain position in the population of consumers—touch on all of the three domains to which we have called attention in this chapter: first, the stereotyped and unrealistic representations common in children's advertising can become templates that shape children's social attitudes and development, particularly in the way they interact with their peers and parents; second, the commercialization of programming has profoundly influenced the quality and emphasis of children's television; and third, the industrial sectors (toys, snacks, and cereal manufacturers) with interests in children's marketing are very limited. In short, the fundamental issue at stake is the *flow of culture to children.*

To date, we have dealt with this issue in only a piecemeal way. For example, we fully recognize that television is the dominant children's medium of communication, largely because American snack, soft-drink, cereal, and toy manufacturers are willing to spend approximately one billion dollars annually in the United States to support children's advertising and marketing promotions through television. We have no estimates of how much the advertising subsidy contributes to the channelling of children's cultural production effort into television alone, or how successful similarly low-cost books, movies, or radio programs would be in the children's market. Certainly, the evidence suggests that limits on commercial time or attempts to ban advertising in particular time slots (especially Saturday mornings) are likely to fail in the current broadcasting environment. Besides, this approach does not recognize that children watch adult programming and advertising at least as much as they watch children's programming. As a TV station owner bragged in an interview: "I have the largest share of the children's audience because I never run children's programs." Likewise, it would be easy to open up new children's "ghettos" (such as weekday mornings), provided the advertising revenue was there. Indeed, syndication and licensing arrangements are making the network broadcast self-regulation increasingly inconsequential to children's marketing. Similarly, attempts to restrict particular types of testimonials for products by the characters in children's programs have been undermined by a new marketing strategy in which the program is itself the advertisement (for example, the "Gem" or "Transformers"). Even attempts to ban advertising to children altogether, as in Quebec, have been undermined by the transmission, by cable, of uncensored foreign broadcasting into the regulated environment. The real problem is that the child's socialization is formulated within a wide cultural kaleidoscope, and in order to be effective our policy formulations must address the entire realm of commercially mediated culture, not just the part of it represented by advertisements.

We have stated our reasons for concluding that the economic view is too narrow a framework to support useful debates about the role of advertising. The economic perspective fails to recognize that advertising is an accomplished and versatile form of social communication. Commercial messages have permeated the entire fabric of life during the course of this century, subtly blending their materials and techniques with those of the consumer culture as a whole, until they became virtually identical with it. As a result, the meaning and impact of advertisements considered in isolation is difficult to pin down. The significance of advertising is not confined to specific ads, to particular product categories or brands, or even to specific effects on a single medium. Advertising should be viewed as part of the institutionalization of marketing communication in our society, for its implications extend to the whole realm of mediated communication and popular culture. Whatever limitations we impose on marketing communication must likewise be grounded in a recognition of advertising as a robust form of social communication.

13

Fantasia for the Citizen: The Nature and Uses of Political Marketing

with ARLENE SHWETZ and LORI YONIN

> "Privately, I wondered how a man who couldn't
> mount an effective ad campaign would be able
> to manage a country."
>
> — ad creator Ed McCabe, on the
> Dukakis presidential campaign

We have shown how important advertising has been throughout the twentieth century as a key part of the transition from industrial to consumer society. As an accomplished technique of persuasive communication, advertising has played a leading part in shaping how consumers think about their needs and what will satisfy them. But advertising's most important social impact is not to be found here; rather, it lies in the diffusion of the advertising model of persuasive communication to other social processes, and especially in the rise of political marketing. Increasingly in North America and elsewhere today, political organizations and electoral campaigns reflect the application of advertising and marketing techniques. The fact that election campaigns are indistinguishable in form (and often in content) from product marketing campaigns is the single most dramatic instance of the triumph of the advertising model of persuasive communication in modern society.

Political marketing is the application of consumer research and advertising-format techniques to politics. Its purpose is, first, to elicit the values, attitudes, and opinions of voters (the "consumers" in the marketplace of politics) about issues of concern to those involved with electoral campaigns, candidates, and politicians; and second, to utilize those findings in the construction of campaign strategies. Here, just as in the realm of consumer goods, marketing cannot offer foolproof formulas for success; it can offer useful procedures for problem solving, but it gives no guarantees (Mauser 1988, 2). Marketing assists those groups who can best make use of marketing to "sell" their ideas and values to the public.

With this reservation in mind, we can begin our analysis of how marketing research operates in the political arena today. Especially during campaigns, such research primarily targets individuals who are either undecided or likely to change their vote before election day. These voters have been called "switchers," the "swing vote," and the "alienated voter." They are important not for their sheer numbers, but because it is generally conceded that elections can be decided by only a 3 percent swing in the total vote (Gargrave and Hull 1979, *viii*). Marketing research points out factors that could persuade those individuals to vote in a certain way.

Pre-campaign polls help to uncover a theme for an image campaign; to appeal to the voter, it is necessary to know what voters "want." Image-makers make contracts with pollsters to determine what the electorate is looking for in both ideal and acceptable candidates. Richard Kirby, television strategist for the federal Liberal Party during the 1988 Canadian general election, in a CBC broadcast indicated that the values of the candidate, the leader, and the party are more important than the issues. According to Kirby, voters tend to ask, "Who is the party that is most inclined to make decisions in as yet unknown situations? Whose set of values do I most trust?" Further, Kirby believes that elections have become contests of images, tactics, and strategies; the parties, thinking they know what the public wants to hear, compete to make the public believe them when they say it.

Political marketing research is also extremely important during elections for the "campaign within a campaign," otherwise known as the "meta-campaign." This aspect of the strategy sees its primary target audience as the media, and various tactics, such as timely releases of the results of privately commissioned opinion poll results, are used in an attempt to get the media to report favourably on a particular candidate.

The significance of marketing research in politics is, at the same time, a reflection of the leading role that ad agencies have come to play in political campaigns. As we saw in Chapter 6, ad agencies were pioneers in marketing research and thus, not surprisingly, the first group to apply marketing research tools to the political arena. The agencies' role in Canadian elections is especially prominent because full-time political consulting firms—which are now a fixture in the United States—are rare in Canada; there are just too few elections to support a consultant who does nothing else. The polling firms are also important actors, but the ad agencies are responsible for orchestrating the campaign as a whole. And more often than not, it is still the agencies who hire the pollsters and pay their bills.

ORIGINS OF POLITICAL MARKETING

The proliferation of research departments in the advertising industry during the 1930s soon led to the founding of organizations specifically concerned with market research. By the mid-1930s, both the American

Marketing Association and the Advertising Research Foundation were well established. Simultaneously, the National Opinion Research Centre was founded in the United States, along with the journal *Public Opinion Quarterly*. Soon the industry was confident enough to broaden its horizons. The increasing use of telephones was making large-scale polls both easier and more cost efficient, and it was in this period that the application of market research to political campaigning was born; specifically, the goal of predicting election results was seen to be achievable. This was by no means the first attempt at political polling (the Harrisburg *Pennsylvanian* had been publishing polls since 1824), but it was the first time that polls were thought to be "scientific" enough to actually mean something.

The first pre-election polling was actually done privately by George Gallup for his mother-in-law in 1932 (she was running for Secretary of State in Iowa). But Gallup was not alone for long. By 1933, the first professional campaign management company, Campaigns, Inc., had been founded by Clem Whitaker and Leone Baxter. The new firm was a natural outgrowth of its founders' prior experience in both public relations and advertising activity, with a new application of their skills to the political arena.

Whitaker and Baxter were quick to make the most of polls (they have boasted that between 1933 and 1955 they won seventy of the seventy-five campaigns they managed [Nimmo 1970, 36]), for by 1936 George Gallup and others were claiming that election polls were indeed "scientific." However, predictions for the 1936 U.S. presidential election turned into a disaster that has since become known as the "*Literary Digest* Debacle." The Crossley and Gallup organizations, *Fortune* magazine, and the *Literary Digest* all issued results that forecast victory for Republican nominee Alfred Landon over Franklin Roosevelt. The blunder was the result of unrepresentative sampling: polling had been restricted to automobile owners and telephone subscribers, and while the average American fitted neither category, many Republicans did. The researchers were quick to learn from their mistake, and by 1946 the first privately commissioned poll on behalf of a political candidate was conducted.

In 1948, however, the pollsters were forced to learn another hard lesson: polls were accurate only if conducted at a number of specific times in the campaign. George Gallup discovered this when he wrongly predicted the loss of Harry Truman to Thomas E. Dewey in the 1948 presidential election. In that fateful forecast, Gallup stopped interviewing on October 15, eighteen days before the election was held. As Gargrave and Hull (1979, 144) note: "A post-election analysis showed that a minimum of 4.5 million votes, nearly one out of five in Truman's total vote, were based on decisions by voters after the middle of October."

By the 1950s, the advent of television made the need for audience data even greater than before, and agencies were once again quick to step in. Agencies in the United States at this time were also closely tied to the Republicans, and in 1952 this affiliation changed the face of political campaigning forever. The presidential election that year was notable for two reasons. First, television was the new game in town, and politicians saw it as an effective tool for their campaigns. Second, campaign managers had little knowledge of the new medium—but the advertising agencies did; the politicians needed the ad agencies' expertise, and the agencies saw political campaigns as a vast new market to be exploited.

In the 1952 presidential election, Republican General Dwight D. Eisenhower ran against Democratic candidate Adlai Stevenson. Taking advantage of the Republicans' close ties to the ad agencies, Eisenhower had both an advertising strategist (Rosser Reeves) on his campaign team and an "Agency of Record" (BBD&O). Reeves made it a habit to follow Eisenhower around and listen to his speeches. Something was wrong, Reeves felt, but he could not figure out exactly what it was. He described his dilemma, and how he solved it, as follows: "Ike made a speech in Philadelphia and he covered thirty-two separate points. I sent a research team down the next morning. We got a thousand people to interview, as I recall it, and said, 'Did you hear Ike's speech?' Then we said, 'What did he say?' Nobody knew." Reeves also knew that voters' memories would be improved if Eisenhower narrowed his focus to several primary issues. To determine what those issues should be, Reeves visited George Gallup, who after extensive polling told the strategist: "corruption, rising taxes and inflation, and the Korean War" (Diamond and Bates 1984, 51ff).

This was probably the first time that what we now call "hot button" issues had been identified in an election campaign through public opinion polling. It was polls such as Gallup's that inspired Reeves to situate Eisenhower as the "Man of Peace." But Reeves apparently believed that Eisenhower would have won with or without market research and the TV spots based on that research—a view shared by the Republican National Committee, which not only refused to allow Reeves to conduct any post-election surveys, but also rejected even the suggestion that Eisenhower had won for any other reason than Eisenhower himself (others were not so sure). The mushrooming campaign costs incurred in the 1952 election, primarily by the Republican candidate, first raised the question that has been with us ever since: Can money buy votes? More specifically, can money buy the expertise that would guarantee the votes?

The Democrats were particularly concerned about this issue because, as Diamond and Bates (1984, 78) note, "in 1955, when the Democrats started talking to ad agencies, no one wanted their business." Meanwhile the tools of Madison Avenue had been spreading to other campaigns as well. As early as 1950, the race for governor in New York was characterized by extensive surveys of voters' attitudes and interests. Sig Mickelson (1972, 48) writes: "The 1950 Dewey campaign for the governorship of New York was a classic. . . . The Dewey staff pioneered in developing strategies and techniques which were to set the pattern for the . . . decades which have followed." Clearly, political marketing research was here to stay.

THE POST-1960 PERIOD

By 1960, a number of significant developments were changing the face of political marketing research. These included a move from quantitative to qualitative research, more precise demographics, the extension of the pre-campaign periods during which market research was undertaken, and a generation of politicians who had grown up on polls.

The 1960 U.S. presidential race saw the culmination of all these factors, primarily in John Kennedy's campaign, which was notable for its extensive research, as well as for the extended time period during which such research was conducted: "John F. Kennedy . . . began campaigning for election the day after he lost the vice-presidential race in August of '56. This was four years and two months before his ultimate election in November of 1960" (Mickelson 1972, 156). Kennedy's campaign team hired two of the best researchers in the country—Lou Harris and Professor Ithiel de Sola Pool of MIT. The independent findings of both these men convinced Kennedy to take a proactive approach to what was then known as the "Catholic issue." Harris and de Sola Pool based their findings on what had been the largest sample of public opinion polling to date—23,000 voters in Wisconsin alone (Nimmo 1970, 85). They used this polling to develop campaign themes, and kept on polling to see if such themes required modification. Continued research throughout the campaign was seen as fundamental to the Kennedy momentum.

Shortly thereafter, increasing numbers of political candidates were following suit. By 1962, two-thirds of all U.S. Senate candidates were using surveys, and by 1966 this proportion had risen to 85 percent (Sabato 1981, 69). In fact, opinion polls had acquired such prominence by the time of the 1964 presidential election that Democratic candidate Lyndon Johnson carried around poll results in his pocket. The 1964 campaign was also notable because it was based on one of those hot-button issues. (Analysts generally agree that this campaign saw the birth of hot-button politics.) Research had shown that voters were concerned about nuclear war, and, more specifically, that Republican candidate Barry Goldwater, if he were to be elected president, might be likely to start one. There followed perhaps the most famous political ad of all—Tony Schwartz's one-minute "daisy" spot: a little girl sits pulling petals off a daisy; the camera zooms in to an extreme close-up shot of her eye, while on the audio track a missile-launch countdown is heard, followed by the sound and sight of a nuclear bomb explosion, and a final audio-video message exhorting viewers to vote for Johnson (Diamond and Bates 1984, ch. 8).

By the mid-1960s, technological changes had greatly enhanced the attractiveness of market research, just as the telephone had done in the 1930s. The significant innovation was the computer, and before long political consultants saw its strong applicability to political campaigns. Computers quickened the pace of information gathering and made the results easier to analyze. More sophisticated manipulation of data meant that it was now possible to obtain virtually any combination of psychographic or demographic factors. The mass audience could be broken down into smaller and smaller components, ushering in the era of specifically targeted campaign themes for different groups of people.

Such advances in marketing research meant that campaign teams who did not employ experts in this area would fall behind. Indeed, as a result of the explosion of information relating to political marketing research and campaign management, even the ad agencies could not stay on top of developments. Thus emerged a new breed of business—independent political campaign consultants. The establishment of the American Association of Political Consultants and the International Association of Political Consultants in 1969 came at a time when politicians were increasingly favouring independent consultants over their own party workers. Political campaign management required the best that market research could offer. The research itself was becoming more meticulous than ever, particularly with respect to its timing; public opinion polls commissioned by both the Republicans and the Democrats were moving from a weekly to a daily basis, and campaigning routinely started at least a year prior to the formal inception of the campaigns themselves. Both sides in the 1968 U.S. presidential campaign were heavily oriented toward market research.

By the mid-1970s, however, market researchers were discovering that quantitative research could not provide all the answers for the successful management of political campaigns. Indeed, the diminishing success of many political consultants (in 1970, they lost as much as they won) made the need for new research techniques imperative, and, once again following the lead of product marketing, these consultants turned to focus group interviews. Focus groups, like many market research techniques before them, grew out of the behavioural sciences, specifically psychiatric group therapy; they are also known as group-depth interviews. The procedure for such interviews is to gather together eight to twelve people who are homogeneous in terms of their voting patterns, and to probe intensively their reactions to issues, messages, candidates, and, indeed, every possible facet of a political contest.

The focus group's greatest strength is its ability to discover motivational factors, a point that was not wasted in the Reagan campaign era. In fact, it was focus groups conducted by Republicans and Democrats alike that, as Diamond and Bates note (1984, 289), "pointed to an electorate that was ready to give Reagan his chance to 'get governments off our backs.' " Reagan's researchers also used focus groups to explore whether or not his former career as a Hollywood actor would hurt his chances at the presidency; their fears were alleviated by the results of large-scale opinion polling, in which only 3 percent of those polled even mentioned Reagan's acting background.

By 1988, focus groups had superseded the public opinion poll as the most talked-about method of political marketing research. And, while public opinion polls still played a very large part in the 1988 U.S. presidential election, it was the focus groups that appear to have been the ultimate factor in determining how this election was played out. Both the Republicans and the Democrats were making extensive use of focus groups as early as May of the election year, and both parties were getting the same results: while Dukakis was seen as tough and competent, Bush was plagued by a "wimp" image.

It was during this same period, however, that the issues Bush was to wield so effectively against Dukakis were uncovered. Early research conducted by both camps showed that American voters had particularly strong reactions about the death penalty, gun control, the American Civil Liberties Union, and the Pledge of Allegiance, all of which became the hot-button issues of the 1988 presidential election. It was the Republicans, not the Democrats, who decided to take the initiative in exploiting the electorate's preoccupation with these issues; and once again it was focus groups—and a motorcycle gang—that told Lee Atwater, the Republican campaign manager, exactly how such an initiative could be carried out (Fineman 10/24/88):

> "Focus groups" of swing voters were exposed to the likely lines of negative attack: Dukakis's record on furloughs, the death penalty, the Pledge of Allegiance, voluntary school prayer, defense spending and taxes. Then, using an actor to play "anchorman," the Bush handlers presented a mock "newscast" of Dukakis's views, and his likely responses, to a selected group of viewers equipped with "people meter" dials to measure their reaction. The result was the Attack Man campaign Bush has been using, in Jekyll and Hyde alternation with the "kinder, gentler" theme.

The use of symbols also gradually became apparent to Atwater. As Elizabeth Drew (1988, 132) has written, "the myths and symbols Reagan had manipulated so well were a gift to Bush."

But it was a coincidental event that provided Atwater and the Republicans with the best symbol ever: Willie Horton. This Massachusetts prisoner had, while on release through a furlough program, violently attacked a Maryland couple. Lee Atwater discovered the tremendous potential for "blaming" Dukakis for the event on the July 4th weekend at a Chinese restaurant in a small Virgina town. His focus group this time consisted of a group of motorcyclists: "The bikers volunteered the one thing they knew about Dukakis; he was the guy who had let Horton, who was black, out of jail" (Fineman 11/07/88). Atwater also knew from focus groups that "liberal" had become a dirty word, and that the release of Horton confirmed Dukakis was a liberal. To Atwater's delight, Dukakis himself personally identified himself with the liberal label. Ironically, attempting to gloss over the blunder, the Democrats tried to invoke the power of polling: "When Dukakis called himself a liberal, his aides tried to convince the press that the mistake was actually a strategy. They tried to give the impression that there was something they knew from their polling that made this a smart move" (Drew 1988, 125).

By September, the Republicans' nightly tracking polls were showing clearly that they had laid claim to the hot-button issues, and their poll results were indicating continuously increasing support for Bush. Dukakis and his campaign team were not lacking in either tracking-poll information or hard-hitting commercials, but it appears that Dukakis was unwilling to take advantage of them. The ad-man responsible for his TV campaign, Ed McCabe, maintains that the Dukakis team produced plenty of good material that was never used because Dukakis simply did not understand the importance of advertising in the election. As Elizabeth Drew (1988, 123) explains: "Dukakis . . . didn't comprehend the importance of symbols." But McCabe (1988, 48) passes the most damning judgment of all on a politician in the modern age: "I wondered how a man who couldn't mount an effective ad campaign would be able to manage a country."

How much did all this finally cost? The Republicans' total 1988 campaign expenditures were $46 million (U.S.) on direct campaign expenses and another $50 million on "soft" expenses, which usually includes political marketing research (Mackenzie 1988). Expenses for Dukakis were about the same.

THE CANADIAN EXPERIENCE

Public opinion polls appeared on the Canadian scene for the first time in 1865, in New Brunswick. Premier Leonard Tilley had been convinced by the lieutenant-governor of the day, Sir Arthur Hamilton Gordon, that the time was right to call an election, based on Gordon's "polling of many citizens." Gordon was wrong, however, and Tilley lost by a landslide. It turns out that Gordon had almost certainly introduced a bias in choosing the people he polled:

> He may have held discussions only with upper class New Brunswickers, such as himself. Perhaps he conducted his poll in his private club and neglected to

talk with the waitresses and bartender. The good Sir Arthur was likely an Anglican; perhaps he overlooked the opinions of the large Roman Catholic community in New Brunswick. . . . Perhaps he erred on all these counts (Comber and Mayne 1986, 63–65).

In any event, while polling took some time to prove its usefulness, the use of ad agencies by political parties was well established by the 1930s. In fact, by this time both the Government of Canada and the ruling Liberal Party had an agency of record—the firm Cockfield, Brown. While it appears that at first this agency did little more than take orders from its "political masters"—buying radio advertisements for the party and so forth—it was only the reluctance of the leading politicians of the day that prevented Cockfield, Brown from taking a much larger role than it did; Prime Ministers Mackenzie King and Louis St. Laurent did not trust the new techniques. Nevertheless, by the 1950s the relationship between Cockfield, Brown and the Liberal Party was one of mutual dependence, so much so that in the 1953 campaign the agency "donated" one of its principals, Bill Munro, to the Liberal cause. Jeffrey Simpson (1988, 143) writes: "The agency provided research assistance for ministerial speeches, wrote some of them entirely, [and] organized free-time political broadcasts." The agency was especially helpful in the 1945 campaign when it "collected money from companies which—by contributing to the Liberal [P]arty through Cockfield, Brown—wrote off the costs as a business expense" (Simpson 1988, ibid).

By the time of the 1988 Canadian federal election, political marketing research had become a guiding light for all three major parties, just as it had in the United States. Prime Minister Brian Mulroney's campaign team attempted to portray him "in a warmer, more humane light—a clear response to opinion polls showing that many Canadians mistrust Mulroney while giving him high marks for competence and administrative ability" (Kopvillem 1988). Similarly, ads for the New Democratic Party (NDP) were based on focus group results that expressed the concerns of many Canadians about issues such as free trade and the environment. According to Charlotte Gray (1989, 15), each of the three parties spent just below the legal limit of $8 million imposed by the 1974 Election Expenses Act. Interestingly enough, however, such limits do not apply to funds spent on research, one of those election campaign expenses known as "soft spending." Gray estimates that, for the Tories, such spending amounted to $18 million.

While both the Liberals and the NDP also spent sizable sums on similar types of research, they did not come close to the Tories' budget. For example, while Decima Research was conducting regular polls in twenty-five ridings across the country and a series of national polls for the Tories, the NDP could afford regular polling only in a few key ridings, with samples of two hundred, compared with Decima's five hundred.

Charlotte Gray concludes: "Polling was crucial in this election because of the volatility of the electorate. The Tories had the edge on the other two parties because they were always the first to know of shifts in opinion." Indeed, public opinion shifted dramatically over the course of the campaign, but the final national poll results produced for the Conservatives accurately predicted the final election results.

The 1988 campaign also produced some effective political ads. Perhaps the best was one done for the Liberal Party on the issue of "free trade" between Canada and the United States. The Liberals had taken the position that the free trade bill, proposed by the governing Progressive Conservative Party, would undermine Canada's autonomy and lead Canada into a greater social, political, and economic integration with the United States. One of their campaign ads showed a map of North America and the long boundary line separating Canada and the United States; as the voice-over attacked the free trade bill, the boundary line disappeared. This spot was further testimony to the impressive communicative power of simple graphical representation, which can convey the gist of an abstract idea quickly and effectively.

THE STRUCTURE OF POLITICAL IMAGERY

The politician's media handlers and strategists focus on attributes that pre-election polls indicate are likely to attract the voter. The politician attempts, especially through television commercials, to associate his or her image with certain symbols, qualities, or themes. Campaign advertising may also provide the voter with issue coverage and information, and may be particularly effective if used by opposing parties to refresh voters' memories of scandals, broken electoral promises, and the like. It is in their commercials that the party and the leader shape and control the message they wish to disseminate. The basic rule is that the advertised image must be a credible extension, and not a contravention, of the candidate's previously established image (Jamieson 1984).

Certainly the term "image," as used in the political arena, often evokes negative connotations. Audiences associate images with the "manipulation of existing characteristics or the conjuring up of new ones" (Hahn 1972, 60). For Dan F. Hahn, this view of image and image manipulation is based on the belief that the so-called image-makers can conceal everything about their candidates that they want concealed, reveal all that they want revealed, and "sell" a largely nonexistent person to the voter. Dan Nimmo (1970, 7) modifies this perspective with his emphasis on the citizen's "interpretive behaviour": People do not simply respond in predetermined or conditioned ways to flags, anthems, political advertising, patriotic or revolutionary appeals; rather, they interpret political signs and sometimes arrive at meanings shared by most members of the community, but at other times reach different—even conflicting—meanings. In any event, each sign does not simply "stand for" something else—it becomes a symbol with an image of its own to each citizen, a meaning apart from the visible referent. Nimmo regards images as the concepts of the essential qualities that people associate with certain objects, products, or individuals.

Other commentators have maintained that as a candidate's image develops, people's impressions of the candidate become progressively more general. The newer opinions that develop are more likely to concern a candidate's personality than his or her leadership (Patterson 1980, 138). The extent to which voters' impressions concern a candidate's style, however, depend on how well formed the candidate's image was before the campaign began. Previously familiar impressions merely increase in proportion; older impressions are not substantially overridden. The image of a candidate, then, is determined by the interaction of his or her personality and orientation to the world with ours. Foremost in media campaigns is the candidate image, in which the campaign organization stresses the human qualities of the candidate, that is, his or her association with key issues and competence for the job.

Thus, two competing theories of political imagery become evident. One is that the image is something a politician, or the group of handlers and aides, creates, projects, and sells; if the image has no consumer appeal, the politician simply creates a new one. The other view sees the originating force for this process as residing in the minds of the voters; that is to say, images of politics are lodged in the minds of people and political leaders adapt their style and messages to them (Nimmo 1970, *vii*).

In Chapter 10 we referred to Daniel J. Boorstin's definition of the uses of imagery in politics as the creation of "pseudo-events," which he defines as "the new kind of synthetic novelty" (Boorstin 1961, 9). According to Boorstin, the pseudo-event is not spontaneous, but rather comes about because someone has planned, planted, or incited it. The pseudo-event is planted primarily for the immediate purpose of getting it reported or reproduced; its relation to the underlying reality of the situation is ambiguous and it is intended to be a self-fulfilling prophecy. Pseudo-events are planned for dissemination, and participants in them are selected for their newsworthy and dramatic interest. The image in this sense rests on a tension between what is seen and what is "really" happening—in other words, a situation that requires decoding by the audience. Thus, for example, the image is the visible public "personality" as distinguished from an inward private "character." The overshadowing image covers up whatever may really be there: the image can always be more or less successfully synthesized, doctored, repaired, refurbished, and improved apart from the spontaneous original of which the image is the public portrait (Boorstin 1961, 186–87).

Dan Hahn maintains that voters are, to a surprising degree, more strongly influenced by images than by issues. He refers to a study conducted by the American Institute for Political Communication, which asked voters in the 1968 U.S. presidential election, "If you had to name just one factor or thing which most influenced your voting decision in the presidential race, what would that one thing be?" The results showed that

> . . . 41% of the respondents said one of the presidential candidates or a characteristic of the candidate was the factor "which most influenced" their presidential vote. Some 25% said an issue or issues was most important. And 13% opted for party affiliation and another 13% for the desire for a change in national leadership and 8.5% specifically referred to one or more of the media (a TV appearance, an editorial, a series of articles, et cetera). (Hahn 1972, 57)

A candidate's image consists of all the subjective impressions voters have about that candidate. The impressions can be associated with a candidate's issue position, political philosophy, family or background, personality and leadership, or even campaign style. Moreover, voters compare these impressions not only to their impressions of the competing candidates but also to their overall vision of an "ideal" candidate.

Although research has consistently found that public perceptions of a candidate's image act as a significant factor in voting behaviour, it has not yet been found *what* qualities constitute the ideal candidate in the public mind (Trent and Friedenberg 1983, 75). One reason for this failure is that voters' priorities can change from election to election. Trent and Friedenberg do, in fact, posit the existence of three overall dimensions or major determinants of a voter's image of the ideal candidate. The first is credibility, represented in terms of such qualities as high ability, good character, and energy; the second is interpersonal attraction, which can be thought of as a candidate's social and physical attractiveness; and the third is "homophyly" (defined by Trent and Friedenberg as "having a common ancestry"), which refers to the similarities in personality, social class, educational background, or beliefs that the voters believe they share with the candidate. These authors argue that the creation and maintenance of images, based on the three dimensions cited above, play a predominant role because voters have a whole series of impressions regarding those who seek elective audience that they compare with a personal vision of an ideal candidate.

Nimmo (1970) likens a candidate's image to the impression voters have of his or her inner character, an impression constructed from the candidate's physical appearance, style of life, bearing, conduct, and manner. Selective aspects of one's personality suitable to the politician's role are emphasized for public exposure. The image is not, therefore, a model of the "whole person," but rather of the dimensions of personality appropriate to the role and its setting. Nimmo also argues that "all serious political pretenders must at least act as though they have the necessary attributes," which means the candidate must select and emphasize the most appealing of his or her qualities, publicize them widely and repetitiously, and at the same time play down any limitations. This process of selectively publicizing desirable attributes is what professional campaigners term "image projection" (Nimmo 1970, 13, 129).

Controlling political images is a primary goal of politics. Lance Bennett (1983, 36-40) suggests that successful image-making involves three components:

1. **Message Composition** Composing a simple theme or message for the audience to use in thinking about the matter at hand. Political messages generally begin with a key phrase, idea, or theme that creates a convenient way for people to think about a political issue, event, or person. Political themes and slogans can get an image started by encouraging people to imagine things about a situation. The image is not some concrete entity that exists "out there" in the world but is the product of human imagination shaped by the suggestive symbolism of political messages. Bennett notes that the symbolic component of an image is so simplistic, abstract, and free of detail that the only way it can make sense is for people to add their own interpretations, fantasies, and concerns. Thus, an image is an impression of something that is anchored partly in a symbolic suggestion and partly in the feeling and assumptions that people have in response to that suggestion.

2. **Message Salience** Saturating commercial channels with messages so that one's own message will become more salient than competing messages. Images come into being only when the symbolic component or message becomes a frequent point of departure for the popular imagination. The need for a message to capture attention explains why the second goal of image-making is to saturate commercial channels with the message.

3. **Message Credibility** Surrounding the message with the trappings of credibility so that, if it reaches people, it will be accepted. Credibility can be constructed by associating the message with arguments that appear to contain sound logic, solid evidence, or reference to authority.

In conclusion, a study of U.S. presidential campaigns from the 1930s to 1972 sums up the four key changes in modes of campaign communication (Agranoff 1977, 4-6). First, the candidate rather than the party tends to be the chief focus of campaigns. Second, the party professional has given way to different types of professionals—the advertising and public relations specialist, the management specialist, the media specialist, the pollster—who perform services for candidates based on the skills acquired in nonpolitical fields. Third, these new professionals have brought to the campaign their habit of obtaining systematic research about products, markets, and audience segments prior to making important decisions, and have made electorates the new objects of their research. Fourth, the new style of campaigning includes communication through a variety of media, but television has become the surrogate party worker and the vehicle for conveying candidate style, image, and message.

In one sense, therefore, the candidate image, which is the sum of the *perceived* personal and professional characteristics of the candidate, is what is really "running" in an election campaign. The candidate image is the mask that the politician presents to the voters.

IMPLICATIONS AND CONSEQUENCES

The justifications that have been offered for the use of marketing research in political campaigns are threefold: first, such techniques have been widely approved in other contexts for many years; second, the candidates who spend the most money do not always win; and third, such research makes politicians more finely attuned and responsive to the electorate. Philip Kotler (in Mauser 1989, *vi*) touches on this last point in his introduction to a text on political marketing: "A marketing orientation should lead candidates to better understand what voters want and to give voters what they want . . . Candidates do not have to guess what voters think and want."

The elimination of guesswork between the politicans and the electorate is seen as one of the fundamental advantages of political marketing research to the democratic system. Harry O'Neill defends the practice in his contribution to a collection of essays entitled *The Political Image Merchants*, stating that political marketing research is communicative, not manipulative. Another contributor to that same volume, John d'Arc Lorenz, concurs, saying that such research represents the only element of a modern campaign that is uniquely "of the people" and "by the people" (in Hiebert 1971, 124, 63). Yet political consultants and columnists often point to the many failures of candidates who have been backed by ample research and message spending. As Sabato (1981, 336) puts it, there is no "foolproof magic that can transform a sow's ear into a silk purse." Other political observers cite the advantages of being an incumbent—the politician who holds office while running for re-election—as the single most important factor in electoral success today.

There exists still another dimension to political marketing research—one that has nothing to do with the success or failure of the techniques devised to vault candidates into office. We may describe this as a fundamental reversal of the basic roles within the process of political marketing. As it was first conceived, the marketing consultants served the politician, for better or worse, bringing new technologies to the front lines of the traditional political battlefields. But recently we have seen the emergence of something different: the politician who seems to be the simple creation of a marketing machine that has its own internal logic and strategic interests.

The rise and fall of Joe Biden, a candidate for president in the 1988 Democratic primaries, is a good illustration of this new development. Biden was forced to withdraw from the primary campaign after a member of Dukakis's staff prepared a videotape showing that Biden had plagiarized a speech by the British Labour Party leader Neil Kinnock. But this was not the real significance of Biden's brief candidacy. As recounted by *Newsweek* reporters Jonathan Alter and Howard Fineman (1987), Biden's entire campaign strategy had been "cooked up by consultants and pollsters trying to find a specimen to fit their airy theories of the American electorate." What happened, according to their report, is that a team of political consultants wanted to test their theory that the baby-boom segment of the 1988 U.S. electorate would respond favourably to the kind of message that is associated with the memory of John F. Kennedy. They looked around for a sitting U.S. Senator who could "present" this type of message and found Joe Biden. The theory did not pan out.

How should we evaluate the significance of the rise of political marketing? Certainly the "manipulation hypothesis" does not appear to be very relevant, for the simple reason that, when voters have a choice between at least two well-established political parties, they are exposed to two sets of competing messages and thus have the opportunity to compare both the "appeal" and the "logic" of one against the other. Commentators are correct in saying that there are no guarantees of success, even with the most brilliant and expensive campaign strategies, but, after all, this is the lesson found in the marketing record itself, as gained in the far more extensive experience with consumer product marketing; there are at least as many, if not more, failures as successes, and since the circumstances that affect consumer purchasing decisions are always changing, the market researchers' work is never done.

Assuming that two or more parties have roughly equal resources, and hence equal call on the talents of political consultants, any short-run advantage gained by one party as the result of a particularly effective strategy is likely to be cancelled out over time. Even when the strategy seems to have been very effective, for example in the Bush campaign's "attack videos" against Dukakis, we cannot leap to the conclusion that the techniques employed had themselves some kind of alarming persuasive power. Studies of the Bush-Dukakis battle show that perhaps the most decisive factor in the outcome was Dukakis's failure to exploit his team's focus-group findings quickly and, above all, to respond quickly and forcefully to the Bush team's attack videos. By the time that Dukakis's handlers convinced him that a response was necessary, the momentum had shifted from Dukakis's side to that of his Republican challenger, and thereafter Bush's very capable team, led by Lee Atwater, made sure that it would not shift back again.

The entrenchment of political marketing in our society means, first of all, that it is now quite possible for short-term advantages in strategy, tactics, and execution by a campaign team to affect the fortunes of an electoral contest, even, in specific circumstances, to become a major factor in the outcome. It also means that there is a minimum "entry fee" for political parties that wish to compete in general elections today—namely, sufficient financial resources to hire professional consultants, and to produce and distribute in the mass media campaign messages that meet a minimum advertising industry standard of sophistication in marketing technique, style, and execution. For those parties already well established (two in the United States and three in Canada), the provisioning of funds for electoral campaign expenses through the tax system is an appealing way of ensuring a certain level of guaranteed support to pay those bills. For new political parties, or for those that have never attained widespread support, the situation differs little from that known to independent innovators of new consumer product ideas, who are faced with almost insuperable obstacles in getting their message across in a crowded marketplace.

In democratic political systems, the difficulty faced by citizens in making their representative institutions serve the best interests of the citizens themselves is a perennial one. Unlike some commentators, we are not persuaded that the rise of political marketing has facilitated the objective of effective control by citizens over the political process; but we would also say that it has probably not hindered it either. The true significance of political marketing lies in another dimension, namely in the observation that, after about forty years of experience with its increasingly adept strategies, it is unlikely that, at least for the foreseeable future, we will be able to conduct our political business in any other way. Advertising and marketing professionals have gained almost universal recognition as the peerless practitioners of the art of selling messages—whether they be for ideas and causes (social marketing), consumer products, or politics—in what would appear to be a logical extension of the enormous and ever-widening influence that the advertising model of persuasive communications has achieved in our society over the course of the twentieth century.

Bibliography

Aaker, D., and J. Myers. 1975. *Advertising Management.* Englewood Cliffs, N.J.: Prentice-Hall.

Advertising Age. 12 March 1984, 1 October 1984.

Agranoff, Robert. 1977. *The New Style in Election Campaigns.* 2nd ed. Boston: Holbrook Press.

Albion, Mark, and Paul Farris. 1981. *The Advertising Controversy.* Boston: Auburn House.

Allemang, John. 1989. "*Ms.* Gives It a Miss: Magazine to Suspend Publication." *The Globe and Mail* (Toronto), 3 November.

Allen, Frederick Lewis. 1931. *Only Yesterday.* New York/London: Harper & Brothers.

Alter, Jonathan, and Howard Fineman. 1987. "The Fall of Joe Biden." *Newsweek*, 5 October.

American Advertising Association Newsletter. 1980. "AAA Measures Miscomprehension of Televised Communications." April–May.

Anderson, Michael. 1984. *Madison Avenue in Asia: Politics and Transnational Advertising.* Cranbury, N.J.: Associated University Presses.

Andren, G., L. Ericsson, R. Ohlsson, and T. Tännsjö. 1978. *Rhetoric and Ideology in Advertising.* Stockholm: AB Grafiska.

Arlen, Michael. 1981. *Thirty Seconds.* New York: Penguin.

Armstrong, Gary, and Merrie Brucks. 1988. "Dealing with Children's Advertising: Public Policy Issues and Alternatives." *Journal of Public Policy and Management* 7.

Ashman, Roy, John Hasenjaeger, and H. Keith Hunt. 1979. "Advertising and Government Regulation." Report no. 79-106. New York: American Academy of Advertising.

Atwan, Robert, D. McQuade, and J.W. Wright. 1979. *Edsels, Luckies, and Frigidaires: Advertising the American Way.* New York: Dell Publishing Co.

Baran, Paul, and Paul Sweezey. 1966. *Monopoly Capital.* London: Penguin.

Barbour, N. 1982. *Those Amazing People! The Story of the Canadian Magazine Industry, 1778–1967.* Toronto: Crucible.

Barnet, Richard, and Ronald Muller. 1974. *Global Reach: The Power of the Multinational Corporations.* New York: Simon and Schuster.

Barnouw, E. 1978. *The Sponsor: Notes on a Modern Potentate.* New York: Oxford University Press.

Barthes, Roland. 1973. *Mythologies.* London: Paladin.

Bell, M. 1966. *Marketing: Concepts and Strategies.* Boston: Houghton Mifflin.

Bennett, W. Lance. 1983. *News: The Politics of Illusion.* New York: Longman.

Berelson, B. 1952. *Content Analysis in Communication Research.* New York: Free Press.

Berger, John. 1972. *Ways of Seeing.* London: Penguin.

Bergreen, L. 1978. *Look Now, Pay Later.* New York: Russell Sage Foundation.

Black, Larry. 1989. "What's in a Name?" *Report on Business Magazine,* November. Toronto: *The Globe and Mail.*

Bohannan, Paul. 1963. *Social Anthropology.* New York: Holt, Rinehart and Winston.

Boorstin, Daniel. 1962. *The Image.* New York: Atheneum.

———. 1973. *The Americans: The Democratic Experience.* New York: Random House.

Borden, Neil. 1947. *The Economic Effects of Advertising.* Chicago: Richard Irwin.

Boyer, Peter. 1988. "NBC Considers Risk of Killing Saturday Morning Cartoons." *The Globe and Mail* (Toronto), 20 September.

Bradburn, N. 1969. *The Structure of Psychological Well-Being.* Chicago: Aldine Press.

Bradburn, N., and D. Caplovitz. 1965. *Reports on Happiness.* Chicago: Aldine Press.

Briggs, Asa. 1961. *The Birth of Broadcasting.* London: Oxford University Press.

Brown, Les. 1972. *The Business Behind the Box.* New York: Harcourt Brace Jovanovich.

Bruce, Dennis. 1987. *Marketing,* December 14.

Campbell, A., P. Converse, and W. Rodgers. 1976. *The Quality of American Life.* New York: Russell Sage Foundation.

Canada, Supreme Court. 1989. *Irwin Toy Ltd. v. Quebec (Attorney General).*

Canadian Radio-television and Telecommunications Commission. 1978. *Attitudes of Canadians toward Advertising on Television.* Ottawa: Supply and Services Canada.

———. 1986a. "Sex-Role Stereotyping in the Broadcast Media: A Report on Industry Self-Regulation." Ottawa: Supply and Services Canada.

———. 1986b. "Broadcast Advertising of Alcoholic Beverages and Food and Drugs." Public Notice no. 1986-247. Ottawa: CRTC, 19 September.

Cantril, Hadley. 1965. *The Pattern of Human Concerns.* New Brunswick, N.J.: Rutgers University Press.

Ceulemans, Meike, and Guido Fauconnier. 1979. *Mass Media: The Image, Role, and Social Condition of Women.* Report no. 84. Paris: UNESCO.

Coleman, R., and L. Rainwater. 1978. *Social Standing in America.* New York: Basic Books.

Comber, Mary Anne, and Robert S. Mayne. 1986. *The Newsmongers: How the Media Distort the Political News.* Toronto: McClelland and Stewart.

Compaigne, B. 1979. *Who Owns the Media: Concentration of Ownership of the Mass Communications Industry.* New York: Harmony Books.

Courtenoy, A.E., and T.W. Whipple. 1983. *Sex Stereotyping in Advertising.* Lexington, Mass.: Lexington Books.

Csikszentmihalyi, M., and E. Rochberg-Halton. 1981. *The Meaning of Things.* Cambridge: Cambridge University Press.

Curran, James. 1977. "Capitalism and the Control of the Press, 1800–1975." In *Mass Communication and Society,* ed. J. Curran, M. Gurevitch, and J. Woollacott. London: Arnold.

Curti, Merle. 1967. "The Changing Concept of Human Nature in the Literature of American Advertising." *Business History Review* 41.

Debord, Guy. 1970. *Society of the Spectacle.* Detroit: Black and Red.

DeFleur, Melvin L. 1970. "Mass Communication and Social Change." In *Media Sociology,* ed. J. Tunstall. London: Constable.

DeFleur, Melvin, and Sandra Ball-Rokeach. 1989. *Theories of Mass Communication.* 5th ed. New York and London: Longman.

De Saussure, Ferdinand. 1966. *Course in General Linguistics.* New York: McGraw-Hill.

Diamond, Edwin, aand Stephen Bates. 1984. *The Spot: The Rise of Political Advertising on Television.* Cambridge, Mass.: MIT Press.

Diener, E. 1984. "Subjective Well Being." *Psychological Bulletin* 95.

Dominick, J., and G. Rauch. 1974. "The Image of Women in Network TV Commercials." *Journal of Broadcasting* 16, no. 3.

Douglas, Mary, and Baron Isherwood. 1978. *The World of Goods.* Harmondsworth, Middlesex: Penguin.

Drew, Elizabeth. 1988. "Letter from Washington." *The New Yorker,* 12 December.

Driver, J.C., and G.R. Foxall. 1984. *Advertising Policy and Practice.* London: Holt, Rinehart and Winston.

Dunlop, Marilyn. 1989. "TV Networks Deny Rejecting AIDs Ads." *The Toronto Star.* 9 June, p. A10.

Dyer, Gillian. 1982. *Advertising as Communication.* London: Methuen.

Earle, Richard. 1984. "Global Advertising: How to Successfully Market World Brands." *Madison Avenue* 26, December.

Easterlin, Richard. "Does Economic Growth Improve the Human Lot? Some Empirical Evidence." In *Nations and Households in Economic Growth*, ed. P. David and N. Reder. New York: Academic Press.

Elliot, Blanche. 1962. *A History of English Advertising*. London: Batsford.

Engelhart, Tom. 1986. "The Strawberry Shortcake Strategy." In *Watching Television*, ed. Todd Gitlin. New York: Pantheon.

Ewen, Stuart. 1976. *Captains of Consciousness*. New York: McGraw-Hill.

————. 1988. *All Consuming Images: The Politics of Style in Contemporary Culture*. New York: Basic Books.

Fineman, Howard. 1988. "Why Bush is Winning," *Newsweek*, 24 October; "Poppy the Populist," *Newsweek*, 7 November.

Firth, Raymond. 1959. *Economics of the New Zealand Maori*. Wellington, New Zealand: Government Printer.

Foreign Ownership and the Advertising Industry. 1973. Report for the Select Committee on Economic and Cultural Policy of the Legislative Assembly. Province of Ontario. June.

Forgas, J. 1981. *Social Cognition: Perspectives on Everyday Understanding*. New York: Academic Press.

Forty, Adrian. 1986. *Objects of Desire: Design and Society from Wedgewood to IBM*. New York: Pantheon.

Fowles, L. 1976. *Mass Advertising as Social Forecast: A Method for Futures Research*. Westport, Conn.: Greenwood Press.

Fox, Richard Wightman, and T.J. Jackson Lears, ed. 1983. *The Culture of Consumption*. New York: Pantheon.

Fox, Stephen. 1984. *The Mirror Makers*. New York: William Morrow.

Frank, Clinton. 1963. *Printer's Ink Advertising: Today/Yesterday/Tomorrow*. New York: McGraw-Hill.

Galbraith, John Kenneth. 1958. *The Affluent Society*. Boston: Houghton Mifflin.

————. 1967. *The New Industrial State*. Boston: Houghton Mifflin.

Gargrave, Anthony, and Raymond Hull. 1979. *How to Win an Election*. Toronto: Macmillan.

Gershman, Michael. 1988. "The Twilight of Advertising." *Management Review*, June.

Gitlin, Todd. 1983. *Inside Prime-Time*. New York: Pantheon.

Goffman, E. 1979. *Gender Advertisements*. New York: Harper and Row.

Goldberg, Marvin. 1986. "The Effects of the Law Intended to Eliminate Advertising Directed at Children in Quebec." Quebec City: Government of Quebec, Office de la protection du consummateur, 30 March.

Gossage, Howard Luck. 1967. "The Gilded Bough: Magic and Advertising." In *The Human Dialogue*, ed. F. Matson and A. Montague. New York: Free Press.

Gray, Charlotte. 1989. "Purchasing Power." *Saturday Night*, March.

Greyser, Stephen. 1972. "Advertising: Attacks and Counters." *Harvard Business Review*, March–April.

Guirand, P. 1971. *Semiology*. London: Routledge and Kegan Paul.

Gutman, Herbert. 1977. *Work, Culture and Society in Industrializing America*. New York: Vintage.

Hahn, Dan F. 1972. "Political Myth: The Image and the Issue." *Today's Speech* 20, Summer.

Hakuhodo Institute of Life and Living. 1982. "Hitonami: Keeping up with the Satos." Kyoto: PHP Research Institute.

Hall, S. 1980. "Encoding/Decoding." In *Culture, Media, Language*, ed. S. Hall, D. Hobson, A. Lowe, and P. Willis. London: Hutchison.

Hall, Stuart, and Paddy Wannell. 1965. *The Popular Arts*. New York: Pantheon.

Hanson, Philip. 1974. *Advertising and Socialism*. London: Macmillan.

Harper, M., P. Harper, and J. Young. 1963. "The Advertising Agency." In *Printer's Ink Advertising: Today/Yesterday/Tomorrow*. New York: McGraw-Hill.

Harris, Neil. 1981. "The Drama of Consumer Desire." In *Yankee Enterprise*, ed. O. Mayr and R.C. Post. Washington: Smithsonian Institution Press.

Harris, Ralph, and Arthur Seldon. 1959. *Advertising in a Free Society*. London: Institute of Economic Affairs.

———. 1962. *Advertising and the Public*. London: André Deutsch.

Heighton, E., and Don Cunningham. 1976. *Advertising in the Broadcast Media*. Belmont, Cal.: Wadsworth.

Hettinger, H. 1933. *A Decade of Radio Advertising*. Chicago: University of Chicago Press.

Hiebert, Ray et al., eds. 1971. *The Political Image Merchants*. Washington, D.C.: Acropolis Books.

Hillier, Beavis. 1983. *The Style of the Century: 1900–1980*. New York: E.P. Dutton.

Hindley, D., and G. Hindley. 1972. *Advertising in Victorian England*. London: Wayland.

Hirsch, Fred. 1976. *Social Limits to Growth*. Cambridge: Harvard University Press.

Hirschberg, Lynn. 1983. "When You Absolutely, Positively Want the Best." *Esquire*, August.

Hirschman, A.O. 1982. *Shifting Involvements*. Princeton: Princeton University Press.

Holsti, O. 1969. *Content Analysis for the Social Sciences and Humanities*. Reading, Mass.: Addison-Wesley.

Horowitz, D. 1980. "Consumption and Its Discontents." *Journal of American History* 67.

Hotchkiss, G.B. 1950. *An Outline of Advertising.* 3rd ed. New York: Macmillan.

Hurvitz, Donald. 1984a. "Broadcast Ratings: The Missing Dimension." *Critical Studies in Mass Communication* 1.

———. 1984b. "U.S. Market Research and the Study of Radio in the 1930's." Paper presented at the meetings of the International Association of Mass Communication Research. Prague.

———. 1985. "The Culture of Business and the Business of Culture: Social Research, Scientific Management and the Collection of Media-Audience Data." In *Proceedings of the Second Workshop on Historical Research in Marketing.* East Lansing: Michigan State University, Department of Marketing and Transportation.

Hutchinson, Allan. 1988. "Opening Pandora's Box." *The Globe and Mail* (Toronto), 20 December.

ID: Magazine of International Design 33, no. 6, November/December 1986.

Inglis, Fred. 1972. *The Imagery of Power: A Critique of Advertising.* London: Heinemann.

Innis, H. 1951. *The Bias of Communication.* Toronto: University of Toronto Press.

Jamieson, Kathleen Hall. 1984. *Packaging the Presidency.* Oxford: Oxford University Press.

Janowitz, Morris. 1978. *The Last Half-Century.* Chicago: University of Chicago Press.

Janus, Noreen. 1980. *The Making of the Global Consumer: Transnational Advertising and the Mass Media in Latin America.* Ph.D. diss., Stanford University.

Jhally, Sut. 1987. *The Codes of Advertising.* New York: St. Martin's Press.

Jhally, Sut, Stephen Kline, and William Leiss. 1985. "Magic in the Marketplace." *Canadian Journal of Political and Social Theory* 9, no. 3.

———. 1989. "Advertising as Religion." In *Cultural Politics in Contemporary America,* ed. I. Angus and S. Jhally. New York: Routledge.

Joyce, W. 1963. "The Role of Mass Media Today." In *Printer's Ink Advertising: Today/Yesterday/Tomorrow.* New York: McGraw-Hill.

Kaldor, Nicholas, and Rodney Silverman. 1948. *A Statistical Analysis of Advertising Expenditure and the Revenue of the Press.* London: Cambridge University Press.

Key, Wilson Bryan. 1972. *Subliminal Seduction.* New York: Signet.

———. 1976. *Media Sexploitation.* New York: Signet.

Kidd, Kenneth. 1989. "New RJR-Macdonald Unit Skirts Ad Ban." *The Toronto Star,* 14 April.

Kirby, Richard. 1988. Interview, CBC Television, October.

Kleefeld, Hans. 1986. "Tide Could Turn in Ocean of Graphic Pollution." *Marketing*, 1 December.

Kline, Stephen. 1977. "The Characteristics and Structure of Television News Broadcasting: Their Effects upon Opinion Change." Ph.D. diss. London School of Economics.

––––––. 1983. "Images of Well-Being in Canadian Magazine Advertising." Paper presented at the annual meeting of the Canadian Communication Association, Vancouver, B.C.

––––––. 1989. "Limits to the Imagination." In *Cultural Politics in Contemporary America*, ed. I. Angus and S. Jhally. New York: Routledge.

––––––. 1990. *Children in the Age of Marketing*. Toronto: Garamond.

Kline, Stephen, and William Leiss. 1978. "Advertising, Needs and Commodity Fetishism." *Canadian Journal of Political and Social Theory* 2, no. 1.

Kohut, John. 1988. "Election Pre-emptions Pose Problems for TV Advertisers." *The Globe and Mail* (Toronto), 19 October.

Kopvillem, Peter. 1988. "Prime Time for a Blitz of Ads." *Maclean's*, 31 October.

Kotler, P., and R.E. Turner. 1981. *Marketing Management*. Canadian 4th ed. Scarborough, Ont.: Prentice-Hall Canada.

Kottman, E. John. 1969. "Truth and the Image of Advertising." *Journal of Marketing*, October.

Lane, Robert E. 1978. "Markets and the Satisfaction of Human Wants." *Journal of Economic Issues* 12.

Lasch, Christopher. 1979. *The Culture of Narcissism*. New York: Warner Books.

Leiss, William. 1976, rev. ed. 1979. *The Limits to Satisfaction*. Toronto: University of Toronto Press.

––––––. 1978. "Needs, Exchanges and the Fetishism of Objects." *Canadian Journal of Political and Social Theory* 2, no. 3.

––––––. 1983. "The Icons of the Marketplace." *Theory, Culture and Society* 1, no. 3.

Lerbinger, Otto. 1978. *Design for Persuasive Communication*. Englewood Cliffs, N.J.: Prentice-Hall.

Levitt, Theodore. 1970. "The Morality(?) of Advertising." *Harvard Business Review* 48.

––––––. 1983. "The Globalization of Markets." In *The Marketing Imagination*. New York: Macmillan.

Levy, Sidney J. 1969. "Symbols by Which We Buy." In *Advancing Marketing Efficiency*, ed. L.H. Stockman. Chicago: American Marketing Association.

––––––. 1978. "Hunger and Work in a Civilized Tribe." *American Behavioral Scientist* 21.

————. 1981. "Interpreting Consumer Mythology: A Structural Approach to Consumer Behavior." *Journal of Marketing* 45.

Levy, Sidney J., and G. Zaltman. 1975. *Marketing, Society, and Conflict.* Englewood Cliffs, N.J.: Prentice-Hall.

Lewis, G.H. 1977. "Taste Cultures and Culture Classes in Mass Society: Shifting Patterns in American Popular Music." *International Review of the Aesthetic and Sociology of Music* 8.

Leymore, Varda. 1975. *Hidden Myth: Structure and Symbolism in Advertising.* London: Heinemann.

Lindblom, Charles. 1977. *Politics and Markets: The World's Political-Economic Systems.* New York: Basic Books.

Linder, Staffan. 1970. *The Harried Leisure Class.* New York: Columbia University Press.

Lucki, D., and R. Pollay. 1981. "Content Analysis of Advertising: A Review of the Literature." Working Paper 799, University of British Columbia.

Lynd, Helen, and Robert Lynd. 1929. *Middletown.* New York: Macmillan.

McCabe, Ed. 1988. "The Campaign You Never Saw." *New York,* 12 December.

McCracken, Grant. 1988. *Culture and Consumption: New Approaches to the Symbolic Character of Consumer Goods and Activities.* Bloomington: Indiana University Press.

McDaniel, C., Jr. 1982. *Marketing.* 2nd ed. New York: Harper and Row.

Mackenzie, Colin. 1988. "U.S., Canadian Campaigns Alike on Surface Only." *The Globe and Mail* (Toronto), 24 October.

McLuhan, Marshall. 1951. *The Mechanical Bride.* London: Routledge and Kegan Paul.

————. 1962. *The Gutenberg Galaxy.* London: Routledge and Kegan Paul.

————. 1964. *Understanding Media: The Extensions of Man.* London: Routledge and Kegan Paul.

McNeal, James. 1987. *Children as Consumers.* Lexington, Mass.: Lexington Books.

Mandel, Ernest. 1978. *Late Capitalism.* London: New Left Books.

Mander, Jerry. 1977. *Four Arguments for the Elimination of Television.* New York: William Morrow.

Marchand, Roland. 1985. *Advertising the American Dream: Making Way for Modernity, 1920–1940.* Berkeley: University of California Press.

————. 1987. "The Fitful Career of Advocacy Advertising." *California Management Review* 29.

Marcuse, Herbert. 1964. *One-Dimensional Man.* Boston: Beacon Press.

Marketing. 1986. " 'Globalization' Year," January 13; "Look What the Winds Will Blow In," January 13; "Supra-national Forces Conspiring against Advertisers: WFA President," June 9.

Marney, Jo. 1988. *Marketing*, March 28.

Marquez, F.T. 1977. "Advertising Content: Persuasion, Information or Intimidation?" *Journalism Quarterly* 54, no. 3.

Marx, Karl. [1867] 1976. *Capital*. Harmondsworth, Middlesex: Penguin.

Mauser, Gary. 1989. "Marketing and Political Campaigning: Strategies and Limits." In Margolis, M. and G.A. Mauser, ed. *Manipulating Public Opinion*. Belmont, Cal.: Wadsworth.

Media Watch. 1985. "Sex Role Stereotyping: A Content Analysis of Radio and Television Programs and Advertisements." Toronto: Media Watch.

Mehr, Martin. 1986. "CRTC Pondering Codes for Booze Advertising." *Marketing*, 2 June.

Mickelson, Sig. 1972. *The Electric Mirror: Politics in an Age of Television*. New York: Dodd Mead.

Miller, Daniel. 1987. *Material Culture and Mass Consumption*. Oxford: Basil Blackwell.

Mills, C. Wright. 1956. *The Power Elite*. New York: Oxford University Press.

Mitchell, Arnold. 1983. *The Nine American Lifestyles*. New York: Macmillan.

Moscovici, S. 1981. "On Social Representations." In Forgas, J. *Social Cognition: Perspectives on Everyday Understanding*. New York: Academic Press.

Moskin, J., ed. 1973. *The Case for Advertising*. New York: American Association of Advertising Agencies.

Mukerji, C. 1983. *From Graven Images: Patterns of Modern Materialism*. New York: Columbia University Press.

Murdock, G. 1982. "Large Corporations and the Control of the Communications Industries." In *Culture, Society and the Media*, ed. M. Gurevitch, T. Bennett, J. Curran, and J. Woollacott. London: Methuen.

National Advertising Review Board. 1975. *Advertising and Women*. New York: National Advertising Review Board.

Nelson, J. 1983. "When the Brain Tunes Out the Admen Tune In." *The Globe and Mail*, 16 April.

Nelson, Philip. 1974a. "Advertising as Information." *Journal of Political Economy* 82.

———. 1974b. "The Economic Value of Advertising." In *Advertising and Society*, ed. Y. Brozen. New York: New York University Press.

Nicosia, Francesco, ed. 1974. *Advertising, Management and Society*. New York: McGraw-Hill.

Nimmo, Dan. 1970. *The Political Persuaders*. Englewood Cliffs, N.J.: Prentice-Hall.

Nowak, K. 1982. "Cultural Indicators in Swedish Advertising 1950–75." Unpublished paper.

Oliver, R. 1981. "Advertising and Society." In *Advertising in Canada: Its Theory and Practice*, ed. P. Zarry and R. Wilson. Toronto: McGraw-Hill Ryerson.

Packard, Vance. 1957. *The Hidden Persuaders*. New York: D. McKay.

Patterson, Thomas. 1980. *The Mass Media Election: How Americans Choose Their President*. New York: Praeger.

Peterson, E. 1963. "The Magazine." In *Printer's Ink Advertising: Today/Yesterday/Tomorrow*. New York: McGraw-Hill.

Peterson, R.A., and P. Dimaggio. 1975. "From Region to Class: The Changing Locus of Country Music." *Social Forces* 53.

Philcox, Brian. 1989. "The Public Has a Right to Know What's for Sale." *The Globe and Mail* (Toronto), 16 January.

Pohlemus, Ted, and Lynn Procter. 1978. *Fashion and Anti-Fashion: A Study in the Anthropology of Clothing and Ornament*. London: Thames and Hudson.

Pollay, R.W. 1979. *Information Sources in Advertising History*. Westport, Conn.: Greenwood Press.

———. 1983. "The Identification and Distribution of Values Manifest in Print Advertising." Working Paper 921, University of British Columbia.

———. 1984. "Twentieth-Century Magazine Advertising: Determinants of Informativeness." *Written Communication* 1.

———. n.d. "Thank the Editors for the Buy-ological Urge! American Magazines, Advertising and the Consumer Culture." Working Paper 831, University of British Columbia.

Pollay, Richard, and S. Mainprize. 1984. "Headlining of Visuals in Print Advertising." In *Proceedings of the American Academy of Advertising*, ed. J. Glover. Denver: American Academy of Advertising.

Pope, Daniel. 1983. *The Making of Modern Advertising*. New York: Basic Books.

Potter, David. 1954. *People of Plenty*. Chicago: University of Chicago Press.

Presbrey, Frank. 1968. *The History and Development of Advertising*. New York: Greenwood Press.

Pulos, Arthur. 1986. *American Design Aesthetic: A History of Industrial Design to 1940*. Cambridge, Mass.: MIT Press.

Querles, Rachael, L. Jeffres, and A. Schnuerer. 1980. "Advertising and the Management of Demand: A Cross-National Test of the Galbraithian Argument." Acapulco: International Communication Association Conference.

Ray, Michael. 1982. *Advertising and Communication Management*. Englewood Cliffs, N.J.: Prentice-Hall.

Real, Michael. 1971. *Mass-Mediated Culture.* Englewood Cliffs, N.J.: Prentice-Hall.

Reynolds, T.J., and J. Gutman. 1984. "Advertising As Image Management." *Journal of Advertising Research* 24.

Ricoeur, Paul. 1977. *The Rule of Metaphor.* Toronto: University of Toronto Press.

Riesman, David. 1950. *The Lonely Crowd.* New Haven, Conn.: Yale University Press.

Roberts, Donald. 1983. "Children and Commercials: Issues, Evidence, Interventions." In *Rx Television: Enhancing the Preventative Impact of TV,* ed. J. Sprafkin, C. Swift, and R. Hess. New York: Hawthorne Press.

Rothenberg, Randall. 1989. "Brits Buy Up the Ad Business." *New York Times Magazine,* July 2.

Rotzoll, K., J. Haefner, and C. Sandage. 1976. *Advertising and Society: Perspectives Towards Understanding.* Columbus, Ohio: Copywright Grid.

Sabato, Larry J. 1981. *The Rise of Political Candidates.* New York: Basic Books.

Sahlins, Marshall. 1972. *Stone Age Economics.* Chicago: Aldine Press.
———. 1976. *Culture and Practical Reason.* Chicago: University of Chicago Press.

Salisbury, Richard. 1962. *From Stone to Steel.* London: Cambridge University Press.

Sampson, Henry. 1874. *A History of Advertising from the Earliest Times.* London: Chatto and Windus.

Sandage, Charles, and V. Fryburger, eds. 1960. *The Role of Advertising.* Homewood, Ill.: Richard Irwin.

Schneider, Cy. 1987. *Children's Television: The Art, the Business and How It Works.* New York: NTC Business Books.

Schwartz, Tony. 1974. *The Responsive Chord.* New York: Anchor.

Schudson, Michael. 1984. *Advertising, The Uneasy Persuasion.* New York: Basic Books.

Scitovsky, Tibor. 1976. *The Joyless Economy.* New York: Oxford University Press.

Sears, Roebuck & Co. 1971. *Catalogue no. 117: 1908.* Edited by J. Schroeder. Northfield, Ill.: DBI Books.

Segall, S. 1971. *Imagery: Current Cognitive Approaches.* New York: Academic Press.

Seldin, J. 1963. *The Golden Fleece: Selling the Good Life to Americans.* New York: Macmillan.

Shapiro, Karen. 1981. "The Construction of Television Commercials: Four Cases of Interorganizational Problem Solving." Ph.D. diss., Stanford University.

Sheehan, P. 1972. *The Function and Nature of Imagery.* New York: Academic Press.

Silverstein, Arthur, et. al. "The Portrayal of Women in Television Advertising." *Federal Communications Bar Journal* 27.

Simon, Julian. 1970. *Issues in the Economics of Advertising.* Urbana: University of Illinois Press.

Simpson, Jeffrey. 1988. *Spoils of Power: The Politics of Patronage.* Toronto: Collins.

Sinclair, John. 1987. *Images Incorporated: Advertising as Industry and Ideology.* Beckenham, Kent: Croom Helm.

Singer, Benjamin. 1986. *Advertising and Society.* Don Mills, Ontario: Addison-Wesley.

Sissors, J. 1978. "Another Look at the Question: Does Advertising Affect Values?" *Journal of Advertising* 7, no. 3.

Skornia, H. 1965. *Television and Society.* New York: McGraw-Hill.

Smith, A. 1979. *The Newspaper: An International History.* London: Thames and Hudson.

Sommers, Monte. 1983. "The Evolution of Marketing Thought and Its Implications for the Study of Advertising." Paper presented at meetings of the Canadian Communication Association, Vancouver, B.C.

Springborg, P. 1981. *The Problem of Human Needs and the Critique of Civilization.* London: Allen and Unwin.

Stephenson, H.E., and C. McNaught. 1940. *The Story of Advertising in Canada.* Toronto: Ryerson.

Stigler, George. 1961. "The Economics of Information." *Journal of Political Economy* 69.

Strauss, Marina. 1989. "Tobacco Firms Start Challenge of Ad-Ban Law." *The Globe and Mail* (Toronto), 25 September.

Sumner, C. 1979. *Reading Ideologies.* London: Academic.

Swingewood, Alan. 1977. *The Myth of Mass Culture.* London: Macmillan.

Taussig, M. 1981. *The Devil and Commodity Fetishism in South America.* Chapel Hill: University of North Carolina Press.

Trent, Judith, and Robert Friedenberg. 1983. *Political Campaign Communication: Principles and Practices.* New York: Praeger.

Tuchman, Gaye. 1979. "Women's Depiction by the Mass Media." *Signs* 4.

Turner, E. 1952. *The Shocking History of Advertising.* London: Michael Joseph.

United States, Federal Trade Commission. 1978. "FTC Staff Report on Television Advertising to Children." Washington, D.C.: FTC.

Varcoe, J.B. 1981. "The Advertising Agency." In *Advertising in Canada: Its Theory and Practice,* ed. P. Zarry and R. Wilson. Toronto: McGraw-Hill Ryerson.

Veblen, Thorstein. [1899] 1953. *The Theory of the Leisure Class.* New York: New American Library.

Venkatesan, M., and J. Losco. 1975. "Women in Magazine Ads, 1959–1971." *Journal of Advertising Research* 15.

Vestergaard, Torben, and Kim Schroder. 1985. *The Language of Advertising.* Oxford: Basil Blackwell.

Walker, David. 1988. "Advertisers' Own Programs Revive Better-Dead Notions." *Broadcast Week*, 12 November.

Walker, John. 1983. *Art in the Age of Mass Media.* London: Pluto Press.

Wernick, A. 1984. "Ideology and Advertising: An Interpretive Framework." *Theory, Culture and Society* 2.

Williams, Raymond. 1961. *The Long Revolution.* London: Penguin.

———. [1962] 1980. "Advertising: The Magic System." In *Problems in Materialism and Culture.* London: New Left Books.

Williams, Rosalind. 1982. *Dream Worlds.* Berkeley and Los Angeles: University of California Press.

Williamson, Judith. 1978. *Decoding Advertisements.* London: Marion Boyars.

Wortzel, Lawrence, and John Frisbie. 1978. "Women's Role Portrayal Preferences in Advertisements: An Empirical Study." *Journal of Marketing* 28.

Zeltner, Herbert. 1984. "Media Buying Calls for Tight Controls." In *Advertising Age*, 1 October.

Index